BUILDING BRIDGES

Nonfictions is dedicated to expanding and deepening
the range of contemporary documentary studies.
It aims to engage in the theoretical conversation
about documentaries, open new areas of scholarship,
and recover lost or marginalised histories.

General Editor, Professor Brian Winston

Other titles in the *Nonfictions* series:

Direct Cinema: Observational Documentary and the Politics of the Sixties
by Dave Saunders

Projecting Migration: Transcultural Documentary Practice
edited by Alan Grossman and Àine O'Brien

Vision On: Film, Television and the Arts in Britain
by John Wyver

Films of Fact: A History of Science in Documentary Films and Television
by Timothy Boon

Building Bridges: The Cinema of Jean Rouch
edited by Joram ten Brink

Forthcoming titles in the *Nonfictions* series:

Documentary Display: Re-Viewing Nonfiction Film and Video
by Keith Beattie

*Chávez: The Revolution Will Not Be Televised
– A Case Study in Politics and the Media*
by Rod Stoneman

BUILDING BRIDGES
The Cinema of Jean Rouch

Edited by Joram ten Brink
Preface by Michael Renov

WALLFLOWER PRESS
LONDON & NEW YORK

First published in Great Britain in 2007 by
Wallflower Press
6 Market Place, London W1W 8AF
www.wallflowerpress.co.uk

A catalogue record for this book is available from the British Library.

ISBN 978-1-905674-47-3 (pbk)
ISBN 978-1-905674-48-0 (hbk)

Book design by Elsa Mathern

Printed and bound in Poland; produced by Polskabook

CONTENTS

FOUNDATIONS AND LEGACIES

ACKNOWLEDGEMENTS

I am grateful to many for the support, inspiration, encouragement and advice in the past three years. To Annette Hill, Rosie Thomas, Wendy Malem and Sally Feldman at the University of Westminster; Julien Plante, Frederic Lavigne and Vincent Melilli and the staff at Ciné Lumière, London; Roy Armes, Jon Dovey, Andy Porter, Julian Henriques, Emilie Bickerton, Johannes Sjöberg and Keith Shiri in the UK; Françoise Foucault and Laurent Pellé at the Comité du Film Ethnographique, the staff at BNF and BIFI, Séverin Blanchet from atelier Varan, Alain Bergala, Jean-André Fieschi and a special thank you to Valdo and Marie Pierre Knüeblehr and to Gabi Mahn in Paris for assisting me in 'finding my way around'; Luc de Heush (Belgium), Mustafa Allasane (Niger) and Peter Wintonick (Canada); in the Netherlands: the European Foundation Joris Ivens/Joris Ivens Archives. Many thanks to Chris Darke for his expert translation of three chapters originated in French, and to Wanda Boeke for her skilled translation of one of the chapters from Dutch to English. Special thanks to Dirk Nijland who first introduced me to Rouch's work and supplied me with a wealth of information throughout and to Brian Winston, the general editor of Wallflower Press's Nonfictions series, for his invaluable advice.

I am deeply indebted to the Comité du Film Ethnographique (CFE) in Paris, to Madame Rouch and to 'the Friends of Jean Rouch' organisation in Paris for the permission to use Rouch's photographs.

I cannot praise enough the hard work and dedication of my students Zemirah Moffat (with the organisation of the conference) and Adam Christopher Snow (with the preparation of this collection); and especially the tireless efforts of Jacqueline Downs and Yoram Allon of Wallflower Press in bringing this book to print. Thank you. And to all the contributors to this volume for their skill and patience a very special thank you.

This book is dedicated to Atalia and Na'ama.

NOTES ON CONTRIBUTORS

BRICE AHOUNOU is an anthropologist and a journalist working in Paris. He collaborated with Jean Rouch on film projects and at the Musée de l'Homme.

DAVID BATE is Reader in Photography at the University of Westminster. He is the author of *Photography and Surrealism: Sexuality, Colonialism and Social Dissent* (2004) and has contributed to many edited collections, including *Art, Education, Photography: The Photography Reader* (2003) and *After Postmodernism* (2004). He is also a photgrapher and has shown his work in many solo and group exhibitions worldwide.

REDA BENSMAÏA is Professor of French literature and philosophy, film theory and French and Francophone postcolonial literature at Brown University. He is the author of *Experimental Nations or the Invention of the Maghreb* (2003) and the editor of *Gilles Deleuze* (1989) and *Recommending Deleuze* (1998). He is on the board of many journals, including *French Forum*, and is a member of the Society of Cinema Studies.

PHILO BREGSTEIN is a writer and filmmaker. His films include *The Compromise* (1968), which won the Golden Dove at the Venice International Film Festival, and *Jean Rouch and his Camera* (1986).

MICHAEL CHANAN is Professor of Film Studies at the University of Roehampton. He is a documentary filmmaker, and author, editor and translator of many books and articles on film and media, including *Repeated Takes: A Short History of Recording and its Effect on Music* (1995) and *Cuban Cinema* (2004). He has contributed to several journals, amongst them *Filmwaves* and *New Left Review*. His latest film is *Detroit: Ruin of a City* (2005).

IAN CHRISTIE is Professor of the History of Art, Film and Visual Media at Birkbeck College, University of London. Amongst many publications, he is the author of *The Last Machine: Early Cinema and the Birth of the Modern World* (1994) and *A Matter of Life and Death* (2000) and co-editor of *Eisenstein Rediscovered* (1993) and *Spellbound: Art and Film* (1996).

ELIZABETH COWIE is Professor in Film Studies at the University of Kent's School of Drama, Film and Visual Arts. She is the author of *Representing the Woman: Psychoanalysis and Cinema* (1997), the co-editor of *The Woman in Question* (1990) and has contributed to several edited volumes, including *Shades of Noir* (1993) and *Collecting Visible Evidence* (1999).

ANNA GRIMSHAW teaches in the Graduate Institute of the Liberal Arts at Emory University, Atlanta. She is the author of *The Ethnographer's Eye* (2001), editor of the *C.L.R. James Reader* (1992) and co-editor of *Visualising Anthropology* (2004). Her work on anthropology has also been published in the *Journal of Media Practice*.

PAUL HENLEY is a social anthropologist and ethnographic filmmaker. He has been on the jury of several ethnographic film festivals and has been the Director of the Granada Centre for Visual Anthropology at the University of Manchester since its foundation in 1987. His publications include contributions to *Applications of Anthropology: Professional Anthropology in the 21st Century* (2006) and *Reflecting Visual Ethnography: Using the Camera in Anthropological Research* (2006).

IVONE MARGULIES teaches film studies at the Film and Media Studies Department, Hunter College, City University of New York. She is the author of *Nothing Happens: Chantal Akerman's Hyperrealist Everyday* (1996), the co-editor of *Rites of Realism: Essays on Corporeal Cinema* (2003) and has written widely about French cinema for several journals and collections.

HAMID NAFICY is John Evans Professor of Communication in the Department of Radio, Television and Film at Northwestern University. He is the author of *An Accented Cinema: Exilic and Diasporic Filmmaking* (2001), the co-editor of *Otherness and the Media: The Ethnography of the Imagined and the Imaged* (1993), and has also produced educational films and experimental videos.

DIRK NIJLAND was Senior Lecturer at the Institute of Cultural and Social Studies, National University of Leiden from 1971 until 1999. He was involved with the production of *Cinémafia* (1980) and *Jean Rouch's Gang* (1993), and played a small part in *Madame L'Eau* (1993).

BERNARD SURUGUE is a French anthropologist, filmmaker and Associate Professor at the Sorbonne. He directed Jean Rouch's last major film *Le Rêve plus fort que la mort* (2002).

JORAM TEN BRINK is a Reader of Film at the School of Media, Arts and Design of University of Westminster and a documentary filmmaker. His latest film work is *The Journey* (2006).

CHRISTOPHER THOMPSON is Emeritus Professor of French at the University of Warwick. He is the editor of *L'Autre et le sacré: Surréalisme, cinéma, ethnographie* (1995) and chaired the Comité du film ethnographique (Musée de l'Homme) 2000–2004.

STEVEN UNGAR teaches French and Comparative Literature at the University of Iowa. He is the author of *Roland Barthes: The Professor of Desire* (1983) and co-author of *Popular Front Paris and the Poetics of Culture* (2005). In 2006, the French Ministry of Education named him Chevalier dans L'Ordre des Palmes Académiques.

MICHAEL UWEMEDIMO is a curator, filmmaker and author. He is a founding member of the filmmaking collective Vision Machine, and Research Fellow at Royal Holloway, University of London and Roehampton University. His recent publications include contributions to *Jean-Luc Godard: Documents* (2006) and *Fluid Screens/Expanded Cinema* (2007).

CHARLES WARREN teaches film studies at Boston University and at the Harvard University Extension School. He is editor of *Beyond Document: Essays on Nonfiction Film* (1996).

BRIAN WINSTON is the Lincoln Professor of Communications at the University of Lincoln. He is the author of many books on documentary filmmaking, including *Lies, Damned Lies and Documentaries* (2001) and *Messages: Free Expression, Media and the West from Gutenberg to Google* (2005). Amongst numerous other accolades, he has been awarded with an Emmy for documentary scriptwriting.

PREFACE
Spreading the Word about Rouch
Michael Renov

I sat forward in my chair, straining to hear the words. It was the 1990 commencement ceremony at the University of Southern California film school and
hundreds of soon-to-be graduates and their families anxiously awaited the be-
stowal of diplomas and the ensuing celebration. But first, the anxious recipients
awaited their charge from the commencement speaker, typically a veteran Hollywood director, actor or writer whose career accomplishments had earned the
respect of all. A few years before, Kirk Douglas had proved such a draw that
the fire marshal had threatened to shut the theatre down requiring a move to a
larger venue ever after.

Now, sitting in the cavernous Shrine Auditorium, for decades the home of
the Academy Awards ceremony, the students saw before them an unfamiliar
figure, an older man nattily dressed in a blue blazer, speaking of the cinema
with a passion that belied his years. The heavy French accent proved difficult for
many to decipher. Most had no idea who he was despite the fact that earlier that
day he had received an honorary doctorate from the president of the university
for his landmark achievements as an ethnographic filmmaker and documentary
pioneer. From my perch on the stage, I could make out the faces of some of my
own students who, I learned later, were busily educating their less learned col-
leagues as to just who this fellow was – the legendary Jean Rouch, doyen of the
ethnographic film, the inventor of *cinéma vérité*, teacher and inspiration to Jean-
Luc Godard and the French *nouvelle vague*!

The present volume is the latest and possibly best opportunity to spread the
word about Rouch. Despite his longevity, legendary exploits and enduring influence – all amply discussed in these pages – it is appalling how under-appreciat-

ed Rouch remains in the Anglophone world. For years, Mick Eaton's important but too-slim *Anthropology, Reality, Cinema: The Films of Jean Rouch*, published by the British Film Institute in 1979, offered the only sustained discussion of the Rouchian oeuvre for the English-speaking scholar or educator. Thirteen years later, anthropologist Paul Stoller's *The Cinematic Griot: The Ethnography of Jean Rouch* expanded the conversation for those whose emphasis was Rouch as ethnographic innovator and Africanist. *Cine-Ethnography* (2003), edited and translated by Steven Feld, consolidated a number of Rouch's writings and interviews for English speakers, devoting a special section to *Chronique d'un ete*, Rouch and Edgar Morin's landmark 1960 film that changed the course of film history. At last, the primary texts by Rouch were available to be read and reckoned with.

Rouch's death in an auto accident in Niger early in 2004 provided tragic closure to a remarkable career. Yet, with the publication of a scant three English-language books over a quarter century – this despite a sixty-year career, scores of films, massive influence on European ethnology and a central position in Parisian film culture – there was still no volume that grappled with the legacy of Jean Rouch; no book for English speakers that adequately assessed the reach and influence of this germinal yet controversial figure. For those of us who knew deep in our bones that the ideas and films of this man constituted one of the crucial genealogical supports for today's nonfiction media culture, this was an intolerable situation.

Can one adequately understand (let alone teach) today's frenetic mediascape, replete with 'reality programming' of all kinds, without some grounding in Rouchian precepts and the debates they have engendered? Amidst the current barrage of hybrid forms, it is vital to know just what Rouch meant by '*cinéma vérité*' nearly half a century ago, why he believed so deeply in 'truth as provoked' rather than as captured and how that put him at ideological odds with his American counterparts such as Richard Leacock, D. A. Pennebaker and Frederick Wiseman. For all the journalists and broadcasters who speak so knowingly of '*vérité*', almost none have any sense of the issues or embedded histories at stake in this version of mediated truth.

But alongside his embrace of provocation and his sense of the camera as a psycho-analytic stimulant capable of eliciting powerful truths from his subjects, Rouch was also committed to the ethical obligations he owed those subjects. (Journalists and broadcasters take note!) He understood the terms of the fragile encounter between documentary maker and subject even as he knew that he, the cineaste, inevitably took control in the editing suite. By way of compensation, Rouch devised such notions as 'audio-visual countergift' whereby the filmmaker showed the rushes to his subjects, sought their responses and even occasionally incorporated them into the final product. Rouch, in writing and in person, always counselled young filmmakers to enter the fray, to mix it up with their subjects rather than occupy the 'observation post'; he rarely used a tripod and categorically opposed the use of the telephoto lens. For his brand of ethnographic filmmaking, the addition of non-source music (the 'opiate of cinema') was anathema. But he was always ready to experiment and improvise with his subjects, to engage in a profound sort of play out of which a film might (or might not) ensue. He was a prolific collaborator who helped incite the creativity of others, in and out of Africa.

Moreover, and here I stress the etymological purity of the term, Jean Rouch was a *cinephile*. He fell in love with the movies at a very early age and remained devoted to them for life and with a zealot's passion. He gloried in the seventh art and took a leadership role in maintaining several of the key institutions – for example, the Cinémathèque Française – that preserved and celebrated the outpouring of cinema from around the world. Some have accused Rouch of cinephilia to a fault, suggesting that he held on to celluloid at the expense of newer technologies but I witnessed first-hand his boyish pleasure in experimenting with digital video amidst a gaggle of grad students on the beaches of Malibu.

But what can a single volume, even a very good one, hope to tell us about Jean Rouch, a figure so protean, so prolific, so provocative? The present volume is not, I hasten to offer, a hagiography. Its perspicacious editor, Joram ten Brink, seems alert to the fact that it is the legacy, the Rouchian birthright, we most deserve and require. Given Rouch's initial occupation as civil engineer, the title of this collection, *Building Bridges*, is most appropriate. Rouch's influence is herein registered in spaces – geographic and conceptual – that may well surprise. The variety of disciplinary perspectives on display in these chapters certainly testifies to the richness of the oeuvre, both filmic and textual.

Finally, and here one can only hope, this book may provide a tipping point of demand for the films themselves. It has long been a scandal that so few of Rouch's films can be seen outside of France. If this book swells the ranks of Rouchian scholars and enthusiasts, it could help build a market for the films' international circulation. Such a Rouchian return would indeed be a bridge-building effort of a very special sort.

From fieldwork in Ivory Coast, 1960

INTRODUCTION

I never met Jean Rouch in person, but I first encountered his films during my visual anthropology classes many years ago in Holland. I never forgot these films for they were the first steps in my education as a filmmaker. Somehow the films shown in my class – *Moi, un noir, Jaguar, Cocorico! Monsieur Poulet* – all made perfect sense. They immediately struck me as clear, true and persuasive in their portrayal of 'the other'. It was cinema made simple: straight-talking and in-your-face. Vivid in their depiction of real lives these films tackled human stories and empowered their subjects. Refreshingly, they were clean of any old-fashioned political notions of 'us' and 'them'. I saw these films only once and for many years afterwards I did not meet Rouch's work again. Nevertheless, as Eric Rohmer describes so beautifully of his first viewing of *Stromboli* (1950) and his subsequent habit of watching films only once before writing about them, Rouch had a profound and lasting effect on me. Like Rohmer, Rouch made films full of belief in humanity. In their different ways both continually posed the question: what happens if? Later, I realised Rouch's films strongly influenced my own work as a filmmaker and film educator. Over the years I also came to realise that his essay 'The Camera and Man' (1973) had become part of my method for teaching films.

Following his tragic death in a road accident in Niger, my interest in Rouch and his work resurfaced. In late 2004, thanks to the help of the Institut français in London, I organised a comprehensive programme of screenings and a three-day conference dedicated to Rouch's cinema. The conference brought together filmmakers and academics from Europe, Africa and the US and attracted a large number of visitors from across a wide and, as it turned out, surprising range of film traditions and academic disciplines – visual anthropology, documentary film, media studies, art history, Africa studies and community and video activism. This book has emerged from that event and, with additional contributions that have been specially commissioned, attempts to recreate the vivid experience of viewing and discussing Rouch's work and offer a critical framework from which further studies on Rouch's cinema will hopefully arise in the future. For Rouch throughout his career, be it in the open air, at the centre of an African village under the stars' gaze, or inside the auditorium of the Cinémathèque in Paris, the presentation of public screenings followed by lively debates were maybe as important as making the films themselves. This collection therefore follows his principle of committed engagement with the practice of filmmaking and shared debate as part of the elucidation of Rouch's films. For this reason the reader may come across certain repetition of descriptive material but each contributor presents a critique of the man and his work from a different angle. This also allows for the multifaceted nature of the contributors' interventions to echo the diverse range of presentations during the conference, from personal reflections to academic papers and all points between.

Jean Rouch occupies a unique position in the history of visual anthropology and film. The filmmaker who was educated as a civil engineer became a true bridge-builder between film and anthropology, film and art, fiction and documentary, Europe and Africa. The importance of Rouch's legacy in the development of visual anthropology, documentary and fiction cinema is substantial; early in his career he rejected established forms of documentary and sought new modes of filmmaking to present more complex images of 'reality' through 'play'. For Rouch, filmmaking was first and foremost about having fun. He changed the relationship between fiction and non-fiction, real and surreal, fantasy and fact, establishing the central position of the filmmaker in the work, and achieved all this over the course of more than 120 films without ever compromising his anthropological scientific pursuit. His hallmarks included technological innovation, relentless inquisitiveness and his use of provocation to unravel deeper layers of 'reality'. In many respects, Rouch blazed a trail for filmmakers from Jean-Luc Godard and François Truffaut to generations of visual anthropologists, documentary filmmakers and television producers. This volume is thus an attempt to begin the process of unravelling the nature of Rouch's rich and complex oeuvre as it seeks to critically investigate in depth his undertakings in both visual anthropology and film. More importantly, it examines the crossovers he created in his extraordinarily prolific output during sixty years of hard work.

The book is divided into three main sections. The first, *Rouch: Friend of Men and Gods Alike – Some Biographical Notes*, starts with a personal sketch, written by one of Rouch's closest collaborators over the last thirty years. It describes Rouch's journey from boyhood to his death in 2004, and maps the main milestones in his career as a visual anthropologist and a filmmaker. This is followed by Rouch's other 'story': his roles as an educator, organiser, politician (with a small p) and instigator of countless initiatives, festivals, gatherings and film screenings. Throughout his life, Rouch established and subsequently left behind large networks across the social sciences, education, governments, film industry and the public worldwide.

The Films, the second part of the book, discusses in great detail a large number of Rouch's films across the whole spectrum of his output – from visual anthropology, ethno-fiction, documentary and the more personal work in the latter part of his career. In 1942, Rouch, a young engineer working for a colonial power, was introduced to the world of Africa through a purification ritual following what was perceived to be the gods' deadly strike upon his road workers. From that point, there was no way back – civil engineering was replaced by filmmaking. By the end of World War Two, Rouch, sent to Africa to build bridges, had started his long journey into the continent via anthropology and film. His unique work with camera, gods and man is uncovered here in studies of some of his major contributions to visual anthropology: the extraordinary *Sigui Project* (1931–2033), *Cimetière dans la falaise* (1950), *Les Maîtres fous* (*The Mad Masters*, 1955), *La Chasse au lion à l'arc* (*The Lion Hunters*, 1957–64), *Batteries Dogon* (1966), *Le Yenendi de Ganghel* (1968) and *Les Tambours d'avant: Tourou et Bitti* (*Tourou et Bitti: Drums of the Past*, 1971). Yet it is impossible to consider all of Rouch's visual anthropology films in Africa under a single heading. To begin with, the films span many decades of fieldwork and often took years to complete because of the nature of the film's subject itself or of Rouch's working method, which often involved continuous feedback sessions with the participants in his films. In discussing Rouch's visual anthropology today, from our twenty-first-century perspective, one becomes quickly aware of his pioneering work in pushing the boundaries of his field whilst simultaneously recognising the fact that he remained faithful to some of the contemporary conventions in visual anthropology of his era.

Two of his most remarkable innovative works in Africa, *Moi, un noir* (1958) and *La Pyramide humaine* (*The Human Pyramid*, 1959) are discussed at length in this section of the book. *Moi, un noir* is perhaps the best known of Rouch's ethno-fiction films. The film not only proposed a brand new cinematic method in presenting the lives of the researcher's informants in visual anthropology but also created enormous interest in the wider world of documentary and fiction films outside the anthropological scientific community, with its fusion of documentary, fiction, improvisation and feedback techniques. Similarly *La Pyramide humaine* was an original and provocative cinematic 'invention', supported by commercial enterprise outside the world of visual anthropology. Rouch's method in setting up the film, his constant provocation of its participants, the highly political, social and emotional content of the film and its unusual formal structure highlight, in retrospect, its importance in considering his most famous film outside visual anthropology: *Chronique d'un été* (*Chronicle of a Summer*, 1960). Equally, *La Pyramide humaine* remains a film that can be seen as 'before its time', in view of the developments since in documentary film and television production up to *Big Brother* (2000–).

Many of Rouch's African films occupy an exceptional place in the history and theory of visual anthropology, not least because of the part played by possession and trance in his journey of discovery. Travelling to the heart of African life and its belief systems, politics and social structures brought Rouch to the forefront of scientific and political debates through his documentaries and ethno-fiction films. Whose voice do we hear? Whose films are we watching? At the height of his career, Rouch's cinematic oeuvre has been misunderstood from time to time by African filmmakers and Western scholars. His ethics and working methods were thrown into question, not least because Jean Rouch, the provocateur, never shied away from controversy and from poking fun at reality by posing his eternal question: what will happen if…? The book revisits many of these controversies of the past and offers a contemporary analysis of Rouch's major work in Africa.

Africa was Rouch's main arena of work but since the early 1960s, with his groundbreaking *cinéma vérité* film *Chronique d'un été* in collaboration with Edgar Morin, he intermittently embarked on a series of film productions in France. The films *La Punition* (*The Punishment*, 1962), *Paris vu par…* (1965), *Petit à petit* (*Little by Little*, 1968–69), *Dionysos* (1984) and *Madame l'Eau* (1992) are also discussed in this section of the book. Here, some of his early surrealist impulses, his ethno-fiction methodology, his contemporary political observations and more personal facets of his work merge together to produce a series of intriguing formal experiments in filmmaking. The story of Rouch's three main male collaborators, Damouré Zika, Lam Ibrahima Dia and Tallou Mouzourane, is frequently told in different guises throughout this volume as they played a crucial role in the development of his work for decades. His unique method of work as a filmmaker is also explored in this section through the accounts of three of his main *female* collaborators in West Africa and Paris – Nadine Ballot, Marceline Loridan and Safi Faye. Each seeks to understand his unique method of work in Africa, in Paris, in *cinéma vérité*, in ethno-fiction and in his other fiction films.

Foundations and Legacies, the third part of the book, starts by considering Rouch's roots in the world of Surrealism and ethnography in 1930s Paris. Adventure, dreams, chance, imagination and the irrational were all celebrated by the surrealists. For many, ethnography brought Surrealism and cinema together. Thus, this volume explores here the similarities and attractions between ethnography, documentary, photography and Surrealism in the context of the film work of Jean Rouch. This world of adventure and dream not only surfaced in Rouch's ethnographic and documentary work but also in his later fiction and cinematic fantasies. The man who had his roots in the 'old' world of pre-war Europe managed successfully to point the way and create, with others, a new order of visual anthropology and cinema after the war. In this latter part, the book engages with Rouch's legacy and the much wider debate about the place that his documentary and fiction cinema occupies in post-war Europe. What is his true legacy to a younger generation of filmmakers and television programme creators? How crucial was his work in developing new technological and conceptual tools for cinematic language in today's visual anthropology, documentary, fiction film and television work across the world? Contributions to this section demonstrate that Rouch was a true innovator and a co-traveller with many of his contemporaries in the new world of European cinema after World War Two. Neo-realism, the *nouvelle vague, cinéma vérité*, reality TV and developments in film production technology are all discussed, as is the work of (among others) Alexandre Astruc, Jean-Luc Godard, Chris Marker, Raul Ruiz, Federico Fellini, Abbas Kiarostami, Michael Moore, Nick Broomfield and television productions such as *Big Brother* and *Wife Swap* (2003–).

The photographs that head each chapter are not intended to offer direct illustration to the material that follows, but to open a window onto Rouch's rarely-seen photographic work. From 1946 and throughout his long career as a researcher in Africa, he used a stills camera as part of his fieldwork in anthropology. Some of the photographs were taken in preparation for a moving image project but the majority were taken as part of fieldwork or as a personal record by Rouch himself. Most of the images appearing in this book are taken from a private collection of over 20,000 photographs that Rouch gave to the Musée de L'Homme in Paris in 2000.

Rouch often cited one of his heroes, Dziga Vertov, in saying that one of the main purposes in making films is to create the possibility for further films to be made. Today, just a few years after the death of Jean Rouch, I hope that this book will primarily enthuse the reader to watch the films themselves and create the possibilities for more studies to be published on one of the most important and innovative filmmakers of the twentieth century.

REFERENCE

Rouch, J. (2003 [1973]), 'The Camera and Man', in *Ciné-ethnography*, ed. and trans. S. Feld. Minneapolis: University of Minnesota Press, 29–46.

ROUCH: FRIEND OF MEN AND GODS ALIKE – SOME BIOGRAPHICAL NOTES

Cine Market, Kumasi, Ghana, 1954

1   JEAN ROUCH AND THE SACRED CATTLE

Bernard Surugue

I met Jean Rouch in Niamey in 1966 when he was Director of the French Institute of Black Africa (IFAN – L'Institut Français d'Afrique Noire) in Niger, and I was a young music teacher. He immediately included me in his fieldwork, entrusting me with studying the music and dance of Songhay possession rituals. According to him, this required an aptitude in mathematics and music, but he made it clear: 'You'll see we understand nothing about them, but they're fascinating.' At the same time, I was ritually initiated by Hamidou Yayé, the custodian of all Songhay religious, magical and liturgical lore. We studied and produced musical and dance portraits of our mythological heroes. To this end, we made hundreds of sound and film recordings, the last of which featured in *Le Rêve plus fort que la mort* (*Dreams Stronger than Death*, 2002) under the virtuoso bow of Yayé, now over a hundred years old. We were all reunited at the open-air theatre of Niamey's cultural centre in February 2004 for the first screening in Niger of the film we had made together.

Here, in the form of a final farewell, are a few key moments in the life of Jean Rouch, a man who made his mark on his time as well as on all those who had the good fortune to accompany him.

An Idyllic Childhood

Jean Rouch was fond of recalling his childhood which, according to him, was among the happiest of his century. He liked to say that his story as an ethnologist and filmmaker started in early childhood when the gaze of one child met that of another: the young Rouch fancied himself as Nanook, another little boy who lived somewhere else. Robert Flaherty's Nanook, the little Eskimo boy, curling up snugly among the huskies, was a primordial encounter for Rouch. Along with dreams and projections a vocation was no doubt born that day.

These were Rouch's first steps in his attraction to the other, another mysteriously brought forth from afar thanks to a wonderful tool, that box of images – the cinema.

The youngest of the Rouch-Gain family, whose members were gifted in combining the arts and sciences, Jean continued the family tradition. Jules-Alfred Rouch, his father, was a naval officer, a meteorologist, an oceanographer companion of Charcot on the 'Pourquoi pas?' in the Antarctic and the author of several works of literature. In this scientifically-inclined family everybody painted, took photographs, sang and travelled. The fertile crucible of this extraordinary family fused art and science. Jean mixed with scientists and surrealist artists, delighted in the latest jazz and discovered peoples and countries according to the whims of his father. The adolescent changed *lycées* seven times and on each occasion had to make new friends by recounting the marvellous adventures he had had elsewhere. Furthermore, the talented and charming storyteller was a brilliant student. He passed his *baccalauréat* at 15 years old which opened the gates to the *grandes écoles*. He dreamt of going to the École normale supérieure to study mathematics and Greek, in his eyes indispensable subjects for dealing with 'these mysteries that are beyond me'.[1] Eligible for the École polytechnique, he went to the École des Ponts et Chaussées (the French National Engineering and Construction Academy).

Elegant solutions

As a young student, Rouch was somewhat 'smooth' in the *zazou* fashion of the day.[2] His precocious love of mathematics fed his taste for the 'elegant solutions' that allowed for the resolution of complex situations and intricate problems and found unexpected order in disorder. For him, the 'elegant solution' brought together tact, audacity and efficiency. It revealed the elementary simplicity of first truths. In order to arrive at it, he advocated the famous 'method of successive approximations' which he adapted after his fashion (see Kérissel 2001: 180). This implied that whatever the circumstances he should never remain passive, he should unflaggingly seek to understand and reflect upon everything he was presented with and strive to interpret it. This at times created complicated situations so it was necessary to know how to disentangle oneself rapidly so as not to become their prisoner. Rouch would take malicious pleasure in seeing certain apparent disturbances that would allow him to search delightedly for the 'elegant solution' in order to set all concerned, especially his companions, on the right path. Rouch approached even the most serious questions with humour and malice, feeling a real need for the power of laughter, saying in the film: 'As I have said, laughter is sacred. So, superior men, learn to laugh!'

Rouch admired one of his professors at the École des Ponts et Chaussées, the engineer Albert Caquot (1881–1976).[3] In 1930, Caquot announced the fundamental theory of adaptation stating that a structure is durable in so far as its distortion breaks down into a reversible process within the capacity of its endurance. This theory demonstrates the ability of materials to 'memorise messages' and to resist pressure. For Rouch, therefore, matter could be educated or influenced. With his indefatigable imagination, humour and poetic appetite stimulated by the surrealists, Rouch, along with his classmates Jean Sauvy and Pierre Ponty, made the fundamental theory of adaptation a rule for life – to resist all alternatives. He also kept in mind one of the other teachings of Caquot: 'First you draw a bridge, then you calculate it.' Rouch took this principle to heart, in the first instance in his real-life construction of bridges and roads in Africa and then in making his films: 'You shoot a film first. You produce it afterwards.'

This charming and happy student life was cruelly interrupted when mobilisation orders arrived instructing Rouch, Sauvy and Ponty to report to barracks at the École Militaire du Génie de Versailles where the three companions had been enrolled. After the German offensive of 10 May 1940, before being able to exercise their *métier*, the future artists were sent as a matter of urgency to blow up the bridges of the Marne to repulse the enemy who had skirted the Maginot Line. Rouch was in charge of destroying the Château-Thierry bridge. Other bridges were blown up. Many died for nothing. The enemy got through. Such was the 'phoney' war, which would remain forever absurd and traumatic: 'We travelled the length of France on bicycles, from the Marne to Limoges. Arriving in Limoges, you weren't the same person. You felt an immense sadness that was infinite and inescapable.'[4]

A ship named 'Providence'

After suffering the shame of defeat and having returned to occupied Paris, Rouch and his friends completed their final year at the École des Ponts et Chaussées. With diplomas nestling in their pockets they decided to leave the capital and enlisted in the Colonial Ministry. They were appointed as 'Assistant Engineers of Public Works in the Colonies' in October 1941, and at Marseilles they boarded the 'Providence' bound for Dakar with a common dream, to build the Trans-Saharian railway together. On arriving in Dakar their dream of teamwork went up in smoke, as they had to respond to the demands of a strict administration. The three friends were separated: Sauvy was appointed to a post in Guineau, Ponty to the navy in Senegal and Rouch to Niger.

This separation would prove providential for Rouch's future. He was immediately fascinated by the great river Niger and the world of Songhay society. He was taken on by the Niger Public Works to build roads from Niamey to Gao and Niamey to Ougadougou with vaulted Roman bridges because of the lack of concrete. Rouch had a veritable army of thousands at his disposal whom he came to know through their shared task. He had the uncanny explorer's knack to transform the many setbacks he encountered in the field into as many advantages.

One day, however, in the summer of 1942, at one of his construction sites at Gandel, not far from Niamey, something dramatic happened that marked a decisive stage in Rouch's ethnographic vocation – the tragic death of several of his workers during a storm of lightning that Dongo, the mythological god of thunder of the Songhay, had launched. Dongo, as was later explained to Rouch by Damouré Zika, one of his young workmen, held Rouch responsible for the deaths because he was building on the god's land. Thus, Zika and his family introduced Rouch to Songhay magic and religion during the burial and possession ceremonies that followed the deaths of the road workers.

> It was Damouré Zika who enabled me first to attend fishermen's ceremonies, then introduced me to his grandmother, at Kalia's house. In the evening or on Sunday morning, in this mud hut in the Gawey district, we would both sit before the old lady who, in her soft voice, would tell 'the stories' that Damouré would translate. It was this worm-eaten wooden door to the hut which, for the first time for me, gave on to the African supernatural. (Rouch 1989: 13)

Despite – and perhaps thanks to – a reticent local administration who understood nothing about his attraction to ethnography, Rouch, attentive to the lives of others, slowly won the confidence of the river people in his own way and was already practising what later became 'shared ethnography'.

The oath of Bamako

At the end of 1942, the Americans landed and the French West African army joined the allied forces. As an anti-Vichyist and a committed Africanist, Rouch was expelled from the colony of Niger to Dakar.[5] On his way, in January 1943, he met up again with his friends Sauvy and Ponty in Bamako. During this short 'historical encounter', Sauvy writes:

> We climbed up to 'G Point', high land overlooking the city. There, sitting on the edge of the cliff we contemplated the bend of the Niger ... And so, Rouch and I, sensitive to the exceptional quality of the moment, became lyrical under the naturally ironic eye of our friend Ponty. 'When the war's over we'll come back here', Rouch declares. 'And we'll travel the length of the Niger

in a dug-out, from one end to the other, from the source to the ocean, adds Sauvy … And Rouch, who had already allied himself with Harakoy Dikko, the all-powerful female 'Boss' of the river, made it clear that the voyage would be made under her aegis. (Sauvy 2001a: 79–80)

In Dakar, Rouch was a faithful attendee of IFAN and its founder, Professor Théodore Monod, in taking part in the military training of the liberation armies in the city. Rouch and his companions trained the sappers from the École du Génie de Versailles to build floating bridges on Senegal's rivers in preparation for the battles in Europe. Later, the same exercise had to be repeated under enemy fire in support of the liberation armies crossing the Rhine. Rouch finally reached Berlin in August 1945.

Like many, Rouch remained discreet about this period – the last years of the war in Europe, the enormous suffering, a terrible test of humility, a human sacrifice that put everything in question. He often described to me this traumatic episode as the 'symphony of the desolation of the world'.

The roads to freedom

During these four mad years Rouch and his companions Pierre Ponty and Jean Sauvy paid their duty and took part in the war. Too many of their comrades paid with their lives or were wounded. They decided to do what they always wanted to and fulfilled their 'romantic-surrealist' oath devised three years earlier on the cliff's edge of G Point in Bamako. By amalgamating their three respective names, Sauvy, Ponty and Rouch invented a unique journalist 'personage' – 'Jean Pierjant'. Their quest was to discover new ways of life and to reveal them to the world.

During preparations, Rouch argued for equipping the expedition with a film camera, making it quite clear that photographs are all very well but they are a waste of time next to a 16mm camera. But how would they pay for it? Sauvy had bought a gold ingot in Guinea in 1941 and had carried it in his belt – like a *gri-gri* charm – throughout the entire war. He offered to trade it for the precious Bell and Howell 16mm camera bought at the flea market a day before departure. None of the three men knew how to handle a camera but all had been trained according to the method of 'successive approximations' that had been applied to engineering, to war and to filmmaking.

Thus they took off, placing all their confidence in the salvaged Junkers transport plane that carried the Liotard Expedition.[6] After a stopover in Touareg country, the plane botched its take-off and broke its undercarriage. Rouch made the most of this stroke of luck to take his first lesson in cinematography with Edmond Sechan, one of the members of the Liotard Expedition.[7] A replacement plane left the trio at Gao where Sauvy wrote in his notebook: 'At last the glorious Niger, shining in the morning sun, as wide as the Thames at Westminster, flowing slowly eastward' (Sauvy 2001b: 18).

Cinema's good fortune: a broken tripod

While shooting the fast-moving water on the Niger river the tripod broke but Rouch continued filming. During the five months of travelling down river he realised that it was perfectly feasible to shoot with much greater mobility with the Bell and Howell propped against his forehead. With his innate sense of improvisation, his taste for 'successive approximations' and 'elegant solutions' he had simply invented a new way of filming which became a new school of film-making.[8]

The 4,000 kilometres of the river from its source to the ocean was covered aboard rafts and canoes in five months from 24 October 1946 to 25 March 1947. In this, the three companions accomplished an extraordinary feat recounted in newspaper articles for AFP, photographs and documentary films. This expedition prefigures the filmmaker's ethnological work: the ritual hunting of lion and hippopotamus, as well as encounters with the river-peoples, the phenomenon of possession, the amazing cattle, and much more. The very first film shot as a test with the Bell and Howell fixed on its tripod took place on an island near Ayorou and was entitled *La Chevelure magique*. The negative, carefully put in a barrel full of sawdust, was entrusted at the nearest airport to be sent to Paris. However, the plane was late arriving and the barrel, along with its precious contents, became dangerously hot having spent several days in the Nigerien sun. The laboratory could not do a thing with it and the film was lost. Only a few photographic images are left to testify to this first virtual film shot with the help of a tripod. The second film completed en route, *Au Pays des mages noirs* (1946–47), was projected at the Cinémathèque Française, as the accompanying film to Rossellini's *Stromboli* (1950). This was Rouch's entry into Cinema.

Liberté, égalité: the theory?[9]

Encouraged in his approach by Théodore Monod, and the anthropologists Marcel Griaule and André Leroi-Gourhan, Rouch threw himself into ethnography. He was convinced that there was a science which, while not exact, with the right questions might establish a new approach. To compensate for the inevitable faults of memory, he advocated photography and in particular the 'camera-stylo'. In September 1948, with a bursary awarded 'in commemoration of the Revolution of 1848', he again left for the field to rejoin his Nigerien friends Damouré

Zika and Lam Ibrahima Dia. One film followed another and, step by step, his Nigerien companions became real ethnographic and cinematic assistants. On returning to Paris, Rouch showed his films to Griaule and Leroi-Gourhan at the Musée de l'Homme. *Au Pays des mages noirs* (1946–47) was not shot as an ethnographic film. *Bataille sur le grand fleuve* (1951), a colour film about a hippopotamus hunt shot from January to May 1951, in which the hippo ultimately wins is without doubt the most obvious moment when ethnographer and filmmaker merge. Working at the same pace, Rouch made *Yenendi, Les hommes qui font la pluie* (*The Rainmakers*, 1951). On returning to Paris he defended his groundbreaking thesis under the direction of Marcel Griaule at the Sorbonne (later published as *La Religion et la magie Songhay*):

> Next I went back to Firgoun to present the film for 'feedback' to those who'd battled with the river. I took a projector, a big white sheet and an electrical generator. There were four projections, one after the other. Mutual stupefaction. They talked about my work, what I was doing. Sound and image made the work about them accessible, which allowed for critique. The lion-hunter, Taillerou Koro, said: 'Come with me to hunt lion and you will indeed see lions.' It was the most important moment in my career as an ethnographer ... their view of my work. I found it was the only way to reconstitute my work.[10]

Rouch established a fundamental practice of ethnographic cinema: the validation of a film by the protagonists themselves. He extolled the method of 'feedback' as necessary to legitimate the work done, shared with the people filmed. For him, this essential step overcame academic caution.

The sacred cattle

The origin of the story of the sacred cattle, like the majority of stories that Rouch filmed, dates back to the period of 'Jean Pierjant' and follows the logic of the 'Oath of Bamako'. When Ponty, Rouch and Sauvy had arrived in Niger at the halfway stage of their journey they left the French empire to venture into British territory.

In 1948 Damouré Zika, who was a French state employee, had been unable to get a visa to leave Nigerien territory. As a replacement, Damouré suggested a young Peul shepherd named Lam Ibrahima Dia. Known as 'Lamido the little prince', Lam quickly became Rouch's cook and assistant cameraman. Later, he would become a sound engineer, then advisor on all matters Marabout, a mechanic and the official driver for the IFAN centre in Niamey and, finally, a rich farmer of the right bank of the Niger river irrigated with the help of the famous

Dutch windmills depicted in the film *Madame l'Eau* (1993). Lam, in 1948, a young apprentice Marabout, was returning from a journey on foot from Abéokuta, a Nigerien city lying between Ibadan and Lagos, to Niamey via Sokoto and had some extraordinary adventures:

> He told us about this adventure and how he had passed through Sokoto where for the first time he had encountered extraordinary white cattle with no horns. Because of this, the Peul cattle breeders could not consume their milk because it was the devil's milk.[11]

In fact, the cattle breeding never amounted to anything despite the recommendations of the veterinarian Mariko.[12] Rouch and his Nigerien friends invented a film, *Les vaches merveilleuses*, that told the story of the 'sacred cattle'. The film was never made but the story reappeared years later in the film *Le Rêve plus fort que la mort* (2002). In 1997, Lam Ibrahima Dia fell ill and died. In 2002 Rouch, who was deeply affected by this death, decided to make *Le Rêve plus fort que la mort* with me, in homage to the deceased. The film, improvised throughout, tells the story of the return of Jaguar who had made a fortune in Ghana and came back to Niamey in a smart Jaguar convertible.[13] Damouré Zika improvised the role. But he understood that things were not the same anymore; everything had changed; the river had become capricious, the Marabout had forbidden sacrifices, nothing was as before. In Rouch's honour, Zika organised a celebration with his 150 children with a ritual including offerings and possession dances which, as before, took place under the 'musical protection' of the player of the single-stringed violin.

This was, in fact, also the occasion of Rouch's – alias Jaguar's – return to Niger to see his African friends again. Very much influenced by ancient tragedies and contemporary drama, Aeschylus' 'Persians', it gave Rouch the opportunity to relate the Dionysian vision of the world and its association with Songhay mythology.[14] For the film, Philippe Brunet, professor of Ancient Greek, dramatist and stage director, rehearsed with Diouldé Laya, ethnologist and Hellenic scholar, at the Cultural Centre of the Niger Republic. He paralleled King Darius with the warriors of the Songhay Empire. The whole production was played and sung in ancient Greek, Songhay, Peul, French and Turkish. This opera of the desolation of the world recalled the origin of tragedy.

Not far away, graceful herds of the 'mythical, sacred' white cattle crossed the river. Guided by their inseparable Peul shepherds, they followed their ancient quest for unlikely pastures under the protection of the gods above and those below. Sitting on a dune by the river, in the shade of a caicedra tree, Tallou Mouzourane, the third member of 'Rouch's gang' in Africa for the past fifty years (alongside Damouré and Lam) cast spells in the sand. Then, in the warm light of evening, in the midst of his herd, he sang and invoked the deceased Lam, the little prince. The departed friend thanked his 'father' Jean Rouch for having come to see him and his sacred white cattle without horns. Then, the hundred-year-old virtuoso Hamidou Yayé, with his 'Godié', a single-string viol, invoked the gods and goddesses of the mighty river.

'Rouch has left, he's not here anymore'

In February 2004, we were in Niger with Jean Rouch to prepare for a new film and for the African premiere of *Le Rêve plus fort que la mort* at the location where it had been filmed, the Franco-Nigerien cultural centre. The screening was to inaugurate a retrospective of cinema from Niger at which Rouch was the guest of honour. On Wednesday, 18 February 2004, I accompanied the daughter and granddaughter of Oumarou Ganda to the French Ambassador's residence to welcome 'uncle Rouch'. Rouch had discovered Oumarou Ganda in the Ivory Coast. This former soldier in the Indochina war was working as a docker; Rouch made him the hero of his film *Moi, un noir* (1958). This cult film marked the start of the *nouvelle vague* at the beginning of the 1960s. Ganda subsequently became a major filmmaker who, alas, was brutally cut down in the prime of life. We left for lunch at the *Roniers* alongside the river a little beyond the village of Goudel. It was here that Rouch and his group of friends used to take Idrissa Maiga's canoe to reach the middle of the river and swim in the fresh waters at the hottest time of day, impervious to the hippopotami while others took siestas in air-conditioned villas. Jean was in fine form and we discussed films in prepara-ration, coming up with possible titles for the next one such as 'Eternity' or 'The True Lie'.

A few hours later on one of Niger's roads, identical to those that this engi-neer from the École des Ponts et Chaussées had built right back at the start of his career, Jean was heading for Tahoua. At nightfall, far from the protection of the Niger river, in the land of 'Mahama le touareg' – the fearsome warrior-spirit with 150 wings depicted in the film *Le Rêve plus fort que la mort* – death came upon Jean Rouch. 'Rouch has left, he's not here anymore' were his last words.[15]

Following both the national and ritual funerals, Jean Rouch lies in an ex-tremely simple tomb adjoining the buildings of the Niger office of Public Works, his first employer in 1941. So, a life punctuated by struggle and creativity, all of which had been dedicated to the human sciences and filmmaking, was com-plete. This great 'zima', friend of men and gods alike, is now the eternal guardian of the curved Niger, the valley of universal culture, from its source all the way to the infinite ocean.

1   One of Rouch's favourite expressions that he used in his later years was borrowed from Jean Cocteau's play *Les mariés de la Tour Eiffel*: 'Since these mysteries are beyond me, let us pretend to be behind them.'

2   Like the elegant young 'zazou man' in *Jaguar* (1967) played by Damouré Zika.

3   Albert Caquot is one of the great engineers and builders of the twentieth century. As well as his role in aeronautics during World War One and World War Two, this scientist (and artist) made a crucial contribution to the field of the resistance of materials.

4   Jean Rouch in conversation with Pierre-André Boutang in *Jean Rouch, collection: Le geste cinématographique* by Patrick Leboutte and Marc-Antoine Roudil, 4-DVD pack compiled with the assistance of Bernard Surugue, Éditions Montparnasse, 2005.

5   He liked to recall one of his clashes with Governor Tobby of the Vichy regime who, after a somewhat stormy discussion, said 'Rouch, do you take me for an idiot?' Quick as a flash, Rouch replied 'No. But I could be wrong.' This reply appears again in one of Rouch's last films, *Dionysos* (1984).

6   In 1945, at the Musée de l'Homme from the war onwards, ethnologists in the resistance gathered as the famous 'Liotard Group' of new, young explorers – named after Louis Liotard who had been murdered in Tibet – under the aegis of the Explorer's Club. Liotard had organised the first major post-war expedition in Africa, the Ogooué-Congo mission, with Noel Ballif.

7   Edmond Sechan was in charge of the cinematography of many French films including *Crin blanc* (Albert Lamorisse, 1952), *Mort en fraude* (Marcel Camus, 1957), *La Grande frousse* (Jean-Pierre Mocky, 1964), *A Cœur joie* (Serge Bourguignon, 1967), *Le Pays bleu* (Jean-Charles Tachella, 1976), *La Boum* (Claude Pinoteau, 1980).

8   In 2002 in Gottingen, Rouch told me that his German friends had organised, much later on, a funeral ceremony at which the tripod would be symbolically buried and therefore abolished, thus freeing the camera and, at the same time, cinema.

9   This was the title of a film in homage to Théodore Monod, *Liberté, Égalité: la thèse* by Jean Rouch and Bernard Surugue (AMIP-IRD, 2003).

10   Jean Rouch in conversation with Pierre-André Boutang in *Jean Rouch, collection: Le geste cinématographique*.

11   Jean Rouch, proposal for the film *La vache merveilleuse* which became *Le Rêve plus fort que la mort* (2002).

12   Abdouramane Keletigui Mariko, esteemed veterinarian, is also the author of many books about the oral traditions of Niger.

13 In reality, it was the famous Bugatti car from *Petit à petit* (1968–69) which had to play the role.

14 'Et l'unique cordeau des trompettes marines' constitutes the entirety of the famous alexandrine 'Chantre' ('Singer') by Guillaume Appolinaire (1880–1918); the single line was added by the poet on the proofs of his 1913 collection *Alcools*. The translation is by Anne Hyde Greet. She notes that the alexandrine contains two puns: *cordeau*, 'cord', is also *cor d'eau*, horn of water (and possible *corps d'eau*, body of water); *trompette marine* is a 'trumpet marine' (that is, a medieval musical instrument with a single string) or, literally, a 'marine trumpet' (Appolinaire 1965: 44–5, 224) [Translator's note].

15 See the end of the Surugue & Riollon 2004 film *Le double d'hier a rencontré demain*.

REFERENCES

Appolinaire, G. (1965 [1912]) *Alcools*, trans. A. Hyde Greet. Berkeley: University of California Press.

Kérissel, J. (2001) *Albert Caquot 1881–1976: Savant, soldat et bâtisseur*. Paris: Presses de l'Ecole Nationale des Ponts et Chaussées.

Rouch, J. (1989) *La Religion et la magie Songhay*. Brussels: Edition de la Université de Bruxelles.

____ (1999) *Dionysos: scénario et storyboard*. Paris: Artcom.

Sauvy, J. (2001a) *Un jeune ingénieur dans la tourmente, 1938–45*. Paris: L'Harmattan.

____ (2001b) *Descente de Niger, Trois hommes en pirogue, 1946–47*. Paris: L'Harmattan.

Surugue, B. and L. Riollon (2004) *Le double d'hier a rencontré demain*. Film 10 min Paris: IRD.

Rouch at the Delta works in the Netherlands, researching *Madame l'Eau*, 1990
(photo: D. Nijland)

2 JEAN ROUCH: A BUILDER OF BRIDGES

Dirk Nijland

Jean Rouch is probably best known for the feature films he made with his African friends Damouré Zika, Lam Ibrahima Dia and Tallou Mouzourane. However, he achieved much more: he produced many ethnographic and other films, took photographs, wrote a considerable number of publications and was extremely active within various organisations. He was renowned in the worlds of anthropology, education, documentary film and cinema in general.

The fact that he was able to achieve all of this comes from his ability to put into perspective the execution of his plans and his own personal life: one must not be too serious and at the same time one should show courage. As to the first, an important principle which formed his personality seems to have come from the name of the vessel 'Pourquoi pas?' on which Rouch's father, serving as meteorologist, accompanied an expedition to the South Pole – one must think differently, outside the fixed paths. Additionally, too much perfection was not a good thing. One must not be afraid to fail. Sometimes courage was indeed necessary in order to apply all this. One test that appealed to Rouch was to cross Trocadero Square towards the statue of Marshal Foch located directly opposite the Musée de l'Homme where there is no pedestrian crossing. The instructions were: 'Do not wait, cross the street and look the person at the wheel straight in the eyes, and then they will use the brakes.'

He himself followed you closely. He did not abandon you. Non-conformism was, however, certainly not a rule by itself. By way of advice, when approaching official organisations, the command: 'Cravate!' was often given. The diplomatic side of his personality was expressed, for instance, in the mimicry of his blue tie and jacket. Towards others, Rouch could be quite amiable, but now and again he could behave like a *monstre sacrée*. Appointments considered not important were often not kept. He then shut himself off for the benefit of his own work or something else considered of greater importance. Ultimately, however, he engaged with many people through his work, his continuous drive for new ideas and his personality, often using storytelling and jokes to neutralise imminent conflicts. He could enthuse, delegate and install confidence in people, and was able to build extensive networks. He himself led a disciplined life and could easily switch mentally from one task to another.

This chapter deals with that part of Rouch's work that not only concerns the establishment of organisations, festivals and training programmes to the benefit of ethnographic film, but also documentary film and cinema in general. As his films and written publications receive attention elsewhere in this volume, they are mentioned here as mere references in the various tables below, making it clear that Rouch, often in co-operation with others, produced an incredible output and worked as a true 'builder of bridges'.

Rouch, his publications and scientific career

The bibliography in *Ciné-ethnography* (Rouch 2003), defined as 'selective' by its editor Steve Feld, forms the point of departure for Rouch's written publications described in the table opposite. Feld counts 107 titles including books, articles, prefaces and catalogues to which others have also largely contributed. The titles can be grouped according to subject as follows: Songhay – 21 titles; migration in West Africa (mainly the Songhay) – 10; Dogon – three; Africa, other subjects – 18; ethnographic film – 26; African cinema – seven; cinema in general – six; remaining – 14.

According to the filmography in that volume, which sometimes offers different dates than earlier publications, Rouch has made 102 films, to which another 26 not entirely finished films must be added (see also Anon. 1955, 1967b; Eaton 1979; Heusch 1962; www.comite-film.ethno.net/rouch/rouchfilm.htm). Amongst the 102 films, 56 are of ethnographic value, thirty were filmed on the Songhay and 13 on the Dogon. Nine documentaries deal with more general subjects such as scientific research and celebrations of independence in Africa. One could classify two films as *cinéma vérité* in *optima forma*. Four other films could be classified as documentary fiction, where the basis for the enacted actions is formed by reality. Furthermore, there are twelve 'pure' fiction films. Several titles were produced together with his inseparable friends Damouré Zika, Lam Ibrahima Dia and Tallou Mouzzourane, supported by Moussa Hamidou as sound engineer. With their co-operation, he produced three advertising films. Next, in the period 1974–81, Rouch made nine film portraits. Finally, after 1985, Rouch produced eight films, presenting a personal and often poetic view on a variety of subjects such as African art, Paris or, for example, constructions by Gustave Eiffel.

Aside from his written material and filmmaking, Rouch produced a large body of work in photography. In 1998, he offered the Photothèque of the Musée

Year (age)	ETHNOGRAPHIC FILM, DOCUMENTARY FICTION & FICTION	PUBLICATIONS, Photography & official position
1940 (23)		Ingénieur Ponts et Chaussées ('41)
		APERÇU L'ANIMISME SONRAI ('43)
	AU PAYS DES MAGES NOIRS ('46–'47)	Attaché de recherche CNRS ('47)
1950 (33)	CIMETIÈRE DANS LA FALAISE ('50)	
	YENENDI, HOMMES FONT PLUIE ('51)	
	BATAILLE SUR LE GRAND FLEUVE ('51)	
	LES MAÎTRES FOUS ('55)	CONTRIBUTION HISTOIRE SONGHAY ('53)
		Le Niger en piroque ('54)
		MIGRATIONS GHANA, GOLD COAST ('56)
	MOI, UN NOIR ('58)	
	LA PYRAMIDE HUMAINE ('59)	
1960 (43)	CHRONIQUE D'UN ÉTÉ ('60)	PhD: RELIGION ET MAGIE SONGHAY ('60)
		Maître CNRS, Directeur IRSH Niamey ('61)
	LA CHASSE AU LION À L'ARC ('64)	
	GARE DU NORD ('66)	
	SIGUI '66 : ANNÉE ZERO ('66)	CINÉMA AFRICAIN ('61/'67)
	JAGUAR ('53/'54–'67)	LE FILM ETHNOGRAPHIQUE ('68)
	PETIT À PETIT ('68–'69)	
1970 (53)	TOUROU ET BITTI ('71)	LES AVATARS DE LA PERSONNE ('71)
	FUNÉRAILLES À BONGO ('72)	
	SIGUI 7; COCORICO, MR. POULET ('75)	THE CAMERA AND MAN ('75)
	BABATOU ('75)	Directeur Recherche Exceptionelle, CNRS ('75)
	CINÉ-PORTRAITS, MAKWAYELA ('77)	
1980 (63)	CINÉ-MAFIA ('80)	
	ENIGMA ('86)	TOT. ANCESTORS + MAD MASTER ('88)
1990 (73)	LIBERTÉ, ÉGALITÉ, FRATERNITÉ..? ('90)	LES HOMMES + DIEUX DU FLEUVE ('97)
	MADAME L'EAU ('93)	Action Musée de l'Homme ('99/'04)
2000 (83)		Récits Photographiques (2000)
	LE RÊVE PLUS FORT QUE LA MORT ('02)	

Table 1 Rouch's publications, photography and official functions against the background of the production of ethnographic films, documentary fiction and fiction films

de l'Homme 20,000 photographs, covering his activities in this field from c.1945 onwards. Only one single publication exists as an independently published photo-essay (1954). The exhibition, 'Jean Rouch, récits photographiques' (Musée de l'Homme, 2000) was the largest to date to include his photographic work. Rouch made clear on various occasions that, due to fieldwork conditions, not every single photograph was shot by himself (Rouch 1954: 24; 1960: 5).

Rouch obtained the status of 'Directeur de la Recherche de Classe Exceptionelle au Centre National de la Recherche Scientifique' (CNRS) at the end of his scholarly career. In the last years of his life he was active on behalf of the Musée de l'Homme, which was seriously threatened as a centre of science by the foundation of the Musée du Quai du Branly.

Rouch, committees and festivals

Rouch's entire personal life was very much dedicated not only to promoting communication between visual anthropologists, but also to communication with interested anthropologists, documentary filmmakers and the broader public keen on ethnographic film.

Before World War Two, a number of anthropologists showed an interest in using film. Marcel Mauss and Marcel Griaule introduced film in France, alongside photography and the phonograph, as documentation, teaching and publication tools (Mauss 1967; Griaule 1938). Film was already used elsewhere in science. During the early 1930s, biologist and filmmaker Jean Painlevé organised conferences on scientific film. In 1947 the International Scientific Film Association (ISFA) was formed and continued to run those meetings in Paris.

That same year, the anthropologist André Leroi-Gourhan, who had just completed an expedition to the Congo and brought back film extracts on 35mm, organised the 'Premier Congrès International du Film Ethnographique et de Géographie' at the Musée de l'Homme. It took place in the same hall now referred to as 'Salle de Cinéma Jean Rouch'. In 1948, Leroi-Gourhan published 'Cinéma et sciences humaines: le film ethnologique existe-t-il?' laying the basis for defining the use of film in anthropology. Rouch, who had already completed several films, founded the 'Comité du Film Ethnographique' (CFE) in 1952, together with Leroi-Gourhan, Marcel Griaule, Germaine Dieterlen, Claude Lévi-Strauss, Enrico Fulchignoni, Henri Langlois and Alain Resnais. Rouch served as the general secretary of the committee for the rest of his life. In the same year, 1952, Rouch was involved with the foundation of the Comité International du Film Ethnographique (CIFE) during the fourth International Conference of Anthropological and Ethnological Sciences in Vienna. In 1959, in Milan, at the fourth World Congress of Sociology CIFE was expanded into the Comité International

Year (age)	ETHNOGRAPHIC FILM, DOCUMENTARY FICTION & *FICTION*	COMMITTEES AND FESTIVALS
1940 (23)	AU PAYS DES MAGES NOIRS ('46–'47)	1e CONGR. DU FILM ETHN./GEOGR. ('47)
1950 (33)	CIMETIÈRE DANS LA FALAISE ('50) YENENDI, HOMMES FONT PLUIE ('51) BATAILLE SUR LE GRAND FLEUVE ('51) LES MAÎTRES FOUS ('55) *MOI, UN NOIR* ('58) *LA PYRAMIDE HUMAINE* ('59)	COM. DU FILM ETHNOGR. + CIFE ('52–) CIFES ('59–)
1960 (43)	CHRONIQUE D'UN ÉTÉ ('60) LA CHASSE AU LION À L'ARC ('64) *GARE DU NORD; SIGUI 0* ('65, '66) *JAGUAR* ('53/'54–'67) *PETIT À PETIT* ('68–'69)	FESTIVAL DEI POPOLI ('59–)
1970 (53)	TOUROU ET BITTI ('71) FUNÉRAILLES À BONGO ('72) SIGUI 7;*COCORICO! MR. POULET* ('75) *BABATOU* ('75) CINÉ-PORTRAITS, MAKWAYELA ('77)	VENEZIA GENTI ('72–74) CINÉMA DU RÉEL ('77–) REGARDS COMPARÉS ('78–)
1980 (63)	CINÉ-MAFIA ('80) *ENIGMA* ('86)	BILAN DU FILM ETHNOGRAPH. ('82–)
1990 (73)	*LIBERTÉ, ÉGALITÉ, FRATERNITÉ..?* ('90) *MADAME L'EAU* ('93)	
2000 (83)	*LE RÊVE PLUS FORT QUE LA MORT* ('02)	

Table 2 Rouch's activities in film organisations and festivals against the background of the production of his films

du Film Ethnographique et Sociologique (CIFES) (office: Musée de l'Homme; members: Belgium, Canada, Czechoslovakia, France, Greece, Italy, the Netherlands, Poland, Switzerland, the UK, US and Yugoslavia). Its aim was to establish a link between the human sciences and the cinematic art, with the view of both developing scientific research and extending the art of the cinema. Rouch, holding a leading position in CIFES, always played an inspirational and crucial role in the organisation (see Heusch 1962). For the first time, the following activities took place regarding ethnographic film:

(i)   inventory of all ethnographic footage: analysis, evaluation and preservation
(ii) production of new ethnographic films
(iii) distribution of the best ethnographic films
(iv) development of new possible applications of the medium of film for cultural anthropological research

Partially through good contacts with UNESCO, where Enrico Fulchignoni played an important role, it was possible to appoint researchers, like the archivist Mrs Veuve, to carry out the work. The scientific staff attached to the Musée de l'Homme and similar institutions (also outside France) were chosen for their regional and thematic expertise. Between 1952–56 some 400 films were analysed and, in 1955, the 'Catalogue des films ethnographiques français' was published including the description and evaluation of 106 films. It was followed by the 'Catalogue des films ethnographiques étrangères' (1956), the 'Premier catalogue sélectif international de films ethnographiques sur l'Afrique noire' (1967) and in 1970, among others, the 'Premier catalogue sélectif international de films ethnographiques sur la région du Pacifique' with 174 films analysed by the CIFES and an additional 167 films reported. Although many people contributed to the compilation of the catalogues, Rouch mostly wrote the forewords and provided some articles. The catalogue of 1967 included an excellent survey titled 'Situation et tendances du cinéma africain' that Rouch had already presented in 1961 during a roundtable conference in Venice organised by UNESCO.

The Comité du Film Ethnographique was also active in producing ethnographic films. Besides Rouch, it produced films for other French anthropologists such as Guy Le Moal, Monique and Robert Gessain, Nicole Echard, Marc-Henri Piault and Edmund Bernus. Two commissioning editors were employed by the Comité for a number of years. Film production took place mainly with support from the Centre National de la Recherche Scientifique. For this purpose, in the beginning of the 1970s, it established a section called SERDDAV, later renamed CNRS Audio-visuel. Next, in the 1990s, the section CNRS Images/Media was set up especially for the distribution of audio-visual productions.

It is by participating in and organising a large number of meetings, and later film festivals, that Rouch slowly but surely began building a very large network of filmmakers and anthropologists. It included visual anthropologists such as Margaret Mead (with Gregory Bateson), Robert Gardner, John Marshall, Timothy Asch, David McDougall and Ian Dunlop, plus various sociologists and many filmmakers across the world. In the early years with support from UNESCO and CIFES Rouch organised the 'International Ethnographic Film Weeks'. These were held at the Musée de l'Homme in Paris (1955) and at the University of Cagliari, Sardinia (1957). In addition, an international conference on ethnographic and sociological films took place in Prague (1957) and a meeting was held at the Anthropology Institute of the University of Perugia (1959).

The Italian section of CIFES became very active and for the first time the Rassegna Internazionale del film Etnografico e Sociologico, named Festival dei Popoli (Florence), took place in 1959, continuing its activities to the present day. Furthermore, within the framework of the festival the 'Premier séminaire pour l'evaluation des films ethnographiques et folkloriques' was organised. Rouch himself presided, strictly but in good spirit, over the discussions following each of the films, copies of which were sent to the participants within a year. Here, Rouch had reached his life-long ambition within the framework of ethnographic film festivals: screening films followed by discussion on form and content and the study of new approaches to social sciences and the cinema.

After 1968, the Festival dei Popoli became too political for Rouch's taste, especially within the framework of sociological films. Again with UNESCO support, Rouch, together with Enrico Fulchignoni, Flavia Paulon and Georges Henri Rivière, organised the Venezia Genti (1972–74), following the same format as the Florence seminars. Venezia Genti was established because of Rouch's good relationship with the Venice International Film Festival. (Rouch had previously received awards there for *Chronique d'un été* and *La Chasse au lion à l'arc*.) The Venezia Genti, however, survived only for a few years. In 1977, in collaboration with Jean-Michel Arnold (founder of the Cinémathèque in Algiers), Rouch set up the 'Cinéma du Réel' in Paris. It quickly became a prestigious annual film festival at the Centre Pompidou, but it lacked the discussions and the rigour of the seminars at Venezia Genti.

These returned in 1982 with the Bilan du film ethnographique, which is held in the film hall (dating from 1937, it is the first cinema hall within an ethnographic museum according to Rouch) of the Musée de l'Homme. Rouch's network once again became evident when the Ministry of Foreign Affairs, the Ministry of Culture and Communication, the Centre National de la Recherche Scientifique, Kodak, the Mission du Patrimoine Ethnologique, and, later, Canal Plus, became major supporters of the festival, admission to which was set to be free of charge. Annually, it attracts a large number of mainly young visual ethnographers from around the world. The discussions were all presided over by Rouch until 2000. Together with Françoise Foucault (Comité du Film Ethnographique) and others, Rouch established another form of annual, themed, film events under the title of 'Regards comparés', to present and discuss films produced across the world in different disciplines (cultural anthropology, documentary, television, art film and so forth). The focus of the 'Regards comparés' events is wide-ranging: on the Yanomamö of Brazil (1978), to the Dogon of Mali (1980), the cultures of Irian Jaya and Papua New Guinea (1986), the Inuît (1989), Brazil and its religions (2002) and the cultures of the island of Madagascar (2003).

Rouch and education in ethnographic film

As mentioned above, as early as before World War Two, Marcel Mauss pointed in his classes to the value of film, photography and phonography in Anthropology. There is no reference to any tuition offered at that time in the use of film equipment. In 1986 Rouch wrote in the introduction to the programme of the fifth Bilan du Film Ethnographique that André Leroi-Gourhan made film practice compulsory at the Centre de Formation aux Recherches Ethnographiques from 1946 onwards.

As early as 1954, backed by the Comité du Film Ethnographique, Rouch started to supervise a course titled 'Introduction au film ethnographique'. It took place in the film hall of the Musée de l'Homme where, besides ethnographic films, Rouch's favourites Robert Flaherty's *Nanook of the North* (1922) and Dziga Vertov's *The Man with the Movie Camera* (*Chelovek s kino-apparatom*, 1929) were screened. Besides Rouch, the ethno-musicologist Gilbert Rouget provided a few classes. In 1959–60 a practical filmmaking course was added. Its supervisors were Roger Morillère and Louis Boucher, working at the time for the Comité du Film Ethnographique. Both assisted in various films including *Chronique d'un été* (1960) and *Le Niger, jeune république* (1961). In 1962, further expansion took place with the introduction of a 'film gymnastics' course under the leadership of Rouch and Maria Mallet, wife of the renowned mime-actor Marcel Marceau. The course took place in a dance studio near Pigalle station. It taught hand-held camera techniques: body movements, squatting, standing up, walking backwards to achieve a wide shot, and walking steadily alongside a moving subject. The practice of controlling the body movements, whereby the head is not allowed to move up and down while walking, was central to this training. After researching in 1965 the 'plan-sequence' with the cameraman Etienne Becker for *Gare du Nord*, Rouch applied this technique himself for the first time, as a cameraman, in 1971 during the filming of *Les Tambours d'avant: Tourou et Bitti*.

When I followed the course in 1967–68, film screenings and theoretical classes still took place in the film hall at the Musée de l'Homme. Morillère and Boucher's practical classes, however, were given at the adjoining 19 Avenue d'Iéna, rooms 203 and 204. The story goes that Claude Lévi-Strauss, who also supported the foundation of the Comité du Film Ethnographique, used to oc-

Year (age)	ETHNOGRAPHIC FILM, DOCUMENTARY FICTION & _FICTION_	COURSES & INSTITUTIONS
1940 (23)	AU PAYS DES MAGES NOIRS ('46–'47)	
1950 (33)	CIMETIÈRE DANS LA FALAISE ('50)	
	YENENDI, HOMMES FONT PLUIE ('51)	
	BATAILLE SUR LE GRAND FLEUVE ('51)	
	LES MAÎTRES FOUS ('55)	
	MOI, UN NOIR ('58)	
	LA PYRAMIDE HUMAINE ('59)	COURSE ETHNOGRAPHIC FILM ('59–'71)
1960 (43)	CHRONIQUE D'UN ÉTÉ ('60)	
	LA CHASSE AU LION À L'ARC ('64)	
	GARE DU NORD; SIGUI 0 ('65,'66)	LAB. AUDIOVISUELLE EPDHE ('66–'75)
	JAGUAR ('53/'54–'67)	
	PETIT À PETIT ('68–'69)	
1970 (53)	TOUROU ET BITTI ('71)	SEMIN. CINÉMA + SCIENCE HUM. ('70–)
	FUNÉRAILLES À BONGO ('72)	FORM. DE RECHERCHES CINÉMAT. ('71–)
	SIGUI 7;_COCORICO! MR. POULET_ ('75)	
	BABATOU ('75)	DEA ('76–)
	CINÉ-PORTRAITS, MAKWAYELA ('77)	
1980 (63)	CINÉ-MAFIA ('80)	ROUCH, CLAUDINE DE FRANCE ('80)
	ENIGMA ('86)	
1990 (73)	_LIBERTÉ, ÉGALITÉ, FRATERNITÉ..?_ ('90)	
	MADAME L'EAU ('93)	
2000 (83)	_LE RÊVE PLUS FORT QUE LA MORT_ ('02)	

Table 3 Courses and educational innovations stimulated by Rouch against the background of the production of his films

cupy those studies. When he left, he arranged that Rouch and Dieterlen, who were to assemble the material to be filmed on the Sigui ceremony of the Dogon, could install an audio-visual unit there as part of the École Pratique des Hautes Études, Section V (Sciences Religieuses).

By the end of 1967 and the beginning of 1968, another teaching unit was added in Nanterre (Université de Paris X) at the Institut d'Ethnologie of Professor Eric de Dampierre. Under the supervision of Rouch and Marielle Delorme 'Introduction d'ethnologie par des films ethnographiques' was taught. An ethnographic film, introduced by the maker, was screened each Friday afternoon. In 1969, the course in Nanterre further expanded when Rouch, Colette Piault, Enrico Fulchigoni and Claudine de France started to train students in filmmaking. One of its upshots was the seminar 'Cinéma et sciences humaines (Nanterre-Chaillot à la Cinémathèque Française)', referred to below.

In 1971 research into the use of film, especially within anthropology, was developed through the foundation in Nanterre of the centre 'Formation de Recherches Cinématographiques'. At Rouch's instigation, this enhanced training which replaced that of Morillère and Boucher, became in 1976 formalised in the 'Formation de Troisième Cycle', with a Diplôme d'Études Approfondie (DEA: Diploma in Advances Studies) and the addition of a doctoral programme. Rouch was the head of the centre until 1980 and was succeeded by Claudine de France who presented in 1979 her significant doctoral thesis 'Cinéma et Anthropologie' (published in 1982 and 1989). In it, she develops her theory based on Marcel Mauss's 'Les techniques du corps' (1936) and on ideas formulated by Leroi-Gourhan and Rouch. De France and, among others, Annie Comolli, Jane Guéronnet, Philippe Lourdou and Jean-Marc Rosenfeld built a strong theoretical and practical training in film, and have also followed 'Cinéma et Anthropologie' with a number of extensive publications in the series 'Cinéma et Sciences humaines'. Rouch was involved with the first doctoral degree combining film as a 'publication scientifique de base' and text in 1980 at Nanterre. The last doctoral degree under his supervision was presented in 1992–93. In February 2002, he was for the final time a member of a commission supervising doctoral degrees.

Rouch and cinema in general

Rouch had already met Henri Langlois, the founder of the Cinémathèque Française, at the beginning of the war. He attended his screenings in the film hall of the Musée de l'Homme and continued attending the Cinémathèque screenings until his death. In the first half of the 1950s Rouch met Godard, Truffaut and others who would form the core of the *nouvelle vague* at the Cinémathèque Française. Prior to this, Rouch came into contact with Italian Neo-realism. His film *Au pays des mages noirs* (1946–47), edited by Actualités Françaises from the footage he shot together with Pierre Ponty and Jean Sauvy whilst floating down the Niger river, was shown as a prelude to the French screening of Roberto Rossellini's *Stromboli*. Rossellini, after viewing one of the first versions of Rouch's film *Jaguar*, with its innovative use of improvisation and 16mm technology, organised with Rouch a film workshop ('Atelier collectif de création') in

1957 in which a number of *Nouvelle Vague* directors such as Godard, Chabrol, Rohmer, Pollet and Truffaut participated.

Rouch played a major role in the technical advancement of film equipment. During the development of the Nagra sound recorder, Rouch regularly updated Stefan Kudelski, its designer, on operating the Nagra in the tropics, leading to continuous adaptations of the sound recorder. Kudelski, in turn, helped Rouch when he planned to record sync sound during the shooting of *La chasse au lion a l'arc* (1957–64). He placed on Rouch's Beaulieu camera, for the first time, a special electrical motor in order to enable synchronic recordings. This motor, hanging on the side of the camera was, however, extremely heavy. The result can be seen in those shots in the film where the 'horizon' is mostly not level.

Another close relationship was developed through the co-operation between Rouch and the camera designer André Coutant on a prototype of the Eclair – a quiet, portable camera, capable of producing sync sound – used during the production of *Chronique d'un été*. Later, Rouch was also involved with the development of the Äaton by Jean-Pierre Beauviola. Rouch, who always preferred the use of 16mm to 35mm, however, was not interested in the new Super 8mm format which his good friend Richard Leacock helped to develop with sound editing devices at the Massachusetts Institute of Technology in the US. In all, Rouch made only one film, *Jomo et ses frères* (1975), on the family life of his friend Damouré Zika, using Super-8. In his written publications, Rouch did pay attention to the Super-8 format, but he believed that it was too delicate and fragile as a working tool in Africa. However, classes in Nanterre changed around 1977 from 16mm to Super-8, as did Les Ateliers Varan's beginners courses. Video also came into use, but Rouch himself, again in contrast with Leacock, always held a negative view towards video. Video became a taboo subject because of the problems he perceived in editing, copying and maintenance. As a result, his contact at the Bilan with the younger generations of anthropologists using video was diminished. Whilst Rouch during the first half of his life can be considered as a very progressive filmmaker in his use of new technology, in the second half of his career he displayed somewhat conservative attitudes.

Although Rouch's technical contributions to the world of cinema have been important these are by far exceeded by his contributions to cinema in West Africa. As early as 1961 he presented, at UNESCO's request, a detailed report titled 'Situation et tendances du cinéma africain' (see also Rouch 1967; 2003). A great part of his activities took place in a colonial framework, but later on he ensured that Africans were presented with an opportunity to become involved with filmmaking themselves. Rouch became Director of the Institut de Recherche en Sciences Humaines (IRSH) in Niamey, Niger in 1961. There he set up in 1962 a production unit which owned its own film equipment, 'Atlas' editing

Year (age)	ETHNOGRAPHIC FILM, DOCUMENTARY FICTION & _FICTION_	ACTIVITIES FOR THE WORLD OF CINEMA
1940 (23)	AU PAYS DES MAGES NOIRS ('46–'47)	
1950 (33)	CIMETIÈRE DANS LA FALAISE ('50)	
	YENENDI, HOMMES FONT PLUIE ('51)	
	BATAILLE SUR LE GRAND FLEUVE ('51)	
	LES MAÎTRES FOUS ('55)	
	MOI, UN NOIR ('58)	ATELIER COLLECTIF DE CREATION ('57)
	LA PYRAMIDE HUMAINE ('59)	FLAHERTY SEMINAR: BRAULT ('57)
1960 (43)	CHRONIQUE D'UN ÉTÉ ('60)	COUTANT, KUDELSKI (1960)
	LA CHASSE AU LION À L'ARC ('64)	
	GARE DU NORD; SIGUI 0 ('65,'66)	
	JAGUAR ('53/'54–'67)	CINÉMA AFRICAIN ('61/67)
	PETIT À PETIT ('68–'69)	
1970 (53)	TOUROU ET BITTI ('71)	SEMIN. CINE SCIENCE HUM. ET CINÉM.
	FUNÉRAILLES À BONGO ('72)	
	SIGUI 7;_COCORICO! MR. POULET_ ('75)	
	BABATOU ('75)	
	CINÉ-PORTRAITS, MAKWAYELA ('77)	ATELIER VARAN (1978–)
1980 (63)	CINÉ-MAFIA ('80)	
	ENIGMA ('86)	PRÉS. CINÉMATHÈQUE FRANÇ. ('86–'91)
1990 (73)	_LIBERTÉ, ÉGALITÉ, FRATERNITÉ..?_ ('90)	
	MADAME L'EAU ('93)	
2000 (83)	_LE RÊVE PLUS FORT QUE LA MORT_ ('02)	

Table 4 Rouch's most important activities in stimulating cinema and filmmaking in general against the background of his films

benches and a complete set of perfo-tape machines facilitating the possibility of sound end mixing. With others, Rouch introduced a number of individuals in West Africa to filmmaking. The stimulating approach was as ever broad: ethnographic film, but also filmmaking in general. Moustapha Alassane, who had already assisted Rouch in some ethnographic films, made a reconstruction of a traditional marriage, _Aouré_ (1962), as well as _Le Retour d'un aventurier_ (1966), a parody on the western genre re-located in Niger where young cowboys wish to take control from the elderly. Furthermore, Alassane made the animation film *Bon voyage Sim* (1966), following a training course at the National Film Board of Canada. He went on to produce many more ethnographic, fiction and animation films. Oumarou Ganda, Edward G. Robinson from *Moi, un noir*, used the centre in Niamey to make *Cabascabo* (1968), describing his experiences during the colonial war in Indochina. Others who were trained in the centre were Inoussa Ousseïni, who graduated in sociology and anthropology, became a minister in the Niger government and is currently Niger's delegate at UNESCO, Paris. His early film *Paris c'est joli* (1974) described the exploitation in France of African immigrant workers. Djingarey Maïga made *Vendredi soir, Aube noire* (1983), after starting his career working with Rouch.

Rouch has contributed indirectly to the education of documentary film-making to many across the world through his initiative to establish VARAN (1978–present). During Mozambique's independence in 1975 Rouch believed that local people should record the events themselves. Thus, two intensive training programmes – 'beginners' and 'advanced' – in which 'cinéma direct' was taught were established in the country by Rouch. Additionally, he made in Mozambique, with Jacques d'Arthuys, an anti-apartheid film, *Makwayela* (1977), depicting the story of the labourers in the gold mines of South Africa. The film was edited in camera and was designed to become a teaching tool for local film students. From the Mozambique experience VARAN continued to grow and develop film training projects across the world organised by d'Arthuys and the brothers Vincent and Séverin Blanchet. Courses are run by VARAN in France, as well as in Madagascar, Vietnam, Papua New Guinea and Afghanistan, to name a few.

In 1970 Rouch established a film screening and discussion programme on Saturday mornings at the Cinémathèque Française in the Palais de Chaillot titled 'Le séminaire "Cinéma et sciences humaines" (Nanterre-Chaillot à la Cinémathèque Française)'. Rouch worked initially in tandem with his old friend Enrico Fulchignoni, later replaced by Xavier de France from Nanterre. Documentaries, ethnographic and fiction films were screened to the general public with the filmmakers themselves in attendance. During the first decades especially, discussions often turned violent and the meetings were nicknamed 'La Boucherie'. Later on, screenings became calmer but could continue to count on a faithful public, intrigued by the choice of films and their contextualisation by Rouch and de France with his famous 'small card' system of notes.

When Langlois, the 'father' of the Cinémathèque Française, died in 1977, Rouch, along with Fulchignoni and others, took a seat at the 'comité des activités'. Soon afterwards, George-Henri Rivière, former director of the Musée des Arts et Traditions Populaire and co-founder of the ethnographic film festival Venezia

Genti, was appointed president of the Cinémathèque. In 1979, Rouch became a Vice President. Jack Lang, the Minister of Culture at the time, increased the budget for the Cinémathèque by 300 per cent. In addition, the authorities developed new plans for a Palais d'Image in the Palais de Tokyo in which the Cinémathèque along with the Centre National de la Photographie and the Nouvelle École supérieur du Cinéma would move in. In 1987 this led to an enormous crisis as the government's plans went too far in view of the supporters of Langlois' legacy. Rouch, who was acceptable to both parties, became the President of the Cinémathèque Française until 1991. The quality of the film programmes remained in Langlois' tradition, but openings were created for young filmmakers to show their work for the first time. After 1991, Rouch remained active as a 'membre de bureau', and continued to actively participate in the Cinémathèque's projects (see Olmeta 2000; Sabouraud 1987).

By the end of his life, Rouch had received at least 16 film awards, three honorary doctorates and countless retrospectives home and abroad. After the fatal road accident, Rouch was put to rest on 24 February 2004 at a cemetery in Niamey, Niger. The Minister of Culture Abdou Labo declared that: 'Nigérien tu l'as été toute la vie, Nigérien tu resteras pour l'éternité' ('Nigerien you have been your whole life, Nigerien you will be for eternity'). When saying goodbye to a friend, Rouch did not like to shake hands: 'We would meet again after all?' Indeed, we continue to meet Rouch through his films.

AUTHOR'S NOTE: Thanks to Claudine de France and Annie Comolli for supplying me with answers to some questions I had, and to Philippe Lourdou and Han Vermeulen for their critical reading and comments.

REFERENCES

Anon. (n.d.) Comite www.comite-film-ethno.net/rouch/rouchfilm.htm (accessed 14 November 2006).

_____ (1955) *Catalogue de films ethnographiques français*. Paris: Comité du Film Ethnographique.

_____ (1956) *Catalogue de films ethnographiques étrangers*. Paris: C.I.F.E.S.

_____ (1967a) *Premier séminaire pour l'évaluation des films ethnographiques et Folkoriques* (mimeographed report). Florence: Festival dei Popoli/C.I.F.E.S, 11.

_____ (1967b) *Premier catalogue sélectif international de films ethnographiques sur l'Afrique noire*. Paris: Unesco.

Eaton, M (ed.) (1979) *Anthropology-Reality-Cinema: The Films of Jean Rouch*. London: British Film Institute.

France, C. de (1938) *Masques Dogons*. Paris: Ph.D. Thesis (with an analyses of mask dances, see 'Sous les masques noirs'). Paris: Institut d'Ethnologie.

____ (1989) *Cinéma et Anthropologie*. Paris: Editions de la Maison des Sciences de l'Homme.

Heusch, L. de (1962) *Film and the social sciences*. Paris: Unesco.

Leroi-Gourhan, A. (1948) 'Cinéma et Sciences: Le film ethnologique existe-t-il?', *La revue de géographie humaines et d'ethnologie*, 3, 42–51.

Olmeta, P. (2000) *La Cinémathèque Française de 1936 à nos jours*. Paris: CNRS Editions.

Rouch, J. (1967) 'Situation et tendances du cinéma africain', *Premier catalogue sélectif international de films ethnographiques sur l'Afrique noir*. Paris: UNESCO, 374–408.

____ (2003) *Ciné-ethnography*, ed. and trans. S. Feld. Minneapolis: University of Minneapolis Press.

Sabouraud, F. (1987) 'Cocorico monsieur le Président, Entretien avec Jean Rouch', *Cahiers du cinéma*, 75, IV.

THE FILMS

A boy from the Dogon during the Sigui ritual, 1970

3   JEAN ROUCH AND THE LEGACY OF THE 'PALE MASTER': *THE SIGUI PROJECT, 1931–2033*

Paul Henley

With every good reason, cineastes hail Jean Rouch as a precursor to both the French *nouvelle vague* and indigenous West African cinema, whilst documentarists acknowledge him as the originator, with Edgar Morin, of *cinéma vérité*. But if Rouch's total oeuvre of over a hundred completed films is taken into account, and not just the small and rather unrepresentative sample that has been made available in English-language versions, it is readily apparent that the overwhelming majority of his films were ethnographic in character.[1] Furthermore, although he may have been highly innovative in expanding the modes and styles of ethnographic filmmaking, notably through the fusion of fact and fiction in his urban 'ethnofictions' such as *Jaguar, Moi, un Noir* (1958) and *Petit à petit* (1968-69), the praxis of most of these ethnographic films was extremely conventional, generally consisting of heavily narrated, straightforwardly descriptive accounts of traditional ritual events in rural regions of West Africa.[2]

The Songhay and the Dogon

Most of Rouch's conventionally ethnographic films concern the ritual practices of two particular ethnic groups whose territories lie along the middle reaches of the Niger River: the Songhay and the Dogon. Rouch worked primarily with the Songhay who, together with the closely related Zarma, live in what is today the western extremity of the Republic of Niger, though there are also some communities in neighbouring parts of Burkina Faso and Mali. Some Songhay-Zarma are settled along the Niger river itself, including the Sorko fishermen sub-group, whilst others live in the surrounding savannas where they farm millet and herd cattle, and include the sub-group known as the Gow, renowned for their hunting skills. Indeed, the Songhay and all these various sub-groups contribute to a complex mosaic of ethnic groups inhabiting this region who are continuously involved in all manner of social and economic exchanges with one another, making the drawing of absolute boundaries between them rather artificial.

The Dogon, on the other hand, live some 500 km to the south and west, in the Bandiagara Cliffs escarpment of eastern Mali. They appear to have migrated there from the Mandingo Mountains, a further 1,000 km to the southwest, possibly to take refuge from the political instability that followed the arrival of Islam in the area in the fifteenth century. At the time that Rouch worked with them, they numbered about 250,000 people (see Prédal 1996: 20; see also Fulchignoni 2003: 170). Compared to the Songhay and the other plain-dwellers of the region, they live in relative isolation and although some scholars would classify the Dogon and the Songhay in the same language family, they are socially and culturally very different. Their system of patronymic clans, age grades and related initiation ceremonies, and most significantly for the present chapter, the various religious cults associated with ancestral masks that are so important in traditional Dogon life are completely absent amongst the Songhay-Zarma. Conversely, the Dogon do not have anything akin to the highly elaborated spirit-possession ceremonies that are traditionally such an important feature of Songhay-Zarma life (see Rouch 2003: 114).

However, one feature that is common to both these groups is that a large proportion of their respective populations are practising Muslims. In both groups, public ceremonial expressions of traditional 'animist' religious beliefs and practices have been increasingly under pressure since the mid-1970s when the current fundamentalist tendency in the Muslim world first began to take hold in West Africa (see Masquelier 1993; Boddy 1995). But during the heyday of Rouch's film work in the region, which ran roughly from the late 1940s to the late 1970s, this historical process was only just beginning and, as he reported it, in everyday life there was generally a very pragmatic accommodation between Islam and traditional religious practices (Rouch 1989: 19–28). In any case, in his ethnographic films, Rouch aimed to deal primarily with the traditional 'animist' religions and Islam is touched upon only briefly, usually when its impact on traditional ritual activities was impossible to ignore.

Amongst the Songhay, the religious practice that most intrigued Rouch, both as anthropologist and filmmaker, was spirit-possession: he himself estimated that as many as fifty of his films concerned spirit-possession ceremonies to some degree (in Taylor 2003: 140).[3] Drought is a chronic feature of the middle Niger region since it lies on the southern margin of the Sahelian desert, and it appears to have been extremely severe during the period when Rouch was most active as a filmmaker there. Particularly common therefore amongst the subjects of his films were spirit-possession ceremonies dedicated to rain-making. These are known locally as *Yenendi*, a term which literally means 'to refresh' in Songhay (see Ahonou 2000). Through dancing to particular melodies played on a monochord violin, the adepts of these cults aim to enter a trance state and become possessed by Dongo, the spirit of thunder, who is thought to control the weather. Once the spirit has been incorporated into an adept's body, the priests of the cult can then ask him what he requires in order to bring rain. The response is usually a demand for an animal sacrifice.

Spirit-possession was not the only aspect of Songhay-Zarma life that Rouch treated in his conventional ethnographic film work. He also made a number of films on other topics, notably about hunting practices, initially about the hunting of hippopotami and, later, lions. Some of these are amongst Rouch's best-known films.[4] But in terms of sheer volume, these are far outweighed in importance in the Rouchian oeuvre by the spirit-possession films. Although most of these ceremonies filmed by Rouch took place in remote rural locations on the edge of the Sahel, the notable exception is the one featured in *Les Maîtres fous*, released in 1955. This was shot in a small village outside Accra, Ghana and, along with the equally well-known ethnofictions, *Jaguar* and *Moi, un Noir*, formed part of the extended study of the migration of Sahelian peoples to the cities of coastal West Africa that Rouch was engaged in from 1954 to 1960.[5] *Les Maîtres fous* caused a scandal at the time of its release because it showed the adepts in trance apparently mimicking colonial authority figures whilst behaving in a bizarre manner. Whilst the spirit-possession ceremony featured in this film is certainly not a rain-making ceremony, its precise motivation remains the subject of much controversy.[6]

Yet if Songhay-Zarma spirit-possession represents the predominant subject of Rouch's conventional ethnographic film work, this is strongly counterbalanced by films about the ritual life of the Dogon. Of these, the films that he made in the period 1966–74 are the best example. These films concern the Sigui, a sequence of world-renewal ritual ceremonies that take place over seven successive years and involve all the male members of the community, from the most ancient to those barely able to walk. Orchestrated by a group of elders chanting in *siguiso*, a secret ritual language, at various culminating moments these ceremonies feature the dramatic display of ancestral masks. But perhaps the most remarkable aspect of the Sigui is that it is only enacted at intervals of sixty years. For most Dogon it is therefore literally a once-in-a-lifetime experience, though they calculate that on the occasion of any given enactment there will be sufficient survivors from the previous enactment to instruct the young people in how to perform the crucial ritual activities.

The Sigui films were not the only ones that Rouch made amongst the Dogon. He also made a number of films about funerary ceremonies and, in conjunction with the distinguished ethnomusicologist Gilbert Rouget, a highly pedagogical film about Dogon music. But although the Sigui films represent the largest single ethnographic film project that Rouch ever carried out and, taken as a whole, his Dogon films represent a monumental labour, they still constitute no more than a secondary seam within his total oeuvre to the Songhay-Zarma films. Whilst the Songhay films grew out of Rouch's own deep and extended experience of their world as well as a dense network of close personal relationships developed over a long period, his direct first-hand knowledge of the Dogon prior to beginning the Sigui project was relatively slight. Indeed, although Rouch invested a vast amount of time and energy in the making of his Dogon films, I would argue that they are best understood not as a development of his own prior work but rather as an elaborate act of homage, both in content and form, to his anthropological mentor, Marcel Griaule, and to the latter's long-term collaborator and Rouch's own close personal friend, Germaine Dieterlen.

The legacy of the 'pale master'

Whilst in the final year of his studies, in 1941, Rouch had his first extended encounter with the teacher whom he would later refer to as the 'pale master' when he attended an introductory course of descriptive ethnography that Marcel Griaule gave in the basement of the Musée de l'Homme.

By all accounts, Griaule was a charismatic figure. A daring aviator in his youth, he had been appointed by the French parliament to lead the celebrated multidisciplinary expedition that travelled across North Africa from Dakar to Djibouti in 1931–33. He had also been the first person to be awarded a doctorate in anthropology in France, having studied with Marcel Mauss, nephew and most distinguished pupil of the foundational sociologist Emile Durkheim. Mauss himself was the author of the equally foundational anthropological text, *The Gift*, first published in French in 1923. Later, Rouch would claim to have learnt nothing from Griaule's 'austere lectures', remembering them only as a series of disaggregated ethnographic tidbits (2003: 103). Nevertheless, he was intrigued by the world that Griaule opened up to him. In particular, Griaule passed on to Rouch his fascination for the Bandiagara Cliffs, home and refuge of the Dogon. Griaule had set up camp on the escarpment for two months in 1931 during the course of the Dakar-Djibouti expedition and had subsequently returned there a number of times in the hope of unravelling the 'mysteries' of Dogon cosmology.

Rouch had been attracted to anthropology in the first place through a prior interest in Surrealism whose exponents, as has been well-documented elsewhere, were engaged in an active dialogue with anthropology in 1930s Paris. A third dimension to this exchange was the contemporary rage for *l'art nègre*. This embraced everything from traditional African sculpture to *le dernier cri* in Afro-American modernity, such as the jazz of Louis Armstrong and the sensuous dancing of Josephine Baker.

Rouch spent most of the war years in West Africa working as an engineer, first in Niger and later in Senegal, during which time he began his first tentative ethnographic enquiries on the basis of questionnaires sent to him by Griaule and Dieterlen (see Clifford 1988, and also contributions to this volume). Shortly after being demobilised he returned to Paris and enrolled on the anthropology doctoral programme at the Sorbonne with Griaule as his supervisor. At that time, Griaule was under something of a cloud because whilst most other leading anthropologists had gone into exile during the Occupation, he had actively supported the Vichy regime, accepting not only a professorship at the Sorbonne but even a commission as a colonel in the airforce. When the exiles returned, they conspired to oust Griaule from the Musée de l'Homme, though he managed to hold on to his chair at the Sorbonne. Although Rouch's own political sympathies were very much with the exiles, he nevertheless signed up to study with Griaule because, he would later claim, he found that the Griaulian faction simply 'had more fun' than their critics (Rouch 2003: 110).

If the cultural influences that had attracted Rouch to anthropology in the 1930s had been distinctly avant-garde, the approach advocated by Griaule in the immediate post-war years was remarkably conservative. Its general methodological principles were those that Griaule himself had learnt in the 1920s from his own mentor, Marcel Mauss. As exemplified effectively by *The Gift*, this method depended in the first instance on the assembling of large bodies of ethnographic information or 'documents' about particular social or cultural phenomena, from which, eventually, through a rigorous process of scholarly sifting, one might elucidate some general abstract principles. Some of the principles that Mauss identified – about the importance of reciprocity in a range of human relationships, or the corporeal embodiment of cultural norms, for example – have been highly inspirational for subsequent generations of anthropologists. But contemporary accounts suggest that in his lectures Mauss often got lost in the ethnographic detail and never arrived at the elucidation of the principles.[7]

Rouch's account of Griaule's lectures suggest that they may have suffered from the same faults as those of Mauss. But what Griaule added to the Maussian intellectual inheritance was a commitment to first-hand fieldwork. For although Mauss actively advocated this, he did not actually do any himself. Griaule, in contrast, was highly committed to fieldwork in practice as well as in principle. Rouch liked to quote Griaule's view that one needed at least twenty years' first-hand experience of a given society before one could begin to achieve a 'deep knowledge' of its systems of thought (see, for example, Rouch 2003: 111).

Griaule's ideas about fieldwork were laid out very explicitly in his *Méthode de l'ethnographie*, which was not published until 1957, the year after his death, but which draws on his experience working with the Dogon since the 1930s. The approach he advocates is very different to that developed around much the same time by social anthropologists of the British school – notably by Bronislaw Malinowski – which, it is probably true to say, has become the orthodoxy in social and cultural anthropology generally, even in France. Whereas Malinowski proposed that the fieldworker should 'plunge into the life of the natives' (1932: 22) usually alone, becoming a relatively unobtrusive 'participant-observer' engaged in the day-to-day life of a community, Griaule advocated instead the formation of teams of fieldworkers, organised along quasi-military lines who would not only maximise the collection of data within any given time period, but at the same time triangulate the results that they were obtaining. Far from the discreet observation of life as it is lived, with minimal interference, as per the Malinowskian formula, Griaule's method was highly pro-active, involving intensive interrogatory interviews based on systematic questionnaires. Rather than observing the subjects interacting amongst themselves, Griaule preferred to work instead with a select group of elite informants, usually through bilingual intermediaries rather than in the native language.[8]

In his essay 'The Mad Fox and the Pale Master' Rouch gives a rather droll account of the fieldwork routines of Griaule and Dieterlen as he observed them whilst visiting their camp in the Bandiagara Cliffs in 1950. First thing in the morning, Griaule would give all members of the team their tasks for the day. Whilst he and Dieterlen worked through questionnaires with their established informants, and other researchers in the team were dispatched elsewhere, traditional musicians would be asked to come and work with Rouch and Roger Rosfelder, the research colleague from the CNRS who was acting as his sound recordist. Alternatively, Rouch and Rosfelder would be sent off to film the daily routine in a nearby Dogon village.[9] At noon, the whole team would meet up in the company of the Dogon informants and interpreters, and exchange the information gathered in the morning. On the basis of these discussions – in which, Rouch emphasises, the Dogon played an active part – Dieterlen would typically develop an inspired series of further hypotheses which Griaule would then order into a new series of questionnaires to be used in the afternoon. With perhaps just a touch of irony, Rouch compares this approach to the Socratic method of successive dialogical approximations to philosophical truth (Rouch 2003: 112).

Rouch's own approach to fieldwork, both as filmmaker and text-making anthropologist, shared certain traits with those of Griaule, though in other respects it was fundamentally different. Like Griaule, Rouch returned faithfully to the same sites over a prolonged period. Like Griaule, he usually worked in French or through interpreters, with a small group of key collaborators. In his 'straight' anthropological fieldwork, he often used formal questionnaires, notably in the migration studies that he carried out in the 1950s. Although he never used interviews of any kind in his films, one can perhaps detect, as James Clifford has done, a certain continuity between Griaule's 'dialogical method', as he calls it, in which interrogatory questions are used to provoke subjects into revealing answers, and Rouch's idea that the camera could act as a catalyst to provoke his subjects into revelatory performances (1988: 77). Indeed, it is tempting to argue that in the same way that Griaule's pro-active methods contrasted with the more passive participant-observational methods of the British school, so too did Rouch's pro-active cinematographic methods contrast with the more passive ones of direct or observational cinema as practised by his English-speaking contemporaries.

However, in my view these relatively superficial similarities mask a more profound difference between Griaule and Rouch's methods of working. For Griaule's 'dialogical method', as exemplified by his *Méthode de l'ethnographie* (1957), was essentially antagonistic, taking as its point of departure the assumption that the informant was lying. To combat this supposedly inherent tendency to lie, Griaule proposed that the researcher, compared variously in his text to a prosecution lawyer, a judge and even a bloodhound, had to use whatever device or assume whatever persona necessary to circumvent the defences put up by the informants. They should be treated, Griaule suggested, as if they were the 'guilty party' in a court of law, whilst the remainder of the society should be treated as if they were 'accomplices' in obstructing the researchers in their mission to find out the truth (see Griaule 1957: 59).[10]

This attitude, shockingly aggressive to modern sensibilities and self-evidently the product of a colonial mentality whereby all indigenous knowledge was fair game, could not be further from Rouch's own attitudes. Rouch thought of himself instead as engaged in a project of what he termed 'shared anthropology' in which there was not only co-operation in the making of a film, but also afterwards, through the screening of the results to the subjects. These screenings, he discovered, not only led to comments from the audience that increased his anthropological understanding of the content of his films, but led the subjects themselves to suggest further collaborative film ventures. Although this method had certain pragmatic advantages, Rouch also thought it had clear ethical implications as well. Indeed, he considered these screenings to be a form of 'counter-gift' for the support and trust that the subjects had shown to him by collaborating in the making of the film in the first place. 'Knowledge', he declared, 'should not be a stolen secret to be later consumed in Western temples of learning' but rather should be arrived at through a series of ongoing exchanges, or as he put it, 'an unending quest in which ethnographic subjects and the ethnographer commit themselves to the path of shared anthropology' (1997: 227). When Rouch spoke of indigenous knowledge as in this way, he could have had no better example of this buccaneering attitude than that of his own former teacher. Whilst Griaule thought of the ethnographic endeavour as a struggle to locate a nugget of truth in a tangled skein of deceit, Rouch's notion of dialogical exchange between subjects and researcher was based on the premise of collaboration in a joint creative project. Where Griaule saw himself as 'the bloodhound of the social fact', (1957: 59) Rouch was the filmmaker who wanted to use his camera as Louis Armstrong had played his trumpet, always hoping to improvise unexpected harmonies with his subjects.

The 'mystery' of the Sigui

In 1966, the year before another Sigui ritual cycle was due to commence, Rouch returned to the Bandiagara Cliffs accompanied by Germaine Dieterlen. Their purpose was to seek permission to film the event from the Hogon, the paramount traditional religious authority of the Dogon. In 1931, during the Dakar-Djibouti expedition, Griaule had recorded extensive details of the Sigui ritual cycle on the basis of purely oral accounts provided by those who had attended the last enactment some twenty years before. Griaule would surely have hoped to live to see the next enactment himself since he would only have been in his late sixties when it was due to begin. But shortly before his death in 1956, when he had already had two heart attacks and knew that his days were numbered, he asked Rouch to film it. Later, as the time for Sigui drew near, Dieterlen also urged him to do so. Initially, although he enthusiastically agreed to collaborate with Dieterlen, he was wary of being drawn too far into the uncomfortable mixture of professional controversy and interpersonal tension that characterised relationships between the leading French Dogon specialists at the time. He also had many other projects in hand, both in Paris and amongst the Songhay. So he proposed that he would act merely as a cameraman for Dieterlen and only for the first year or two, before finding someone else to work with her. But, as things turned out, he became progressively drawn into the project, eventually shooting the entire cycle and sharing the directorial role with Dieterlen (see Rouch 1995b: 228–9; Prédal 1996: 20–1).

Despite the obstacles put in their way by the recently independent Malian socialist government unhappy about this recording of 'tribalism', as well as by

Muslim Dogon who disapproved of traditional religious practices, and even by the threat of great encampments of tourists attracted in large numbers to the event, Rouch and Dieterlen went back to the Bandiagara Cliffs for three months, year after year, not only to shoot, but also to screen the material shot the previous year and listen to the feedback. After six years, they brought their principal guide and informant, Amadigné Dolo, to Paris and worked with him in the editing suite. Then they suffered something of a setback in the seventh and final year when the Malian government forbade them to film. The country was in the grip of an intense drought and it was deemed inappropriate to record the celebration of festivities in which large quantities of millet beer would inevitably be consumed. Rouch and Dieterlen therefore had to content themselves with returning the following year, 1974, and filming a highly reduced reconstruction of the event.

Rouch allowed himself to become more involved in this project despite his initial reservations, because, like Griaule before him, he became fascinated by the prospect of unravelling the 'mystery' of the Sigui.[11] When he and Dieterlen began, having only the oral accounts collected by Griaule to go on, they were not even sure how long the cycle lasted – it could have been anything between four and eight years. But as the project proceeded they gradually identified a pattern that was rather different from the one that Griaule had discerned. In doing so, they were greatly aided by the fact that they were able to witness the complete sequence of ritual events, something that no Dogon would normally get to do since the Sigui is peripatetic, moving to a different village every year. In a strictly geographical sense, this movement is in a northwest to southeast sense, up and down, and along the escarpment of the Bandiagara Cliffs, though the Dogon themselves think of the Sigui as moving in an east to west direction, 'on the wings of the wind'. An individual Dogon normally sees no more than three stages of the Sigui: the celebration in his own village, in the village from which his village receives the Sigui and in the village to which his own village passes it on.

At first, the Dogon were disturbed by the fact that Rouch and Dieterlen would see more than three stages of the Sigui and insisted that they consult the Pale Fox, a powerful trickster spirit, to determine whether this would bring unfortunate consequences. This was effected by a Dogon elder, using the normal technique for consulting with the Pale Fox – drawing out a particular pattern in the sand on top of a nearby plateau and then leaving it overnight with a few peanuts as bait, so that it would be walked over by the Pale Fox. By the disposition of his footprints across the pattern the following morning, the Dogon could tell whether or not the Pale Fox approved of the project. In the morning, the anxious filmmakers returned to the scene to see what the verdict had been. Although certain difficulties were foreseen (correctly as it turned out), the decision proved to be essentially favourable and Rouch and Dieterlen were given permission to continue with the filming for the full seven years (see Rouch 2003: 122–4).

The overview that this witnessing of the complete sequence afforded, coupled with the benefits of the feedback garnered from the public screenings in Bandiagara and from Amadigné Dolo in Paris, gave Rouch and Dieterlen all manner of insights into the significance of the Sigui. This process was greatly facilitated by the fact that they were able to view the rushes repeatedly in the editing suite, progressively refining their understandings of the full ritual cycle as they went along. In effect, whereas even a Dogon elder would generally only witness the enactment of a Sigui at most twice, and then only for part of the sequence, Rouch and Dieterlen were not only able to see the whole sequence but, due to the filmic record, to see it many times over. This placed them in a uniquely advantageous position to offer a comprehensive anthropological interpretation of the event.

What they concluded, in summary, was that Sigui represented the re-enactment of the various stages of the Dogon myth of origin which, in its turn, paralleled the various stages of the human life cycle as the Dogon conceive it. Taken as whole, as outlined by Rouch, the Sigui appears to represent the collective triumph over death, not just by the physical process of birth, but by the cultural forms of language and nurturing and, finally, circumcision conceived as the ritual launching of a new generation. In presenting this interpretation, Rouch acknowledged that it was merely a working hypothesis about which not even he and Dieterlen were entirely agreed (Rouch 2003: 121). Certainly, there would appear to be other possible strands of interpretation. There are also some more general theoretical questions that one might raise about the status of an interpretation made from a perspective normally not available to any active participant. But these are matters that should be taken up elsewhere since our present concern is not so much with the hermeneutics of the Sigui itself as with the praxis of the films that Rouch made about it.

The praxis of the Sigui project

The Dogon material was first released as a series of individual films, each corresponding to a different year of the Sigui. Rouch and Dieterlen are credited as the joint directors of all the films, whilst Gilbert Rouget, the ethnomusicologist with whom Rouch collaborated on a number of other occasions, is also credited in some sources with the co-direction of the film corresponding to the first year, L'enclume de Yougou (1967). However, these were 'documents' rather than documentaries; little more than an assembly of shots that could then be used for feedback purposes. Rouch only did a voice-over commentary for one of them, giving up this practice when the Dogon complained in the feedback screenings that his voice prevented them from hearing what they themselves were saying. In 1981, these individual films were amalgamated into the so-called 'Sigui synthèse'. The formal title of this synthesis is *Sigui 1967–1973: L'invention de la parole et de la mort*, and for this version the material has been reduced to just over half the total length of the original films. With the addition of an introductory section about the history of the Dogon and an overview of their principal rites of passage, the result is a film of a running time of approximately 120 minutes.

In both forms, these Dogon films are highly descriptive, in some ways representing a surprising reversion to the praxis of the films that Rouch made in the initial phase of his career in the late 1940s and early 1950s. There are certainly some significant differences due to the technological advances made in the interim. One of the most obvious is the synchronicity of sound and image, whilst another is the length of the shots. Whereas the maximum length of shot allowed by the spring-wound Bell & Howell camera that he had used in earlier films was only 25 seconds, with the cameras available by 1967 it was possible for a take to last for up to 11 minutes. This enabled Rouch to indulge his preference for the long, unbroken take and there are certain passages in the films when he uses this technique to good effect. But for all the technological advantages of the new equipment the cinematography, taken as a whole, is strangely disengaged. With Rouch resolute in his determination not to use a tripod, there are many shaky shots of both the dramatic escarpments of the Bandiagara Cliffs and of the ritual action. The wide-angle lens predominates and for much of the time the camera remains outside the action, a seemingly distant and uncertain observer, even in the later films by which time he would surely have got to know the subjects reasonably well. Notwithstanding his strictures at other times on the zoom lens, there are a number of awkward examples of its use in these films (see Rouch 1995a: 89).

The soundtrack of the 'Sigui synthèse' features an unrelenting voice-over commentary. This is performed by Rouch himself and explains what is going on, translating the synchronous sounds (mostly the songs of the dancers and the ritual chanting of the elders, but also a few passages of more everyday speech) or providing some simple interpretations of the symbolic significance of ritual paraphernalia, the movements of the dancers and so on. All this is voiced in a poetic tone clearly intended to reinforce a sense of the epic nature of the ritual event but, after a while, it has to be said that this becomes rather wearing. Given that by this time Rouch was working with fully synchronous sound, he could have used subtitles if he had wanted to, at least for the subjects' chanting and speech, but he retained a life-long antipathy to subtitles on the grounds that they 'mutilate' the image (Rouch 1995a: 92).

Perhaps even more surprising than these relatively banal technical features is the absence of any clearly established characters in these films. After all, they were shot many years after Rouch's own migration ethnofictions *Jaguar* and *Moi, un noir* had revolutionised ethnographic film praxis by giving the central characters names, identities and voices, and by building the central narrative around them. During the early part of the Sigui project, Rouch was even simultaneously shooting *Petit à petit*, which took ethnofiction into new terrain by following the adventures of his long-time Nigerien collaborators, Damouré Zika and Lam Ibrahima Dia on their explorations of Paris. But in the Sigui films, although a few of the most eminent men are given a name (notably Anaïs Dolo, said to be 120 years old and witnessing his third Sigui, the first having been sensed whilst he was still in his mother's womb), there is no systematic attempt to establish any characters. Apart from a few rare moments, such as when some male elders explain the significance of certain cave paintings, no subject ever directly addresses the camera.

Women are also particularly notable by their absence in the Sigui films, other than appearing in occasional glimpses, though there are some important exceptions to this. There is, for example, a moment when some elderly women known as the *yasigine*, 'the sisters of the Sigui, twins of the Pale Fox', represent the community of women amidst the male dancers. In another brief moment, there is a shot of a woman dancing whilst suckling a child. Rouch does not comment on her presence but given the predominantly male orientation of the event, my entirely uninformed guess is that the child is male and that woman is dancing on his behalf rather than in her own right. There are also some significant interludes in the dancing when women are shown supplying the millet beer or helping their men dress in ritual paraphernalia which, interestingly enough, often consists of the women's own clothing and jewellery. Whilst the absence of women clearly reflects the general emphasis of the ritual event itself, the striking displacement of women from this rite celebrating the generational renewal of Dogon society is commented upon only in passing.[12]

The absence of women in the films would appear to be related in part to the fact that the Sigui films are almost exclusively concerned with the ritual action itself or on preparatory processes directly associated with it. There is no attempt to set the event within the everyday life of the Dogon, nor within any kind of broader political or organisational context of Dogon society, though the impingement of the wider world does break through at various points. This is hardly surprising since, as is explained at the beginning of the 'Sigui synthèse', many of the participants are migrants who have returned for the event from Abidjan and Accra. Thus, for example, at one moment in the film when a village chief dies, a mortuary mannequin in his likeness is set up on his house, and we are surprised to discover that this is dressed in a soldier's uniform because, it transpires, the deceased had been a veteran of the French colonial army.

For the most part though, this impingement of the wider world is not present in the film in the form of symbols of modernity such as music or fashionable dress, as in Rouch's migration ethnofictions, but rather in the form of the threat represented by Islam to the continuation of traditional religious practices. This is illustrated most dramatically towards the end of the material relating to the third year when there is a brief shot which appears to show that in front of the caves where the young men will be initiated and directly overlooking the cleared area where the dancers have been enacting the *dama*, a memorial ceremony, of the first culture hero, there is a mosque with bright white walls and surmounted by a gleaming golden crescent. Later, a similarly striking moment occurs in the material relating to the sixth year, when the dancers make a dramatic about-turn as they reach the point beyond which the Sigui cannot travel since, due to the dominance of Islam, it is no longer welcome in the villages further to the west.

At first sight, it seems rather extraordinary that Rouch should be making films in a manner reminiscent of the first phase of his career at precisely the same time as he was making *Petit à petit* which, although considered by some to be one of his weaker ethnofictions, undeniably involves an intimacy and a direct personal engagement with the subjects of the kind that had marked out all of Rouch's Songhay films since *Jaguar*. But in his defence, as it were, it could be said that in many ways Rouch found himself in the same situation with respect to the Dogon in the late 1960s as he had been with the Songhay-Zarma in the 1940s. Although he had visited the Dogon for short periods on previous occasions, he did not have a personal network that he had developed over the years amongst the Songhay. He did not speak the Dogon language and though he used local people as sound recordists, as was his custom, these included his trusty Nigerien collaborators, Damouré, Lam and Tallou, none of whom spoke Dogon either. As Rouch admitted, it was often the case during the shooting of the Sigui ceremonies that neither he nor Dieterlen had any idea what was going on. It was only later in the editing suite that they realised the full significance of what they had recorded.

But I suspect that there is a more profound reason why the Sigui films turned out the way that they did. For many of the characteristics – the heavy emphasis on the exegesis of the ritual, the absence of any treatment of the organisational or political aspects of the event, the absence of any reference to everyday life, to the world of women or of work and the exclusion except when absolutely necessary of any reference to the pressures from the outside world – echo the criticisms that have been made of the textual accounts of the Dogon produced over five decades by Griaule and his various associates. Clifford, for example, comments that despite the comprehensiveness of the documentation, the account of the Dogon by the Griaulian team remains 'curiously skewed' with little attention to 'just how daily life is conducted, how circumstantial political decisions are actually made'; the heavy emphasis on elaborately cross-referenced native theories of ontology and cosmology in Griaule's work, Clifford suggests, 'never satisfies the nagging question: What are the Dogon really like?' (1988: 137–8).[13]

Exactly the same could be said of Rouch's films of the Dogon, suggesting that here too we may detect the influence of Griaule on his former student. After all, these films were in some sense originally commissioned by Griaule, and Rouch made them in close collaboration with Griaule's long-term partner, Dieterlen. In this sense, the Sigui films could be interpreted as an extraordinary homage to the 'pale master', which in its sheer extravagance masked the ambiguity that is sometimes evident in the sentiments that Rouch expressed about his late mentor (see Henley 2006: 758, n.3). Yet even though there may have been these extenuating circumstances, it is difficult to avoid the conclusion that relative to the vast amount of time and energy that Rouch put into the filming of the Sigui, the result in terms of finished films is disappointing. Even to this day, not merely the original films but even the 'Sigui synthèse' remain difficult to get hold of. In some cases, even those versions that are available appear to be unfinished. It would seem then, almost tragically, that the sheer volume of material rather overwhelmed Rouch and, in a manner that is poignantly reminiscent of the circumstances of his even more distant intellectual ancestor, Marcel Mauss, he never managed to bring it fully under control.

On to the next Sigui

Rouch completed the filming of the Sigui in 1974. This year marked the end of a period of intense filmmaking activity on Rouch's part. For, almost incredibly, the Sigui films were not the only films that Rouch made amongst the Dogon during this phase of his career. He also made three films relating to funerary rites: two of these were of funerals, namely those of the ancient Anaïs Dolo who died in 1971, by then reputedly 123 years of age, and of the Hogon who had first authorised the filming of the Sigui, and who died suddenly in 1973.[14] The subject of the other funerary film, shot in 1974, was generally offered a number of years after the death of the eminent individuals. In this case, the *dama* was for Ambara Dolo, one of the informants who worked with Griaule in 1931.[15] Although these films are more tightly structured than the Sigui films, if only perhaps because they cover events that were more restricted in time, in other regards they are similar in terms of general cinematographic praxis. That is, they are highly descriptive and are composed of long unbroken takes explicated by a sonorous voice-over, with little development of character.

Even more extraordinarily, as if this work amongst the Dogon and the shooting of *Petit à petit* back in Paris were not enough, Rouch continued to visit the Songhay throughout this phase of his career, shooting several further films about *yenendi* and other spirit-possession rites. A number of these also appear never to have been finished, though they also include the impressive *Yenendi de Ganghel*, released in 1968 and one of Rouch's best-known films, *Les Tambours d'avant: Tourou et Bitti* released in 1971. The latter is a film of only 11 minutes, consisting of a single 'sequence-shot' (a take lasting the full duration of a 16mm magazine), but it was very significant in Rouch's development of the concept of the 'ciné-trance' (see Rouch 1997).

After such a vast expenditure of creative energy, it would have been quite understandable if Rouch had been feeling somewhat anomic, given that he was by now in his mid-fifties. Indeed, many years later, he would confess that he did not know quite what to go on to after the Sigui (see Taylor 2003: 141). Lying chronologically almost exactly midway in his filmmaking career, this moment appears to have been something of a watershed for him professionally. Thereafter, conventional ethnographic films become progressively less frequent in his repertoire, though he continued to make ethnofictions with his Nigerien collaborators at regular intervals until the end of his life. The films from the second half of Rouch's career have not been accorded the acclaim given to those from the first half, but he did not forget his intellectual roots in the latter part of his career, even if he made few ethnographic films. Interestingly, in the period immediately after the Sigui, when he was casting around as to what to do next, one of the things he chose was to make three films in homage to Marcel Mauss. These consisted of portraits of three of Mauss's former students: the Japanese abstract sculptor and painter Taro Okamoto, the sociologist and theologian Paul Lévy and last but far from least, Germaine Dieterlen.[16]

Nor did Rouch think only about the origins of the tradition from which his own work sprang. Just as Griaule asked him to film the Sigui of 1967–73, so too has Rouch arranged for two of his own students to film the next Sigui, which is due to run from 2027–33. In approaching the Centre Nationale de la Recherche Scientifique to set aside funds for this, he argued that the study of the Sigui should be conceived on the model of the natural sciences whereby an experiment must be repeated four times for its results to be considered valid. More specifically, he proposed that Griaule should be considered the first person to have conducted the experiment to understand the Sigui, Germaine Dieterlen the second and himself the third. Some years before he died, he provided for his successors, Nadine Wanono and Philippe Lourdou, to carry out the fourth and final experiment in the sequence (Rouch 1995b: 230–1; Prédal 1996: 22–3).[17]

If the Dogon conceive of the Sigui as being a collective triumph over death, Rouch thought of his ethnographic filmmaking as being an enterprise of the same kind. On this matter, he liked to quote Henri Langlois, first president of the Cinémathèque Française, who once observed that 'filmmakers never die, for every time their work is screened, they come to life again'. However distinguished Jean Rouch's contribution may have been to other arenas of cinema, not only was he a uniquely productive ethnographic filmmaker, but he was also one to the last, remaining committed to ethnographic filmmaking throughout his life – and beyond.

AUTHOR'S NOTE: I am much indebted to Nadine Wanono and Philippe Lourdou for the advice that they generously provided on an earlier version of the material presented in this chapter. Even though I could not agree entirely with all their comments, this version has undoubtedly benefited greatly from their superior knowledge both of the Dogon and the films made about them. The faults that undoubtedly remain are entirely my responsibility.

NOTES

1   Even Rouch himself was not entirely certain of how many films he made, though in his later years he would refer to having made 140. This is probably something of an exaggeration since the most thorough listings of his work (Pellé 1997; Feld 2003) suggest that he completed just over 100 films, with a further 25 or so projects consisting of no more than unedited rushes. Nevertheless, Rouch remains by far the most prolific of all ethnographic filmmakers to date.

2   In using the term 'praxis', my intention is to refer not just to the techniques, strategies and stylistic devices that Rouch employed in the making of his films, but also to the more epistemological and ethical postures embedded within them.

3   This too may be a slight exaggeration – West Africanist anthropologist, filmmaker and film historian Marc-Henri Piault calculates that the actual figure may be around forty (1997: 13). Even so, it is still a remarkably high number of films on a single ethnographic subject.

4   They include such celebrated works as *Bataille sur le grand fleuve*, *Chasse au lion a l'arc* and *Un Lion nommé l'Américain* (1972).

5   These investigations were funded by a combination of the CNRS, IFAN, a French colonial research institute based in Dakar and the International African Institute,

a multinational research agency supported by all the European colonial governments of the time.

6 The now-orthodox interpretation of this film is that it represents a counter-hegemonic critique or parody of European colonial power. I have recently published a detailed 'reviewing' of this film in which I argue that this interpretation is mistaken. Amongst other weaknesses, it ignores the continuities between the ritual event shown in the film and the more traditional spirit-possession rituals shown in other Rouch films and described at length in his writings. See Henley 2006.

7 This characteristic, combined with his unselfish commitment to ensuring the publication of the works of his contemporaries killed in World War One, is the reason usually given for his failure to publish any substantial monographs (see Clifford 1988: 65, 123–5).

8 The *locus classicus* for the description of Malinowski's fieldwork method is the Introduction to his *Argonauts of the Western Pacific*, first published in 1922 (see Malinowski 1932).

9 Rosfelder, who was of North African origin, would later become a distinguished novelist under the *nom de plume* Roger Curel.

10 Clifford (1988: 80ff.) suggests that having been initiated into the arcane '*parole claire*' in the latter stages of his work amongst the Dogon, Griaule underwent some sort of conversion, coming to consider his informants as wise 'doctors' rather than base liars. However, *Méthode de l'ethnographie* was published in 1957, shortly after Griaule's death, and some ten years after his supposedly transformative encounter with Ogotommêli, the most eloquent of the Dogon elders with whom he worked.

11 Unless otherwise stated, the ethnographic detail about the Sigui in this section comes from Rouch's 1980 interview with Enrico Fulchignoni (2003: 169–79) or from the Sigui films themselves.

12 When challenged some time later about the absence of women in his films more generally, Rouch explained that he had found that it was quite impossible for a European man to film African women since this would not be permitted by the local people (Georgakas *et al.* 2003: 217). In the particular case of the Dogon, Nadine Wanono reports (personal communication, April 2006) that she encountered no difficulty in filming the women, though this may be on account of her own gender. Regardless of the precise reasons for the relative absence of women from the film, there is clearly a very interesting gender-related theme in the Sigui that Rouch touches upon only briefly in the commentary. Although he links the evident transvesticism in the ritual to the theme of nurturing and motherhood, which is particularly pronounced in the sixth stage of the Sigui, he does not comment on the fact that men appear to be ritually arrogating this reproductive role to themselves – a pattern that is encountered in connection with male initiation

ceremonies in many other parts of the world.

13 Later this shortcoming would be rectified when Nadine Wanono, advised by both Rouch and Dieterlen, was specifically charged with the task of making films about everyday Dogon life (personal communication, April 2006).

14 These films were *Bongo, les funérailles du vieil Anaï* (shot in 1972, but not edited until 1979) and *L'enterrement du Hogon* (1973). In this latter year, he also made an unfinished 20-minute film about a Dogon woman's funeral at Bongo (see Prédal *et al.* 1996: 221).

15 This film, *Le dama d'Ambara* (finally edited in 1980, although shot in 1974), was also co-directed by Germaine Dieterlen.

16 The portrait of Okamoto was shot in 1974, whilst the portraits of Lévy and Dieterlen were both shot in 1977.

17 Clearly Rouch was expecting Wanono and Lourdou to be blessed with his own energetic longevity since they will both be around eighty years of age by the time the next Sigui is concluded.

REFERENCES

Ahonou, B. (2000) 'Les dieux se fâchent a Ganghel: Divinités en colère et anthropologie visuelle', *Afrique contemporaine*, 196, 4, 17–26.

Boddy, J. (1995) 'Managing Tradition: "Superstition" and the Making of National Identity among Sudanese Women Refugees', in W. James (ed.) *The Pursuit of Certainty: Religious and Cultural Formulations*. London and New York: Routledge, 17–44.

Clifford, J. (1988) *The Predicament of Culture: Twentieth Century Ethnography, Literature, Art*. Cambridge, MA: Harvard University Press.

Feld, S. (2003) 'Annotated Filmography', in J. Rouch, *Ciné-ethnography*, ed. and trans. S. Feld. Minneapolis: University of Minnesota Press, 345–84.

Fulchignoni, E. (2003) 'Jean Rouch with Enrico Fulchignoni: Ciné-anthropology', in J. Rouch, *Ciné-ethnography*. Minneapolis: University of Minnesota Press, 147–87.

Georgakas, D., G. Udayan and J. Janda (2003) 'The Politics of Visual Anthropology', in J. Rouch, *Ciné-ethnography*. Minneapolis: University of Minnesota Press, 210–25.

Griaule, M. (1957) *Méthode de l'ethnographie*. Paris: Presses universitaires de France.

Henley, P. (2006) 'Spirit Possession, Power and the Absent Presence of Islam: Reviewing *Les Maîtres fous*', *Journal of the Royal Anthropological Institute*, 12, 4 731–761.

Malinowski, B. (1932 [1922]) 'Introduction: the subject, method and scope of this enquiry', in *Argonauts of the Western Pacific: An Account of Native Enterprise* and *Adventure in the Archipelagoes of Melanesian New Guinea*, second edition. London: Routledge, 1–25.

Masquelier, A. (1993) 'Narratives of Power, Images of Wealth: The Ritual Economy of the Bori in the Market', in J. Comaroff and J. Comaroff (eds) *Modernity and Its Malcontents: Ritual and Power in Post-Colonial Africa*. Chicago and London: University of Chicago Press, 3–33.

Pellé, L. (1997) 'Bibliographie et filmographie de Jean Rouch', in J. Rouch, *Les hommes et les dieux du fleuve: essai ethnographique sur les populations songhay du moyen Niger 1941–1983*. Paris: Éditions Artcom, 271–78.

Piault, M.-H. (1997) 'Préface: Regards croisés, regards partagés', in J. Rouch, *Les hommes et les dieux du fleuve: essai ethnographique sur les populations songhay du moyen Niger 1941–1983*. Paris: Éditions Artcom, 7–21.

Prédal, R. (1996) 'Le ciné-plaisir', *CinémAction*, 81, 19–37.

Prédal, R., with D. Tessier, F. Foucault and A. Pascal (1996) 'Filmographie', *CinémAction*, 81, 214–26.

Rouch, J. (1989) *La Religion et la magie songhay*, second edition. Brussels: Éditions de l'Université de Bruxelles.

_____ (1995a) 'The Camera and Man', in P. Hockings (ed.) *Principles of Visual Anthropology*, second edition. Berlin & New York: Mouton de Gruyter, 79–98.

_____ (1995b) 'Our Totemic Ancestors and Crazed Masters', in P. Hockings (ed.) *Principles of Visual Anthropology*, second edition. Berlin & New York: Mouton de Gruyter, 217–32.

_____ (1997) 'Essai sur les avatars de la personne du possédé, du magicien, du sorcier, du cinéaste et de l'ethnographe', in J. Rouch, *Les Hommes et les dieux du fleuve: essai ethnographique sur les populations songhay du moyen Niger 1941–1983*. Paris: Éditions Artcom, 211–28.

Rouch, J. (2003 [1978]) 'The Mad Fox and the Pale Master', in *Ciné-ethnography*, ed. and trans. S. Feld. Minneapolis: University of Minnesota Press, 102–25.

Taylor, L. (2003) 'A Life on the Edge of Film and Anthropology', in J. Rouch, *Ciné-ethnography*. Minneapolis: University of Minnesota Press, 129–46.

From fieldwork in Niger, 1967

4 JEAN ROUCH AND THE GREAT SAHELIAN DROUGHT: VISUAL ANTHROPOLOGY AND THE WRATHFUL GODS AT GANGHEL

Brice Ahounou

The premonitory menace

Just before the 'Great Drought' broke over the Sahelian strip of West Africa, the traditional Songhay-Zarma deities made a menacing intervention during a ritual possession at Ganghel (Niger) announcing that a major climactic event was imminent. As a witness to their revelation, in August 1968, Jean Rouch captured on film (in *Le Yenendi di Ganghel*, 1968) the warning of the calamities to come. At the peak of the *Yenendi* ceremony the divinities, having been consulted, pound out in the film the words 'No pity, no pardon!' In front of the camera, these wrathful spirits accuse men of having transgressed. As punishment, they predict an unparalleled heat wave which indeed came to pass.

The famous West African drought began in the late 1960s. A period of low rainfall, lasting roughly from 1968 to 1973, spread uninterruptedly across the Sahel right up to the mid-1980s. While restricted in time, two particularly severe periods of drought are acknowledged, from 1972 to 1973 and 1982 to 1984 (see Sircoulon 1984/85). These are sadly famous for the succession of catastrophes that ensued: decimated herds, poor harvests, populations starved and often displaced. The initial critical impact was in keeping with the anxious messages and warning signs that Songhay deities had been issuing since 1968. After its first peak in 1972–73, the drought eased somewhat and stabilised for a short period before reappearing again in a second, more severe phase in 1982–83, which at the time caused some 21 countries of the continent to declare themselves 'devastated' (Sircoulon 1984/85: 76). For a sustained period, the lack of water thoroughly transformed the daily life of the societies affected and changed their worldview. In diverse ways, the drought tested the centres of human activities to their very core. In some cases, it caused migrations, 'enforced mobility' or even an all-out exodus in the Sahelian-Saharan region (see Bernus 1999 for a detailed analysis of the aftermath of the drought).[1] Elsewhere, the severe consequences took the form of repeated onslaughts against the social and cultural spheres. Surprisingly, the pressures to which the Songhay villages of the Eastern valley of the Niger found themselves subjected to had been foretold through mythological interpretations, concrete divinatory predictions and sometimes followed by attempts (such as the making of new sacrifices) aimed at containing the coming disaster. Thus, the work of anthropology was in direct contact with the upheavals indicated above.

In emphasising the observations of Rouch, an 'initiate'-researcher in Ganghel for almost sixty years, this chapter will choose as its cinematic reference point the moment before the catastrophe took place. The beliefs of 'the other' in relation to the ethnographic filmmaker will thus be examined here from a new perspective.

Drought of the gods[2]

It was at Ganghel (a village around 30 km from Niamey) that the gods first warned men who were accused of having failed in their duties by violating a ritual sermon. At the outset, in 1968, significant events took place: the storm burned down a hut, broke a Peul shepherd's shoulder and killed cattle. The possession ritual organised to purify the storm-damaged site contained, against all expectations, its share of surprises. Catastrophe was on the horizon and its imminence did not leave the ethnographer-filmmaker feeling indifferent. Before examining in detail the events concerning the damaged site at Ganghel, let us pause over a few religious particularities necessary to an understanding of the subject.

One of the specificities of the Songhay-Zarma of the Eastern valley of the Niger is to make contact with the gods during possession rituals or the 'Holey' cults. The *Yenendi* (literally meaning 'to cool down') is the most celebrated of the annual ceremonies during which the sky-gods, notably Dongo the thunder-spirit, are petitioned to bring rain but to spare people from the 'sky's fire'. The *Yenendi* takes place in the seventh month of the dry season, approximately in May. Its place in the ritual calendar is calculated according to the seven lunar months from the last tornado of the preceding October. In the case of overwhelming circumstances (as during the years of drought) it is possible to override the ritual calendar. In the ceremonial arrangements the dance of possession remains a centre point of the *Yenendi*. And under the iron rule of a priest (*zima*) calabash-drummers and single-string viol players accompany proceedings as the ceremony unwinds leading to the entry into a trance of the 'spirit horses' of whose bodies the gods take possession in order to engage in discourse with the community. This is the right moment to ask the gods questions, in order that the truth can be revealed before everyone. And it is often the two principal divinities of thunder and lightning, Dongo and his brother Kirey the Red, who are invoked in these frightening encounters. Masters of the belief system concerning rainfall, Dongo and Kirey the Red are sometimes supported by Sadiara the Rainbow or Manda Haoussakoy, another fearsome storm-bringer.[3] It is these fiery invitees that are petitioned by men and when the formidable ancestors reject them, the times are indeed bad. The 'tooru', as the gods are called, share in doling out punishment: Dongo brings fire and storms, Marou Kirey (the spirit of light) brings lightning and Harakoy Dikko (spirit of water) rain.

The majority of the material assembled by Jean Rouch in this region showing the relations between gods and men began with the film *Le Yenendi, les hommes qui font la pluie* (1951), made when the gods still had a modicum of respect for men. Among the analytical films made about the possession cults in the Niger delta between 1948 (*Initiation à la danse des possédés*) and 1978 (*Simiri Siddo Kuma*) Rouch considered several of them as portraits of Dongo, the thunder god, taking place under the internal organisation of the *Yenendi*. During the mid-1960s, his project was to collect as much footage as possible showing different people of all ages and both genders, in different places, and all possessed by the same spirit. Next, through a work of synthesis, he attempted to sketch, through editing, a 'film-portrait' of the thunder god. 'In this way, through a cinematic process and no doubt through this approach alone, a mythical personage could be defined in greater detail. We hope to be able to show his behaviour, his character, his way of speaking which, for initiated viewers, are completely recognisable', Rouch explained in a note for *The Yenendi de Boukoki* (*Rain Dance at Boukoki*, 1972) .[4] So, both before and during the drought, he filmed the *Yenendi* in such places as Gamkallé (1967), Ganghel (1968), Yantala (1971), Simiri (1971) and Boukoki (1973).[5] A part of this documentation covers the first phase of the drought that struck the Sahel. The sound and fury of Dongo and his acolytes had been gathering since 1968. Rouch was there and had filmed them thanks to his privileged links to the cohorts of the sky. His quite particular relationship with Dongo should be emphasised.[6] As reflections of the climactic dramas that affected the lives of men, his many research films illustrate, through the prism of ethnography, the position of the gods according to systems of local thoughts and beliefs, where the gods of the sky would bring about the great drought.

Ganghel, or the first 'fire of the sky'

A record of the eve of the drought, *Le Yenendi de Ganghel* is perhaps the best of this rich filmed material because the gods' sententious and premonitory message comes through clearly despite its complexity. The work is a visual document – essential for the study of the phenomenon of possession – taking us back to the village of the Sorko fishermen, which was struck by lightning in August 1968 at the outset of the drought. Without waiting, a *Yenendi* was organised to allow the gods to speak. From the first sequences witnessing the ceremony, Rouch recalls in the film the beginnings of his ethnographic concerns:

> In 1942, lightning had struck the Ganghel public works site, which I was in charge of, and killed ten workers who were building the road from Niamey to Ougadougou. The next day, guided by Damouré (my faithful source of information) and his grandmother Kalia Daoudou, I came across a ritual dance of possession ... Since then, I have never stopped trying to get to the bottom of these fascinating and terrifying ceremonies. Twenty-six years later, in August 1968, the village of Ganghel was struck by lightning again. The following day, as in 1942, Sorko priests who were successors of the old woman Kalia Daoudou, musicians, ritual dancers and the faithful, led by Pam Sambo Zima, came from Niamey to Ganghel. Daouda Sorko inspected the burnt-out hut where, that night, the thunderbolt had shattered a Peul shepherd's shoulder. The musicians called on Dongo the thunder spirit and Kirey the Red the lightning spirit to ask why they had attacked and to solicit forgiveness. This was the *Yenendi*: the cooling of the sky's fire.

After this introduction, the ceremony can begin in the film. The drummers beat out the ancient rhythms of the possession ritual: 'Hey, Dongo, we are calling you! Hey you! The wrathful one with the big testicles! Welcome Dongo! Welcome to the Man!' Dongo takes possession of Arguza, a farmer from Gamkallé and an esteemed 'spirit-horse'. Beside him, Kirey the Red takes possession of Kadi, a Niamey housewife. On their knees before the drummers beating their upturned calabashes, the possessed pair stamp their 'hooves' firmly in the sand, with alternately abrupt movements and rhythmic accelerations. The Sorko fishermen flatter Dongo with foreign currency: 'It is for the best if he strikes a man! If Dongo has killed a man, the *hampi* (holy vase) will take care of it. You must bury it. But if Dongo is not here, do not bury it! The sky and the earth are in Dongo's hands alone.' The attributes of this singular divinity are endlessly extolled: 'Dongo strikes hard! ... He is powerful, he is bad, he causes harm! He strikes the back, the belly! The man is dead, he is laid out stiff, he is shrivelled up! Fear god! Fear Dongo! The devious ones who hear him but don't believe, Dongo gathers termites nests and flat stones to hurl at them!'

At the crucial moment, in the film and the event itself, a dialogue begins: 'Why have you summoned me?' demands Dongo angrily. Aided by Kirey the Red he complains of an underhand trick. Without further ado an explanation is given by a viol player: 'Two months ago at Niamey, Dongo told us to hold the *Yenendi*, the rain ceremony, with a strong black horse ... which we did, but Dongo came on two horses at the same time. A Dongo came who was not the right one.' The conclusion was that a fake Dongo, a counterfeit double, had been involved in religious matters. A grave error, men had tarnished themselves and so the gods promised an unprecedented heat wave. To the officiating priest, Dongo said: 'Ah! Tell the truth, Sambo ... You know what happened! You'll see if there will be any millet crops this year! ... If we spared the shepherd it wasn't out of pity ... I can burn down the whole village if I wish! I want to leave!' Dongo is begged to stay. 'Don't go before you've sorted out this problem.' Furiously, the god insisted: 'I've said what I have to say and done what I have to do. I have no pardon, I have no pity, I want to leave!' Backing him up, Kirey the Red said his piece: 'You Sorko fishermen will have plenty of work this year. There will be fire and water and the village will be covered in millet ... but all this millet will become sterile flour because the millet field is Dongo's.' Blame and threats rained down.

'We need water given to our fields, if you don't do that we'll all die!' implored one of the participants. 'No pardons!' replied Kirey the Red. The gods' anger was unstoppable. 'No pity, no pardon!' they hammered out at the congregation. 'Dongo must strike powerfully! It is Dongo who brings storms! It is Dongo who brings furious fires! In the stomach, on the back, it's all over! The sky is cold! The earth is burning!' the agents of the cult were obliged to recite again.

The gods departed, death was cast, misfortune was on its way and there was no way of stopping it. The predictions had to be fulfilled. The film's epilogue states that the millet of August 1968 'despite the farmers' efforts, did not grow. There would be no pardon. For seven years the Sahel would suffer from the great drought that Dongo had announced. There would be no pity. Around Niamey, during the single rainy season, 100 had died in storms...'. In 1970, the count was 120 dead in an area of 100 km around the Nigerien capital, according to sources other than Rouch and from which the supremacy of Dongo is linked to the fact that the storms kill an enormous number of people (see Anon. 1975).

When Dongo fertilises the earth

Need one believe in the gods of the sky? To consider some of the phenomena that appeared after Dongo struck brings to light certain indications that are surprising, even rational. When the lightning struck, the Songhay said it hurled down stone axes that could be found buried in the earth. It was enough for initiates to make use of antidotes and cures prepared from the bark of trees known only to them. Rouch was present on several occasions when 'lightning stones' were extracted and was able to handle these extraordinary objects with their glazed coating: the sand surrounding the 'thunder axes' having melted under the effects of high temperatures. These Neolithic axes are known to have been used to make talismans against the fire from the sky (see Rouch 1997: 264).

To these certainties, agronomic discoveries can now be added. Within the sphere of the lightning storm was a tree, the *Gao beri*, an *Acacia albida* (or *Acacia faidherbia*), which has dealings with the fiery god of the sky whose attention it is able to attract. It is by no means rare that the same tree should sometimes be repeatedly struck by lightning. It occasionally makes for a disconcerting spectacle in the Nigerien landscape – even when ruined by the sky's fire and flattened to the ground the *Gao beri* goes on living. Recent discoveries made by research teams working on the micro-organisms that act as nitrogen-fixatives at the foot of the acacia emphasise the symbiotic powers of this tree-like leguminous plant whose roots can reach as deep as 35 metres, as far as the earth's phrasal layer. At the end of the roots of the *Alcacia albida* a mutual relationship is formed with a species of underground mushrooms (*Bradyrhizobium*) which manufactures nitrogen essential to food-producing cultures. From this symbiosis, which allows young plants to not suffer from the thin reserves of mineral nitrogen in Sahelian soil, is born the hope of improving the fertility of African lands and gives the cultivation of the trees of the Sahel a fresh impetus. This was a watershed for agronomists.[7]

Regularly struck by lightning, the *Gao beri* puts Dongo in the context of the agronomic sciences. According to this hypothesis, lightning releases nitrogen. To put it plainly, Dongo could be fertilising the earth – a fascinating avenue by which to establish the true agricultural capacity and the fertilising power of this god, the paradoxical liberator of nitrogen.

True to his method of successive approximations, Rouch is convinced he is confronted with knowledge of natural sciences based on a firm foretelling of weather conditions. After more than fifty years' worth of direct experience of Songhay beliefs and despite the fascinating results of his observations, the ethnographer insisted in all modesty that he was far from understanding everything, preferring to abide by the system of thought being studied and to believe the beliefs of the other.

If the Songhay had an explanation – religious, magical, social and political – for climactic changes affecting their way of life, Rouch demonstrated that he was open to it. In dealing with their cults he took

> seriously the beliefs and the values of 'the other' ... Granting his hosts the full responsibility of their proverbs, knowledge and beliefs, Rouch undertook, as regards the possession cults, the astonishing project not only of identifying

the gods at the moment they took visible form but above all to make a portrait of them ... He is therefore one of the first to have understood that one must deal with these systems of projection as reality, and that the production of gods is not a simple fantasy but a concrete procedure whose object took the shape of perceptible truth. (Piault 2000: 13)

For this reason, he took the predictions of Ganghel seriously, for it was decided by the nature of the gods' message: the inevitability of a climactic disaster.

To see the gods

When, by way of warning, Ganghel was struck, Rouch was in the right place at the right time: in between the gods and men. His camera was able to capture the results of the 'wrath of the gods' and to record men's words. The gods accused men of having tainted the ritual system by introducing Dongo's counterfeit double into it. Apart from this fault, why did the gods make their accusations in front of 'the man with the movie camera'? Why choose this instrument to make recriminations and utter threats before carrying them out?

Over a long period the gods had grown used to Rouch's working methods and his films. To best understand this one must go back to the filmmaker's first involvement in this area. His very first 'initiation' into Dongo took place in Ganghel in 1942. While he was Chief Engineer of the Western Subdivision of the Niger Public Works the fearsome divinity showed himself to Rouch by striking at his workers. The purification ritual that followed introduced Rouch to a troubling and unexpected realm: the thunder god accused him of having built a road over his lands without consulting the gods. Anxious and fascinated, Rouch was thrown into the belief system which thenceforth he strove to relate to. From then on, he 'grasped reality from close up', to use the expression of Dziga Vertov.

First and foremost in Rouch's world of cinema there were humans who metamorphosed into gods while in a trance state. The groups with which Rouch worked throughout the years had taken the time to get to know him, to come up with an account of his personality and to construct an image for him. At the symbolic level the engineer-turned-ethnographer/filmmaker was not a disruptive influence in Songhay society. He was not felt to be a bringer of 'misfortune'. Children born since his arrival had not succumbed to bad influences. His presence in the villages did not bring with it deep troubles but seemed rather to be a bearer of wellbeing to these communities. This earned him a privileged status and his lasting integration extends across two or three generations of Nigeriens.

Returning to Niger at the end of the war, the imprudent 'Mr Engineer' who had violated Dongo's lands in 1942, when his workmen died in a thunder storm, began to cross the country 'barefoot' with a strange piece of equipment (the camera), all under the eyes of the natives who were intrigued by his new activities. Experimenting with 'feedback', the ex-engineer would show the first images he had shot to the persons filmed.[8] The gods and their assistants were not slow in spotting the interest in his research. Little by little they would alert him to a ritual being held, speak to him without fear, show themselves before the camera in complete confidence, taking him as a witness. This confidence did not fade. The gods had grasped the interest of cinema, the power of images. It was also their way of evaluating the qualities of the one who was observing them. In the field of 'shared anthropology', Rouch has the reputation of 'seeing gods' via his camera, so say those who embodied the gods for the ethnographer. The camera facilitated their possession just as much as the viol and the calabash-drums. Beyond this interpretation, what is at stake has to do with the complex role played by the 'participant-camera'. If the camera captured certain key moments of the Ganghel *Yenendi*, did it not also serve to provoke them, at least in the long term?

At this point the issue of induction and instruction via 'feedback' arises. To show to 'the one observed' images taken of him or her incites the reciprocal reconsideration of how he or she perceives things and the modification of behaviour. By dint of showing the people filmed their own images, they are to a certain extent influenced by them. However, this retroactive self-image cannot be limited to an inductive process. The gods appear before the cameras to get their message across and threaten society's deviance. Familiar with ethnography, they long ago assimilated the communicative – indeed, quasi-magical – capacities of cinema. 'For the Songhay-Zarma, who were very much used to cinema' Rouch wrote, 'I changed before their eyes just as the possession-dancers changed during the "ciné-trance" of the person filming the other's real trance. This is so real that I know, on looking through my viewfinder and by the reactions of the spectators, if the sequence works or not and if I've succeeded in throwing off the weight of ethnographic and cinematic theory to rediscover elemental invention' (1997: 226).

In Rouch's case, the theory of 'feedback' as the 'productive echo' of the ethnographer's work is obvious. Serious visual anthropology is not possible without restoring 'the Other's' image to him or her, without making them share in the film that has been shot. He recommends soliciting the views and reactions of 'the Other'. Even if the power-relations (non-egalitarian) leave the last word to the film's auteur, the only way of guaranteeing the seriousness of his work, of validating it, is to practise this double approach, to share the risk and, for the first time in ethnology, to share the rights of the auteur.

Rouch laid down the ground rules of this particular game very early on:

The ethnographer has the possibility to project, before the population he is studying, the images he has shot of them. The actors of the film are induced to critique the images at the camera operator's request and a dialogue of incomparable richness can thus arise from this confrontation. We therefore have, through this possibility of 'screening' the film, an opportunity for the 'ethnographised' to revise the work of the ethnographer. For example, if the researcher is studying a priest carrying out a ritual he obviously doesn't have the opportunity to interrupt the priest during the sacred activity, and that is a serious limitation in the classical form of research. On the other hand, if the same researcher films the ritual, he has the opportunity to show the film to the priest who, in contemplating his own image, can explain, analyse and comment in detail on his actions. 'The object of the research' can, therefore, thanks to the film, interpret his activity himself and supply the researcher with a host of supplementary information which the research would otherwise risk missing. It is worth adding that it is stimulating for the one being researched to see the film and leads him or her to yield up interesting commentaries. One should not forget that an informant only responds to the questions one asks them and it is as if to screen the film is implicitly to ask these questions. (1968: 437)

The problem of visualisation

A key moment in the story of the wrathful gods, a concrete illustration of the relations between gods and men, *Le Yenendi de Ganghel* also brings up the problem of visualisation in anthropology. Would we have believed this ritual existed had images of it not been brought back? Not necessarily, or at least not to the same extent given the doubts surrounding written ethnological accounts. Already suspect in various different fields, the written word is even more so when it comes to 'exotic' creations recorded at the far ends of the earth. It is hard to believe in what we cannot see. The pioneers and practitioners of ethnographic film have done everything possible to get the phenomena they have studied in the can. Thus, ethnography has been able to go beyond the written evocation towards moving image representation, for the written word no longer suffices to reconstitute the world of 'the Other'. From this point of view, visualisation remains an important act for it makes visible through film what would otherwise appear indistinct.

The problem of visualisation arises among anthropologists themselves. It is a little-known fact that it was in watching *Ambara Dama, echanter la mort* (1974), a film by Jean Rouch and Germaine Dieterlen devoted to a mourning ceremony in the land of the Dogon involving an extravagant masked display, that an impressed Margaret Mead confessed in confidence that, up to then, she had barely believed in the former descriptions of Dogon cosmogony set out in the works of Marcel Griaule and Germaine Dieterlen. The masked dances documented in the film were suddenly a reality for her: the American anthropologist was finally able to believe in them. Reality engraved on acetate established observable shapes and convincing expressions. The image was outstripping the written word. 'As strange as it might seem, cinema is the only instrument that allows one to show how man lives in his environment. Cinematic shots reconstitute authentic reality and put man in context' Rouch declared as early as 1968 (ibid.). This has not prevented observers from believing only what they want to see.

The moving image, too, was once tainted with suspicion within academia, but in ethnology it was immediately stripped of the doubts attached to it. Through the image – and this is its paradox – the texts describing distant societies assumed new or revitalised complementary visual dimensions. Since 1966, one could go to the cinema to see the Dogon people of the Bandiagara Cliffs celebrating the 'Sigui', their sixtieth anniversary commemoration of the invention of speech and death filmed by Dieterlen and Rouch. Well before, the works of Griaule were dealing seriously with the subject. But they were missing the definitive guarantee of the moving image that his successors contributed and by which they destroyed the baseless accusation of mythological inventions sometimes levelled against the author of *Masques Dogons* (1938).

Let us imagine undertaking a project *in situ* with the inhabitants today: this would pave the way for a theory of change and social transformation combined with climactic variations and other religious phenomena. Visual anthropology today contains so many avenues of exploration torn between film and other visual means of expression. As a discipline of the visible, of visibility and 'visualisation', the ethnographic film remains at its heart despite the temptation to be pulled in many different directions. And even while one of its branches – and its strict avatar – 'filmic anthropology' has traced its own path better adapted to the approach of documentary filmmaking, the ethnographic film, in its classic form just as in its more recent innovations, remains the base of this sometimes disputed discipline.

As a dynamic witness to the changes in the societies it studies, has it not become a place where the culture of 'the other' and representation of the self come face-to-face? A critical space of alterity, identity and diversity? A moment of readjustment, even of tension between the naïve and the historic conscience? A more equitable distribution of images between self and other? The proof lies in the richness of Rouch's work. As the reasoned demonstration of the visible and invisible, visual anthropology, faced with many challenges, searches for its identity at the intersection of disciplines. Far from the exoticising taste for origins, its scientific progress has not stopped bearing fruit. In Anglo-Saxon countries, *Visualising Theory* (Taylor 1994), a collection of essays assembled in the mid-1990s, illustrates recent tendencies of this extremely lively field while attesting to its relative vitality.

Epilogue

The study of possession cults initiated by Jean Rouch has brought about an advance in the use of the moving image in ethnology, both in terms of quantity and quality.[9] In the documents shot by the ethnographer-filmmaker, the gods lay the blame. Troubled, the Soghay people implore them and make sacrifices. To have recourse to film as a research tool immediately implies that one reflect on the questions posed by this practice. At Ganghel, the use of the camera made clear the intentions of the wrathful gods who invoked the climactic catastrophe that resulted in the 'great drought'. In inscribing this passage from word to deed in a process of innovating the methods by which the imaginary of 'the Other' can be approached, this strange discipline which connects the observer with the observed delivers an exercise in 'better shared anthropology'.

AUTHOR'S NOTE: An earlier version of this chapter first appeared in *Afrique Contemporaine*, 196, 17–26, 2000. This version has been translated by Chris Darke.

NOTES

1 Here, the geographer describes the migratory strategies employed by the Touareg peoples during the droughts of 1968–73 and 1983–85.

2 Gods, divinities, spirits: the terms are used interchangeably here to designate the local pantheon.

3 See also Rouch's 'Culte des genies chez les Sonrai' (1997: 45).

4 In an internal note in the film archives of the Committee of Ethnographic Film, Musée de l'Homme, Paris.

5 The *Yenendi* was also filmed in 1967 in Kogou, Kirkissey, Goudel, Gourbi Beri, and in Karey Gorou in 1969.

6 Marc-Henri Piault recalls this in his preface to *Les Hommes et les dieux du fleuve* in which Rouch's texts on the Songhay published between 1941 and 1983 are collected (1997: 13).

7 This information is taken from two articles published in *La Recherche*: 'Les acacias fixateurs d'azote du Sahel', 22, 223, June 1991, 802–4 and 'Acacias du Sahel,

un espoir pour l'agriculture', 25, 269, October 1994, 1045–7.

8 Feedback: the central notion and essential stage in Rouch's philosophy of ethnography in which he unflaggingly recommends researchers to show the images they have shot to the people filmed with the sole aim of provoking a reaction that helps advance the research. His films were made according to this method of investigation specific to 'shared anthropology'.

9 Roughly a third of Rouch's films are about possession. Within this area the presentations are varied, including dances of the possessed, hunting rites, *Yenendi* or rain rituals, *hauka* cults invoking 'new gods of strength' and much more.

REFERENCES

Anon. (1975) 'Les calendrier mythique chez les Songhay-Zarma (Niger)', in *Systèmes de pensée en Afrique noire*, Laboratoire 221. Paris: CNRS/EPHE, 52–62.

Bernus, E. (1999) 'Exodes tous azimuts en zone sahélo-saharienne', in V. Lassailly-Jacob, J. Y. Marchal and A. Quesnel (eds) *Déplacés et Réfugiés. La mobilité sous contrainte*. Paris: IRD, 195–208.

Piault, M.-H. (1997) Preface to J. Rouch, *Les hommes et les dieux du fleuve: essai ethnographique sur les populations songhai du moyen Niger, 1941–1983*. Paris: Artcom, 1–15.

_____ (2000) *Anthropologie et cinema: passage à l'image, passage par l'image*. Paris: Nathan.

Rouch, J. (1968) 'Le film ethnographique', in *Ethnologoie générale, Encyclopédie de La Pléiade*. Paris: Gallimard, 429–71.

_____ (1997 [1945]) 'Culte des genies chez les Sonrai', in *Les hommes et les dieux du fleuve: essai ethnographique sur les populations songhai du moyen Niger, 1941–1983*. Paris: Artcom, 45.

Sircoulon , J. (1984/85) 'La Sécheresse en Afrique de L'Ouest, comparaison des années 1982–1984 avec les années 1972–1973', *Cahiers de l'Orstaom, série Hydrologie*, 21, 4, 75–86.

Taylor, L. (ed.) (1994) *Visualizing Theory: Selected Essays from V.A.R. 1990–1994*. New York and London: Routledge.

From fieldwork in the Dogon, in preparation for the Sigui, 1972

5   A CINEMA OF CRUELTY

Réda Bensmaïa

Despite the two or three hundred years since the inhabitants of Europe have been pouring into other parts of the world and constantly publishing new collections of voyages and travel, I am persuaded that the only men we know are the Europeans ... that every author writes under the pompous title of the study of man only a study of the men of his own country. (Rousseau 1994: 106)

In opening this study of Rouch with a text that is taken to have inaugurated 'modern' ethnological thought my intention is not a display of erudition but, rather, a return to the sources.[1] As soon as the question arises of the traffic of one people to another and of one culture to another, the 'study of man' (*anthropology*) poses almost insurmountable problems. Because the 'material' of the ethnologist and ethnographer has, until recently, been constituted by formerly colonised peoples or those on the way to being made extinct through elimination (the Indians of Brazil, for example), one can readily understand the suspicion of such work among indigenous people.[2]

It appears, therefore, that as a technology which only came to be transplanted into ethnology and ethnography after the event and quite late in the day, cinema should automatically be liable to the same kind of political condemnation: that it is a cinema of voyeurs, of slave displays or of official images (or not, it matters little) of an 'imperial' vision of the world.

Now, what I would like to suggest in this chapter – and against not a few detractors of this genre of cinema, European and African alike – is that Rouch is among the rare ethnological filmmakers who has known how to elude the dangers lying in wait for the ethnological 'gaze' in general and to make of it a political weapon (in a way I will go on to define), as well as a kind of surrealist machine for pleasure, for play and the transformation of the world (see Bensmaïa 1978: 26–37).

Because and despite of the difficulties and traps that this cinema, dedicated to voyeurism and ethnocentrism,[3] carries with it, I believe it is possible here to defend the idea that, contrary to appearances, Rouch is not the filmmaker or the ethnologist we take him to be. In writing this I do not want, moreover, to suggest that ethnology for Rouch has only been a pretext for making films at any price, any more than cinema has only been a means to serve ethnology, knowledge, science or whatever of the same ilk. On the contrary, to my mind it is, on the one hand, a certain 'idea' of cinema which has led Rouch to go as far as to change the project of classical ethnology and to end up by gradually putting its 'object' in question. On the other, it is as an ethnologist, as a man who has always been in touch with a 'terrain' fundamentally other than his own, that Rouch has known how to endow his cinema with the style that it has taken on.

The ethnologist, the cinema and the reality effect

What interests Rouch the ethnologist in cinema as a technology is not the enormous possibilities it offers him to do his ethnological work – in other words, to bring back 'living' images, to establish 'archives' in order to analyse them later and to do 'scientific' work. Cinema as a technology interests Rouch less as a passive instrument for the recording of 'raw' facts or for amassing visions or knowledge for the future than as a relay or a medium that allows for direct contact with a reality (cultural, for example), which at first sight demonstrates no structural similarity with one's own.

Where the pen and even the photograph – which freezes the body, disrupts rhythm (even while it may have its own intrinsic rhythm) and extinguishes sound – fail, as a complex of movement and sound and an irreplaceable means of communicating with the other *sine medio*, cinema succeeds. Now, it is clearly this that fascinates Rouch about cinema and which has made him privilege it above all other means: as Rouch has said, 'in the end, we very often noticed that nothing was impossible if the camera was there' (in Téchiné & Fieschi 1967: 19.

One might think it a statement of the obvious to say that what interests Rouch about the cinema is the doubled movement of sound and the 'reality effect' it makes possible; this is essentially true for almost any filmmaker. It was as an ethnologist and not only as a filmmaker that Rouch was fascinated by cinema. In fact, the 'reality effect', as we know, resides less in allowing direct contact with a given reality in the first place than in producing the 'illusion' that the things one sees on screen are 'real': the audience is frightened by the arrival of the Lumière brothers' train!

But it is clear that this 'possibility' offered by cinema can be used for the most diverse ends: fiction, documentary, storytelling, scientific observation and so forth. As a filmmaker, Rouch does not neglect this 'dimension' of cinema but, like everybody else, makes use of it. It is important to signal here that, in some ways, it is the secondary effects of the 'reality effect' that seem to count most for Rouch, less the illusion of truth than the possibility to see, to record before understanding, to communicate (indeed, to commune) without the intermediary of language and, one could say, to feel (an emotion, for example) without protocol, as if from within. From such a perspective, the fact that things appear 'real' or 'true' – a phenomenon first of all linked to cinema as a technological 'device' – is less important than the fact they can appear in the first place, despite the cultural distance, despite the linguistic obstacles and, finally, despite the primitive 'strangeness' of what we are given to see and hear.[4] For Rouch the ethnologist, cinema – cinematic technology – is not an instrument subject to the scientific and didactic ends of the accumulation of knowledge but, on the one hand, a means of discovering and provoking events and, on the other, a privileged instrument of the immediate communicative and physical connection with the other.[5] In this sense, cinema for Rouch is a quasi-magical tool – the word would certainly not frighten him – which allows one to enter directly into contact with that which presents itself as the very figure of otherness and which, to a certain extent, would be inaccessible without cinema.

Subversion of the dominant forms of Western cinema

With Rouch, this first movement – from cinema to ethnology, allowing one 'reality' to be connected to another 'foreign' to it, as if immediately to mix two heterogeneous discourses – is systematically twinned with another 'movement' but which, despite everything, is different, as if through the intermediary of cinema. Rouch considers himself able to renew his relationship with ethnology in general and through this to give a radically new version of the study of man. Inversely (dialectically) when it is his experience as an ethnologist that we privilege, one realises that at the same time 'ethnological reality', the permanent contact with alterity – in essence resistant to all recuperation and hasty rationalisation – becomes the instrument of a radical subversion of certain dominant forms that have taken hold of cinema in the West, either as instrument of the representation of Western 'good conscience' or as a mirror in which to analyse, admire or criticise oneself. It matters little which position one takes: both act principally in domesticating the forces that would threaten in some way to 'shatter the screen' with the use of shouts, non-coded affects, unsimulated trances, 'irrational' types of behaviour, wasteful expulsions of energy – these in terms of content – and, above all, the formal side of things, raw de-narrativised images, or narrative sequences not integrated into a story, without a real beginning, middle or end.[6]

It is this movement which allows one to understand the exact meaning of certain recurring statements by Rouch about what he calls 'cinema-religion'. 'I am against the cinema-religion', he told Guy Hennebelle, 'I'm for slow films. One is liberated from the cinema of set design and the actor but not from certain artifices such as the curtain of the theatre or, from another point of view, the framework of the novel. My films will never have a beginning, middle or end. One can walk into them at any moment whatever' (in Hennebelle 1971: 80).

One could call on a number of other spoken or written statements by Rouch along exactly the same lines which clearly show that one of his most abiding concerns consisted not only in changing cinema through ethnology and vice versa, but in reinterpreting and challenging each through the other to the ends, at least in the first instance, of transforming and deconstructing the space of the classical cinematic setting – the set, the curtain, characters, endings, beginnings, the 'whole story' in short! – by means of the metamorphosis of the 'real' itself.[7] The adjoining principle of an apparently equally 'idealistic' problematic is as follows: for someone to have truly recognised the existence of the other, for whom to study the other is not to compare similarities but to recognise differences for what they are, the 'world', 'reality' will henceforth appear as a 'theatre' that one must learn how to value preferably from within it.

What is important to signal here is that in 'de-ethnologising' the ethnological 'gaze' through cinema and, at the same time, in deconstructing cinematic rhetoric through a transformed ethnological practice, Rouch's oeuvre – but is it an oeuvre in the traditional sense, that is, 'a whole'? – rapidly abandoned the specifically ethnological (speculative) realm to take shape as a true 'conspiracy'. This one consists less in acting directly on its times through classical revolutionary means than in preparing for the ruin of the political and ideological structures of Western society and the setting up of elements of a new civilisation through the means of an other cinema.[8]

Reconsidering the classical ethnological approach

Now, in order to carry out this seemingly 'unhinged' project, Rouch, as one of his first tasks, completely reconsidered the dominant ethnological approach and turned its basic principles upside down to make them serve incredible ends.

What were the principal characteristics of ethnological cinema when Rouch produced his first films?

(i) It was practically the only cinema which, on account of its 'object', appeared as essentially Western.

(ii) It was the only cinema which, on account of the permanent crisis which had shaken ethnology since its North American origins, had not succeeded in finding a coherent language, the correct 'tone'; in fact, whatever the politics of ethnologists, they could not ignore the existence of colonisation and be completely blind to its certain effects. Thus, ethnological discourse has always remained balanced between the 'scientific' desire for objectivity (a desire which inevitably leads to the pseudo-neutrality of the report) and the sincere desire to communicate and understand, which in certain cases has led to the most violent interventionism (see, for example, Gualtiero Jacopetti's *Monde Cane* (1962)).

(iii) It is a cinema which, intending at the outset to reach the rawest reality, indeed, a certain simple 'origin' of humanity, has – on account of the fundamental alterity of its object – opened on to the most fantastic fictions. From this it is only one small step to wallowing in moronic exoticism or racism. As we know, this step has often been taken.[9]

Now, to consider what passes generally for the purely ethnological part of Rouch's films – I am thinking here of such exemplary films as *La Chasse au lion à l'arc* (1957–64) and *Les Maîtres fous* (1955) – one realises that it is absolutely impossible to categorise them without testing them against the configuration just outlined. In fact, concerning the first point, it is clear that one of the initial pitfalls that Rouch avoids is of maintaining the 'distance' that makes this cinema – such as it is! – specifically Western: *Les Maîtres fous*, for example, is no longer content to exhibit the other in the isolation that is the mark of radical foreignness. In filming these men in the grip of the *haukas*, Rouch has paid no attention to reconstituting the small, closed world of the professional ethnologist or, to put it otherwise, that world which would allow the ethnologist to update his stock of 'disinterested' knowledge, 'internal laws', constitutive systems and other symbolic expressions.

On the contrary, it is around the character (and *personae*) of the British governor that the *haukas* ritual is organised. The film's alternating editing makes it perfectly obvious that what is taking place before our eyes is neither strange in itself nor foreign to us, but is indeed the pre-recorded rehearsal and consequently the 'theatricalisation' of a situation in which, owing to colonialism, men risk madness and death every day. Thus madness and death are acted out in order to be conjured up and made survivable.

But the essential thing is that this 'game' is obviously not gratuitous: it acts as the 'malign inversion' and the violent reversal of the 'drama' of colonisation and the submission of men to a regime which annihilates them. What is therefore exhibited here is not the inferiority or savagery of certain men in relation to others but the 'cruelty' of the relations that links the colonised to his 'master', the coloniser. This is a strange kind of theatre that relates back not to voyeurism or exoticism but poses, admittedly in a way that is quite violent and unexpected, the question of colonisation. So it is less to the Orphic myth and Cocteau one need turn in order to understand the spirit of Jean Rouch's political process than to Antonin Artaud,[10] who assigned to the first 'Theatre of Cruelty' production, *La Conquête du Mexique 1931–1933*, the following objectives:

> It will bring to life in an implacable, brutal and bloody fashion the perennial fatuousness of Europe. It will allow the idea of her superiority to be deflated. It will oppose Christianity to much older religions. It will do justice to the false conceptions that the West has been able to entertain of paganism and certain natural religions and will emphasise in a moving, impassioned way the splendour and poetry of the still current metaphysical depths on which these religions are based. (1964: 151–2)

Better still, in filming *La Chasse au lion à l'arc*, Rouch explodes another ethnological hobbyhorse, namely the taste for abstract 'particularities' lacking any dialectic relation to time or actual spaces marked by the differences between culture; in fact – and is this not why the film opens like a child's story? – what really emerges in the film is the inanity of any exotic vision of the other. If the preparations for the hunt are filmed according to artistic criteria, if the rituals are scrupulously reproduced, then the presence of the Land Rover, the painful use of mantraps, but above all the terrible sequence in which a wounded hunter is tended to as if he were a baby by a doctor administering an anti-tetanus shot, clearly shows that it is impossible to remain outside the events shown here. The 'difference' that allowed ethnologists to make Africans an 'object of study' by referring to their cultural and technological 'backwardness' or their 'particularity' – in short, a certain intellectual comfort linked to the anti-ethnocentrism of progressive ethnologists – is this not itself only a myth fabricated to conceal the hard factual reality: the material and technological presence of the West annihilates and destroys African values once and for all. The African lion-hunters have already become legends!

Jean Rouch and colonialism

The lesson is therefore clear. We know that among the Hopi Indians, once the initiation was over, the adults removed their masks and revealed themselves as fathers and uncles! We also know the reactions of the initiates. 'When the Katcina entered Kiva without their masks' writes a young Indian, 'I had a great shock. They weren't spirits. I knew all of them and I felt very unhappy because for all my life I'd been told that the Katcina were gods. I was most shocked to see all the fathers and uncles of the clan dancing in Katcina. But it was even worse to see my own father!' (Mannoni 1969: 16).

Rouch's films do something similar. They are 'initiations', but in reverse. For if, as with the Hopi, the man at the mercy of his *hauka* (spirit) can, on returning to daily life, carry on as if nothing has happened (denying possession) and say 'I know well that the *hauka* are (only) spirits but, all the same, I am still the General when I go into a trance', the spectator absolutely cannot carry on as if nothing has happened. Because, confronted with the two scenes at the same time – that of the British presence and that of the exploitation of the Africans – and their *mise-en-abyme* in cinema he cannot deny what ails Africa which is first and foremost the inequality of economic and political relations, the domination and exploitation of one people by another.

These two examples allow it to be understood that Rouch very quickly found the 'correct' tone: Rouch's way is correct not only because it does not ignore colonialism but because, in constantly departing from its underside and exhibiting its nature through the massive effects it produces elsewhere, he does not allow the spectator to remain indifferent for a moment and compels him or her if not to take a position then at least to shift around.

In doing so, one understands that Rouch was never simply looking for 'raw' facts or even seeking to make one believe they exist. As far as one goes looking for them, 'origin' or absolute alterity have always already been 'trafficked' somewhere and always to the detriment of the people that the West has colonised. One also understands what made Rouch never settle for objectivity, as 'scientific' as it might be: having understood that decolonisation as a whole should, for a European, begin with decolonisation of the self,[11] Rouch did not hesitate to sign up for the political path of the 'plot' in which cinema should be one of the principal weapons.

In analysing some of Rouch's statements, it is this hypothesis that I would like, at present, to give all the weight it deserves. But to start with, let us listen to Rouch:

> I am now going to make an eleven-hour-long film which will show in a cinema where one can enter and leave as one wishes: one can sit on the floor, smoke, talk … This film will be called *The Owl's Testicles* (precisely because owls don't have testicles) or *Grand à grand*. It will be a 'political sci-fi' film. (In Hennebelle 1971: 80)

But perhaps the essential element is not to be found here. For as soon as he made this statement, which is disconcerting for its 'anarchistic' content, he added:

> Damouré and Lam will become gurus consulted by hippies, politicians and intellectuals. They will have a captive who will be called Jean Rouch who will

film what people imagine in order to show it to them. I am going to shoot eleven hour-long sequences which will deal respectively with the family, death, religion, the proletarian Left, politics and everything, everything, the entire world! If I can't shoot it in Africa, I'll shoot it in Levallois-Perret or in Italy where I'll also film an hour dealing with the Vatican with Carmelo Bene in order to have done with this problem that's gone on far too long. It won't act as a suppository but a little Molotov cocktail. (Ibid.)

This is how Rouch establishes that for him filming is not simply a game or a *métier* but truly the equivalent of revolution: a 'little Molotov cocktail'! But aimed at who or what? What is it that is literally to be blown up?

Given that this is a revolution undertaken through cinema, the most straightforward way of learning what it involves and what its aims are requires asking the following question: what sort of cinema are we talking about? Or, better still, what sort of cinema does Rouch want to make? In order to respond to this double question – which I tried to suggest a little earlier in demonstrating the strange dialectic that Rouch has always wanted to establish between cinema and ethnology – the only possible way is to start by avoiding the misinterpretation that is habitually made regarding Rouch in associating him for example with the *cinéma vérité* movement, with realism and goodness knows what else. In other words, what is to be avoided at all costs when dealing with Rouch is to ask him the wrong questions and to submit him to problems that do not concern or interest him. In short, to avoid starting false proceedings against him. And in particular to avoid at least three misinterpretations which, when all is said and done, are three types of condemnation.

The first is that of the Africanists, whether European or African – they exist – who accuse him of promiscuity of means and lack of seriousness as soon as he moves away from 'fieldwork' and starts to utter prophecies and do cheap ethnology (for example, certain responses to *Chronique d'un été* (1960) which, it is too often forgotten, is a film of 'shared anthropology').

The second is that of Africans themselves who take it at face value the fact that Rouch has, as Godard put it, the title of 'Researcher at the Musée de l'Homme' and accuse him of being a 'slave exhibitor', a voyeur, an entomologist, a racist and imperialist like all his brothers (which is the reported attitude of Ousmane Sembène).

Finally, the third is that of progressive intellectuals and in particular that of Marxists – out of naivety or habit? – who, while condemning certain of Rouch's films (*Les Maîtres fous* for example) because they risk reinforcing the incomprehension and racism of Westerners, have the merit of making clear the obvious character of 'plot' in accusing Rouch of 'political triviality'. For example, one cannot make a revolution with images or even worse they will claim: revolution is a far too serious business to play with.

To these, as with others, Rouch – in his haste? in his impatience? – has not hesitated to supply as many arguments against himself that they might wish. Has he not taken this 'vice' as far as suggesting that for him 'the only revolutionary act that African states must undertake is to stop thinking'? (Hennebelle 1971: 80). Has he not shamelessly affirmed that 'this, for me, is also what the young French revolutionaries should do'? Has he not himself said that this is his 'message' in *Petit à Petit* (1968–69) (ibid.).

An unclassifiable, hence controversial oeuvre

Despite rather overwhelming evidence, there is a deep misunderstanding regarding Rouch. Or, better still, what is essential in his cinematic oeuvre has perhaps not yet been clearly perceived. And there is at least one reason for this. Constantly caught between at least two cultures, two civilisations, Rouch is a bit like the 'Mana' that Lévi-Strauss discusses; he is never where you go looking for him, and inversely you never find him where he is. He is there and not there. But he is also missing his own identity, his own resemblance; he lacks his own origin.[12] Like his films, like *Petit à petit*, like his *Les Maîtres fous* who are not (only) female or male, neither powerful nor powerless, neither labourer nor General, Rouch is neither black nor white, occupying instead the atopic position of the crazy man and joker of cinema and ethnology. At the same time, it is not something that 'policed' societies, to use the euphemism of Rousseau's epoch, are very keen on: 'I am neither black nor white. I spent a part of my life in Africa. I've been there since 1941. I'm like a character from Lawrence who lives in two civilisations and who is condemned, either to madness or death! According to Dr Lawrence's diagnosis, I am condemned to madness!' (Rouch in Hennebelle 1971: 82). 'I am condemned to madness', Rouch says, harking back to 'Doctor' Lawrence and wanting in some way to ward off the fourth set of accusations that threaten his work and menace his undertaking: that which attributes the apparently wild or in any case unclassifiable character of his contradictory oeuvre to 'madness' or, worse still, to psychological or political irresponsibility.

Now, it is at this point that an element may be introduced which, while having been practically ignored, is no less than at the heart of what constitutes Rouch's genius. If we manage to disregard the arbitrary frontiers delimiting cinematic genres – fiction films, adventure films, experimental films, and so on – Rouch's work no longer appears as a shapeless patchwork of 'bric-a-brac'. From one perspective, it is serious-minded, with reports, analysis, knowledge; from the other it is fictional, improvisational, wild, with an 'anything goes' approach – but like an open totality in search of a public-to-come. From the ethnological film to the fiction film, thanks to Rouch's work, the limits have become increasingly fluid – when Touré Mohammed 'plays' at being 'Lemmy Caution, FBI Agent' in *Moi, un noir*, which is supposed to be a fiction film; when one of the 'maîtres fous' takes himself to be 'the doctor's wife' or 'the General', in *Les Maîtres fous*, which itself passes for a documentary – one understands why it is absolutely necessary to start by reconsidering the notion of genres and the attitudes (and expectations) they demand. We must dispense with a fixed hierarchy of genres; instead let us rethink these set hierarchies of discourse and hence the morals, cultures and values they determine.

For all these reasons, it seems to me that when Rouch talks – whatever the circumstances – about his project of 'shared/divided anthropology', of the 'Molotov cocktail' (in 'cocktail' there is the idea of an explosive mixture), of 'Parisian ethnology undertaken by Damouré' or of the 'postcard for the imagination', it is with a precise intention every time: it always involves, according to the vow of another 'maître fou', Artaud, the attempt to liberate the myths of men from the modern world. 'What I propose to return to through theatre is an idea of the physical knowledge of images and the means of provoking trances, just as the Chinese doctor knows all the points across the human anatomy where the application of a needle can control even the most subtle functions' (1964: 97). This declaration of principle is from Artaud but for those who have seen *La chasse au lion à l'arc* or *Les Maîtres fous* it could just as well have been from Rouch.

Because, for him, making films – of whatever kind – is not about liberating the imagination, or at least not solely; but is, in a way, about injecting a dose of the possible into reality.[13] Meaning that, thanks to film, new dimensions of reality become possible. In this sense, for Rouch, filming is not only about dreaming (by means of images) but about living his dreams. Or rather, thanks to cinema, living in his dreams for real. Let us remind ourselves: nothing is impossible once the camera is there.

This is to say that there is something of the 'demiurge' about Rouch – a creator of modern myths – flanked on one side by a midwife who delivers up the 'real' of fears and fantasies, and on the other by a 'photothète', a bearer and creator of new images and representations. This is also to say that, for Rouch, cinema must operate in at least three directions at once:

(i) It must explain (and deploy) a certain 'reality' of the world, its irreducible and non-totalisable 'being-there', using all available means to the point of exhaustion. This is why, for him, the film of his dreams, the total film, should last at least 24 hours and during which one could enter, leave, talk – in short, live.

(ii) It must be a method of physically intervening in life, into the feelings and representations that it would reactivate in order to unmask or transform them.

(iii) Lastly and above all, it must be a means to metamorphose the 'real world' and to connect and mix it with his dreams, desires, political convictions, fears and so on. This explains why, whatever his basic subject – Rouch never departs from a subject – Rouch's films always appear as a multitude of heterogeneous things: 'A sort of symphony, an opera or even a cowboy film ... jazz, a poem, a song, a tragedy, a comedy, a farce and so on....'[14]

Today, when one re-reads the pages in which Artaud explains his choices and the nature of the effects he expects from his 'Theatre of Cruelty', it is as if they were a commentary anticipating Rouch's films (including the so-called 'ethnological films') and the cinema he wanted to make: the modern cinema of cruelty.

AUTHOR'S NOTE: An earlier version of this chapter first appeared in *CinémAction*, 81, 1996, 59–68.

NOTES

1   Less those of Rouch, as we will see, than those of modern anthropology and ethnology.

2   See the analyses of the American anthropologist Paul Rabinow in *Reflections on Fieldwork in Morocco*. Quantum Book: University of California Press, 1977.

3   Jean-Jacques Rousseau already observed in his *Second Discourse*: 'However much individuals come and go, it seems that philosophy does not travel, so true is it that the philosophy of one nation is ill-suited for another' (1994: 106–7).

4   This explains some of Rouch's most recurrent statements. See for example 1960: 27, where Rouch says: 'For me, the only way to make a film is the method of successive approximation. Up to now, I've made it a rule never to write before shooting a film. It's not for nothing that our friend Astruc invented the "caméra-stylo", without ever using it.' Further on, presenting the *La Pyramide humaine* project, Rouch writes: 'there was no script or dialogues to speak of but a continual improvisation before the cameras ... the camera was not an obstacle but, on the contrary, the indispensable witness which motivated this expression' (1960: 27).

5   The 'prise de langue' and the 'faire signe' by Hubert Damisch (1978).

6   I can do no better than indicate here the beautiful article by Claudine Eizykman (1973) 'Que sans discours apparaissent les films', *Revue d'esthétique*, 2, 3, 4, 159–71.

7   See for example, Téchiné & Fieschi 1967, 19: 'For me (the cinema, filming) are like surrealist painting: the use of the most realistic and photographic methods

of reproduction but in the service of the irreal, the presentation of irrational elements (Magritte, Dalí). The postcard in the service of the imagination.' And above all this: 'So I'm working in two registers: I make ethnological films in which I try to express a reality (which, anyway, is mine, but that's not the issue) and I use the same methods to depict the oneiric world that people carry with them...' (ibid.). Or this, which is essential: 'I'd like to make a 24-hour-long film, I was talking about it with Langlois, a film exactly 24 hours long ... people would enter and leave when it felt right. Myself, I don't believe all this stuff that says there has to be a beginning and an end.' As we see, the most abiding aim is above all to explode the classical frame of theatre and cinema which remains in place.

8   See Derrida 1967 and Artaud 1964.

9   See Noguez 1977: 90cf.

10 'Rouch and Cocteau, the ethnographer and the poet, are very similar in having the same sure instinct in avoiding the two contrasting traps of inane poeticism and false critical distance' (Phillipe 1971: 222). It is not a matter of challenging such an appreciation but of enlarging its scope. Besides, one can find it put in almost the same terms by Claude Jutra (1960: 33).

11 'Twenty years ago I started my own decolonisation in a way that I don't in the least renounce, I find only that it was nothing but a step ... It wasn't enough. It wasn't enough that it led to saying that to be Black had neither meaning nor importance: for the Black cannot believe in it and finds on the contrary that it has a great deal of importance and meaning' (Rouch in Mannoni 1969: 30).

12 See Deleuze 1969.

13 See for example Téchiné and Fieschi (1967: 18–19) where Rouch says: 'The most extravagant, the wildest fiction is finally the most real depiction of a given reality.' Or this: 'One enters a realm that is not reality but its provocation, which reveals reality' (ibid.). And finally, this passage: 'This introduction of fiction into real world, with an immediate breakdown, fascinates me' (ibid.).

14 Malcolm Lowry describes his novel *Under the Volcano* in these terms. These descriptions suit Rouch's oeuvre well.

REFERENCES

Artaud, A. (1964 [1946]) 'Le théatre et son double', in *Idées*. Paris: Gallimard, 135–94.

Bensmaïa, R. (1978) 'Le cinéma ethnologique est-il encore possible?', *Les Deux Écrans*, 7, 26–37.

Damisch, H. (1978) 'La "prise de langue" et le "faire signe"', in *Pretexte: Roland Barthes*. Paris: UGE 10/18, 394–406.

Deleuze, G. (1969) *Logique du sens*. Paris: Les editions de Minuit.

Derrida, J. (1967) 'La parole soufflée', in *L'écriture et la différence*. Paris: Éditions de Seuil, 253–92.

Eizykman, Cl. (1973) 'Que sans discours apparaissent les films', *Revue d'esthétique*, 2, 3, 4. Paris: Éditions Jean-Michel Place, 159–71.

Hennebelle, G. (1971) 'A propos de *Petit à petit*: Interview with Jean Rouch', *L'Afrique littéraire et artistique*, 19, 75–86.

Jutra, C. (1960) 'En courant derrière Rouch', *Cahiers du cinéma*, 114, 32–46.

Lowry, M. (1947) *Under the Volcano*. London: Jonathan Cape.

Mannoni, O. (1969) 'Je sais bien, mais quand même', in *Clefs pour l'imaginaire or l'autre scène*. Paris: Éditions de Seuil, 9–33.

Noguez, D. (1977) *Le cinéma, autrement: Collection 10–18*. Paris: UGE.

Phillipe, C-J. (1971) 'Dossiers du cinéma', *Cinéastes*, 1, 221–222.

Rabinow, P. (1977) *Reflections on Fieldwork in Morocco*. Berkeley: University of California Press.

Rouch, J. (1960) '*La Pyramide Humaine*: Scenario', *Cahiers du cinéma*, 112, 15–27.

Rousseau, J-J. (1994 [1754]) *Discourse on Inequality*, trans. Franklin Philip. Oxford: Oxford University Press.

Téchiné, A. and J-A. Fieschi (1967) 'Jean Rouch 2 *Jaguar*', *Cahiers du Cinéma*, 195, 17–20.

A group of drummers performing in Niamey, Niger, 1961

6 ROUCH, MUSIC, TRANCE

Michael Chanan

One of the features of the renovation of documentary in the 1960s, when sync-sound location filming first became easy, was a growing number of documentaries about music and musicians. These films have not been treated well by documentary film studies, except for isolated examples like *Dont Look Back* (1967) and *Gimme Shelter* (1970), and the subsequent minor genre sometimes known as the 'rockumentary' (which is still very much alive). The music documentary as such, biographies or portraits of musicians that let us in on the secrets of their art, have been thoroughly neglected, as if music were a specialist pursuit – despite it being a central feature of contemporary culture – and the issues it raises marginal to the main agenda of critical and theoretical concerns. That is not all. Despite the growing interest in questions of film music, another area of neglect is the use and function of music on the documentary soundtrack.

This chapter on Rouch and music in his ethnographic films from West Africa – especially the films about possession cults, where music and dance are inseparable from the subject portrayed – is therefore undertaken within a context of inattention, and it is necessary to begin by sketching in some background.

The arrival of the sound film was a mixed blessing for the documentary, as sound was introduced to serve the purposes of shooting fiction in the studio, and for many years remained deficient for location sound recording. The earliest sound systems, being technically not much more than prototypes, could only record live with the picture; the sound could not be re-mixed and re-recorded until post-production techniques were introduced around 1932. Location recording was difficult because the microphones then in use were unselective and omnidirectional, fragile, sensitive to wind and other ambient sounds, resulting in excessive background noise and lack of detail. Not least, the necessary gear was bulky and heavy and needed a truck of its own; hardly practical for most documentary, and certainly not in far-flung locations.

There were a small number of attempts to overcome these restrictions. Esfir Shub demonstrated the quality of Soviet sound technology in a little-known film of 1932, *K. Sh. E. (Komsomol, Patron of Electrification)*, which contains extensive location filming with synchronised sound, including both speech and musical performance, four years earlier than the GPO Film Unit's *Housing Problems*, the film usually cited as the earliest example of the new filmic trope of the interview. By then Jean Renoir had managed to shoot a feature film called *Toni* (1935) on location in the South of France, with synchronous dialogue – an extraordinary example of Neo-realism *avant la lettre*. And of course Leni Riefenstahl had all the resources she needed to shoot location sync sound at the Nuremberg Rally in 1934. For the most part, however, the technological limitations were too restrictive. Fiction filmmakers learned to shoot exterior dialogue scenes in the studio using back projection to ensure aural clarity; documentary was left stranded. While hankering after location sound, documentarists preferred the agility and immediacy of the clockwork camera, for which filmmakers like Joris Ivens, or the Russian Roman Karmen, developed a formidable hand-held shooting technique.

Jean Rouch as cinematographer belonged to this tradition, famously abandoning the tripod at the very start of his career in the late 1940s and almost never going back to it. The imperative for this was a mixture of the practical and the theoretical. Using a tripod for Rouch defeated the purpose of making a film at all, since to show anything ethnographically useful you had to be able to move around your subject and not do what they did in studios: move things around in a way that suited the camera (and the lights and the microphones). If the introduction of sound led to what Rick Altman called the return of the silent cinema's repressed – that is, the voice – then in the case of documentary this had the paradoxical effect of depriving it of what it never previously possessed, namely, the instrument of direct speech (1985: 51). If the fiction film reverted to the primacy of dialogue, which for many critics represented a regression to theatricality, then documentary was largely condemned (with a few notable exceptions) to use of a commentary that could be added to the edited film, an invisible and disembodied voice that inflects the film's whole mode of address. Many documentarists chafed against its semantic domination, which tended to limit and reduce the power of the image, and its authoritarian impression of omniscience, which Paul Rotha called the 'voice of God', which together end up distancing the film from both its own image and the perspective of the viewer. The English tried experiments like using poetry instead of prose. Ivens worked with Ernest Hemingway on *The Spanish Earth* (1937) to turn the commentary into the voice of the camera as witness, at once functional, sparse and terse; at the same time, partisan and spoken in the first person plural. Rouch would develop his own strategy, speaking the commentary in his own voice but generally not in the first person, yet still communicating the effect of the camera as witness. Guided by ethnographic principles, his method recognised the value of commentary for conveying necessary information and elucidation, while remaining aware of the danger of tendentious interpretation (although sometimes falling foul of it).

But this leaves the problem of music, because music is not factual or descriptive but always performative and expressive. It therefore cannot be neutral, and inevitably functions as a form of implicit commentary, sometimes all the more insidious for not declaring itself as such. Buñuel parodied the commentary-and-music documentary to devastating effect in *Las Hurdes* (*Land Without Bread* aka *Tierra sin pan*, 1933). Others were driven by a sense of experiment to seek the radical integration of the whole soundtrack. Joris Ivens had turned to the composer Lou Lichtveld for *Philips Radio* in 1931, which was shot silent. Lichtveld used a small band, playing somewhat fragmentary music in a modernist style similar to Honegger, Poulenc or Milhaud, combined with a whole range of noise effects. The Paris studios where the film was recorded were equipped for mixing but not re-recording, so everything had to be recorded simultaneously. All they could do was break the film up into sections, and turn the recording session into performance (which is why it made sense having a composer in charge). Hollywood developed a similar technique, which later came to be known by the name of its progenitor, Jack Foley, but there is a critical difference: the Foley artist became a specialist within an elaborate division of labour, in which sound effects were separated from both dialogue and music, rather than all elements in the soundtrack being treated as a musical ensemble. Ivens later succumbed to the American method when he came to make *The Spanish Earth* a few years later, with post-production in the United States. The results were professional but not very interesting, and here another problem set in. The music was selected by the composer Marc Blitzstein from records Ivens brought back from Spain. But the music came from a different region of the country from the places portrayed in the film.

In Soviet Russia, Vertov's first sound film was *Enthusiasm* in 1931, incorporating a soundtrack composed of noises recorded on location in the mines and villages visited by the camera, which Georges Sadoul, from the distance of France after World War Two, described as 'the clash of hammers, of train whistles, of the songs of workers at rest', adding that Vertov edited the sound 'as freely as he cut visuals, creating a kind of *musique concrète*' (1972: 104). Benjamin Britten took a similar approach to Lichtveld in composing for *Coalface* (1935) and *Night Mail* (1936) a few years later. The steam engine gathering energy, for example, its pistons beginning to drive the wheels, is scored for a very unorthodox seven-piece percussion group consisting of compressed air, sandpaper on slate, a small trolley, clank, drill, hammers, siren and so forth. As the musicologist Donald Mitchell remarks, this is more like the sound-world of Varèse than Britten, but comprises, in the name of documentary realism, 'a kind of a musical factuality' (2000: 83). And again he calls it a kind of *musique concrète.*

One thing these examples make clear is the strong affinity that then existed between documentary and the modernist avant-garde, and films like *Enthusiasm* and *Philips Radio* represent a signal moment not just in the construction of the sound documentary but also in the line of experimentation which leads from the noise machines of the Italian Futurists to the sound art of John Cage and Pierre Schaeffer, two of the key figures at the roots of the post-war musical avant-garde (it was Schaeffer who coined the term *musique concrète*). But in matters musical this quickly became difficult to sustain in the face of the cultural populism of cinema as an institution, which would only much later come to incorporate the outlandish inventions of the avant-garde, when a new aesthetic emerged, in the shape of postmodernism, which took away the sting.

Rouch would later complain of the old-fashioned music, along with its 'Colonial Exposition' style of commentary, in early films of African ethnography like *Sous les masques noirs* (1938) by Marcel Griaule. His own first efforts, shot in silent 16mm, suffered the same fate. Released in the cinema in 1947 under what Rouch called the 'abominable' title of *Au pays des mages noirs*, it had been bought by a commercial producer who blew it up to 35mm, reduced it from thirty minutes to ten, and put it out along with Rossellini's *Stromboli* (1950). 'In the absence of real sound, it was accompanied by idiotic music and a narration spoken by the commentator of the Tour de France bicycle race, in his characteristic voice … My reaction after this film is to say, "No! It's not possible!" The music is worthless; the tone of the commentary is insufferable. It's really an exotic film, a film that should not have been made. I've never shown it in Africa. I'd be ashamed' (Rouch in Fulchignoni 2003: 161).

Another example, from a different quarter, was Basil Wright's *Song of Ceylon* (1934) for which the score by Walter Leigh was an example of the kind of musical orientalism that Pierre Boulez described as 'the clumsy appropriation of a "colonial" musical vocabulary' to be found in the numerous *rhapsodies malgaches* or *cambodgiennes* of the early years of the century (1986: 341).

One documentarist of the 1940s used music very differently. For Humphrey Jennings, music was not to be relegated to the background, but belonged to the social space of the film's subjects, which in wartime Britain always meant the nation. Jennings bathed the nation in its music, with the benefit of improved equipment and government propaganda resources which enabled him to film, with synchronous sound, on location. The shots are all set up and carefully composed, but the circumstances are such that people are relaxed in front of the camera. If *Listen to Britain* (1942) comprises, as Ian Aitken puts it, 'an expression of the connectedness of experience' in the nation at war (1998: 216), then the most important component in this portrayal is the performance and enjoyment of a variety of music according to their proper social settings. For Jennings, music's most important quality is what Theodore Adorno often called its anthropological function, its capacity for bringing together communities, affirming the social nature of life.

As remote from Rouch as the work of Jennings may seem, this attitude to music as part of living cultural experience might be thought of as a secret bond between them, which is expressed in both as a commitment to uphold the sociological or ethnographic integrity of the music in the film. The first chance Rouch had to approach this aim was in 1951, making *Cimetière dans la falaise* with the aid of a prototype portable magnetic tape recorder. For the first time in a film from Africa, we are hearing – as indicated in a title at the start of the film – the actual music of the people we are seeing. In its cinematography, Rouch faced the common problem of shooting continuous actions, as he was, with a spring-wound camera that limited the maximum length of individual shots to about twenty seconds; to answer this difficulty he developed his technique of moving around while winding the camera and continuing to shoot from a slightly different angle. The sound tape recorder has no such limitation. Not yet capable of synchronous shooting, this meant that in the edit continuous location sound could be used to bind sequences together.

In the early scenes of the film, music is used to provide cultural atmosphere while filling the gaps between passages of commentary; the sung words are not translated, though it would later become Rouch's practice to do this. In the later part, where Rouch is following the funeral ceremony, the visual and aural material (including the voices of the villagers as well as drums and instruments) allow the editor to introduce some cleverly cheated impressions of sync sound. This requires from the editor a skill in putting music to images – in matching the rhythms of bodies in movement and the rhythm of the music they move to – which is little commented on, despite becoming part of the editor's expert practical knowledge, because its effects are inevitably invisible: it is only when it is badly done that the viewer notices the lack of confluence.

If the technique is largely derived from the codes of narrative continuity, documentarists of the 1950s made extensive use of it, as in *Momma Don't Allow* (1955) by Karel Reisz and Tony Richardson, a wordless film about a jazz club where the editing expertly disguises the fact that the film was shot without synchronous sound. Rouch's most sustained application of the technique comes in his most famous film of this period, *Les Maîtres fous* (1955) though here the narrative is carried by a commentary running through the length of the film. It is certain that without it these strange and bizarre proceedings, with their unique and syncretistic symbolism, would make no sense at all, but the commentary also allows Rouch to have his cake and eat it by dipping the level of the location soundtrack the better to hide its non-synchronicity. He even allows himself to use close-ups of people speaking – albeit in a language completely unknown to the European viewer, who probably is not bothered because there is so much else going on to grab the attention (and in any case, when people speak on screen we tend to look at their eyes, not their mouths).

For the most part, Rouch would drop this kind of invisible sound editing when it was no longer needed because 16mm synchronous shooting permitted long continuous takes. Look at a film like *Le Yenendi de Ganghel* (1968), shot with sync sound in 1968, and what you find is long takes with a mobile camera moving smoothly between drummers and musicians and participants in the ceremonial, with no cutaways. The microphone, judging by a moment when it appears in frame, is a directional gunshot microphone that moves with the camera. This means that on the one hand the sound perspective – the balance between the different groups of drummers, or between drums and voices – changes, but on the other, it retains the camera's perspective, and the viewer hardly notices.

Rouch is closely linked, through *Chronique d'un été* (1960) and other films, to the concept of *cinéma vérité* and the self-reflexive documentary, as against the fly-on-the-wall transparency of direct cinema in the New York style. Yet a film like *Le Yenendi de Ganghel*, which apart from the opening and closing sequences consists of nothing but a series of long takes joined end to end in the order in which they were taken, is perhaps the purest example of direct filming one can find, the commentary notwithstanding (since mainly, the commentary does nothing more than the same job as subtitles: it supplies a translation of what is spoken or sung). Yet there are crucial differences with fly-on-the-wall and its myth of invisible presence. In Rouch, the camera is not on the edge but moves around within the scene as a tacitly acknowledged observer, entering the circle of the possession dancers. Occasionally the acknowledgement is explicit, like the moment in the middle of *Le Yenendi de Ganghel* where one of the principal participants comes up and greets Rouch-the-camera and his entire team, without stepping out of his ritual persona (or Rouch out of his). Explaining in the commentary what is happening, this is one of the few moments when Rouch speaks in the first person. The general effect is a common one nowadays in the age of the video diary, but this is more than 35 years ago and the context quite different.

The film which raises the question of the relation of music and trance most acutely is *Les Tambours d'avant: Tourou et Bitti* (1971). According to one of

Rouch's associates, the musicologist Gilbert Rouget who has written extensively on the subject, the relation between trance or possession and the music which attends it and seems to play a role in initiating it is subtle and paradoxical. We know that music has definite somatic or kinaesthetic effects, and given the right kind of beat our autonomic system responds with a quickening of the pulse, yet there is no simple or direct correlation of trance states with particular types of music, but rather a repertoire of both which interact in various ways. Further, the musician who plays the music does not himself go into trance. The phenomenon of trance is a social one, in which the effect of music depends on its insertion within a social code in which trance becomes an allowable form of behaviour. Moreover, nobody falls into trance who is not predisposed to do so (whether one is speaking of possession cults, or in Rouget's own comparison, the trance-like behaviour of 'Beatlemania'). Music, says Rouget (1985), can undoubtedly sensitise a subject to the call of possession, but it is not responsible for the psychological condition which leads to such a vocation. In *Tourou et Bitti*, Rouch has been invited to film a festival for the spirits, but for three days nobody has become possessed, despite the two special old drums, *tourou* and *bitti*, which have been brought out for the occasion. On the last day, Rouch tells us, several hours pass without possession taking place, but he decides to film anyway, to get some footage 'of this beautiful music, which is in danger of disappearing'. He filmed in one continuous shot and when the drumming stopped he was about to turn off when the lute player started up again, playing solo: he had 'seen a spirit', and immediately one of the participants became possessed. Rouch was left with the feeling that it had been his own 'ciné-trance' that 'played the role of catalyst that night', and subsequently wrote one of his most trenchant essays on ciné-ethnography, where he explains: the Songhay-Zarma among whom he was filming have a theory of self in which everyone has a double who lives in a parallel world, which is also the home of the spirits, the masters of the forces of nature, and of the imaginary (dreams and reveries). Shamans, sorcerers and possession provide a connection between the real world and its double. 'I now believe', said Rouch, 'that for the people who are filmed, the "self" of the filmmaker changes in front of their eyes during the shooting ... For the Songhay-Zarma, who are now quite accustomed to film, my "self" is altered in front of their eyes in the same way as is the "self" of the possession dancers: it is the "film-trance" [*ciné-transe*] of the one filming the "real trance" of the other' (2003: 99).[1] But Rouch also considers this strange condition, where the filmmaker 'looks at them only through the intermediary of a strange appendage and hears them only through the intermediary of a shotgun microphone', as a paradoxical effect of the technology of filming which produces 'a strange kind of choreography, which, if inspired, makes the cameraman and soundman no longer invisible but participants in the ongoing event' (ibid.). This is why he never believed the claims of the New Yorkers of the direct cinema that the camera could attain some kind of impartial, objective and transparent rendering of the scenes that it filmed.

From a musical point of view, the most interesting and unique film is *Batteries Dogon*, made with Gilbert Rouget in 1966. This film, a study in drumming, has no commentary at all after the opening few words (which also serve to announce the credits). In the first half of the film, we watch a series of shots in which boys are learning the rhythmic complexities of West African drumming, using stones on rocks. A boy, or his teacher, plays a rhythm; the other listens then plays another, then they put the two together. This happens several times, each exercise separated by a title announcing the kind of rhythm. The scene is the entrance to a cave (presumably because this is where suitable rocks are plentiful) and the camera, unusually for Rouch, is on a tripod, allowing it to gently zoom in and out. The second half of the film is a funeral ceremony of the kind where the boys will perform when they are men. Here the camera is hand-held and moves around in Rouch's more usual manner, coming to concentrate on a succession of energetic, agile and graceful dancers. This film is immensely instructive. Simply showing us the boys practising is to enlist the eye to provide a lesson in listening. First we hear individual rhythms, then a cross rhythm, then the two together, different ones several times over, with our eye fixed all the while on one or other of the drummers as they beat them out, our eye teaching us to differentiate what arrives at our ears as a complex unitary flow of audition. This is practically the purest form of record-footage you can get, and many viewers will not even recognise it as being what is properly called a film. But it provides the distant viewer with a sensuous deconstruction of a music whose inner complexity is normally beyond the uninitiated listener. This is perhaps the difference between music and trance. The uninitiated viewer seeing the images of trance is watching something that remains beyond their experiential capacity as members of a totally other culture. Music, however, reaches across cultural boundaries and enters foreign bodies even at the remove of a comfortable cinema in the distant metropolis, because, as Adorno once put it, music is indeed a universal language without being Esperanto. And the same, of course, is true of film.

NOTE

1   See also Elizabeth Cowie's contribution to this volume.

REFERENCES

Aitken, I. (ed.) (1998) 'Humphrey Jennings', in *The Documentary Film Movement: An Anthology*. Edinburgh: Edinburgh University Press, 215–36.

Altman, R. (1985) 'Evolution of Sound Technology', in E. Weis and J. Belton (eds) *Film Sound: Theory and Practice*. New York: Columbia University Press, 44–53.

Boulez, P. (1986) *Orientations*. London: Faber and Faber.

Fulchignoni, E. (2003) 'Ciné-Anthropology: Jean Rouch with Enrico Fulchignoni', in J. Rouch, *Ciné-Ethnography*. Minneapolis: University of Minnesota Press,147–87.

Mitchell, D. (2000) *Britten and Auden in the Thirties*. Rochester: Boydell.

Rouch, J. (2003 [1973]) 'On the Vicissitudes of the Self: The Possessed Dancer, The Magician, The Sorcerer, the Filmmaker and the Ethnographer', in *Ciné-ethnography*, ed. and trans. S. Feld. Minneapolis: University of Minnesota Press, 87–101.

Rouget, G. (1985) *Music and Trance: A Theory of the Relations Between Music and Possession*. Chicago: University of Chicago Press.

Sadoul, G. (1972) *Dictionary of Films*. Berkeley: University of California Press.

Stills from *La Chasse au lion à l'arc*, 1957–64

7 ETHNOGRAPHY AND AFRICAN CULTURE: JEAN ROUCH ON *LA CHASSE AU LION À L'ARC* AND *LES MAÎTRES FOUS*

Hamid Naficy

Some thirty years have passed since I interviewed Jean Rouch on the lush banks of the Zayandehrud river in Isfahan, where his films, including his then latest work, *Babatou, les trois conseils* (1975), were being screened and he was a guest of honour at the Festival of Ethnographic Film, 1977. The full interview was published in 1979.[1]

As an anthropologist primarily working in Africa, he was an exile of sorts both in Africa and France. He was a white European working sympathetically amongst, and with, the peoples of former African colonies and a critic of his own native French society and anthropology, who was simultaneously an insider and an outsider in both places. Like him I lived most of my life outside the country of my birth, Iran, and was always an insider and outsider there and in Europe and the United States where I lived and worked professionally. This connection was in my thoughts when I wrote *An Accented Cinema: Exilic and Diasporic Filmmaking* (2001). Although not a true exile in the sense discussed in that book, Rouch was a liminal figure and made his films with what I theorised as interstitial and collective production modes, characteristic of those deterritorialised filmmakers and films.

The tensions inherited in his methodologies, theories and ethics are intertwined in the two seminal African films that are covered extensively in this interview, *La Chasse au lion à l'arc* (1957–64) and *Les Maîtres fous* (1955).

I will first, briefly, summarise these practice-derived methodologies, theories and ethics, as extracted from the interview, many of which have since become commonplace; some of them have been exploited and distorted, while others have been contested or gained additional traction.

Rouch's African films were interstitial in that he performed multiple functions in making them; he occupied both an interstitial social position and a liminal personal identity in societies where he made them; he had access to multiple cultures, societies and languages; he benefited from his national, racial, colonial and bureaucratic capital (as a civil servant French filmmaker) which freed him from local African exigencies and limitations; and he worked in the interstices or outside the film industry, where he engaged in various ad hoc, contingent and improvisational film practices. His filmic subjects were also often liminars and outsiders themselves, whether these were the natives of his African films or the natives and foreigners of what he called his 'Parisian tribe' in *Chronique d'un été* (1960).

His modus operandi was collective and participatory. It was collective to the extent that he almost always collaborated with indigenous African youngsters interested in cinema, who assisted him and actively participated in the production process. It was participatory in that he shrunk the distance and blurred the traditional unequal power relations between ethnographer and subject. This collective and participatory approach led to what he called 'shared anthropology', whereby he engaged his subjects in the process of shaping the films' ideas, plots and characters, and he sought their advice and critique of the filmed footage about them. He hoped that such engagements of indigenous filmmakers and subjects in the process would produce results that approximated the ethnographic reality more as well as confer value and dignity on the ethnographic situations and subjects. This involved not only making manifest the invisible processes of film production but also incorporating the commentary and critique of the ethnographic subjects into the final film. It also involved other features of reflexivity – self-inscription and self-referentiality – which positions the filmmaker to be both an author and subject of their films' discourse. One of Rouch's remarkable achievements was that he developed his various methodologies and theories during practice and in an ad hoc, unplanned and improvised fashion. As he and his cohort ran into difficulties and contingencies, they exhibited flexibility and inventiveness. He was engaged in collective improvisation which encompassed the form of the film as well, leading to textual experimentation, such as the mixing of fictional and non-fictional elements. In this improvisatory process of ethnographic fieldwork and filmmaking, he also developed a set of ethics in the field.

Interstitial production, collective and participatory production, shared ethnographic self-reflexivity and improvisation all necessitate achieving a judicious balance between commitment to unvarnished reality (revelation) and responsibility to the ethnographic subject and subjects (secrecy). Sometimes, it is important that ethnographic filmmakers refrain from revealing certain indigenous practices the subjects do not wish to be shown, or scenes that should not be shown, because exposure may be unethical or because it may invalidate or debase the practices or dishonour and shame the practitioners, or because if revealed governments, religious leaders and political pressure groups may seek to censor them or commercial enterprises may attempt to exploit them. It may mean refraining from screening the films in certain circumstances, or to certain people, because of the unwanted effects they may have either on the subjects or on the viewers. In addition, shared ethnography and collective production required sharing with the subjects both the production credits and profits of the film.

On *La Chasse au lion à l'arc*

HN: *Why do they hunt lions?*

JR: Sometimes there is a disruption of the normal system when a lion kills animals, but does not eat them. It seems to be killing only for the pleasure of killing. Once a lion begins to behave in this natural way, it is very dangerous, because it might start killing people, so they must kill it. Also the cattle herders live in close relation with the lions and haven't the right to kill the lions. They think that the lion is good for the cattle, since it forces the cattle to move and to be active. Normally the lions kill the animals who are weak or ill. The lions move behind the cattle like dogs and they eliminate the sick and the weak by natural selection. But this is a very delicate equilibrium between the wild animals and the domestic animals. When a lion begins to kill for pleasure, then you have to destroy it. It is then that the shepherds ask the lion hunters to kill the particular lion. Lion hunting as I said is really very dangerous. Not only physically (guns are strictly forbidden!) but from the cosmological point of view, it is a very difficult thing to kill this animal. It requires a great deal of preparation. That is why there are so many tales about the relationship between human beings and the death of animals, and the methods used to avoid the revenge of the dead animal, driving out the soul of the animal and so on. Another important thing! The heart of the lion which was killed during the filming was sold to a statesman from the Ivory Coast for about $2,000, because the lion was killed with an arrow in the heart, and this really is a potent magical charm. All these hunters earn their income by selling the flesh of a lion killed by poison because the flesh is a very good medicine. In fact, this is another very important point which is not in the film. The poison from strophantin trees, which contain an alkaloid substance like cortisone, reacts with the adrenaline in the body of the dying animal; we know exactly how it works. During the twenty minutes of agony, the animal's body is a kind of laboratory in which there is this mixing of the cortisone, adrenaline and so on. And the flesh of the animal, as a result, is very good, and the fat is used against rheumatism. Many other things are derived from the flesh as well, but the hunters asked me not to say these things in the film because they said that, 'you (technologists) now will take our lions! That is why there are lions in the zoos in the townships of Niger.' They said they now know the reason why the Europeans asked them to have lions alive. 'It is in order to learn all our skills, to use the *nagi* [poison] and make medicine to cure your rheumatism. Then you will take our income from us.' I had to avoid giving this information in the film, because to an extent they were not wrong.

HN: *One sees a lot of films from the US about violence of one sort or another, and always the death-throes are dramatised extraordinarily. In The Lion Hunters the deaths are very quiet. Was that because of the poison?*

JR: Yes, it was the poison and the fact that they were speaking to the lion at the time of filming. I myself could not understand much. They were chanting for the lion to be courageous. And the lion gets quieter and quieter. And it dies quietly. You must calm the animal to die. They insult it at the same time that they admire its courage. And they describe the situation to it, saying, 'Your heart is like a boiling pot.' They describe what is cooking in the body of the lion and what is happening with the poison in its body. And when the lion vomits they say to it: 'You vomit your death! You are finished. Vomit your death!' Vomit your death is the last thing said in the film. All these words are very, very difficult to translate. I tried to translate it, but that is also another problem in this kind of film. Even if you translate these sentences you need maybe two pages of footnotes to explain the real meaning of the words.

HN: *Can you give us a breakdown of the financial aspects of The Lion Hunters?*

JR: I used three hours of film to shoot the film. It was shot on Kodachrome and the first editing was done on the original itself. It is not an expensive film, not at all. The National Centre for Scientific Research sponsored the film, but it is difficult to estimate the budget because the film was shot over a period of years; and I did not have to pay for the journey, I was already there. We decided to give the hunters forty per cent of the profits of the film.

HN: *Did the sponsor retain any control of the film?*

JR: When I showed the film to the sponsors, they said nothing. For them the preparation of the poison was more important than the hunting itself.

HN: *Did you also show the film to the hunters themselves?*

JR: Yes. When I showed the film to them they said, 'There are not enough lions.' And that is the reason that I had to go there a second time, to film more lions.

HN: *What was their criterion for the judgement? Did they want more dramatic shots of the hunt?*

JR: No, they wanted to show the lions alive. I had only shown a lion dying. In fact the film portrayed a true picture of the situation because you never see a lion alive in this part of Africa; it is not the same in East Africa. Also, they complained about the fact that it was not sync sound. Since only the beginning and the end of the film is sync sound, that was a big problem. So the adventure of the film was that the hunters themselves said, 'No, it is not good for us.' And I went and re-shot the film, and that version met with approval.

HN: *Did you ever ask the villagers or the hunters in your films to participate in the act of filming, to give you ideas about what to and what not to do?*

JR: Of course, all the time. I was not the director of the film. They said, 'We'll go to this place and that place', and I followed them, working like a newsreel cameraman, trying to follow what was happening. It was very, very difficult, because very often nothing would happen and there were a lot of problems. There is the question of censorship. During the first hunting party when everything went wrong and we did not find any lions to hunt, suddenly the chief of the hunters started to cry in the middle of the bush because it was a shame not to have hunted. He realised that everything was against us and that there would be no lions to hunt. He felt responsible and ashamed and he thought I would be discouraged, and that would stop the filming or the showing of this film, which would be a defeat for these lion hunters. So I stopped filming because they said it would shame them to reveal their secret. It would have been impossible to show that film to other people. This is a very important thing because for them to be courageous it is necessary first to be afraid. To surmount your fear, that is courage. If you have no fear, there is no courage.

HN: *In The Lion Hunters there are several shots, at the moment of the death of the lion, where you show close-ups of hunters' faces. Their eyes are filled with fear and tears, the faces are intense and there seems to be a special kind of communication between the hunters who are watching the death of the lion and the lion itself. Am I reading too much into it?*

JR: You see, this young lion was caught in a trap and there was no way out. We could not free him. It was a young lion and ready to kill everybody. So they had to kill him by poisoned arrows. But they say (and I think it is mentioned in the commentary also) that if a hunter kills a young lion he will lose his own children in the same year. So the hunters will have no descendants. They kill lions and all their sons die. And that is the reason for this strange relationship you mentioned. They try to avoid their fate by using magic charms. The man who was there, Isaka, who is a fiddle player, and who shot the lion, did in fact lose his eldest son during that same year. He had to kill this lion, even though he knew that by killing the lion he would lose his own son. I was very moved in the middle of filming that sequence, but I cannot say those things in the commentary. Because it would cause the hunters shame, and the reason for it is very interesting! Perhaps I can say these things now because there are no more lions left. They say that in northwest Africa the lion hunters were the first group of men ever organised. Their organisation was copied after the organisation of the lion community itself. The lions are polygamous; the lionesses hunt for the lion. In the African community there is one man and women work for him. They also say that the advantage is that a good hunter has no descendants, which means that there is no inherited power. In the beginning, the chiefs were hunters. But to be a chief you could not be the son of a chief. You have to achieve it by yourself. Unfortunately, at some time in the past one of these big hunters decided not to hunt but to be the chief of his group and this was the beginning of all the trouble, which is brought about by power inheritance. That is a very important point in this film, but I could not say so at the time because all these people were involved in this kind of adventure. It was potentially very dangerous. I learned later that one of the hunters involved in the first hunt had been in love with the lioness, and had made some efforts to thwart the hunt. Later on it was reported that he had died and it was not clear what the cause of the death was. I knew then that we were playing with fire. You have to be very careful with all this and you have to be careful with the editing of the film.

HN: *If you were not to show the film to the hunters themselves you could presumably have included these segments in the film?*

JR: Well, the problem with anthropology is that there are some things you have to keep secret. You cannot tell everything. It is impossible. And that is a very important thing. It is not a question of film alone. At present we are making a film on oral tradition in connection with history, and we know that the history the people are teaching in school is not true, absolutely not true. But it is impossible to tell the truth now because the truth is officially censored.

On *Les Maîtres fous*

HN: *Are you working on collecting examples of possession ceremonies from all over the world?*

JR: No, I am trying to film samples among the people I know quite well. Although I know a lot about possessions, I don't understand everything.

HN: *Early on you recorded peoples' reactions to your films and then included them in your films. Have you continued doing that in your later films?*

JR: Yes and no. It is very difficult to do that with possession films. It is impossible to show the film on possession to the people who were themselves possessed because there is a kind of electro-shock effect. Suddenly they become possessed again.

HN: *Didn't you show Les Maîtres fous to the people who were involved?*

JR: No. The priests wanted the camera to be used as a tool in their cult, to show the film to the people and shock them into possession. They were crazy! They didn't know what the risk was. I think that they were very lucky not to have the authorisation to show the film. It was censored in Gold Coast by the British Government. They said that it was an insult to the Queen because the British Governor, who is the Queen's representative, was insulted and also the Society for the Prevention of Cruelty to Animals considered the film violent and cruel to animals.

HN: *I see. So they did not get a chance to show this film to their people?*

JR: The priest saw the film, but not the people who were possessed.

HN: *The priest was not possessed?*

JR: Not during the filming. If you are not possessed in the film, you can see other possessed people, but you must not see yourself on the screen, possessed.

HN: *Have you shown any of your possession films to the people who were possessed?*

JR: I did it twice, and it was a mistake. The men became possessed there and then, and it was really a very traumatic experience. It was like an electro-shock treatment. While in shock they said to me, 'You disturbed me! Why did you call me? Why? Why have you come here and what do you want?' And they talked to other people also. It was very difficult because it was really a shock for them.

HN: *When they came to see the film they were not possessed?*

JR: No, they saw the film and in one second they were possessed. Like this [snapping his fingers] they were possessed, and it was a real possession. It was very tragic, there was shouting and so on. We had to stop the film. And they were absolutely angry at us.

HN: *After you shot Les Maîtres fous, when you were returning home that evening, you mentioned that everybody, including your assistant, felt that it was a very exhausting experience; you could smell blood all over. Was what they did uncommon?*

JR: These specific ceremonies happen only once a year, and it is a long trip to the site. That was the reason we spent an hour or two in the car, driving back to town. We were all very tired. Then the day after the possession ceremonies I saw the same boys, they looked so well! I thought to myself, 'Well, my goodness! It is all right! These people know what we don't know!' And I am sure of that.

HN: *In the film, the day after the possession ceremonies, you see a great change in their facial expressions and also in the colour of their skin and virtually everything else. Did they put on make-up for the ceremony?*

JR: No, no make-up at all. They were exactly different persons. These people have found a real way to cure this kind of sickness. I don't know what it is even now. Studies have been made, but nobody really knows what it is exactly.

HN: *You said that the possession ceremonies that you showed in Les Maîtres fous have since changed.*

JR: Yes, because the British Colonial rule ended in 1957. Since then the region has come increasingly under the influence of Islamic politics. They gave a new sense to the traditional possession ceremonies. There was this new blood coming from outside and even the mythology is changed. The importance, for me, of these ceremonies is the importance of changing ritual and mythology. The origin is life, everyday life, changing the beliefs of the people! There are new possessions. For example, in Niger a dance on death and sex has developed which is very strange. It is forbidden because people become naked and make love in public and so on. But since it is forbidden, it becomes stronger and stronger every day.

HN: *Possession ceremonies are conducted all over the world. What are the reasons for these ceremonies, which are apparently very similar from country to country?*

JR: A *zar* [possession] party is the only place where people can meet together, and men and women can dance together. They enjoy dancing, because it is not just a ritual. The joy of being a good dancer, to hear wonderful music and so on is pleasing to them. At the same time, this is the only way people in the village can mix together. I understand why possession ceremonies are often forbidden, because when people are possessed it is the *zar*, which is speaking through their tongues, and very often in the village they speak of everything. They speak of the political development and social problems. The things they say may be politically dangerous and have to be censored. I think, however, that is the effect, not the cause. The cause is that we all live in both reality and in dream. The relationship between man and nature has been extremely important and is based on subjective impressions. The old civilisations, before Islam or Christianity, were based on the system of trance, which means communication with something outside the normal realities. In our society we have that with television, theatre, film and so on. When you have a trance or possession ceremony there is a mixing of everybody, there is no social barrier. The participants may be slaves, rich, Muslim, non-Muslim, male or female. Everyone has the same stature. That I think is very significant, and is the reason why these ceremonies have often been forbidden. But nowadays all around the world you see that this technique of possession and trance is becoming more and more prevalent. The new theatre is based on that. What Peter Brook and the Living Theatre have done is based on this idea of trance. But like any other drug, if you use it for religious activity and as a means of getting in touch with the problems, not of your own but of your society, and try to solve them, then possession ceremonies are absolutely all right. But if you use the drug just to escape and to solve your own personal problems, I have no interest in it. I think that these techniques are becoming more necessary. In the US the Holy Rollers are using these techniques. We have the same thing with the Gypsies in France now. And it is becoming more important all around Africa. For example, when thirty years ago I wrote my thesis about possession rituals in Niger, I thought that I was recording the last manifestations of possession dance in that place because Islam was spreading and a new form of civilisation was taking root. But since then the *zar* or 'possession phenomenon' has become more and more important every year. All the students in anthropology, all the field-workers in Africa, even all the prominent men in Niger are members of these possession groups, or they have in their own family people who are possessed. The Africans practise possession to revenge the Arabs, because they were slaves to Arabs and as slaves they were the dancers and people who provided entertainment. They claim that they will play a role similar to the American slaves in the American culture, giving to them the gift of rhythm and music, jazz music. They think that the ex-slaves, the black people in Namibia and Ethiopia, will be the saviours of the Arabs, because they will give the Arabs what they have lost: imagination. If these manifestations are censored or banished, this will give to the manifestations a new strength. If you forbid something it means that it has some value. When you forbid something, you create martyrs and you will see that within ten or twenty years possession ceremonies will gain a great deal of importance because they are forbidden.

HN: *I am always uncomfortable with the purist point of view that one must belong to a group in order to make a film or write about it, in order for the opinion to be of value.*

JR: Yes, there is no logic behind it! You are a foreigner to everything. You are a foreigner in your own family. When you are making a film there are only two motives. You have to either like the people you are filming or dislike them. Maybe that is the reason why it is so difficult to make films on everyday life.

HN: *Does the presence of the camera interfere with people's self-expression, or does it allow people to reveal themselves more?*

JR: I am sure it reveals if you are using it properly. When shooting *Les Maîtres fous* I was alone. I had a native sound recorder, and I myself have known these people for 25 years. I made maybe 20–25 films on this village and the life of this very strange community of people. Also, my camera is not passive. The camera, from my point of view, is a kind of provocation. The provocation can be good or bad. Right now we are speaking into a microphone and we are not speaking as if we were just sitting and talking. I think that is the reason why it is so difficult to make films about everyday life. For example, I made a small film about the relationship between rhythm and work. One part of the film is about some girls who were carrying food, and as I started to film, they started singing. The song was really a very, very good one. I didn't stop because the song got better and better. It was a kind of collective improvisation. I think that is the role of visual anthropology. It is a very difficult role and one from which you can't escape. The anthropologist can no longer be a man with a notebook, not asking questions. When he starts to ask questions, there is some change because he is there, even if he is from the same tribe. If he is a sociologist studying, for example, the nature of work, when he goes to a factory and he interviews the workers, he is changing them, because they have to answer questions they have never been asked before. Filming possession ceremonies like in *Les Maîtres fous* in some ways was dangerous because it was a very important ritual. If something had gone wrong, I would have been responsible. But I think you have to take risks. The same thing was true with *The Lion Hunters*. If a man had died I would have been responsible because I was there and had provoked it. You have to take risks when you are making an ethnographic film. But I think the old attitude of anthropologists who think that they are there and that they do not disturb the people they are studying is incorrect. Human sciences are not like physics or chemistry or even natural history. You are disturbing your subjects. Perhaps in natural history one disturbs one's subjects very much also. I don't know.

HN: *You have mentioned that the process of filming and watching the film by the subjects who are in the film is a dramatic experience for them because they sometimes reveal things about themselves they were not aware of, and that this experience is so traumatic sometimes it affects their minds greatly.*

JR: I spoke of this dramatic effect after the film *Chronique d'un été*, but all the films that I shot in Africa had the same effect. When you are using this system of filmmaking you are really using a kind of drug. It is very difficult for the people to resist it. When the first time they see themselves on the screen, they discover a new personality in themselves. And after a while they get accustomed to it. When I was shooting *Chronique d'un été* it was very difficult to stop the film because people wanted to be filmed all the time. The camera was their reason for life. You can see in the film a girl like Marceline who at the beginning is very shy, and at the end of the film is very responsive. The reason was that all these people were included in the filmmaking; all the people in *Chronique d'un été* became involved with film.

HN: *Do you see this as your main role, making films that will stimulate the production of other films?*

JR: Yes. Vertov's idea was and is a very good one. He said, 'What is important is not to just make films. It is to make films that give birth to other films.' I think that is the best thing people can say about a film.

NOTE

1   The full interview, entitled 'Jean Rouch: A Personal Perspective', was first pub-
     lished in 1979, in the *Quarterly Review of Film Studies*, 1, 3, 339–62. The version
     published here is a revised, shortened version.

REFERENCE

Naficy, H. (2001) *The Accented Cinema: Exilic and Diasporic Filmmaking.* Princ-
     eton: University of Princeton Press.

A page from a collection of photographs taken in Accra, Ghana, 1954–55

8 WHOSE VOICE? WHOSE FILM?: JEAN ROUCH, OUMAROU GANDA AND *MOI, UN NOIR*

Steven Ungar

Becoming another?

Can one put the West to flight? Can one flee oneself? In *Cinema 2: The Time-Image* (1985), Gilles Deleuze describes the problems faced by the filmmaker in Africa among peoples colonised by those who impose their stories from elsewhere and appropriate local myths to their own ends. In answer to this question, Deleuze cites the trance sequences in Jean Rouch's film, *Les Maîtres fous* (1955), in which characters on screen become others by storytelling, while the filmmaker becomes another by fashioning characters drawn from real life. He conceptualises this reciprocal interaction as a double-becoming and concludes: 'It may be objected that Jean Rouch can only with difficulty be considered a third world author, but no one has done so much to put the West to flight, to flee himself, to break with a cinema of ethnology and say *Moi, un noir* [1958]' (1985: 223).

Some 27 years earlier, Jean-Luc Godard referred to Rouch's film, *Moi, un noir* (1958), as audacious and humble because it showed a free Frenchman freely setting his free gaze on a free world (1998: 177).[1] But if – in terms of this composite portrait – Rouch was a free Frenchman (Godard) who tried more than anyone to flee himself (Deleuze), it remains unclear what *his* freedom and *his* ability to become another imply concerning those portrayed in his film. This chapter studies *Moi, un noir* in conjunction with urban modernity in late colonial Africa and as a prod to *Cabascabo* (1968), film by Oumarou Ganda, whom Rouch had recruited to play the lead in his film a decade earlier. Its emphasis on colonial history and African film goes against the received understanding of critics and historians who consider *Moi, un noir* almost exclusively in terms of visual style linked to *cinéma vérité* and the French *nouvelle vague*. Rouch in 1958 is indeed a white French male – 'free' in Godard's choice of term – working in apparent good faith to record the daily lives of Africans living under French colonial rule (see Dine 1994: 178). But exactly what image of urban Africa in 1957 does *Moi, un noir* disclose? How does its narrative structure bear on its place in the histories of African film and late colonial Africa? My intention here is not to judge Rouch *ad hominem* on the basis of circumstances that empowered him as a 'free' French male working in a colonial setting. At the same time, reconsidering *Moi, un noir* from this perspective provides a means of reassessing Rouch's African films of the 1950s with reference to perceptions of overseas territories occupied by France during the final decade of colonial rule.

One Africa or two?

Moi, un Noir is a 70-minute colour film shot in 1957 in the Ivory Coast capital of Abidjan. The French first occupied the lagoon area of Abidjan in 1842. Fifty-one years later, it became a colony, soon to be part of French West Africa. Railway links facilitated transport of natural resources such as wood, cocoa and coffee, for eventual exportation. In 1958, the Ivory Coast evolved from overseas territory to a republic, to be led from 1960 until 1993 by President Félix Houphouët-Boigny.

Rouch centres his film on a group of young Africans who come south from Niger to find work in Abidjan. In line with their efforts to adapt to the 'new' Africa they encounter in the Treichville section of the city, four of the new arrivals adopt nicknames – Edward G. Robinson, Eddie Constantine (in the role of US federal agent, Lemmy Caution), Tarzan and Dorothy Lamour – inspired by actors and characters of feature films made in the US and France. Global mass culture thus furnishes identities and stories tailored to 'the new universe of the young Africans moving almost without transition from the griot to Hollywood, from tribal myths to the mythologies of contemporary societies' (Gauthier 2002: 72).[2]

Modernity in *Moi, un noir* extends from image to process; that is, from scenes of daily life in Treichville to Rouch's efforts to relocate filmed ethnography from 'folkloric' rural settings to urban spaces. Georges Sadoul links Rouch's long-term involvement with the Songhay people of Niger to the phenomenon of migration towards urban capitals of the 'new' Africa (see 1979: 376).[3] In such terms, the film is arguably a case study of colonial modernity in which migrant workers involve themselves in new socio-political formations linked to but also between existing Western institutions and their African counterparts (see Wilder 2005:

8–9). Rouch first engaged the phenomenon of migration in two films – *Les Maî-tres fous* and *Jaguar* (1967) – he undertook in Africa earlier in the decade. Unlike these two, *Moi, un noir* is shot almost entirely in urban settings, with pastoral images of childhood in Niamey appearing only in flashback towards the end of the film. In *Les Maîtres fous*, Rouch had filmed the cult of the *hauka* (literally 'the new gods') whose retreats and possession rituals he described as a means of compensating for the realities of their daily lives in the 'new' urban Africa. By contrast, the value attributed to imagination and fantasy in *Moi, un noir* is ambiguous and not clearly redeeming.

Of special interest throughout the film is the use of voice-over alternating bet-ween description and the cinematic equivalent of a free indirect discourse that seemingly expresses the thoughts of characters on screen.[4] The words spo-ken by Oumarou Ganda in his role as Edward G. Robinson are especially moving as he fantasises about himself alternately as the world champion boxer Sugar Ray Robinson and husband of the woman who calls herself Dorothy Lamour. Con-sistent with the film's emphasis on role-playing, the character played by Ganda is never referred to as anything other than Edward G. or Sugar Ray Robinson. Accordingly, the adoption of a stage or professional name can also assert a self-styled identity that is often at odds with lived origins. (For the record, Edward G. Robinson was the stage name of Emanuel Goldenberg, born in Bucharest, Romania in 1893; Walker Smith Jr changed his name to Sugar Ray Robinson in 1940 when he became a professional boxer.)[5]

Moi, un noir's opening sequence includes no fewer than 21 shots before any title credits appear. The first – hardly conventional as an establishing shot – shows a man from behind, sitting on the curb of an urban street, with a truck, houses and pedestrians in the background. Successive shots follow him as he meets two acquaintances and walks through the streets of Treichville. Ambient sound enhances this initial vision of urban Africa, with gas-powered motors, automobile horns and background conversations accompanying an extended voice-over from shots 1–14:

> Each day, young people ... like the characters of this film arrive in the cit-ies of Africa. They have left school ... or the family home in order to try to enter the modern world. They know how to do nothing and everything; they are one of the illnesses of the new African cities ... unemployed youth. This youth caught between tradition and the machine world, between Islam and alcohol, has not renounced its religious beliefs but devotes itself to the mod-ern idols of boxing and cinema. For six months, I followed a small group ... of young immigrants from Niger living in Treichville, a section of Abidjan. I proposed to make a movie about them in which they would play their own

roles, in which they would be able to say and do everything. This is how we improvised this film. One of them, Eddie Constantine, was so faithful to his character, US federal agent Lemmie Caution, that he was sentenced to three months in prison while we were still shooting the film. For another, Edward G. Robinson, the film became a mirror in which he discovered who he was, the army veteran of Indochina, chased away by his father because he had lost the war. He is the hero of the film; it is time for me to let him speak. (Rouch 1981b: 8)

After this initial voice-over Ganda states: 'Ladies and gentlemen, here is Treichville' (ibid.). Only after the voice-over ends might the spectator infer that the first voice heard had been that of the filmmaker Jean Rouch. The transition recalls practices of ethnography in which a primary investigator – typically a white European male – draws on local informants to interpret words, gestures and actions whose meaning he presumably fails to understand. Some spectators may recognise the first voice right away as that of Rouch, even though nothing identifies him by name until later in the film. But since others may associate the unidentified voice with anonymous and omniscient narration, it is fair to ask in which mode Rouch means to speak. Is the framing 'I' heard in the initial voice-over personalised and identifiable? Or is it abstracted within the conventions of filmed ethnography and travelogue? Does Rouch speak as a white French 'insider' collaborating on an equal basis – by 'becoming another' – with those whom he films? Or does he speak instead as an outside observer removed from his subjects?

Even in the intermediate role of participant-observer, the identity of the 'I-sayer' in the opening sequence is ambiguous and is disclosed only in stages. The ambiguity derives in part from technical constraints of the period that required the soundtrack to be added in post-production and in part from models of narration and discourse that warrant scrutiny. As with many of Rouch's films of the period, *Moi, un noir* blurs received distinctions between fiction and documentary film. Documentary can arguably be seen as a mode of fiction built on the basis of heterogeneous images and effects that often mobilise elements of the cinematic apparatus – point of view, field of depth editing and sound – to produce representational systems on a par with the (so-called) fiction film (see Rancière 2001: 202–3).

The arrest of the actor Petit Touré during the film shoot led to a three-month delay before he and Ganda were able to record their voice-overs while they viewed a rough cut of the film in an Abidjan radio studio. Rouch described the interval as formative and crucial because it underscored the extent to which unforeseen aspects of real life are integrated within the filmmaking process:

This imprisonment changed the tone of the film. At first, it was somewhat like 'The Treichville Zazouman', the initial title chosen, except that because of this interruption, the narrative became much more dramatic ... It should be said that the film was reconstructed only after the initial shooting because the need to rewind our little movie camera manually [meant that] hardly any single shot lasted more than 20 seconds. As a result, the art of editing completely recreated continuity in a film narrative, an operation that was simultaneously a stimulus and a hindrance for the actors who were often unable to say all that they wanted to say because we had to move on to the following shot. (In Piault 1996: 143)[6]

While Rouch recognises the extent to which the three-month delay and visual editing affected the final film, I want to look more closely at how the voice-overs spoken by Ganda produce what I have characterised above as the cinematic equivalent of free indirect discourse.

Who is speaking?

Three sequences disclose the scope and force of Ganda-Robinson's comments that are framed initially within conventions of filmed ethnography and travelogue. The first sequence (shots 304–29) occurs after Robinson and his friends spend an afternoon swimming on the Atlantic coast. As Robinson sits across from Dorothy, he confesses his sadness: 'Dorothy Lamour, you see, I need a wife and – later on – children, too. I, too, need to be happy like everyone else' (Rouch 1981b: 22). The next shot shows Robinson entering a boxing ring dressed in a striped robe on the back of which we see the words 'Edward Sugar Ray Robinson'. An accelerated sequence shows Robinson raising his hands in victory, with sights and sounds of jubilation, until his voice-over brings the fantasy back to reality: 'This is what I'd like to be, champion of the world Ray Sugar [sic] Robinson. I ain't no boxer, it's only a dream and here's the real boxer' (Rouch 1981b: 24).[7] Robinson's words to Dorothy are a plea. The two are betrothed in Niamey before Robinson leaves to join the French army. By the time he returns, the betrothal has broken and Robinson's relations with his fiancée have devolved to a point where he fantasises about himself becoming a champion boxer whose prowess and celebrity will help him regain the affection of his erstwhile fiancée.

The second sequence (shots 620–8) occurs as Robinson wanders drunk at night through the city streets, just after passing a poster of Marlon Brando advertising a French version of *The Wild One* (1953). As Dorothy Lamour is seen standing in a doorway, Robinson says in voice-over:

And Dorothy Lamour will be my wife, and I'll be an actor like Marlon Brando ... and Dorothy Lamour will wait for me in front of our door because the house could belong to me and I could be master of the house ... with Dorothy Lamour as my wife. She will always wait for me and at night she will close the door. We don't want anything to bother us, we want to be at ease ... in our very own house. I have my Dorothy Lamour! The radio is turned on, she speaks words of love to me, she will take off her dress because I like to see her breasts, she is thirsting for love; there on our bed, what we do is our business alone. (Rouch 1981b: 30)

In fact, Dorothy Lamour is a prostitute who spends the night with an Italian who picked her up the previous evening while she sat next to Robinson in the ironically named Bar de l'Espérance (Bar of Hope). Robinson bangs on her door the next morning and the Italian emerges, hurling insults that provoke a fight between the two men. When Robinson loses this physical encounter he also loses the fantasy of Dorothy as his wife that he had linked to the virility and fame embodied in the boxer, Sugar Ray Robinson.

The physical encounter with the Italian leads to a final sequence in which Robinson laments his decision to leave Niger: 'What the hell are we doing here in the Ivory Coast? We really made a big mistake. See, we are sleeping on the streets, in the market, on the sidewalks. The others are happy! Look how they live while for us there is nothing except prison and for three whole months, at that!' (Rouch 1981b: 34). This voice-over continues for four minutes over 35 shots. Unlike earlier sequences that project idealised desire towards the future, the images accompanying this voice-over evoke the past of a lost innocence in Niger. Curiously, this sequence added after the shoot to enhance the dramatic force of Robinson's disenchantment conveys a picturesque Africa – pastoral setting, naked bodies, children with toothy grins – at odds with the realities of daily life in Treichville. Where did this sequence come from? Even if the sequence is intended as an ironic critique, reverting to images seen in interwar colonial films such as Léon Poirier's *La Croisère noire* (*Black Journey*, 1925) is troubling and at odds with almost all other narrative elements of the film.

Robinson is next seen walking with Petit Jules through deserted areas near the large lagoon in Abidjan. Suddenly, he heaves a stone he has picked up, jumps forward, lies flat on the ground, gets up and jumps again, as though he were sprawling into a trench. He repeats the gesture as a lengthy voice-over begins:

I'm in a hell of a mess! I have done everything in my life, everything. You know, Petit Jules, I served in the war, the war in Indochina. I killed the Vietminh with a submachine gun, a knife, a hand grenade. And that's how you do it with a hand grenade, you throw it right away and you lie down flat on the ground ... It wasn't worth it at all! Petit Jules. I did everything! Everything! Everything! But nothing worked for me. Listen, old friend, I just don't know; me, I did everything that a man should do. Everything! But nothing has any importance ... For nothing, for nothing, old friend! And just as I am walking alongside you ... I am dead ... a grenade explodes ... All this does nothing. We are not happy. Look at how happy these other people are. (Rouch 1981b: 35–6)

This sequence culminates Robinson's account of his daily life in a Treichville still under French colonial rule. He contrasts his life as a day labourer (*bozori*) with what he had done after leaving home ('I did everything! Everything!'). As he recounts the deaths he has seen, Robinson adopts the perspective of a French soldier by objectifying the enemy: 'To kill a Vietminh, you raise your knife and wham! You knock him to the ground' (ibid.). He also identifies positively with his soldier comrades: 'I've seen blood flow and buddies die two metres away from me! I've seen buddies with whom I'm drinking coffee, and right after drinking it, they die right there! And all of this, what good is it?' (Rouch 1981b: 35).

Robinson vents his frustration, but he also asserts a sense of accomplishment and courage that turns to resolve: 'Me, I fought in the name of France and I am brave. I'm a man, but I have nothing; I'm poor, but nevertheless I'm brave!' (Rouch 1981b: 36). Robinson's account is personal; yet his references to French policies that made the occupied territories a prime source of recruiting soldiers are among aspects of the film that motivated authorities to cut twenty minutes of it before it could be shown.[8] Subjectivity in *Moi, un noir* builds on post-shoot voice-overs and visual editing overseen by Rouch. The mixing of Rouch's voice with that of Ganda-Robinson generates the central story through the disjunction between Robinson's fantasies and the reality of his daily life. Are Robinson's statements subject to censorship exercised in the form of visual and sound editing? Is censorship of one kind or another unavoidable?

Nearly a decade after *Moi, un noir*, the Senegalese writer and filmmaker Ousmane Sembène asked Rouch what he thought Europeans might do once Africans began making films on their own. Rouch answered that being a European was both an advantage and a liability, because when placed in front of a culture that is not his own, the European saw things that those within the culture did not always see. Sembène countered that especially in the realm of cinema one had to analyse as well as see. So that instead of saying merely that a man whom one sees is walking, one needed to know where the man on screen was coming from and where he was going. He added:

There's a film of yours that I like, that I have defended, and that I will continue to defend. It is *Moi, un noir*. In principle, an African should have made it, but none of us at the time was in a position to do so. I think that a follow-up to *Moi, un noir* is needed. To continue – I think about it continually – the story of this boy who, after Indochina, no longer has a job and winds up in prison. What happens to him following independence? Would anything have changed for him? I don't think so … In the end, for me there are only two films on Africa that count: yours, *Moi, un noir*; and then there's *Come Back Africa* [1960], that you do not like. And then a third that's somewhat special, since I mean *Les Statues meurent aussi* [*Statues Also Die*, 1953]. (In Cervoni 1996: 105–6)

Sembène's words cut two ways. For while he acknowledges what Rouch had tried to do in *Moi, un noir*, the anger that he directs toward ethnologists who study Africans 'like insects' neither detaches nor absolves Rouch from the damage caused by films from the United States and Europe that portray Africans negatively. This damage is exactly what Deleuze describes as the colonisation of Africa by stories from the outside. The fact that Rouch casts *Moi, un noir* as a break with conventions of documentary practices by involving the filmmaker more directly in the film does not preclude taking Sembène's anger as a measure of his advocacy of African films to be made by Africans.

An African made it

Ousmane Sembène's 1965 call for an African follow-up to *Moi, un noir* did not go unheeded. Oumarou Ganda first met Rouch in Abidjan a year or so before Rouch cast him as Edward G. Robinson. Starting in 1966, Ganda made eight films of his own before his death in 1981, at the age of 45. Among the eight films is a 45-minute feature, *Cabascabo*, released in 1968 and shown at the Cannes Film Festival the same year as part of the Semaine Internationale de la Critique. *Cabascabo* (a word in Zarma dialect that translates as 'hard to cook') 'continued' *Moi, un noir* by portraying problems encountered by a young native of Niger who, much like Ganda, returns home after serving in Indochina in the French army.

Statements by Ganda during an interview in December 1980 underscore his ongoing ambivalence concerning the collaboration with Rouch on *Moi, un noir*:

Personally I did not like this film very much for a number of reasons; first, at a certain point it all sounded false; in addition, I thought that the way my thoughts were shown should have been different, because in a way, I was co-director of this film, I brought my share to the film; from one day to the next, we were working together, and then Rouch did the editing...

Rouch profited from my life experience; besides at first there was no question about making a film about a veteran of the war in Indochina; it was supposed to be a film about immigrants from Niger; it was supposed to be called 'Zazouman de Treichville', a film short, and we ended up with a feature-length film, *Moi, un noir*. I tried in my first film to set things straight, to say almost the same things as I saw them with a lot more detail, and this is why I made *Cabascabo* to express what I was feeling ... because I did not have the means to do so earlier. This is how things were, but in *Moi, un noir*, things are true...

There are moments when Rouch exaggerated, for example when he stated in his commentary that my father could not stand the defeat in Indochina; it is exaggerated, my father knew nothing about it; it had nothing to do with him. (In Haffner 1996: 97–8)

Ganda's openness about the differences between Rouch's concerns and his own points to the singular ability of film practice to record from a specific point of view affected by the physical placement of the movie camera and by editing. Rouch wanted to convey (what he took for) the reality of the lives of *bozori* such as Ganda. But he could not do so except from a point of view that necessarily diverged from that of Ganda. Relations of power and knowledge affecting Rouch's status as a 'free' white European male filming in an Africa under colonial rule also return us to the question raised by Deleuze at the start of this chapter concerning the extent to which Rouch succeeded in fleeing himself.

In retrospect, the denunciation of colonial society implicit throughout *Moi, un noir* had only limited impact on structures and institutions of colonial rule against which individuals such as Ganda were powerless, even when afforded with a public venue to screen his film throughout Europe and the West. Rouch understood this bind. In a notice published in January 1981 shortly after Ganda's death, he wrote:

There was no word 'end' to the story of the man who dreamt of being simultaneously Edward G. and Sugar Ray Robinson, an actor or a boxer but who, by moving to the other side of the camera, became quite simply a filmmaker. The 'to be followed' were eight films that today are classics in the history of film: *Cabascabo* [1969], *Le Wazzou polygame* [1971], *Saïtine* [1973]. Or even his last film, his last adventure, *The Man in Exile*, about a diplomat who, just before dying, recounts with marvel the exemplary legends of an Africa forever lost. (Rouch 1981a: 40)

Cabascabo responds to Sembène's call for an African continuation of *Moi, un noir*. Yet Ganda's account of the hard re-adaptation faced by a young native of Niger following French military service in Indochina soon yields to a critical portrait of daily life in rural Africa dominated by predatory friends and exploitative working conditions. Once the small fortune Cabascabo brings back from Indochina is exhausted, he finds himself as much an outcast among his family, friends and neighbours as he was within the French army in Indochina. But unlike Edward G. Robinson in *Moi, un noir* who leaves Niamey to seek a new life in Treichville, Cabascabo heads out in the film's last scene to work in the local fields because he realises that he must remake himself among his peers before deciding where (in Sembène's formulation) he is going and (Deleuze again) whom to become.

A strident critique of Rouch's shared anthropology of the 1950s is implied in a passage written by Chris Marker several years before *Moi, un noir*, in conjunction with his 1950–53 collaboration with Alain Resnais on *Les Statues meurent aussi*, a film commissioned by the journal *Présence Africaine*. Characterising Europeans who justify their presence in Africa in the name of a civilising mission, Marker writes:

> We are the Martians of Africa. We arrive from our planet with our ways of seeing, our white magic, our machines. We will cure the black man of his illnesses, this is certain. And he will catch ours, this is certain, too. Whether he is better or worse off in the end, his art will not survive. (1961: 21)

What makes this statement different from those of many anti-colonialists is Marker's refusal to set himself apart from his critique of the damage inflicted by Europeans on Africans and their cultures. Like Marker and Resnais earlier in the decade, Rouch makes films critical of colonisation and colonial culture while neither asserting nor aspiring to the title of committed filmmaker (*cinéaste engagé*). His decision to portray modern urban Africa in human terms makes *Moi, un noir* less militant than *Les Statues meurent aussi* and René Vautier's *Afrique 50*.[9] Yet Ganda-Robinson's long monologue is arguably as forceful in denouncing French colonial policies as the direct critiques in the other two films.

Rouch's African films of the 1950s do not call for the end of French colonial rule (see DiIorio 2005: 60). Instead, his efforts to balance fieldwork, narrative and improvisation recast local informants as agents of a narrative over which – within limits imposed by technology and editing – they exercise an unprecedented degree of control. Rouch often gave equipment to those whom he filmed so that they might make films of their own. Unlike Jean-Paul Sartre who wrote *Orphée noir* a decade earlier as an advocate for – and thus in place of – others,

Rouch's intentions were more in line with Michel Foucault who, during the late 1960s and early 1970s, actively transferred the power of self-representation to those who had formerly been denied it. In spite of the tensions to which I have pointed above, *Moi, un noir* promoted a cinematic practice for and by Africans to which Rouch and Ganda were committed, each in his own way.

Rouch may never have succeeded in fleeing the West, but his 1958 experiment in voice-over prodded future African filmmakers such as Sembène and Ganda to make films on their own terms. In the context of late colonial Africa, *Moi, un noir* marked a necessary phase in a progression towards autonomy and self-representation whose relevance persists both in relation to Rouch himself – see, for example, Manthia Diawara's *Rouch in Reverse* (1995) – and in light of new African cinema since the 1960s.

NOTES

1   The review was first published in *Arts*, 713 (11 March 1959). (The sentence in French reads, 'un Français libre qui pose librement un regard libre sur un monde libre'.) Godard's early enthusiasm for *Moi, un noir* centres on Rouch's ability to transform his collaborators into characters who played out their lives – both real and idealised – in front of the movie camera. Some twenty years later, this enthusiasm persists: '*Moi, un noir*, it affected me a lot. It's somewhat like [Robert] Flaherty: making fiction out of lived experience. Take characters from real life and make fiction with them' (in Douin & Remond 1983: 179). After *À bout de souffle* (*Breathless*) was released in 1959, filmmakers and critics such as Luc Moullet referred to Godard at the time as the 'Jean Rouch of contemporary France'. See Nemer 2006: 19. Unless otherwise indicated, all translations are mine.
2   Nicknames illustrate the extent to which *Moi, un noir* portrays this transition as neither smooth nor definitive. I thank Sam DiIorio for reminding me that they can also be a means of remaining anonymous in a labour market that exploits those whose transitional status often forces them to work illegally and for minimal pay.
3   Elsewhere Sadoul inadvertently confuses the characters of Lemmy Caution and Edward G. Robinson (see Sadoul 1962: 134).
4   My remarks on voice-over do not extend to what Deleuze, building on writings by Jean Mitry and Pier Paolo Pasolini, explores as free indirect images. See Schwartz 2005.
5   Six years later, Robinson was the world welterweight champion. After moving to middleweight, he held the world title five times between 1951 and 1960. In a career of 200 fights, Robinson earned 109 KOs, and finished with a record of

175-19-6 with two no-decisions. Muhammad Ali called him 'the king, the master, my idol'. Dorothy Lamour (1914–96) played in more than fifty feature films. She is best remembered as the sarong-clad co-star of Bing Crosby and Bob Hope in seven *Road to...* movies (including *Road to Morocco (1942)* and *Road to Rio* (1947)) made between 1940 and 1962.

6   This issue is an updated reprint of *CinémAction*, 17 (1982), titled 'Jean Rouch, un griot gaulois'. (The earlier issue carries the imprint of the publishing house, L'Harmattan.)

7   A brief clip of the real Sugar Ray Robinson in the ring discloses the irreality of Ganda-Robinson's fantasy. It also recalls footage of black athletes in the final ten-minute section of Alain Resnais and Chris Marker's film, *Les Statues meurent aussi (Statues Also Die,* 1953) that government officials refused to authorise for public distribution until 1965.

8   Louis Faidherbe, governor general of French West Africa, instituted the practice of training Africans to serve French military units in sub-Saharan Africa in 1857 because he realised that they could be effective under the conditions of climate and health to which French troops were ill-adapted. Over the next century, thousands of Africans were drafted; some volunteered and others were bought from slave traders. In August 1944, Africans made up more than half of the French troops who landed in southern France under the leadership of General Philippe Leclerc.

9   See Vautier 1998: 29–47 and 2001.

REFERENCES

Cervoni, A. (1996) 'Une Confrontation historique en 1965 entre Jean Rouch et Sembène Ousmane: "Tu nous regardes comme des insectes"', *CinémAction*, 81, 104–6.

Deleuze, G. (1985) *Cinema 2: The Time-Image*, trans. Hugh Tomlinson and Robert Galeta. Minneapolis: University of Minnesota Press.

DiIorio, S. (2005) 'Jean Rouch: the anthropologist as auteur', *Film Comment*, 41, 3, May–June, 58–63.

Dine, P. (1994) *Images of the Algerian War: French Fiction and Film, 1954–1962.* Oxford: Oxford University Press.

Douin, J.-L. and A. Remond (eds) (1983) *La Nouvelle Vague 25 ans après.* Paris: Cerf.

Gauthier, G. (2002) 'Jean Rouch, gourou nouvelle vague', *CinémaAction*, 104, 70–5.

Godard, J-L. (1998 [1959]) 'Étonnant, Jean Rouch, *Moi, un noir*', in *Jean-Luc Godard par Jean-Luc Godard, vol. 1 (1950–1984).* Paris: Cahiers du Cinéma, 177–8.

Haffner, P. (1996) 'Les Avis de cinq cineastes d'Afrique noire: entretiens avec Pierre Haffner', *CinémAction*, 81, 89–103.

Marker, C. (1961) '*Les Statues meurent aussi*', in *Commentaries, vol. I*. Paris: Seuil, 8–25.

Nemer, F. (2006) *Godard (le cinema)*. Paris: Gallimard.

Piault, C. (1996) 'Parole dominée, parole dominante...', *CinémAction*, 81, 140–7.

Rancière, J. (2001) 'La fiction documentaire: Marker et la fiction de mémoire', in *La Fable Cinématographique*. Paris: Seuil, 201–16.

Rouch, J. (1981a) 'Hommage à Oumarou Ganda', *L'Avant-Scène Cinéma*, 265, 40.

_____ (1981b) '*Moi, un noir*', *L'Avant-Scène Cinéma*, 265, 7–36.

Sadoul, G. (1962) *Le Cinéma français, 1890–1962*. Paris: Flammarion.

_____ (1979) 'Du folklore à l'ethnographie moderne: *La Chasse au lion à l'arc* de Jean Rouch', in B. Eisenschitz (ed.) *Chroniques du cinema français, vol. I, 1939–1967*. Paris: Union Génerale d'Éditions, 374–80.

Schwartz, L.-G. (2005) 'Typewriter: free indirect discourse in Deleuze's *CinemaI*', *Sub-stance*, 108, 34, 3, 107–35.

Vautier, R. (1998) *Caméra citoyenne: mémoires*. Rennes: Apogée.

_____ (2001) *Afrique 50*. Paris: Les Cahiers de Paris Expérimental.

Wilder, G. (2005) *The French Imperial Nation-state: Negritude and Colonial Humanism Between the Two World Wars*. Chicago: University of Chicago Press.

Photographs taken in Ghana, 1954–55

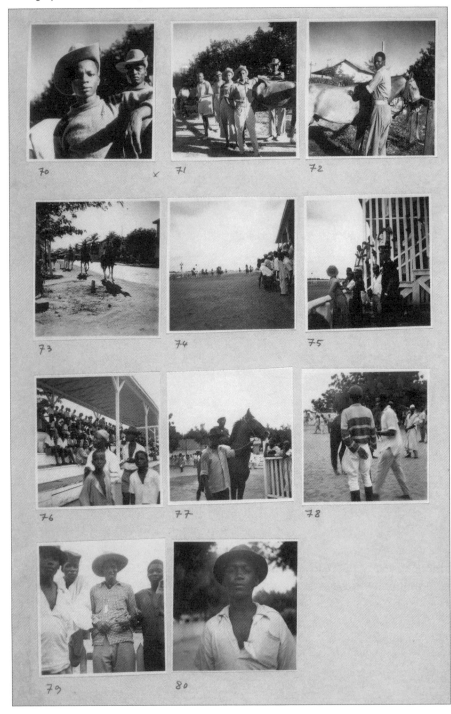

9   THE REAL IN-BALANCE IN JEAN ROUCH'S *LA PYRAMIDE HUMAINE*

Ivone Margulies

In 1959, the *annus mirabilis* of the *nouvelle vague*, yet another film about adolescents tested the limits of realism.[1] *La Pyramide humaine* (1959) is Jean Rouch's experiment in racial integration. Without making any reference to the Ivory Coast's colonial relationship to France just prior to independence, the film addresses the alienation between Europeans and Africans in a high school in Abidjan. The project is simple: get black and white students from the graduating class to meet each other outside the classroom. Following a loose scenario Rouch instructs the students to play themselves, and in search of fruitful psychodrama he warns that some of them will have to play racists.

La Pyramide humaine was filmed during the school holidays in a classroom made of film set boards in a construction site by the Abidjan lagoon and in a studio in Paris. With no teacher present and desks and a blackboard as the only real props, the film presents, a year before the famous screening scene in *Chronique d'un été* (1960) the film projector as signifier and transformer of reality.

This didactic film seeks to extend interracial relations beyond the classroom, and then beyond the film itself. It matters very little, therefore, if Rouch's social modifiers – flimsy fictional ploys and forced performances – cannot produce a seamless spectacle. That these students are graduating and about to move into their adult lives is much more relevant for the filmmaker who conceives of film as a liminal stage propitious to change.

Like *Chronique d'un été* and *Moi, un noir* (1958), *La Pyramide humaine* advocates filming as a process of performative revision. Screenings and even dubbing can promote self-knowledge through a revisitation of one's image in film. In *Moi, un noir* Oumarou Ganda records his dialogue and comments on the scenes, performing a poignant meditation on his social place and the condition of migrant workers. This reflective dimension of the films is only possible because of the temporal lag between filmed scene and recorded commentary.

The lack of synchronised sound defines, however, a problematic of particular significance to *La Pyramide humaine*.[2] In his application for funds to complete his project Rouch explained that the first, silent shooting had taken place during the July vacations, necessitating two extra shootings for dubbing (see Rouch 1960: 16–18). At these occasions the students were at a different stage in their knowledge of each other and of themselves. Passages of the film contradict others. Some of the students became fascinated by contemporary problems of Africa, and grew progressively more articulate about it. 'In July', said Rouch, 'they spoke like Tintin, at Christmas they sound like a *Figaro* editorial and by Easter, they felt like contributors to *L'Express*, or *France Observateur*' (1960: 18). This difference in tone was frustrating for the author who confirmed his opinion that this kind of film had to be shot in sequence and only once (ibid.).

Rouch's ideal was to install a pure continuum between a pro-filmic reality which, charged with made-up scenarios and role playing, would then bring about an improved social reality. Because it depends fully on performance this humanist cinema is haunted by its potential insincerity. To counter the effects of theatricality, immediacy and presence are called to the rescue: 'It seemed to me that the only way not to lie was to film very fast a single subject in real time' (ibid).

Still, technical difficulties are not the sole reason for the film's broken texture. The film is, in Michel Delahaye's words, 'its own motor, its own means' (1961: 8). It is pure scaffolding. Unravelling in continual self-deconstruction, the film has five different beginnings. It is held up by an excess of explanatory frames at both of its ends. And this unwarranted propping up results in eroding the film at the same time that it justifies its goals. Rouch's anxiety regarding the film's status intimates a persistent awareness that this activist film can do very little to address the irresolvable banality and residual racism between the two groups.

I am interested in *La Pyramide humaine*'s fault lines. It is when the film changes gears from activist documentary to poetic reverie, from creating images of a willed, exemplary future and back to exposing impossible, difficult relationships, when it is at its most contradictory and untenable, that it is most exciting.

'What matters if a film is born or not', asks Rouch at the film's close. 'What really matters happens around the camera.' 'This small film', he says, 'accomplished in its daily improvisations what years of being in the same classroom could not' – namely the friendships it sparked between blacks and whites. Even before the credits roll, three separate caveats are issued: firstly, an inter-title announces the film is an experience 'provoked on' a group of adolescents and that once started, the director simply filmed it. Secondly, two parallel scenes with black and white students present Rouch answering their initial hesitations related to acting and plot. Finally, a commentary over images of Jean Claude and Elola (white and black, respectively) strolling together completes this lengthy introduction to the film: 'Instead of mirroring reality the film created another reality. This story did not happen but the actors made up their lines and reactions during shooting. Spontaneous improvisation was the only rule,' says Rouch in the film.

Immediately after the credits, to prove the film's success, Denise, an African student, and Nadine, a European woman, are shown as friends in Paris. Rouch intimates that a year ago it was not so. For the beautiful Nadine, Rouch creates the pivotal role of initiator. Her recent arrival from France makes it plausible for her to question the limited social integration between black and white students. Denise assumes a matching role as a sympathetic black student, in part, because we have access to her thoughts. They become Rouch's emissaries. Both Nadine and Denise introduce the other characters. Through an affectionate verbal description of their friends the two women portray with a precise ethnographic texture the two worlds inhabited by Europeans and Africans: loose images of Alain and Nadine (a European couple) on a motorbike against the striking background of the Abidjan port and scenes of going to the club's swimming pool are inter-cut with Elola and Dominique (an African couple) strolling through the Treichville market meeting Natalie and at night in the dance hall. These parallel depictions indicate, in their symmetry, the equality Rouch wants to establish.

The film's plot mimics the alternate rhythms of leisure and homework that govern these students' lives. Opportunities are never missed to raise the issue of racial integration. A long discussion is occasioned by Denise's outrage at being referred to with *tu*, a misplaced intimacy lacking in respect. Elola and Denise are adamant about this expression of racism in Abidjan. At this point, and for the first time, the film's exemplary purpose is announced when Dominique suggests that by being together they will create a model for change.

The mixing of Africans and Europeans is visually enacted as they play soccer together, as they race and embrace. Grand topics are introduced. But the filmmaker obviously relishes scenes that pair a looser camera movement to a musical soundtrack. As Nadine comes to ask Denise what she means by the term 'apartheid', Alain stands up and runs towards his new black friends, followed by the camera's parallel sweep. The pairing of the camera movement to Alain springing into a mixed-race grouping under an African guitar tune conveys a sense of ease and pleasure that matches Rouch's ideals for a new community.[3] Such scenes seem to hastily bypass conflict, creating, almost too soon, idyllic pocket-images of co-existence.

Split between providing an actual forum for discussion and freely plotting scenes of integrated relationships, the film seems as uncomfortable as its actors are in their performances. Each step in the students' relations is preceded by group discussions, scenes that serve their conventional function in activist documentaries representing a collective perspective. Rouch uses role-playing in loose variations of socio-drama.

In an effort to generate conflict, Jacqueline, one of the white girls, overdoes her character's racist opinions, making them vehement and simplistic: she talks about the blacks' lack of traditional culture, how dumb they are. Here role-playing backfires. Her hammy performance hints at an insincerity that is hard to place. If one associates her over-acting with the crude and biased views she spouts one would tend to assume by default that these could never be Jacqueline's own opinions but only available racist clichés ready for appropriation in a schematic characterisation. Instead of provoking the likelihood of real debate, the exaggerated acting represents an extreme position that can be safely distanced both by the group of students and by the film's audience. The nuanced and unspoken racism they live amongst remains untouched.

Poor acting is particularly revealing of the film's quandary. The phoniness of the acting amplifies the awkwardness of relations to such a degree that the film seems to create through its wooden acting the very stiffness in these relations it supposedly addresses. When actors exert themselves in their roles, or when flimsy pretexts generate repetitive arguments, the project's malaise is exposed.

As if to awaken its dormant psycho-dramatic potential, a sequence begins in the film that could be called 'Le Caprices de Nadine', following the famed source of Jean Renoir's *La Règle du jeu* (*The Rules of the Game*, 1939). The film's second part is headed by a reading of a poem by Paul Éluard, *Les Dessous d'une vie ou la pyramide humaine* (1926). As Jean Claude reads on youth, on loving love itself and women replacing each other endlessly, the camera solemnly crosses each of the students' faces registering a pensive expectation: 'It was after the Human Pyramid that all changed, poetry infected us as poison, love entered our lives.'

Éluard is an obvious choice for a switch into enchanted territory as Rouch had associated his own entranced verbal commentaries in *Les Maîtres fous* with the poet's voice and Surrealism in general.[4] Poems, anchored or not to homework scenes, float over the bright blue and white images of a ship, while a beached old cargo is reinvented as their favourite playground and Alain's haunt. Rouch positions his characters in magical childish spaces. Jean Claude, for instance, plays music and confides in Nadine in a ruined house. A dream scene showing Raymond, one of the African classmates, and Nadine getting married in a syncretic religion church cuts between close-ups of statues and Nadine's coquettish masking of her face with her long hair.

The sequence's motif becomes Nadine's flirtatious manner and the frustration arising from her familiarity with everyone. From now on almost every scene pivots around her and one of the male characters – Alain, Baka (another African participant), Jean Claude, Dominique – who, infatuated, will either argue or physically fight about her. A series of contrived gossiping and small disputes is set in motion when the young men interchangeably claim Nadine, Nathalie (one of the Europeans) or Denise's attentions. Each dialogue scene relays the same information – she loves me, not you – in multiple character permutations.

Even if these infatuation scenarios are understood as generated by a limited adolescent imagination, ultimately they have a structural function. Their common denominator – Nadine – becomes less innocent as a flirt as her narrative role becomes clearer. She is, after all, Rouch's surrogate provocatrice. The consequence of Nadine's inconsequential actions is quite dramatic. After a beach outing and some dancing on the cargo boat, Alain starts a fight with Jean Claude over Nadine and, in a show of bravado, jumps into the water and is drowned.[5]

The violence of this rupture deserves pause. How does Alain's death and its surplus of fiction aid the narrative of progress towards interracial friendship? Up to this point the film has developed in the realm of compatibility between representation and reality. The friendship between the two groups poses no real questions to a more insidious racism, as it does not disturb the film's calm navigation of its documentary course.

Like the former passage from activist docu-drama to Nadine love story, this move into dramatic fiction is a pedal pressed to step up the dynamic between these students. The casual love innuendos introduce interracial sex and marriage as their thematic undercurrent. As imperturbably as Nadine's serial flirtation, these scenes up the stakes of the film, forcing a recognition of the unspoken racism in the Ivory Coast. But the incredible length to which Rouch takes the theme of Nadine's flirtation leads ultimately to a confrontation with another taboo, the sudden and radical dip into dramatic fiction.

In *Gare du Nord* (1966), his only strictly fictive film, one can see with greater acuity the mechanics of the Rouchian drama. A wife, played by the same Nadine, nags her husband about his eating manners, his lack of imagination and the view about to be blocked from their apartment's kitchen window. The speedy crescendo of complaints and the leaps in reasoning suggest the pressure to accommodate the plot to the film's short length. This time constraint generates an interesting dramatic curve reproduced formally in the film's use of a mobile camera and a long take following Nadine until her exit into the street.[6] The resolution of Rouch's little story is both concrete and conceptual. In a chance encounter, a man appears in answer to Nadine's fantasies. But the formulation of his desires in the exact same terms as hers qualifies him as a dream, a bracket in reality. When Nadine refuses to follow him he kills himself, jumping onto the Gare du Nord's rails.

An equally unmotivated approach to drama is evident in *La Pyramide humaine*. Drama has a conceptual import for Rouch and like a *deus ex machina* Alain's leap into the sea is supposed to open a magical door of sorts. Alain's death in the story precipitates the film's end, as his action provokes the two groups to resume their former segregation, the blacks accusing the whites of being superficial. The function of Alain's death in the film's texture, however, is much more complex. Before setting up the boy's disappearance, Rouch applies the brakes twice. Two scenes are clearly wedged in between the serial flirtation and Alain's drowning scene, thus denaturalising their fated link.

The first scene takes place in the classroom. After their final exams, the group naturally gathers around Denise who, pointing at a newspaper, initiates a discussion around France and Britain's duty to make a statement concerning South Africa. Dominique states that he understands why France would want to resist meddling in South Africa's internal affairs, since other countries would then bring up the matter of Algeria. The scene corresponds to the group's developing sophistication and engagement with African and apartheid questions, when Rouch ironically commented that after eight months they sounded like *L'Express*. But this scene is also the film's most explicit positioning of the French group's ambivalence *vis-à-vis* Africa, and of the Africans *vis-à-vis* France.

A cut from Alain centrally framed defending France's neutrality introduces the next shot, his face now close to a film projector. The camera pans over a group of students watching a screening. Rouch re-introduces each student through their identifiable personas. 'These roles are now a part of their reality' states Rouch, who proposes to push the experiment to its limits: 'Why not test their reality with a tragedy, a fiction that once filmed becomes reality, freeing those who believe too seriously in their role?' Alain's death had been decided by the group because he had become too identified with his character. The screening scene seemed crucial to the author to remind all involved, including us, that the film is only fictional. But this insistence on the film's fictional status is itself problematic in a film that has flirted so emphatically with its potential to effect actual changes in an extra-textual reality.

Why does the film stress this precise and deadly disjunction? The significance of this interruption becomes clear if we see the reflexive screening scene not as a preparation for the next scene, the leap into dramatic artifice, but related instead to the prior discussion scene. In the long classroom conversation all seem even more ingrained in their differences than before. Baka's reference to Algeria as France's Achilles heel, Alain's use of the phrase 'it is normal' to justify France's reluctance in taking positions against apartheid suggest a level of discord that belies the humanist fraternity Rouch hoped the film would affirm. The screening scene and Rouch's insistence that the students needed to free themselves from believing too seriously in their roles is actually an attempt to contain the difference of opinion that emerges in the discussion.

Catherine Russell's notion of narrative mortality helps explain Rouch's invocation and dismissal of closure through a death scene. Like other filmic practices 'moving beyond formalist categories of open and closed endings as well as mythic categories of fate and romance' (1995: 2), *La Pyramide humaine* uses a death scene to open up the question of cinematic realism. But the film's restless reframing of its reality cannot be seen separately from the problematic of European and African racism, a topic to which the film returns.

The discussion scene and real conflicts represent possibilities that had been deflected by the light *ronde*-like sequence of adolescent caprice. These three scenes – the discussion, the screening and Alain's death – equate the complex and unresolved state of racism between the French and Africans to the equally suspended status of the real in cinema. By grafting his obsession – the confusion of real and fiction – onto the genre of consciousness-raising film, Rouch can only exacerbate the paradox proper of activist films. Poised between promoting process and creating evidence of progress, the film's narrative continually halts. The demand to represent both the fluidity of changeable living relations and to provide a quotable image for the film's accomplishment creates for its agents and improvised actors an unstable resting point. *La Pyramide humaine* acts out this restlessness through a series of breaks and impossible endings.[7]

The framing of Alain's death raises questions not easily solved by the film's final optimistic message. For Rouch's struggle to shape reality to the measure of his fantasy depends not only on sudden reversals but on a resurrection. In the film's very last image, alternating by race and gender, two couples – Alain and Denise; Nadine and Baka – move together in a purposive frontal stride towards the camera. This Family-of-Man image follows a close-up of Denise who, in voice-over, says, after Rouch's self-congratulatory remarks: 'Our story is both simple and complex, it is up to us to make it.' Alain's presence in this picture-perfect poster for integration revives the film's main questions. He is the white student who had 'died' in the film's most arbitrary directorial decision. His first appearance after 'drowning at sea', his resurrection, is yet another reminder of the film's fictive nature. But when he reappears just for the last shot he taints this model image of success with a phantasmal dimension. His re-emergence exposes the film's strain in trying to create out of its meandering plots and stilted conflicts an exemplary ending.

I want to rewind to a slightly earlier moment, before Rouch's dutiful return to a humanist and exemplary agenda. The surreal beauty of the rollercoaster of realities traversed during *La Pyramide humaine* is condensed in an image seen from above, from a plane. After Nadine leaves for Paris and before Rouch dismisses the film's failure as irrelevant when compared with the actual friendships it successfully created, we see again, from the air, the beached cargo ship. First slanted to the right and then slanted to the left it occupies the full frame. It floats as if redesigning the ground, sand, sea and sky. Instead of the Family-of-Man tableau that means to suspend the issue of racism, I end my *Pyramide Humaine* with this unhinged image. Its romantic evocation of Neverland and a permanent state of play is, I believe, as essential to Rouch's humanist aesthetics.

NOTES

1   The *nouvelle vague* filmmakers enacted their rite of passage into feature filmmaking with films about growing up or young adult life as in, for instance, François Truffaut's *Les Quatre cents coups* (*The 400 Blows*, 1959) and Claude Chabrol's *Les Cousins* (*The Cousins*, 1959).

2   Trying to synchronise the speech of non-actors in *La Pyramide humaine*, Rouch mentioned it was not possible to repeat what he had done in his prior film *Moi, un noir*. He explained that the words spoken by Oumarou Ganda (Edward G. Robinson) were autobiographical, and that he relived directly and completely the scenes during the dubbing projection. In *La Pyramide humaine* the relationships created were ultimately fictional, and the people involved never felt directly concerned with their screen images. Only when there was a conflict did they feel that their acting abilities were called for (See Rouch 1960: 17, n.8; this text consists of Rouch's script of the film for the most part already shot, as he applied for extra shooting funds from the Centre National de Cinématographie. The footnotes establish what subsists of the project in the final print of the film).

3   On Rouch's predilection for images of play see Morin 2003: 241, 262.

4   Rouch is quoted as saying that while speaking the commentary for *Les Maitres fous* 'he heard himself speaking in a singular voice (the toneless voice of Éluard or Jean-Louis Barrault reading surrealist poems in the Theater of Champs Élysées in 1937)' (in Piault 1996: 142).

5   Rouch's sequence of misguided love functions structurally in the same way as Renoir's mobilisation of the lengthy sequence of Christine's directionless flirtations. Both are meant as distractions from the serious matters that hover in the background. In *La Pyramide humaine* this sequence of inconsequential flirtations demands, as in *La Règle du jeu*, a tragic consequence. But the film does not finally confront racism. Serge Daney has remarked how modern narratives resort to a logic of permutation and vicariousness, as they avoid psychological motivation. He cites Renoir and criticises Rouch's humanist manoeuvres to have blacks and whites exchange positions, 'to preserve rhythm and symmetry' (2003: 38).

6 The long take is broken once she enters the lift.

7 I discuss the uses of *cinéma vérité* to circumvent an image of authority (see Margulies 2004). The extended dialogue between Morin and Rouch at the end of the film, as well as the innumerable post-film publications, exemplify this difficulty of ending on a note of dissidence.

REFERENCES

Daney, S. (2003) 'The Screen of Fantasy (Bazin and Animals)', in I. Margulies (ed.) *Rites of Realism: Essays on Corporeal Cinema*, trans. M. A. Cohen. Durham: Duke University Press, 32–41.

Delahaye, M. (1961) 'La Règle du Rouch', *Cahiers du Cinéma*, 120, June, 1–11.

Éluard, P. (1926) *Les Dessous d'une vie ou la pyramide humaine*. Marseille: Les Cahiers du Sud.

Margulies, I. (2004) '*Chronicle of a Summer* (1960) as *Autocritique* (1959): A Transition in the French Left', *Quarterly Review of Film and Video*, 21, 3, 173–85.

Morin, E. (2003) 'Chronicle of a Film', in J. Rouch, *Ciné-ethnography*, ed. and trans. S. Feld. Minneapolis: University of Minnesota Press, 229–65.

Piault, C. (1996) 'Parole interdite, parole sous contrôle', *CinémAction*, 81, 140–7.

Rouch, J. (1960) '*La Pyramide humaine* (Scénario)', *Cahiers du Cinéma*, 112, October, 15–27.

_____ (2003) *Ciné-ethnography*, ed. and trans. S. Feld. Minneapolis: University of Minnesota Press.

Russell, C. (1995) *Narrative Mortality: Death, Closure, and Cinemas*. Minneapolis: University of Minnesota Press.

Nadine Ballot (right) in *La Pyramide humaine*, 1959

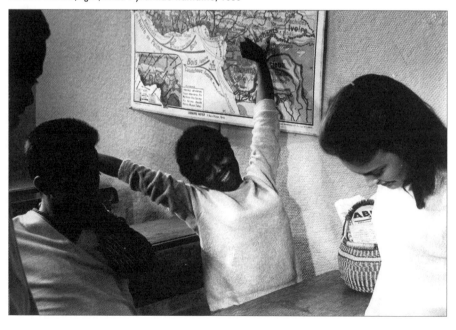

10 *LA PYRAMIDE HUMAINE*: NADINE BALLOT

Joram ten Brink

Nadine Ballot appeared as herself and as an actress in *La Pyramide humaine* (1959), *Chronique d'un été* (1960), *La Punition* (1962) and *Paris vu par...* (1965). She is currently an editor at the Cité de la musique, in Paris. The following interview took place in Paris, April 2006.

Joram ten Brink: *Where and when did you meet Jean Rouch for the first time?*

Nadine Ballot: In the Ivory Coast, I was 17. It was strange. He was a kind of role model for me. He told me that it was important for me to study, so I went later to the Sorbonne in Paris and I had fantastic a time at the Sorbonne.

JtB: *Were you born in the Ivory Coast?*

NB: No. I went there with my parents and brothers in 1945 or 1946. It was just after the war. My father was a banker. I followed my parents everywhere – we came back to France for a while, and after that we went back to Africa. When I was 16, my parents arrived to Abidjan in the Ivory Coast and stayed there for two or three years. I stayed with them and went to study in the local *lycée*. I met in Abidjan people like Jean-Luc Tournier. He was the manager of IFAN, the Institut Français d'Afrique Noire, in the Ivory Coast. Everyone who came to the Ivory Coast passed through his house. In his home I met all those people, including Jean Rouch and Germaine Dieterlen.

I was 17 and by myself. My parents were living in another part of Abidjan, and the people who were visiting Tournier's house became my second family. I found them very interesting and my parents, who were always working very hard, thought it was a good idea for me to meet people who were different from those working at the bank. They were clever people, my parents. I met Jean there, at that house. He was not living in the Ivory Coast. He was not living anywhere except in Paris. He was travelling from Nigeria to the Ivory Coast. He went through Ghana to make films but never lived there. I travelled with him after the completion of *La Pyramide humaine*. We travelled together in a car and went to Ouagadogou in Burkina Faso, to Togo, Ghana, Niger. We met Germaine Dieterlen on the way and the three of us went on to Niamey.

JtB: *Were you a pupil at the lycée during the production of the film La Pyramide humaine?*

NB: Yes. It was just before independence. Independence came in 1959 and I met Rouch in 1958 or something like that. He decided to make the film *La Pyramide humaine* after I told him about the conditions at the *lycée*. Like everyone else, Jean was constantly asking me about the 'situation', in other words, race relations at the school. I told him that we had no relationship at all. We didn't mix.

JtB: *Were you taught in the same class or separately?*

NB: No, no there was no apartheid in the Ivory Coast. We were in the same classroom but there was no social contact between us. Jean explains this and his reasons for doing the project at the start of the film. He explained that he was interested in bringing people together.

JtB: *And Jean-Luc Tournier from IFAN helped to put the film together?*

NB: No, he was not really connected with the project. We shot scenes in his house, but if I remember correctly, he was in France with his wife and he left us the house for the film. It was a big house with lawns and a lagoon. It had a large open space and it was easy to shoot the scenes for the film there. We also shot scenes everywhere else in Abidjan, on the football pitch etc.

JtB: *And the school? They didn't have a problem with the film?*

NB: No. It was holiday time and many scenes that were supposed to be filmed in the classroom were actually filmed later at Gaumont Studios in Paris after the main shooting period in the Ivory Coast was over. Jean never wrote any scene down – neither those shot in the studio nor back in Abidjan. It was a kind of improvisation on his part and for our part and we were constantly sharing our ideas with Rouch and with one another. It was a true improvisation, but Jean was the 'chief of improvisation'.

JtB: *Provocateur?*

NB: Naturally. And there was another person in the cast, Denise, who was very important to the story, because she was the daughter of a very close friend of the president of the Ivory Coast at that time. She was more clever than we were, a little older, maybe two years. She was not exactly in our class. Many people who are in the film were not in our class. Only five classmates of mine were in the film.

JtB: *How did you find the other people for the film?*

NB: Well, just like that.

JtB: *So you started working by improvising?*

NB: Yes, Jean was telling us: now you are beginning to discuss something – go and discuss segregation in South Africa for example. Or: Nadine, who is new to Africa and doesn't know about the problems between black and white people here and therefore is very 'innocent' is arranging a party with everybody. It becomes a scandal, because for the first time black boys can approach white girls, and they can approach Nadine in particular because she is without a 'history' in Abidjan. I guess that it was probably exciting for Jean to see all those things going on because some people in the film got carried away. In the end they believed in these kinds of possibilities. It was, if anything, very funny. It became a kind of a game. I did not believe in it all, but maybe some of the boys believed in the possibilities suggested in the film.

JtB: *Those ideas of the constant changes, the acting and the game came naturally to you all? Or was there a lot of prompting from Jean Rouch? Did the group really start to enjoy themselves and come together as a group?*

NB: I think so. We all knew that it was all fake. But it was very interesting because during filming people spoke like it was all real. It became a very strange situation.

JtB: *Do you think that at a certain point people were starting to believe in the game?*

NB: I suppose it was the case, for example, with Jean Claude. Jean Claude was the romantic man who played piano. He was convinced that he loved me. I don't think he did. 45 years later I discussed it with him and I told him – but you were not in love with me? He told me – yes I was. I don't know if it is true. I don't know. I'll never know. It was a very strange situation.

JtB: *How long did it take to shoot the film?*

NB: The main part was done in one month, I think.

JtB: *Everyday?*

NB: Yes, everyday. But Rouch was on his own with his camera, so it was not very difficult to organise it. When Rouch returned to Paris the producer, Pierre Braunberger [Les Films de la Pléiade], told him he could not sell the film in the state it was in. He thought the project was very interesting but the material was too raw. As a result, Jean asked the participants of the film who were still in Africa to come to France for two weeks to continue the filming. They all lived in a hotel and filming took place at Gaumont Studios. I was already living in France because I had decided to continue my studies there. Being together again in Paris was a very happy occasion, but it was not the same because it was a studio shoot with lots of lights and a cameraman other than Jean. It was a very different way of filming and it felt very different to us too. It did not have the same ambience and we were six months older and not the same as we were in July back in Africa. It was obvious that we were not the same people anymore. It was difficult for Jean too – to match the different scenes, between Africa and Paris. He managed this because he had to, and in the end there were enough scenes to make a film. And Jean was very skilled at it. It was a difficult project to do – to build a story from all those elements, but he did it.

JtB: *Then, of course, there is the very famous scene in the sea with the ship…*

NB: It was during the first shooting period. The sea in Abidjan is very dangerous and you have to dive and try not to drown under those huge waves. Many died every year in the sea. We decided to use the ship because we thought it would be a very dramatic and spectacular scene and something was bound to happen on the ship. Alain, the big man, decided that he was in love. I don't know if he was really in love with the beautiful black sexy girl, Natalie. Jean Claude challenged him. Alain responded and to prove himself he jumped into the waters. It was very clever of Jean to film it with a slight twist of the camera angle. It was completely improvised and completely fake.

JtB: *Did you as a group of young people begin to mix socially after July, after the* *shooting ended?*

NB: Yes, we became friends because we met and we got to know each other.

JtB: *So it started to happen...*

NB: It started to happen...

JtB: *...because of the film.*

NB: Because of the film.

JtB: *Without the film it wouldn't have...*

NB: It was an occasion to meet and speak and get to know the different people in the group. It became important later to keep up the contacts. This film made us different people in the context of the relationships between white and black, black and white.

JtB: *You personally, did you change?*

NB: Yes, but it was a very special period in the Ivory Coast during the 1950s. White people who were living there were either in the military or owned plantations. It was a difficult situation. The military and especially the plantation operators needed workers. It was a situation where you could not have relationships between white and black.

JtB: *Was the film screened in the Ivory Coast?*

NB: Oh yes, but much later because the film was banned for a long time.

JtB: *What was the reaction of the film in Paris?*

NB: I don't remember very well. I remember screenings at UNESCO or places like that but it was not distributed widely. The festivals were sympathetic. It was such a new way of filming, and it was done with no money at all. It was so cheap and inexpensive compared to the usual way of filming. Afterwards many people like Godard and others began to make films with improvisation.

JtB: *Where do you think Rouch got the idea from in the first place?*

NB: He was generally a very curious person. All his life he observed people and tried to think what was going on and what he could do with them. Jean wanted to have fun in life. That is the real reason that he made so many films. He wanted to work and to be happy.

JtB: *Whilst you were making the film, did he explain what he wanted from you or did he just 'play the game'?*

NB: He explained everything to us. He was always very frank about what he wanted and what his point of view was, but I think that he never knew exactly what the end result of his work with us would be. It was an osngoing experience and he was experimenting every day. I think he never knew exactly how it would all end. I think all his enterprises were impulsive – made for fun. It depends on what you understand as fun. He loved life.

JtB: *Then came Chronique d'un été?*

NB: Then came *Chronique d'un été* in 1960, and it was another kind of experiment because he was working with Edgar Morin. There were two groups: Edgar's and Jean's, and we were not the same people at all. Jean was following his ideas about the film and Edgar was doing the same. Edgar knew many people who were involved in leftist politics, while Jean's group were not very involved in politics. I was supporting the left but not in the party. It was a very funny experience. It was the same system as with *La Pyramide humaine*. Things were following a kind of chaotic improvisation because we did not know exactly where Jean and Edgar would take us. It was difficult to build something credible. It was a kind of strange marriage between them. They had much respect for each other, but their ideologies were difficult to match.

JtB: *And the two groups of actors...*

NB: No problem. It was very exciting to meet the others. You had Michel Brault filming us and Jean or Edgar constantly asking us to do things. Sometimes the result was interesting and sometimes it was not. What is funny is that people were either authentic or not, they were kind of playing or they were not. Marceline was playing, overplaying but being very honest. Laundry was very honest. Angelo, the worker from Renault, was overplaying, too. It's obvious. Angelo was one of Edgar Morin's 'actors'. Rouch did not like those scenes around the table – he thought they were a little too static. Edgar felt it was necessary to have long scenes around the table. He was mainly interested in intellectual discussion.

Rouch, on the contrary, was somebody who was constantly moving. He wanted more action. It was necessary for him to move, so it was difficult for him to sit and have long discussions, but he played along with Morin's game. I know that Edgar was exasperated, disturbed by the differences in points of view.

JtB: *Which was a more successful experience for you: Chronique d'un été or La Pyramide humaine?*

NB: I'm not very good at improvisation. I was trained by all the others in the films but I was not able to follow the improvisation all the time. Generally, when I see *Chronique d'un été* I think that it is a very interesting experiment and a very forced one at the same time. It is only partially real; it is only part of the reality. If now young people see the film, they don't understand anything described in it. They do not know about Renault and the working conditions in the 1950s. Then there are the scenes between Laundry and Angelo…

JtB: *But at the time it was something new, like the scenes of the pupils in the classroom in Abidjan?*

NB: Yes, this was an important thing for us as pupils but was it as important for the cinema? I don't know. Yes, the films were interesting experiences and they opened doors for other filmmakers but they were only one step.

JtB: *What is the relationship between reality and the truth as we see on the screen in Chronique d'un été and La Pyramide humaine?*

NB: There is always a truth in experiments, but what is the truth? It is something you cannot define. During the final scene of *Chronique d'un été* we all reacted differently … we all had different 'truths'. It is a difficult experience to see oneself on the screen explaining your life and being filmed at the same time. It is very difficult because this is the distance between what you really are and what people see and hear of you.

JtB: *When Chronique d'un été came out in the cinema did it received more attention than La Pyramide humaine?*

NB: Yes, because of Edgar Morin. Ethnology was not as well known as sociology or politics – Morin's areas of expertise. The reactions were very mixed.

JtB: *Then you did another two films with Jean? Did you enjoy making the films?*

NB: Not at all. It was always somehow difficult for me in both the films *La Punition* [1962] and *Gare du Nord*. *La Punition* was less difficult because I knew Michel Brault and it was very interesting to work with him. He was a wonderful man and incredible cameraman. To see him working with a camera and being able to react to any situation was remarkable. I did not have the sensation that he was filming. Michel knew exactly how to do it. Jean Rouch and Michel Brault were a very strong team together.

La Punition was a very interesting experience because it was filmed with direct sound and I was 'wearing' the Nagra. I did not like working on *La Punition* because I had to improvise a lot. The boy, Jean Claude, was courting me and I was not interested in him at all. It was very difficult. I didn't like it. *Gare du Nord* was very different because it was filmed in my apartment. It was shot very quickly after we wrote the script together, Jean and me. *La Punition* was not scripted, it was completely improvised.

JtB: *You never saw yourself as an actress?*

NB: No, I was not an actress.

JtB: *But by this time it was your fourth film, so you must have started to understand the idea of acting?*

NB: It was not acting, believe me. Really, it was not.

JtB: *After Gare du Nord, you stopped working in film?*

NB: I appeared in a François Truffaut film, but it was just a private joke. We had dinner one night together and Truffaut asked me to appear briefly in a scene at a bar ... and I appeared with no make-up.

JtB: *But you didn't make films with Jean anymore?*

NB: No, I didn't. He wanted to make *Chronique d'un été* and *La Pyramide humaine* forty years later. He planned it with Jacques Attali but it wasn't possible.

Edgar Morin (right) during the filming of *Chronique d'un été*, 1960

11 *CHRONIQUE D'UN ÉTÉ:*
MARCELINE LORIDAN IVENS

Joram ten Brink

Marceline Loridan Ivens, filmmaker, appeared as herself in *Chronique d'un été* (1960). Following that she became a prolific filmmaker, often working with her late husband Joris Ivens. Her latest film, *La Petite prairie aux bouleaux*, was released in 2003. The following interview took place in Paris, April 2006.

Joram ten Brink: *Did you meet Jean Rouch before taking part in Chronique d'un été?*

Marceline Loridan Ivens: I did not know Jean Rouch before *Chronique d'un été*. I knew Edgar Morin. I was a friend of his. I was involved in the Algerian War movement and in the underground movement in Paris and the project began from that.

JtB: *Were you at all connected to the film world?*

MLI: No, no. I came from the camps. I had a difficult life. At that time I was working in market research. I worked for the first company in France to create an American-style marketing office. I was hired to do statistics. A friend of mine became the head of the psychology department in that company. We had met before. He was a Hungarian Jewish refugee and every week he would come to my mother's house to eat dinner because he was so poor. We helped him to survive. After a couple of months, I told him that I understood the work he was doing and offered to assist him. He refused because I did not have a university degree. I persisted, so he put me on a special team working with tobacco products. It was a big success – I came back with the best results. Consequently, they encouraged me to continue, gave me more interesting assignments and paid me more money. But, I was also a woman interested in the trade unions movement. I attempted to organise the workers in the company and they threw me out. It was good though because I found a job in another company and earned even more money.

JtB: *And Edgar Morin?*

MLI: I do not remember how I met Edgar Morin. He was a sociologist working for the CNRS [Centre national de la recherche scientifique]. He was not very well known at the time. He was writing books about the Communist Party when I met him and I was involved in leftist politics; opposed to the Communist Party.

JtB: *Anti-communist?*

MLI: No, more to the left than the communists, especially concerning the communists' attitude towards Algeria. So, Morin and I became friends. He had this project with Anatole Dauman.[1] Edgar Morin told me that he met Rouch at a festival in Florence, and proposed to him to work together. But I think that they were introduced to each other by Anatole Dauman and Dauman proposed to Morin that he and Rouch should work together on this project. By that time Jean Rouch had made *Les Maîtres fous* [1955] and finished *La Pyramide humaine* [1959] [with Nadine Ballot].[2] That's how I met Rouch for the first time. Quickly, their differences were apparent. I was not part of Jean Rouch's 'gang'. I was Morin's 'friend' first. Nadine was part of Jean Rouch's group.

JtB: *Were the differences political?*

MLI: No, they were about the film's concept. Morin was a sociologist. He brought with him some 'proletarian' people – the workers from Renault, the Trotskyites and other groups, Régis Debray etc and me, but I am a person incapable of belonging to one group. Jean Rouch always tried during the production of the film to make everything lighter, full of creativity, invention and confrontation.

JtB: *Provocation?*

MLI: Yes, he became more and more provocative. I worked on the preparations for *Chronique d'un été*. Most of the scenes were shot in my apartment.

JtB: *What did you learn from Rouch's filming method?*

MLI. We started with old-fashioned equipment. We had an Arriflex and a 50kg blimp with quite a formalist-orientated director of photography. Not so much a formalist, but definitely an 'academic'. Jean Rouch was not happy with that, and he had the idea to ask Michel Brault to come to Paris from Canada to take part in the experiment. I did not have the inclination to go behind the camera and to start to work on the production side of the film. At that moment I had the feeling that I could become an actress.

JtB: *You were happy with your acting in Chronique d'un été? You enjoyed it?*

MLI: At the beginning I saw myself as a timid, shy person, between Jean Rouch and Edgar Morin. When I saw for the first time the sequence in the film with Marilù Parolini I understood everything – I understood how one could act oneself. I understood how one can use emotion and look good on film. At the end I was furious because they [Morin and Rouch] cut a beautiful sequence with Jean Pierre and myself near the sea. They said that it was too beautiful and that no one would believe that scene. Some of my friends who were with me at Auschwitz were furious at my role in the film. They asked me: how could I take part in such a film? It is shameful. They were furious at the scenes at the beginning of the film when I ask: 'Are you happy?' They did not understand how I can talk about happiness after the camps.

JtB: *And the scene where you walk through Les Halles?*

MLI: During that scene I became the filmmaker. I proposed the scene to Rouch and Morin. I told them that I had to be alone and that they had to be far away from me. I took the Nagra and put it under my coat with the microphone. And the scene was beautiful. Later on, many years later, Jean Rouch spoke about this scene as his contribution to *cinéma vérité*.

JtB: *But what was the impact of Chronique d'un été in France?*

MLI: Many people were quite disappointed with the film, but Anatole Dauman asked me to go to Cannes for its presentation. I told him, 'Okay, but you have to buy me some clothes'. So, he brought the money and I bought new clothes and went to Cannes.

JtB: *When did you meet Joris Ivens?*

MLI: I met Joris in 1962 or 1963.

JtB: *Was he part of any of the 'groups'?*

MLI: No. No. Anatole Dauman asked Joris to watch *Chronique d'un été* after its completion and to give his comments. After watching the film, Joris asked Jean Rouch who I was and later said to Rouch that he could fall in love with me. But, I did not know this at the time.

I made my first film about the Algerian War. I came back from Algeria and started editing it with Jean Pierre (we made the film together). It was our first experience. It was a difficult experience. During the work, I was invited by Anatole Dauman to a premiere of a Joris Ivens film. After the screening I met him and as I had so much admiration for him, as a young cineaste, I asked for his advice on my new film. He told me that he did not have time because he was going to another film festival, but he gave me his editor's address. After eight days, I received a beautiful bouquet of flowers and a small note. Two or three months later, by chance, I was at a photographic exhibition when we met again.

JtB: *How did you start to make films yourself after Chronique d'un été?*

MLI: Because of *Chronique d'un été*, I went to Cannes, and there I received a proposal to work in television as a journalist by, among others, Jean Pierre Chartier. He offered me work with another filmmaker as a journalist and asked me to come up with new subjects. So, I proposed a lot of progressive ideas. For example, I proposed to film the Communist Party's night school. After that I worked on some of my friends' short films and went to Algeria immediately after independence and decided to make a film.

JtB: *And Jean Pierre was working in film?*

MLI: He stopped very soon afterwards.

JtB: *What was the reaction in Paris to the film, when Chronique d'un été came out?*

MLI: People were either for or against it. It received the critics' international prize at Cannes. It was something so new…

JtB: *What was new for you in Chronique d'un été?*

MLI: The method of filmmaking. The new equipment made it possible to be close to the people to have another approach to actuality. It was a big transformation. Beforehand the cameras were very big and noisy. And, of course, later I had this experience in my film, the *17th Parallel* [1968], because we were too poor to have a 16mm Éclair.

JtB: *Do you see Chronique d'un été as a documentary film?*

MLI: It is difficult to answer. It is not a feature film, but in a certain way it is. It could be seen as a kind of documentary. These days you can see the importance of the film with the evolution of cinema since. Joris Ivens, after he watched the film, saw immediately the danger in it. He said: 'People will not think any more. They will just shoot.' For him it was a big danger. I think he was right. He thought that the new method in making films, following the example of *Chronique d'un été*, might become too narcissistic. That was the danger in Joris's view.

JtB: *In the 17th Parallel Ivens started to shoot...*

MLI: No, no, it's different – when you are going to shoot a scene you have got to think of it, prepare the scene and reflect upon it and to work out how scenes are linked together.

JtB: *But in the 17th Parallel it was the first time that Joris Ivens used sync sound.*

MLI: Yes.

JtB: *This is because of you?*

MLI: Yes, because of me. We received the equipment from Felix Greene in England, from his Documentary Studio Group. It was fabulous: Felix taught me how to use a Nagra and what you can do with the microphone and with different types of microphones. So I was very happy because, of course, we were limited without a mobile camera but we could find a way to reach a little further, with the new microphones.

Earlier, in 1965, right after the Tonkin Gulf incident when the USA began bombing the North, Joris was in Hanoi. He made a beautiful film with archive footage and with new footage he shot there – *The Sky and the Earth*. Afterwards I told him we cannot make another film like that – just a montage film – a beautiful montage of images and commentary. We must go deeper to understand why the people support the war. We needed sound. We could not go on making films without sync sound. For political reasons too, absolutely, so that people could express themselves. They exist after all!

JtB: *What did Joris Ivens say?*

MLI: He agreed, of course, because I was very 'fresh', youth-oriented, from the young generation.

JtB: *But for him, it was a big change?*

MLI: For him it was not a big change, but definitely something new. He ended up mixing non-sync-sound editing and the 'new way' of making films, with sync-sound. That came partly because I did all the sound work with him. I was night and day standing outside with a long cable and the microphone with a big boom pole six metres away from the camera. After *17th Parallel* we made the series of films in China using this method of direct sound.[3] It became a very important series of films.

JtB: *17th Parallel and later on in China everything was shot with sync-sound?*

MLI: Yes. After the 12 films in China, we went on trying new techniques. We wrote a script, an experimental kind of script about the city of Florence. This film was sponsored by the city, by the region, by the province and by the RAI [Radio Audizioni Italiane], but in fact all these organisations could not find a way to work together, so we did not make that film. It was a very inventive project.

JtB: *With sync sound?*

MLI: Yes, and Joris planned to use video for the first time. Nobody used video at the time. Joris also planned to act in the film.

JtB: *Like in A Tale of the Wind...*[4]

MLI: Yes, the film *A Tale of the Wind* exists between reality and the imagination. The film reveals the essence of Joris.

JtB: *It is the most beautiful film. But again, A Tale of the Wind is not a documentary film.*

MLI: No.

JtB: *It's a performance. He is like a performance artist in that film.*

MLI: Yes, it was a very liberating and 'free' experience. It was an invention of ours. Soon afterwards, Joris passed away. Joris's death was a big shock to Jean because he realised that it was the end of something. After the funeral he organised a big banquet for Joris. He presented *A Tale of the Wind* and later the film inspired him to make *Madame L'Eau* [1992]. I created the Association of Friends of Joris Ivens, and Jean became the association's president immediately.

JtB: *Did you keep in touch with Rouch when he was in Africa in the 1960s after he finished Chronique d'un été?*

MLI: It was in 1978 or 1979 when I was in New York to try to sell the series *How Yukong Moved the Mountains*. Jean knew I was there, I don't know how. He knew I was in New York. One morning I received a telephone call from him: 'I am in Boston and I am presenting *Chronique d'un été*. Please take the first plane and come here and join me. I will help you. You will be very happy to be with me. I am here with Richard Leacock. Come immediately.'

JtB: *At the Harvard summer school?*

MLI: Yes, and he waited for me in a park in Boston with beautiful flowers. He cut a rose and offered it to me. It had been nearly twenty years since I had seen the film so I was a little afraid to see myself again. The beginning of the screening of the film was a terrible experience for me. I saw that young girl ... that nice girl, so shy and so sad. I had the feeling I wanted to talk with her on the screen and tell her not to worry, to tell her that her life is not so bad, you will be happy and you'll find everything you want to find. Don't worry ... And I was holding this rose in my hand, and do you remember the scene in the film in the Musée de l'Homme? The sequence starts with a rose in my hand. And I remembered that at the time of making the film Jean had given me a rose too. It was fabulous and I got up and spoke after the screening in Boston.

Chronique d'un été is a very beautiful film and I did not realise that at the time of making it because I was so involved in it. I think it is a film that never ages, will never become 'old'. Some films you keep in your memory and they will stay with you as during the first screening.

NOTES

1   Anatole Dauman (1925–98), French producer, was one of the key film producers in post-war France.

2 See the interview with Nadine Ballot in this volume.

3 *How Yukong Moved the Mountains* (1976) Dir. Joris Ivens and Marceline Loridan Ivens. 763 min.

4 *A Tale of the Wind* (1989) Dir. Joris Ivens and Marceline Loridan Ivens. 80 min.

Safi Faye in *Petit à petit,* 1968–69

12 *PETIT À PETIT*: SAFI FAYE

Joram ten Brink

Safi Faye, the Senegalese filmmaker and ethnologist who has made her home in Paris, is the first and best-known woman filmmaker from sub-Saharan Africa. Her film career started with her role in *Petit à petit* (1968–69), where she appeared as herself. Since then she has directed *La Passante* (1972), *Letter from the Village* (1975), *Fad'jal* (*Fragile*, 1979), *Selbe* (*One Among Many*, 1983), *Mossane* (1996). The following interview took place in London, June 2006.

Joram ten Brink: *How did you get involved in Petit à petit?*

Safi Faye: I worked as a teacher in Senegal from 1962 after completing a teacher-training course. In 1966 many free and independent young women, like myself, attended the Dakar Art Festival – the first festival of African art ever organised in Senegal. A great number of African scholars from around the world attended the event. It was organised by President Senghor of Senegal. I was curious. I wanted to know who was who. We knew that many Europeans knew Africa better than us. Young people like myself tried to meet them and learn about African art. Jean Rouch was one of those 'experts'. I asked for permission to take a break from teaching and go for two weeks to work as a hostess at the festival and help the organisers. I was very young, very dynamic, very beautiful. That's how I met Rouch and got to know him well. After a few days I brought him into my family. He met my mother, my father, my sister and the people of my village. At the end of the festival he told me, 'I would like to make a film with you.' I said, 'Make a film? I'm a teacher!' And he said, 'We will see. I have to see my producer in Europe and we will see.' And, so one day…

JtB: *Did he show his films during the festival?*

SF: No. No one saw the films. There was a large exhibition during the festival, of sculptures and other African art, all shipped from Europe to Senegal. There were a lot of discussions about building a new museum for African art for it to stay in Africa after the event. We Senegalese were fascinated to learn about our culture and to hear why Europeans created different interpretations than our own about our native art. We felt that we, African intellectuals, must correct all that because some of the interpretations were wrong. We had to discover what belonged to us. I remember the festival very well because I was around twenty; it left a great impression on me and I was very eager to learn.

JtB: *You belonged to the first generation of young people after independence?*

SF: Yes, or maybe the second generation after independence to become intellectuals, to gain knowledge, to be educated like Europeans not like Africans. I was thinking like the French because that's what I always learned. I was confused myself because I received a French education but my mother had an African education. She never went to school, but she didn't give me an African education either because she wanted her child to become French-educated. She wanted me to succeed in life, to have a good job. We really were French people, up to 1960. We had French nationality, and so in my head we were always French; but what about our own personal culture? I had to hear about it from all those French and European experts who stimulated me to learn more. Maybe the people I met for the first time in Dakar drove me later to go to the Sorbonne and study about my own culture. So, after seven years I stopped teaching because I wanted to know more about my own society. But let's go back to Rouch. He told me that he wanted to make a film about me, because he said he had a lot of admiration for me. Rouch was born the same year as my mother but I never felt the age difference between us. When he was with me it was as though we were the same age. In his mind and behaviour he was like a young boy with a young lady. One day he came back to Senegal and said, 'I want to make a film' and I said, 'if you want to make a film, you'll have to talk with my father and my mother because I still live in their house'. When he talked with my father he said, 'You know, once a Senegalese asked her to act, but she offered her so little money that I told her, "it's better to work as a teacher". My father wanted me to continue teaching because teaching was a secure job. Acting was not. So my father said to Rouch, 'Okay you like her, she likes you, you can make a film but only whilst she is not teaching, during the school holidays: Christmas and two weeks in April and three months in the summer.' Rouch accepted those conditions. In Christmas we would go somewhere in Senegal, or we would go to Niger or the Ivory Coast or to Europe, and that's how it was. There was no script. There were no plans. I did whatever I wanted to do during the filming. He would stay for the whole day with me with his camera. He never stopped shooting, he never had a script, he never cut. I did whatever I wanted to and after that he would choose the scenes.

JtB: *Did you ever ask him during the filming of Petit à petit 'What is it about? What do I have to do?'*

SF: Even when I asked, he said, 'You do whatever you want.' It was like that. He told me what he did with Damouré [Zika] in Niger. They dreamt of building a skyscraper, and I listened and said, 'Yes, I can go to Paris. I can do this, I can do that, I don't care.' All the scenes in the film came from us – from all the actors – not from Rouch. He couldn't show us a piece of paper telling us what to do. He just followed my exchanges with all the other actors. They played my game and invented the idea that I was to be the wife of the one and the other would be jealous and so on; that I have to show my body; that I must drive on the Champs Elysées with the Bugatti of Jean Rouch because I can't drive at all and so on. It was a game. Rouch would come in the morning to pick me up and take me to the big apartment where Damouré and Lam [Ibrahima Dia] were staying. He turned on his camera and let us do whatever we wanted in the apartment. When we ran out of ideas indoors and wanted to go outside, he followed us in whatever weather.

JtB: *In order to organise a tale that starts in Niger, goes to Paris, Switzerland and back to Niger, he must have had an idea about the story.*

SF: He told me about the company name for *Petit à petit* … but for my role he didn't have any storyline. It was the same for the white girl in the film, Ariane, the secretary. Because every time we asked about it he didn't say a thing and he continued shooting all day and never stopped.

It took one week to view the rushes. He would bring us to watch them, but I slept through it for the whole day … I didn't see anything because it was far too much. I kept thinking, 'What is he going to do with all that material?'

JtB: *Who was the producer?*

SF: [Pierre] Braunberger

JtB: *And did you meet Braunberger?*

SF: I met him for one and a half minutes – a very kind person. But what I knew was that he never gave one penny, he never invited us.

JtB: *But he paid for so much film stock.*

SF: I remember how much he paid me, but I cannot say it. I would have told you if Rouch was still alive. The only advantage was travelling where I wanted. That was like a dream for me – like a young lady dreaming of travelling. It was wonderful, coming back from my travels and telling my friends I was in Zurich, I was in Geneva, I was in Paris.

JtB: *What did your father say? Was he happy with the film?*

SF: I don't know if he ever saw the film.

JtB: *Was he happy with you working as an actress?*

SF: It was not work! Because in my father's mind I was a teacher. But he was proud that his girl was crossing the world. And when I came home he would always ask about my travels.

JtB: *How did you work with the other actors? Damouré and Lam had worked for a long time with Rouch already...*

SF: I felt that there was a lot of respect between them and between us all. I could say what I wanted, when I wanted, while working with them. We did not know at the end of the filming if it was a game or not. I saw it when I went to Niamey with Rouch. I saw that there was a long history between them, they worked very well together.

JtB: *You later became a filmmaker yourself – how do you view now the way Rouch worked with the camera and the actors?*

SF: For me it was an anarchist system but I was also an anarchist in my mind and I appreciated what he was doing. I understood exactly what he wanted. I never operate the camera myself. With Rouch, he had the camera on him all the time. He made all his own plans for the camera and shot it himself. I dictate to my camera operator what I want.

JtB: *Can you talk about your film Letter from the Village?*

SF: Two years ago, in the final week before Rouch left Paris to go to Niger for the last time, he screened *Letter from the Village* in the Musée de l'Homme and he asked me to come, but I wasn't well enough. If I had known that I would never see him again, I would have come to the screening of my film. But you see ... the last film that he showed in Paris was *Letter from the Village* and then he left to go to Niger. It was a premonition. Why my film? Why did he go there to die? When I think about it, it makes me sad. Before completing any of my films, Rouch would organise people to see the film's rough cut. But I did not become a filmmaker because of him. When I got my PhD he was part of the examination team. He always followed my career – but from a distance.

JtB: *So after you finished Petit à petit you decided to go back to Paris?*

SF: Yes. It was 1968. I visited Paris every year, with or without Jean Rouch, ever since I began earning money as a teacher in Dakar because I liked Paris. It was a dream – the big city. I came to Paris with a man I met in Senegal and this man didn't want me to work in Paris. He may have been jealous, so I decided that if I have nothing to do I should go and learn about my country. I went to the École pratique des Hautes Études where a lot of Rouch's friends were but he came from time to time only to show his films. Before doing my PhD I decided I would record my research on film rather than write a book. I applied to the Lumière film school and I was accepted. I wanted to combine research and film. After one year I decided to make my first [short] film. My film studies were not finished yet, but I had the opportunity to meet a cameraman from the USA. He offered to do the camerawork for me and because of my literary education my first film was *La passion de Baudelaire* [1971]. I was the first black African woman to make films. When I finished that film I realised that in the meantime, as a result of my studies, I had also a large amount of research material about farmers in Senegal because I came from a farming family.

JtB: *And what was the subject of your research?*

SF: Primitive religions. I was fascinated by non-Catholic religions in Senegal. My family has lots of mystics. You will call it animism, but it isn't really animism. I link it to my ancestors. I got my tape recorder and I talked with the farmers about religion, about life, about food, about drought. When I finished my research, I came away with all their pain and all their criticisms. I kept wondering – why can't they live like normal people? So that became the subject of my first long film, *Letter from the Village*. Everybody said: she's an intellectual; she's beautiful; she is a lady; she's emancipated and she talks only about famine. That's how my career began. I continued with my PhD; I was always studying and stopping to film ... until now. I am curious. I will be curious until I die.

JtB: *Why was Letter from the Village censored in Senegal?*

SF: Because I gave, for the first time, voice to the people who suffered from famine and let them talk for themselves in the film. The title is actually 'words from the famine people', not a letter, but Europeans translated it as letter because there is a letter in the film. I showed in the film that my family were simple farmers. The government had a monopoly on agriculture and they didn't want their policy and the famine to be criticised.

JtB: *Was it President Senghor who banned the film?*

SF: He was a son of farmers too...

JtB: *And he decided...*

SF: It was not him, it was his cousin, the Minister of Agriculture.

JtB: *And Senghor did not agree with the film?*

SF: Yes, because I had to go and fight alone with the people from the government. They asked me to cut the film in places. They wanted to cut the scenes with the peanuts being sold to the government.

Jt:. *Did you show the film in France?*

SF: Yes. I showed it also in Senegal but I couldn't show it in public, only in closed meetings. It was maybe the first break between myself and the government.

JtB: *And now?*

SF: Now, I have no problems making a film in Senegal. Once President Senghor asked me to go to Haiti because they also had problems with agriculture. He asked me to go with *Letter from the Village*, but I refused. First, because of the dictatorship in Haiti, and second, I hated my government because they tried to stop my work, but Senghor himself never told me, 'Don't shoot anymore.' I made 13 films without any problems and they invested money in my last film because my work goes to Cannes.

JtB: *So, after you made Letter from the Village you made the film Fad'jal?*

SF: The film *Fad'jal* came out of my PhD research. Now I realise that a lot of my films came out of my study of ethnology and anthropology. When I finished my PhD, I wanted to make my PhD in film, because its subject was memory and storytelling and the stories themselves were never written down. But *Fad'jal* is a very intellectual film. That's why it circulates less and it is only shown in universities. But this was also the first black African film selected for Cannes in 1979. Jean Rouch and Germaine Dieterlen watched the film and said: 'You brought the dead people back. Maybe one day it will become a myth.' Germaine was very proud of my film and Jean too. They felt I brought myth and life together in the film, but the difference is that when you see a Jean Rouch film it is scientific. With me, I make fiction, only fiction.

JtB: *And Petit à petit or Moi, un noir [1958]?*

SF: *Petit à petit*, I think, was reality [she laughs].

JtB: *Documentary?*

SF: No, it was reality. It was not documentary, because I knew that he was shooting me and I kept saying, 'Do you want me like this or like that?' I acted, yes, but he didn't tell me, 'act!' I did whatever I wanted and he shot it all.

JtB: *Yes, but the stories behind Moi, un noir, Petit à petit and Jaguar [1967] are real, 'scientific', using your term, about black men going to...*

SF: Yes, he told me about the men in Ghana. Yes, it is fiction in a Jean Rouch method. In a 'normal' fiction, a story exists at the beginning of the work. Rouch wrote his fiction after shooting.

JtB: *You never asked him why he didn't write a script?*

SF: I never asked him because it was all a game. When I worked with him I did not understand what he was doing. I never really thought that he could do something with all the material he shot until I saw *Petit à petit*.

JtB: *And did you like Petit à petit?*

SF: I liked it.

JtB: *But you were not attracted to work in your own films in the same way?*

SF: I went to a film school and they taught me properly how to make films. I learned 'the right way'. But I also like the way Rouch worked because, after all, he is the one who made the largest number of films on Africa since before I was born. He made so many documentaries to 'serve' African culture that...

JtB: *Is Jean Rouch's contribution to African culture significant?*

SF: Sure. I am sure of that. People like my mother, who never went to school, see in his documentaries with their own eyes – 'Jean Rouch telling the story', showing life. He was the first one to try to preserve the images of Africa.

JtB: *Is he an African filmmaker or is he a European filmmaker?*

SF: Jean Rouch? He is black and he is white, but I think that he would have liked to be black all his life. Positive black, yes. He was much happier in Africa. I always felt that in Europe he was restless, he always wanted to go back to Africa.

JtB: *What do you mean, 'positive black'?*

SF: Because there are Europeans who feel that they are black, but in a negative way. He is positive; all he ever wanted to do was the best for Africa. Like his people say, 'He died in Africa because he preferred Africa.' That was his destiny.

JtB: *Do you think that your films, or other West African filmmakers, developed a different cinematic language to European cinema?*

SF: I don't know. Every African filmmaker, like myself, went to a different film school in Europe – French, Italian, Rouchian – and this influenced us all. I don't make films like Sembène who studied in Russia. I was taught in France. We come from the same country but we were all educated differently.

JtB: *Earlier, you described that as young African intellectuals in the 1960s you were eager to learn from the Europeans about Africa. Forty years later, is the knowledge now with African people themselves?*

SF: Yes, but they [the Europeans] don't leave Africa. There are more French people in Senegal today than there are Senegalese in Europe. The old generation will die in Africa. This is sad, because once they leave Africa they will not leave us with an alphabet, an African alphabet. They leave us with a European one, a French one. We will need more than a hundres years before we can go back fully to our culture. During 300 years of occupation they didn't do anything for us. Forty years is too short for us to learn it all.

Damouré Zika, Ghana, 1954

13 JEAN ROUCH, FICTION FILM PIONEER: A PERSONAL ACCOUNT

Philo Bregstein

Since his death, worldwide homage has been paid to Jean Rouch, with extensive discussion of his pioneering role in the area of anthropological and documentary film. I would now like to emphasise here the originality of his fiction films, often considered to be interesting but relatively less important. They are frequently called 'semi-documentaries' that cannot really be taken seriously as fiction films.

These hybrid fiction films, which Rouch often made on the sidelines of his anthropological work, are what have fascinated me since the 1960s. Because I was personally involved later in the making of several of these fiction films, I was able to experience his special way of working first-hand.

The films

I see various phases in Rouch's fiction film work. Initially these films really were 'semi-documentaries'. In *Jaguar* (1967), Damouré Zika and Lam Ibrahima Dia played the roles of Nigerien emigrants to the Ivory Coast, as Damouré explained in my own film portrait of Rouch and his Nigerien friends, *Jean Rouch et sa camera au coeur de l'Afrique* (*Jean Rouch and His Camera in the Heart of Africa*, 1978). In *Moi, un noir* (1958), Oumarou Ganda improvised his own role as a longshoreman, also in the Ivory Coast. Both of these films still relied on the documentary tradition.

Illustrative of a second phase are his genuine fiction films, like *Petit à petit* (1968–69) and *Cocorico! Monsieur Poulet* (1975). Together with his co-directors Damouré, Lam and Tallou Mouzourane, Rouch would think up a basic story, inspired by an actual situation, on which they would embroider by way of improvisation. The theme of *Petit à petit* was based on the time Damouré spent in Paris completing a pharmaceutical degree. In *Cocorico!* a Citroën 2CV car, also known in France as 'the ugly duck', was dismantled and transported by pirogue across the Niger river in order to avoid the police-controlled bridge further on.

These films are clearly inspired by the capricious, nonlinear structure of African tales or legends as recounted by griots in the oral tradition. It is curious that it is only recently that a younger generation of African filmmakers, such as Idrissa Ouedragou, has begun recreating this typical African story structure in film. Rouch clearly played a pioneering role in this respect.

The historical narrative film *Babatou, les trois conseils* (1975) is based on a script by the Nigerien historian Boubou Hama, a leading specialist in Niger's oral tradition. This fiction film was produced by an association of Nigerien filmmakers headed by Rouch. It has rarely been seen, though, mostly because General Seyni Koutché, the Nigerien dictator who came to power via a coup during the film's production, did not appreciate its antimilitarist message. Hama was inspired by the stories sung by griots about the heroic deeds of Babatou. Babatou was a war-mongering mid-nineteenth-century king who was known for his bloody wars to catch slaves before the French and English colonisation of Africa. In the film, after years of fighting in Babatou's army, 'Damouré' and 'Lam', two soldiers, return home with their booty, which includes donkeys and a female slave. As a counterweight to the war stories, Hama inserted a moralistic tale. En route, the two soldiers meet an old wise man, who, in exchange for the slave, offers them three pieces of advice they must follow strictly in order to get home safely. Rouch applied his typical improvisational approach to the film, so that the war story becomes an ironic anti-heroic parody. Damouré and Lam can simply play themselves, having no need to transform into historical figures – nothing in the Niger bush has changed in a hundred years. Of course Rouch grabbed his chance to film rituals performed the way they had been for very many years, thus again emphasising the continuity between past and present.

In his next fiction film, *Dionysos* (1984) the world of fantasy fully gains the upper hand. It is based on one of the rare scripts Rouch himself wrote over the course of many years. With support from socialist Minister of Culture, Jack Lang, he had a reasonable budget at his disposal for the first time, so he wanted to gather all his friends together so the film could be a huge celebration. Even his Nigerien friends flew over to the location – an old factory outside Paris – to commemorate the cult of Dionysus. As with another of his film celebrations I attended when I was playing a small role as Nietzsche, the festivities were more successful, in my opinion, than the film itself. As a trade-off for the ample budget, Rouch had to comply with the official rules of filmmaking and work with aides, a cumbersome camera crew, script assistants and according to a previously established script. Even the editing had to be done on schedule in a short time, although Rouch, together with his editor, was accustomed to tinkering at length with his films. The result was that he could not freely follow his inspirations. Master of his mini-domain, Rouch suddenly seemed at a loss in the role of the 'big' movie director. It would be interesting to analyse the failure of *Dionysos*, particularly since Rouch himself – and rightfully so, I think – considered the film to be one of his most important projects. The philosopher Gilles Deleuze, I might add, was full of praise too (1985: 197–9). Rouch regained his freedom to improvise with *Enigma* (1986), a commissioned film intended to be a 'semi-documentary' about the city of Turin, for which his Italian co-directors had written a script. Since I was allowed to play a minor role in both *Dionysos* and *Enigma*, I was able to compare the two production experiences. With the low budget for *Enigma*, Rouch was completely in his element again. He was able once more to improvise from day to day, working together with his actors and co-workers. Instead of Niger, it was now the city of Turin that moved Rouch to let his imagination blossom. Playing an expert on Nietzsche this time, I had to recite Nietzsche texts in Italian on top of the Mole Antonelliana. A Swiss painter friend of Rouch's played a forger who had been commissioned by an art patron to paint a fake De Chirico of Turin. The name of the Italian actress who played the art patron's wife happened to be Sabina, which gave Rouch the idea of having her abducted, like a Sabine virgin, by the forger. He consequently lures her away in the film's final scene after presenting the fake De Chirico to the art patron. Once again, the original script was completely swept aside by the improvised shooting.

Madame l'Eau (1992) was based on an idea of mine that Rouch and his Nigerien friends eagerly followed up. They were to play themselves, 'Damouré', 'Lam' and 'Tallou' and come to the Netherlands to look for a windmill that would be able to irrigate the land from the banks of the Niger. Rouch looked for an inexpensive windmill that could also be built on site in Niger, a metaphor for his ideas about development aid, which opposed giving 'poisonous gifts' as he called them – making the impoverished third world continually dependent on aid from rich Western organisations through expensive technology. As always, Rouch simultaneously lent his images poetic meaning with his camera eye. The windmill became a magical object in *Madame l'Eau*, a surrealistic Tingelyesque structure that bravely pumps a tiny trickle of water from the Niger, letting it run into a dry ditch in the desert sands, as an expression of optimism over and against better judgement. As if by magic, a large field of black plastic tulips sprouts up, which Damouré and Lam had planted there only ten minutes before. Dutch friends fly over in solidarity like *deus ex machina* to help to erect a second windmill that was put together on site. Instead of being a 'semi-documentary' about a windmill for irrigation on the Niger, *Madame l'Eau* is more a tale about making impossible pipe dreams come true.

In his next fiction film, *Moi fatigué debout, moi couché* (1977), nothing but the imaginary world is left. There is no longer any script, just an idea developed together with his co-directors and actors Damouré, Lam and Tallou scribbled on a single page. Back to inexpensive low-budget production, Rouch was no longer accountable to anyone. He was able to work without time constraints, just like he worked on his documentaries. As he did every time he returned to Niger, he would always improvise a few scenes with his friends. The film turned into a genuine African tale in which the three actors improvise being mythical figures 'Damouré', 'Lam' and 'Tallou' – the same roles they played before in films like *Cocorico! Monsieur Poulet* and *Petit à petit*. After years of working together, it seems they have grown into the skins of the figures they portray, which they do with verve in front of Rouch's camera in an African *comedia dell'arte*.

In Rouch's last fiction film, *Le Rêve plus fort que la mort* (2004), for the first time in his life he was unable to physically handle the camera, so his co-director and assistant, Bernard Surugue, did the camerawork. The film, too, is steeped in the collective imagination of Rouch, Damouré Zika and Tallou Mouzourane. The point of departure of this new film was the question of whether, after the death of their friend Lam Ibrahima Dia, they would be able to fulfill their original plan for the film *Les vaches merveilleuses*. They quickly let go of the preliminary story structure, though, in favour of a poetic rhapsody. Like the strange objects that Rouch always liked to insert into his films, scenes from Sophocles' *The Persians* acted out in ancient Greek in the theatre of the Sorbonne in Paris suddenly crop up. These are alternated with possession rituals in Niger, clearly to show the Dionysian similarities between them. Although Rouch himself always provided the commentary to the rituals, this was the first time it was done by Damouré, who was surprisingly matter-of-fact in doing so, the way he was in *Madame l'Eau* when he explains to 'Lam' how the windmill works.

The film script

In order to analyse in detail the methods Rouch utilised in his fiction films, I will start with the script. Contrary to the myth of Rouch as the father of *cinéma vérité* who improvised all the time, it appears that the script phase for Rouch was always an intensive one, paralleling the lengthy and meticulous preparations for his anthropological films, particularly the ones about rituals. Damouré Zika played a big role in establishing contacts and initiating Rouch into the knowledge of ritual. Rouch assumed the same student-like anthropologist's attitude in preparing documentaries like *Jaguar* and *Moi, un noir*. Both Oumarou Ganda and Damouré Zika have said that they had thought up practically all the situations they acted out and that they had the feeling that Rouch had done nothing more than follow them with his camera.

I discovered the script phase that is typical of Rouch's fiction films during my first visit to Niamey in 1976 when I was there to cover Rouch, and later during the shooting of my film about him in December 1977. Even the way this Dutch television documentary came about typifies Rouch. I was the first voyeur to try to infiltrate his workplace and playground in Niger, so I encountered a lot of defensiveness at first. Rouch did not want a television crew on site and convinced the Dutch television programmers to let me come down for a month by myself, staying free of charge at the Institut de Recherche en Sciences Humaines (IRSH) that Rouch had helped found. A Nigerien cameraman and an IRSH sound technician were to shoot the film using the IRSH film centre's equipment, something that had been supported by Rouch, but which has since then foundered due to lack of financial support.

The filming of my documentary was improvised, although over breakfast and dinner, Rouch and I would extensively work out the plans for the next day's shoot. I had a script for it, based on my first visit in spring 1977. During this production, I learned about Rouch's way of living and working, along with that of his Nigerien friends – and came to understand the African rhythm of life. Every day I would wait patiently for hours until some sudden film activity would take place, undertaken very professionally and efficiently.

Rouch and his Nigerien friends' script ritual went like this: he would eat breakfast early each morning in the garden of the IRSH, where both of us had rooms. There he, together with Damouré, Lam and Tallou would think up projects, including their next fiction film. True to oral tradition, a pen was never put to paper. Often they would go together on location reconnaissance in order to work out situations on site, including camera positions. When they did this, it was obvious that Damouré, Lam and Tallou knew all the tricks of film technique, the result of decades of working together as assistants to Rouch. The same thing was the case years later, during preparations for *Madame l'Eau*. Breakfast discussions at Rouch's bistro on the Boulevard de Montparnasse would lead us to think up all kinds of versions of the story, which I would record on my tape recorder. He would also tell me what he had come up with, with his three partners. On the basis of these thoughts I made a synopsis, which allowed Rouch to receive a subsidy from the Rotterdam Film Festival to write a script for *Madame l'Eau*. This entailed a research trip through the Netherlands in search of new and old windmills to see if the idea to build a windmill on the banks of the Niger to irrigate the land could be realised. On the grounds of the University of Enschede, Rouch discovered a simple wooden windmill from Crete that had been developed by engineer Frans Brughuis for water irrigation. Only at that moment did Rouch decide that the film could be made. A windmill like that could be put together with materials on site in Niger as well. Engineer 'Frans' immediately became one of the main characters in the film, as did the production assistant, Wieneke, who drove him around the Netherlands (in the film, Wieneke is the Nigerien visitors' guide to Holland, to 'the land of cows, cheese and windmills').

The script seemed to serve primarily as a means of obtaining financing as well as a way of preparing the shooting. In practice, it turned out to be more important, which is what it always had been for Rouch. His seemingly free improvisation hides the thorough preparation, which can be defined as a script according to the oral tradition. It served as a springboard for diving into the film, at which point the script often fell overboard. An important step in this script phase was an extensive visit to the location before the actual shooting, which is when the scenes were really worked out. I myself witnessed hours of preparations near the dyke along the Niger where the windmill was to be erected, or in the Dutch dunes for the scene with 'Tallou', who uses shells to consult an oracle. The *mise-en-scène* was thoroughly prepared down to the last detail without a camera, and Rouch would look for camera positions while Damouré, Lam and Tallou like veteran professionals, walked the trajectories for his imaginary camera, before playing 'their' characters. It is interesting that Rouch often followed his friends' suggestions, which is not customary among movie directors.

When I became involved as an actor in *Enigma* (1988), and later as co-scriptwriter and actor in *Madame l'Eau*, I could see how intensively Rouch worked out each scene beforehand, often over breakfast on the very day of shooting. The basic attitude, however, was that each idea, no matter how attractive, might be subsumed by a new and better idea. His experience as an anthropological filmmaker clearly determined the preparation of his fiction films, whereby he deviated considerably from typical movie script methods.

Cinematography

Regarding the actual filming, it is noteworthy that Rouch's manipulation of the camera in shooting his fiction films was definitely influenced by his anthropological approach. He was always his own cameraman with the 16mm camera, and he used direct sound as soon as it was possible. In this regard, he was clearly also influenced by his engineering background. Rouch was acquainted with all the technical quirks of the camera and often repaired it himself, which of course was a good thing when shooting in isolated spots in the bush.

Generally speaking, directors rarely wield the camera themselves. Most of the *nouvelle vague* filmmakers even had professional cameramen shoot the footage on 35mm using post-synchronisation, with the exception of a number of pioneers such as John Cassavetes, Vittorio de Sica, Jacques Rozier and Jean Eustache. Rouch also worked with the same minimal crew for his fiction films as he did for his documentaries, which consisted of the Nigerien technicians he had trained, like the soundman Moussa Amidou. Damouré, Lam and Tallou were all-round technicians as well as being actors, so there were no 'white intruders' to disrupt things.

At the level of production, it was of course necessary to work on a shoestring budget. Rouch was able to finance his anthropological films as principal investigator for the Centre National de la Recherche Scientifique (CNRS). His fiction films were a hobby that he funded out of his own pocket if he did not find a producer. This was at the same time a stylistic choice; with his tiny crew and mobile equipment, Rouch could quickly respond to the most unexpected situations. This 'lightweight' shooting technique fitted in well with improvisation using non-professional actors in real locations.

In the camerawork for his fiction films, Rouch's anthropological experience is clearly visible. He shot almost exclusively with natural light, usually without the use of special lights. This was one of the reasons that 'Rouch's gang' in Niger often did little all day, jumping into action only between four and six o'clock in the evening. It was only then, for one and a half hours, that the sunlight was not blindingly harsh. This heightened the adventurous atmosphere on the shoot. Filming had to be finished before the sun sank below the horizon an hour later.

Rouch shot his fiction films as he did rituals or documentaries. He would plunge into scenes with his hand-held camera, without worrying about the traditional image aesthetic. It was not that he was not searching for aesthetic expression, it was just that the excitement of the moment was more important to him. Together with his friends, he cultivated an attitude where everything was at stake every minute. Each take was an opportunity for failure or success. For Rouch, there was hardly ever a second take, the same as when he shot rituals, which obviously precluded other takes.

Camerawork and *mise-en-scène* were inextricably linked for Rouch. Each scene was usually shot in a single take, with one or two so-called sequence shots (a single take lasting ten minutes, the length of a roll of 16mm film). Scenes were never rehearsed. At most, the actors' positions were tried out once in front of the camera. Scenes were also rarely repeated; the take either worked or it did not. In the latter case, the scene would be omitted from the film, a risk element that was taken for granted when shooting rituals, but which had a different function in fiction films. Rouch wanted to create extra excitement in all those involved, characteristic of his ideas about 'ciné-trance'. This is precisely the way he often succeeded in arousing the suggestion of authenticity and improvisation.

Obviously this was again determined by the extremely low-budget conditions under which he had to work with a minimum number of film rolls. Yet he transformed this handicap into a stylistic element. To my knowledge, Jean Eustache has been the only one to successfully apply this approach once to a fiction film, *La maman et la putain* (*The Mother and the Whore*, 1973), not just out of economic necessity, but really to stimulate the actors.

With the 16mm synchronous filming technique he developed himself, using Eclair and Aaton cameras, Rouch was actually the forerunner of a contemporary generation of video filmmakers. It is striking that at the same time he remained old-fashioned, resisting the use of video cameras. His biggest objection was that video techniques allow for lengthy and frequent filming, in contrast to using 16mm film where you pay a high price for every roll. It is exactly for this reason, according to Rouch, that concentration is often lacking in videos. Filming should remain an 'unrepeatable adventure' – relevant advice for today's videographers.

From his work with rituals, Rouch also learned to think about the editing while shooting. Whereas he pre-edited *Les Maîtres fous* (1955) during the shoot, with every shot of his Bell & Howell camera, he later transposed this editing in the camera to sequence shots with the 16mm Eclair. Again his documentaries seem to have influenced his fiction films. He shot rituals like *Les Tambours d'avant: Tourou et Bitti* (1971) in two ten-minute sequence shots, the same approach he applied to fiction films. A breathtaking example is *Gare du Nord* (1966), which is a twenty-minute fiction film shot in Paris in just two sequence shots of ten minutes each. Using a hand-held camera, Rouch also shot several plays, such as *Folie ordinaire d'une fille de Cham* (*Ordinary Folly of a Girl of Cham*, 1987) and *Bac ou mariage* (*Diploma or Marriage*, 1988), according to this method. Like the American underground filmmaker Jonas Mekas, who shot Jack Gelber's play *The Brig* (1964) this way, Rouch let the actors go through the play without interruption while he filmed them in a few continuous takes, with two hand-held cameras alternately at his disposal. *Folie ordinaire d'une fille de Cham* was shot in a single day in a psychiatric ward at St. Anne's (Centre Hospitalier Sainte Anne). For *Bac ou mariage*, he travelled with the actors to Senegal on a charter plane, where the scenes were acted and shot in a week at actual locations. This recording of theatre with a hand-held camera was, for Rouch, a physical adventure, similar to the filming of rituals, and miles away from the current television videos of operas and plays.

Mise-en-scène

It was characteristic of Rouch's *mise-en-scène* that, contrary to what usually happens, the story was filmed in chronological sequence. Here, too, he applied his documentary experience. There was no shooting a new scene if it chronologically preceded one that had already been shot. Rouch preferred to return three times to the same location, because he placed the actors' experiential world within the continuity of the story above all else. The first part of *Madame l'Eau* was filmed in Niger, then there was a visit to the Netherlands, and only afterwards came the building of the windmill in Niger – which is very uneconomical and unprofessional according to commercial production norms.

Rouch had clearly developed the lessons of Neo-realism and combined them with his experience as an anthropologist. For years, Damouré, Lam and Tallou were assistants, technicians and investigators for Rouch's anthropological films. What was new, in contrast to the documentaries, was the playful element in the fiction films. These films were really a game to them, as compared to their serious anthropological work. Stimulated by Rouch's camera, they created their own characters. An 'anthropology shared' among Rouch and his Nigerien friends in the anthropological films became a 'cinema shared' in his fiction films, as Michel Keita, a brilliant Nigerien sociologist and a Rouch co-worker at IRSH, aptly put it in my 1978 film portrait of Rouch. (Keita unfortunately died in a car accident not long after this interview.)

Editing

When I became involved in the editing of *Madame L'Eau*, I again discovered the surprising 'kitchen' of Rouch's fiction films. There is a myth of Rouch as a documentarist whose films were effectively done when he completed shooting. As an anthropological filmmaker, Rouch always worked long and intensively on the editing, receiving feedback from those involved in the shoot by having them assist with the editing as informants. The filmed material was used to understand the rituals that had been shot. Rouch applied an analogous method to his fiction films, and he often asked those in the film to give their opinion at the time of editing. He was able to do this because he had patched together his own editing room and mixing studio at the Musée de l'Homme, where he could work free of charge for as long as he wanted.

As with his anthropological films, Rouch also used an 'approximate edit' on his fiction films. Firstly, the material was spliced together and then the film slowly took shape. In contrast to standard fiction film editing, which is based on a script written beforehand, Rouch's films came into being only during the editing process. During this process he would, to my amazement, note everything down systematically, as if it involved scientific, anthropological documentation, so that a detailed script emerged in the editing room – a strong contrast to the custom in the television world of slapping documentaries together. I also discovered how passionately Rouch edited. Every cut, every sequence was tried over and over again and re-edited. I witnessed the surprising re-editing of sequences in *Madame l'Eau*, such as that of 'Damouré', 'Lam' and 'Tallou's' return to Niger from the Netherlands, as well as the final scene containing the 'windmill, windmill' poem. By regrouping various shots that sometimes appeared by chance, they became poetic highlights in the film. Often, Rouch would not touch his fiction films for a time, picking up the editing only after months had passed, since he was consumed by other projects as well. Sometimes I would have my doubts and be afraid that the film would never be completed. The maturation process, however, only served to improve the editing. In any normal film production this is obviously unthinkable due to production pressures and the financial investment. Once again the influence of his documentaries – where Rouch would spend years freely editing and reshooting – was revealed.

Precisely because Rouch's fiction films were made inexpensively and on the fringe, with no prospects of commercial distribution, he could tweak them for a long time, just as he did with his documentaries. *Petit à petit* was six hours long in its first version, and it was reconstructed as such fifteen years ago and broadcast on television in three parts.

Rouch's gang

Although the French film critic Serge Daney professed admiration for Rouch as the father and forerunner of the *nouvelle vague*, he formulated his disillusionment on closer contact with 'Rouch's gang' in his posthumously published diary. He criticised 'the somewhat boorish parasitism' of Rouch, 'whose ego always brings him to surround himself with slaves or friends who support him materially. The master makes no alliances because he knows he needs servants, "negroes", "buddies", underlings he very well knows are not equals, although it appears like they're his "brothers"' (see 1993: 270–2, 281–4). A few African directors and intellectuals, like Ousmane Sembène, also criticise Rouch because they claim his films present a paternalistic, colonial view of Africa. A similar reproach was launched against Rouch from left-wing circles in the Netherlands, particularly among third-world idealists. Rouch supposedly characterised his Nigerien friends using colonial stereotypes like 'cheerful and childlike'.

My years of observation on site in Niger convinced me the opposite was true. The fundamental equality and the openness of the relationship Damouré Zika, Lam Ibrahima Dia, Tallou Mouzourane and other Nigerien friends had with Jean Rouch struck me on my first visit to Niger. The so-called childlike cheerfulness in Rouch's films that bothers ponderous third-world idealists in Europe belongs to a game that is deeply rooted in African culture. For Rouch, that *savoir vivre* is often superior to much of the seriousness and formality in European behaviour patterns. In this respect, Rouch clearly thought multiculturally, where our 'European ways' do not set the standard by a long shot. For instance, Rouch often lamented that 'we' had lost the playful element to life. One of its attributes was the 'joking relationship', which he got to know in Niger as a superior form of friendship. Precisely because you are true friends, you can tease and make fun of each other. Jane Rouch, his first wife, said it very well in the title of her book about Rouch at work on site in Niger during the 1950s: *Le rire n'a pas de couleur* (*Laughter Has No Colour*, 1956). It is true that in Dirk Nijland's film *Rouch's Gang* (1993), Damouré Zika stated that he considered Rouch to be 'a father' who had helped him get out of poverty and achieve a certain level of comfort. The relationships inside 'Rouch's gang' were in fact very complicated, with a clearly personal history as a backdrop. Rouch got to know Damouré when, as a colonial engineer, he had to build roads in Niger with forced labourers in 1941 and 1942. They immediately became friends, and from the very beginning Rouch distanced himself from the French colonial elite. When he returned to Niger after 1946, as an anthropologist, his friendship with Damouré grew to one of working together. Rouch helped him find work and complete a pharmaceutical degree in Paris, resulting in the latter managing the pharmacy at the Niamey hospital up until his retirement. After he retired, he was able, again with Rouch's support, to set up his own clinic outside Niamey. From the beginning, though, it was an equal relationship of give and take between them. Damouré did a lot for Rouch's anthropological work, as Rouch's other Nigerien friends did later on. They provided local inside information as well as their indispensable support in making his anthropological films.

The distribution of Rouch's fiction films deviates from that of movie production in general, including that of the so-called low-budget ones. Rouch always contractually established that he and his Nigerien friends would share equally in the revenues. Regarding the anthropological films, Rouch paid his co-workers personally, but where the fiction films were concerned, everybody took part without pay in making the film and shared equally the money it brought in. So Damouré was able to build houses and a medical dispensary from the money made with *Cocorico! Monsieur Poulet* (one of their few commercial successes); Lam Ibrahima Dia was able to acquire a Land Rover for transport to and from the bush. Even for the films that had real producers, like *Petit à petit* or *Madame l'Eau*, Rouch stipulated equal earnings for his Nigerien friends and himself.

This 'equality in inequality' that characterised their relationship is disputed in Daney's criticism of Rouch as a manipulator of his co-workers and friends. On site, Damouré, Lam and Tallou were often more master of the situation than Rouch was. They were also aware of how much Rouch depended on them, and it was not always taken for granted that in return he would help them monetarily or support them in other ways. Contrary to Daney's view of the situation, they were the ones who spearheaded the game, particularly in the fiction films, and Rouch was often their student and follower. Had Daney been able to go to Niger he would certainly have analysed this 'equality in inequality' in his usual, original way.

Of course Rouch was not free of traces from his colonial past, but he was a pioneer in his attempt to break through the colonial relationship between 'rich whites' and 'poor blacks' and to arrive at a relationship based on equality, not least because of his great respect for and love of African culture. As Lam puts it in the film *Rouch's Gang*, as a counterbalance to Damouré's paternalistic view, 'we're cousins.' And in a family relationship, a cousin is your equal. Rouch succeeded, particularly in his fiction films, in arriving at a unique exchange with his Nigerien friends. I am thinking of Amadou Hampâté Bâ, the famous African expert on the oral tradition for whom Rouch had great admiration, and whom he often cited, saying for example, 'When a griot dies, a whole library is lost.' At a memorial gathering shortly after Rouch's death, Inoussa Ousseini read aloud another of Bâ's texts: 'When the chameleon arrives in a place, he takes on the colour of that place.' In contrast to the frequently negative significance of the chameleon in Europe, in Africa it is honoured as an exemplary creature, and it expresses Rouch's view of life: he, 'the white man', takes on the colour of his black Nigerien friends. I recall Godard's definition of Rouch, 'Even though Rouch is white, he says just like Rimbaud, "I am another", meaning, "Me, I'm black."' Rouch strove to identify with his Nigerien friends, both in their behaviour and in the world of their imagination. This is why the fiction films he made with them in Niger are in the end truly African films.

Epilogue

The fiction films that Jean Rouch and his Nigerien friends made turn out to be pioneering work even today, perhaps even more clearly than before. They are an example of the struggle to close the gap between the white West and the Third World. They fly in the face of stereotypical contrasts such as rich/poor or developed/under-developed, and break through the frequently simplified 'for or against' stance regarding multiculturalism. They demonstrate that we, as 'cousins', can learn much from one another's customs and traditions as long as we are open to playing one another's games and do not take ourselves or others too seriously. Their fiction films are an antidote for any form of fanaticism or dogmatism. They continue to stimulate us to make the impossible come true; by joining forces you can get cars across broad rivers and turn deserts into fertile land with simple windmills.

AUTHOR'S NOTE: Translated from the Dutch by Wanda Boeke.

REFERENCES

Daney, S. (1993) *L'Experience a été profitable, Monsieur*. Paris: P.O.L.
Deleuze. G. (1985) *Cinéma 2. L'image-temps*. Paris: Les Editions de Minuit.
Rouch, J. (1956) *Le rire n'a pas de couleur*. Paris: Gallimard.

FOUNDATIONS AND LEGACIES

From fieldwork in Niamey, Niger, 1961

14 CHANCE AND ADVENTURE IN THE CINEMA AND ETHNOGRAPHY OF JEAN ROUCH

Christopher Thompson

That Surrealism played an important part in Jean Rouch's development is evident from some of his most personal films, and what we have to grasp is how this interest encouraged him to free up cinema and ethnography and fed his passionate enjoyment of the world and his work up to the very end. One of the best ways to do this and to capture the unity of his extraordinary oeuvre, from the energetic and discreetly lyrical but still essentially sober documentaries of his youth to the extravagant cinematic poems and fantasies of his old age such as *Dionysos* (1984) and *Liberté, égalité, fraternité et puis après…* (1990), is to follow a thread which runs throughout and constantly recurred in his conversation: the idea of adventure.

Adventure was inscribed in his genes. His father, Jules-Alfred Rouch, was an eminent meteorologist who had accompanied the explorer Jean Charcot on the 'Pourquoi pas?' to the Antarctic from 1908–10 and subsequently wrote numerous books, including the study *Orages et tempêtes dans la littérature* (*Gales and Storms in Literature*, 1929). Now, while it is interesting that the son of a scientific specialist on storms became the leading authority on Dongo, the spirit of thunder in Songhay mythology, more important to notice is that the father pursued his taste for adventure in letters and that Jean would head to Africa instead of the Poles and seek adventure in literature and art, and make it central to his cinema. Easy to say, you may think, when we are speaking of a filmmaker famous for his improvisation and experimentation. But there is more to it than that.

The evidence for this emphasis in his work, and for the sympathy with Surrealism which it created, is there in two of his films from the 1960s, *La Punition* (1962) and *Gare du Nord* (1966), both built on the well-known surrealist love of spontaneous interrogations of strangers and on their favourite theme of happy encounters between inner desires and reality – the famous *hasard objectif* (objective chance). These films portray Rouch's compatriots as desperate to escape their over-regimented society. In *Gare du Nord*, Odile is imprisoned in a depressing flat and a crumbling marriage; in *La Punition*, Nadine is an adolescent victim of deadening educational constraints. Both dream of leaving 'at random, to anywhere' (as in *Gare du Nord*) to recapture a sense of freedom and mystery in life – Odile full of common fantasies and Nadine with more spirit and the ideas suggested by that trigger of dreams which a museum can become, as in the film. One will leave, the other not, after their respective encounters, even when a stranger invites Odile to break out into an 'adventure about which I can say nothing. Anything is possible'. And *La Punition*, which is certainly among the most revealing (though not the best) of Rouch's films, analyses the idea of adventure and its paradoxes with references to ethnography, as well as with the help of quotations from André Breton's *L'Amour fou* (1937). Rouch stresses here how relative the idea of adventure must be to everyone's desires, imaginations and practical circumstances. The young man whom Nadine meets in Luxembourg Gardens only wants an ordinary amorous adventure; the scientist met by the Seine is really more interested in his experiments than in the attractive Nadine; the African friend she meets at the museum stresses that he lives his adventures in the jungle of Paris. As for Nadine, she does admit to him that wanting to do ethnography in Africa, 'the classic land of adventures', is in many ways escapist, without realising as yet how disturbing for scientific ideals such an admission might be, nor how the escapist element in classical ethnography risked reducing Africans to something like the stuffed animals in front of her in the museum at the Jardin des Plantes, a place historically at the heart of early French adventures in Natural History and Ethnography.

Nor did Rouch disassociate his own career and that of many ethnographers from Nadine's daydreams and quandaries. To Enrico Fulchignoni he admitted to wanting the poet Arthur Rimbaud's legendary shoes, swift as the wind,[1] and he would often count himself among the young men leaving for Africa after World War Two portrayed in Jacques Becker's *Rendez-vous de juillet* (1949). But beyond recognising this taste for adventure in classical ethnography (the mythic dimension of which anthropologists such as Johannes Fabian (2000) have now subjected to devastating analysis), Rouch had an original take on this human foible. Instead of endlessly deploring the distortion of scientific objectivity, he chose to stress a similar taste for adventure (and even for escapism: see *Moi, un noir* (1958)) in the African subjects of his ethnography, as if it were one of the essential traits common to all humans, across all divides. One soon understands that it was not just the power of cinema to follow hunts (*La Chasse au lion à l'arc* (1957–64)), or migration (*Jaguar* (1967)) or a war (*Babatu, les trois conseils* (1975)), that drew Rouch to such topics. The poetry of adventure inherent in such activities brought out the extent to which the bush (*la brousse*) was for local communities a dangerous 'no man's land' endowed with, and defended by, magical powers, into which one should not venture without propitiatory rites and consultations of auspices (*Jaguar, La Chasse au lion à l'arc*). The commentary of *Jaguar* tells us that the migrants leave 'to look for money of course, but also for adventure' just like the lion-hunters and their forefathers left to bring back stories of heroic trials and trophies as much as money. But beyond the simple pleasure of realising and enjoying this common bond with his African friends (a bond celebrated once again at the beginning of *Madame l'Eau*),[2] there is more at issue here for the filmmaker and the ethnographer. All the more so, as in all adventures, the concept of borders and frontiers and their crossing is central, as it is in Rouch's work.

For what does adventure speak of, after all? It speaks of what is unforeseeable, dangerous and perhaps irresistible in life. To go on adventures is to choose to leave the routines imposed by daily work and by fathers, to leave for an elsewhere where everything becomes possible again, including hope. That is why there will also often (but not always) be a specific goal – be it wealth, a woman, a magnificent prey ('le vieux mâle de Tamoulé' in *Bataille sur le grand fleuve* (1951)), or the mysterious blend of attraction and repulsion generated by certain occurrences, such as storms and rites of possession. Unlike many anthropologists, Rouch did not reject, in the name of science, ecstatic experiences of Africa (see Fabian 2000). Instead, he said that to be allowed to join rites of possession as a filmmaker is to learn a little about why others lend their bodies to such dangerous adventures and about the qualities needed to succeed (see Fulchignoni 1981: 11).

What are these qualities? They are the traditional heroic ones needed to deal with the inevitable uncertainties of life. To bring such a perspective to bear on migration, on hunting or even on war, as the Africans in Rouch's films do, is to accept the immense role of chance and disorder and hostile forces in lives which are more precarious than ours, and to see the human need for proprietary rites to put luck and the gods on their side. Moreover, Rouch saw clearly that the same need applied to him as filmmaker and ethnographer, dependent on the whim of sponsors, on the weather, the hazards of technology or simply the luck of being there at the right time and having the camera running, as in the unique and magnificent *Les Tambours d'avant: Tourou et Bitti* (1971). Elsewhere, he reminded us that for the filmmaker, the lion hunt of *La Chasse au lion à l'arc* was also a difficult chase for footage and the story, just as the hunters themselves are finally shown to have sought a story as much as a lion.

Now to say all this of himself, as a Frenchman with an inherited taste for adventure, and as a filmmaker and ethnographer, and to say it too of his African subjects and friends, is to confirm what Rouch always maintained about the un-redeemable, unscientific nature of the desire for knowledge of 'the other' which lies at the heart of ethnography, as of poetry and fiction – a desire, the ambiguity of which Lam Ibrahima Dia stressed at the beginning of *Jaguar* when he said that, 'when you arrive in a country, it's the country that changes you, not you the country'. Anthropology has increasingly recognised the role of this subjec-tive drive, and Rouch stressed that what it means for the ethnographer is that he must make the best of being an adventurer, in the sense of remaining open to what chance may bring, however much it thwarts expectations, ruins all closed systems of thought and blocks all Faustian desires to build a complete map of mankind. So Rouch insisted on the need to seize chance effects and on the value of risky first takes. His wish to remain a specialist in fieldwork and refusal to lock himself into any system of thought or procedure liable to blind him to accidental revelations may have made him seem naïve to some. But his unusual insistence on chance and the spirit of adventure at the heart of all ethnography and explo-ration is also what allowed him to avoid rigid systems of thought that hide their initial assumptions. He was able to create a style which was paradoxically both naïve and modern in its refusal to hide the all-too-human desires feeding eth-nography and its acknowledgement of the changes produced by the intrusion of the ethnographer, both on the group visited and on the intruder himself – not to speak of the change which the resulting film might produce (like a powerful surrealist object) on the future viewer.

This banking on adventure and chance sometimes produced totally unclas-sifiable works such as *Cocorico! Monsieur Poulet* (1975) a film which also illus-trates perfectly the ambiguous place of frontiers and borders in the Rouchian adventure. Rouch is famous for his questioning of these, whether as the limits set to science, to technology or to systems and subjects. And his interest in migrant workers made him especially sensitive to the arbitrariness and fragility of the national frontiers left by colonialism in Africa (*Jaguar*). But it is perhaps because *Cocorico! Monsieur Poulet* is not an ethnographic film, conventionally speaking, but above all a picaresque comedy, that his critique and transgression of limits can become more radical. The film follows the adventures of three small-busi-nessmen trying to make a living by selling chickens and transporting millet in an old Citroên 2CV car. Mostly, however, their work is neglected and pure chance directs their lives – and I suspect the film – to such an extent that this comic odyssey becomes a celebration of African open-mindedness and adaptability before the unexpected and ingenious use of modern technology. Truly off-hand credits introduce a film that respects neither the narrative rules of any genre, nor the descriptive conventions either of travelogues or ethnographies. Even the difference between dream and reality is not respected since the travellers will be plagued by the surprise appearances of a sorceress who will make Damouré Zika mad from time to time, until the appropriate sacrifice is made. But that is not enough for Rouch, who after presenting us with an authentic sorceress – apparently endowed with real powers – confuses issues again when the sacrifice has been made, by using the exaggerated grunts of the actress to stress the deliberately theatrical nature of her appearances and, by implication, of many other such African sorceries. Yet more confusion and satire occurs with respect to the conventional borders between the sexes and ethnic groups. The businessmen comment on the sorceress's taste for cross-dressing and ethnic prejudices provoke spats between them. It is true that all ends well between the three (and with the sorceress), while the only white person in the film, a presumptuous young agent charged with implementing some truly exotic development plans, will no doubt always remain ignorant of the local culture, the social organisation and long agricultural experience that he does not understand or respect. So Rouch was not afraid to show, here and elsewhere, that all groups tend to define themselves by prejudices against others, even if this does not seem too tragic in *Cocorico! Monsieur Poulet*, a film of a country where a considerable margin of personal freedom seems to exist in the great spaces between rare figures of authority and villages of nomadic shepherds that can disappear overnight. And should the European spectator have failed to grasp Rouch's lack of respect for all that limits our freedom and creativity, there is more fun to be had with another of his beloved cars, for the film delights in the comic invention that the travellers bring to using modern technology in a country where everything may become unavailable, including roads. A series of gags on how to drive a 2CV without windscreen wipers, rear mirrors or even brakes climaxes in three crossings of the Niger in which the car is reduced to its basic carcass and turned into a boat. Need one spell out how this violation of all norms of technology (not to speak of the dignity of the river) reinforces the film's satire of all limits, frontiers and classifications? In cinema, the random events of an adventure have rarely led to a more joyous over-turning of our expectations.

Elsewhere, the same radical spirit allowed Rouch to bring to an urgent political question – Republican France's continuing illusions about equality and racism in the bicentennial year of the Revolution – a freedom of poetic invention in *Liberté, égalité, fraternité, et puis après...* which openly refers to modern art and Surrealism with a nod to Douanier Rousseau on the walls of a classroom;[3] its free and abrupt movements in time between 1989, 1789 and Napoleonic France with the help of Haitain songs and rites on the esplanade of the Invalides,[4] and finally by the reading of Baudelaire's hymn to the swaying rhythms of a magnificently beautiful woman (*Le Beau Navire* (The Beautiful Ship, 1857)) over a sublime montage of the Eiffel Tower feminised in its illumination for the Bicentennial. André Breton, who years before had charted Paris onto the body of a woman in his novel *Nadja* (1928), would have liked it, as he liked *La Punition*. Built on a series of improvised interventions in, and hijacking of, the official celebrations of the Bicentennial, the subversiveness of *Liberté, égalité, fraternité, et puis après...* is likewise surrealist in spirit.

A final word. The subversive and ultimately constructive implications of Rouch's cultivation of adventure to free up cinema and ethnography has been recognised by one of France's greatest filmmakers and one of Rouch's greatest admirers in Jacques Rivette's monumental 12-hour masterpiece, *Out 1, Noli me tangere* (1971).[5] In the course of this mysterious improvisation, loosely based on Balzac's *Histoire des treize* (*History of the Thirteen*, 1833–35) and much in-debted also to Surrealism (as is all of Rivette's work), two different theatre companies rehearsing plays by Sophocles, together with other assorted Parisians, find themselves struggling to break out of their respective routines, mindsets and circles of friends, and to see other connections in this and older worlds. At one point, an actress talks to her ethnographer admirer about his current projects. He tells her about his wish to break out of his adherence to the boxes and frames of conventional ethnography and its exotic subjects ('ma clôture à moi'), and praises the initiative of another ethnographer who is doing so ('en train de réussir une expérience de rupture de monde clos') by moving on from working with fishermen on the Niger river to studying fishermen back home in Brittany with the help of a Nigerien. The reference to Rouch is unmistakeable, all the more so as the ethnographer is played by Michel Deshayes, who had just finished acting in Rouch's epochal experiment in so-called 'reverse ethnography', *Petit à petit* (1968–69), and as all his scenes are played on the roof of the Musée de l'Homme. And the tribute is even more telling in that this discussion is an essential *mise-en-abyme* (a miniaturised reflection) of a central theme of Rivette's film and occurs towards its centre.

One could hardly ask for a better tribute to the significance of Rouch's risky, boundary-breaking adventures in cinema and ethnography. Always self-reflexive and sceptical of cultural codes of representation as well as of ethnographic authority, but at the same time deeply committed to the usefully subversive potential of ethnography, Rouch's cinema generously, sometimes a bit madly, helped to open the way for much of the best of subsequent innovation.

AUTHOR'S NOTE: This chapter is a translated expanded version of the article 'Aventure, ethnologie et hasard', published in *CinémAction*, 81 (1996), 69–73.

NOTES

1 'Chausser les semelles de vent d'Arthur Rimbaud'. See Fulchignoni 1981: 7.
2 Where he reminds his regular actors that they have already been 'accomplices' in many adventures.
3 In a picture painted especially for the occasion by a Lebanese painter.
4 Notably a 'casser canaris' to reconcile the spirit of Haiti's liberator Toussaint Louverture with that of the man responsible for his death, Napoleon.
5 Rivette acknowledged Rouch's importance for all French cinema of the 1960s in an interview in *Cahiers du Cinéma*, 204 (see Aumont *et al.* 1968), and for himself after *Out 1* in *La Nouvelle critique* (see Eisenschetz *et al.* 1973) .

REFERENCES

Aumont, J., J-L. Comolli, J. Narboni and S. Pierre (1968) 'Le temps débord: entretien avec Jacques Rivette', *Cahiers du cinema*, 204, 7–21.

Breton, A. (1992 [1937]) 'L'Amour fou', in *Œuvres*, II. Paris: Bibliothèque de la Pléiade, 673–785.

Eisenschetz, B., J. A. Fieschi and E. de Greorio (1973) 'Interview with Jacques Rivette', *La Nouvelle critique*, 63, 244, 65–74.

Fabian, J. (2000) *Out of Our Minds: Reason and Madness in the Exploration of Central Africa*. Berkeley: University of California Press.

Fulchignoni, E. (1981) 'Entretien de Jean Rouch avec le Professeur Enrico Fulchignoni', in *Jean Rouch: une retrospective*. Paris: Ministère des relations extérieures, 7–29.

Rouch, J-A. (1929) *Orages et tempêtes dans la littérature*. Paris: Société d'Editions Géographiques, Maritimes et Coloniales.

'Introduction Méthodologique' by Marcel Griaule, *Minotaure*, 2, 1933

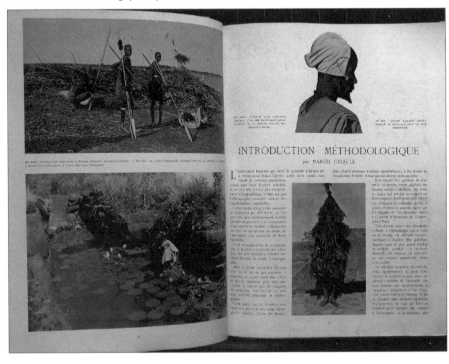

15 EVERYDAY MADNESS: SURREALISM, ETHNOGRAPHY AND THE PHOTOGRAPHIC IMAGE

David Bate

> There is an image that needs to be obliterated, I think – that of André Breton as a poet of unreason. A different one should be placed, not over it, but on top of it, that of Breton as a writer of knowledge. (Foucault 2000: 172)[1]

It is often noted that ethnography and Surrealism emerged in France at the same time, a remark meant to suggest some kind of affinity between them and which is projected forward into the image of Jean Rouch. This chapter explores that idea of an affinity between ethnography and Surrealism in the context of the film work of Jean Rouch.

Although Rouch studied ethnography in Paris just after World War Two when he was 29 (in 1946), his encounter with Surrealism and ethnography had begun much earlier in his cultural life in Paris *prior* to such study. Rouch had returned to Paris for education in 1930, sent there by his parents from Casablanca when he was 13.[2] It was during these early formative years in 1930s Paris that Rouch precociously encountered Surrealism and ethnography. This was the era of the more politically conscious *Second Surrealist Manifesto* (from 1929), the *International Colonial Exhibition* in Paris of 1931 and a politically volatile culture.

The following discussion is thus framed by two questions. The first is quite simply to ask: what was the relation between Surrealism and ethnography? Although it is true that Surrealism and ethnography often overlapped, appearing in the same place and interested in the same objects, exactly what that means in terms of their relationship as 'disciplines' is not clear. To accept that Surrealism and ethnography emerged at the same time in France and seem to parallel one another is not necessarily to endorse the argument made, for example, by James

Clifford who claims that a general hybrid *surrealist ethnography* had emerged at that time.[3]

This issue is important for my second question, which relates to the use of *photographic images* by Surrealism and ethnography. Surrealism and ethnography both shared an enthusiasm for new visual technological media: photography and film. From the mid-1920s the Surrealists increasingly used photographs, not only as a technology of reproduction in their magazines (for paintings and drawings and so forth), but also for the image itself in its potential for Surrealism. Over the 1930s, variously estranged and enigmatic objects, shot from peculiar viewpoints or montages of dream-like contradictions appeared more and more. This enthusiasm extended, where funding permitted, to film too, as most famously in Luis Buñuel and Salvador Dalí's *Un chien andalou* (*An Andalusian Dog*, 1929) and Buñuel's *L'Âge d'or* (*Age of Gold*, 1930).

There was a similar enthusiasm in ethnography. Marcel Griaule, the famous French ethnographer teaching at the Trocadero, also strongly advocated the use of photography and film and argued that photographic images were a key, significant addition to live fieldwork practice. This was a view he had formed during his experience of reconnaissance photography during World War One. It was later, of course, when Jean Rouch, a student of Griaule's, took up precisely the project of using film and developed it in his own way beyond that of Griaule.

The parallel fields of interest in using photographic images in ethnography and Surrealism were brought closer together in the two journals of the early 1930s, *Documents* and *Minotaure*. The short-lived *Documents* (1929–30), edited by George Bataille who was never actually a member of the surrealists (but who has since been re-visioned as one), accrued the status of a forum for 'dissident surrealists'. It was here that the work of ex-surrealists (kicked out by Breton) appeared alongside ethnography, thus bringing them together in print at least. One figure from that journal, Michel Leiris, an early but marginal figure among the literary surrealists during the 1920s, made a distinct leap towards ethnography. But it is *Minotaure*, the second and longer-lasting journal (1933–39), which represents the strongest link between Surrealism, dominated by Breton, and ethnography. It was also the magazine that Rouch acknowledged as having a marked impact upon him.

The first two issues of *Minotaure* came out simultaneously in June 1933. Issue one, organised by Breton, boasts a cover by Pablo Picasso, while issue two, with a cover by the lesser-known Gaston-Louis Roux and edited by the lapsed surrealist Michel Leiris, was totally dedicated to a report of the Dakar-Djibouti Mission. *Minotaure* is a brilliant example of a cultural journal that combined exciting visual imagery and sophisticated texts from numerous disciplines without making any one subservient to another. In this respect, it was an eclectic compromise between different intellectual factions rather than a Surrealist journal proper. This is indicated by the fact that Breton and Bataille, who were asked to co-edit it, refused to work together.[4] Although often described as a key surrealist magazine, the surrealists did not own it and only dominated its pages occasionally and as time went on. Because they did not control it, it was also different from their own previous journals. There were no dreams or automatic writings published in it and a definite lack of the famous 'inquiries' and investigations that dominated their earlier magazines. It also excluded the more direct political dimension of Surrealism that, given the polarised politics of the 1930s, is still shocking in its absence (see Lewis 1990). But it is here, in this second issue of *Minotaure* that a totally ethnographic project emerged, which took a different approach to cultural politics, one less bound up with the culture of politics than it was involved in a politics of cultural difference – under what was still, after all, a colonialist state. The 'Dakar-Djibouti Ethnographic and Linguistic Mission', as it was properly called, was led by Marcel Griaule in a journey that travelled from West to East Africa, from Dakar to Djibouti, between May 1931 and May 1933. The expedition brought back a huge amount of ethnographic data and artefacts, the purpose of which was to provide exhibitionary materials for the new African displays at the Trocadero Museum, the Institute of Ethnography in Paris (where Rouch later studied) to increase awareness and knowledge of African culture.

Griaule's ethnographers gathered a staggering 3,500 objects, including about 100 masks and headdresses, 150 dolls, paintings, rocks and sixty square metres of murals, the notations of thirty languages and dialects, 300 manuscripts and several live animals including a lion, a leopard and 5,000 insects. Each object was labelled, indexed and filed with written information on them, and two copies for safety. In addition to this, 6,000 photographs, 200 sound recordings and 16,000 metres of film were also part of the material brought back.[5] The sounds, stored on 24 cylinders, were mostly recorded simultaneously to the cinematographic recordings, so that the images could be shown with live sounds to accompany them. The photographs were developed in the field as they travelled, which enabled them to be identified, catalogued and labelled with information quickly and as accurately as possible. Griaule took many of the Dakar-Djibouti Mission photographs himself. With the use of photography and film as crucial recording apparatuses, for Griaule the special issue of *Minotaure* was a good opportunity to demonstrate and disseminate the visual work of the Dakar-Djibouti Mission to a wider public.[6]

As the whole function of the Mission was premised on bringing new ethnographic knowledge to its French audience, this visibility, this aspect of *seeing-as-knowledge*, was crucial. Here in *Minotaure* were photographs, accumulated during the expedition, of the actual rituals seen, the masks collected, ceremonial instruments used in circumcision rituals, photographic images of Abyssinian paintings and – one of the celebrated items in the Mission work – pictures of the funeral ceremonies of the Dogon. Such events were heavily photographed, recorded and filmed and, when reprinted in *Minotaure*, accompanied by essays describing these diverse cultural practices in Africa.

Griaule favoured 'direct observation' methods, so the recording of information derived from it was crucial, hence the use of photography and film. In his six-page essay, 'Introduction Méthodologique' (1933) published in *Minotaure*, Griaule spells out the ethnographic techniques adopted for the Mission and his principles and practical rules for ethnographic fieldwork in general. He is keen to establish and justify the scientific parameters of the Mission, its concerns for objectivity and the techniques for achieving it. At the outset, Griaule distinguishes two methodological principles of ethnographic fieldwork: the *extensive* and *intensive* methods. The extensive method is the study of given questions in the largest number of societies possible, whilst the latter is the opposite, a deep study of one society. Although these methods sound like an opposition between 'breadth with no depth' and 'depth with no breadth', Griaule makes a good case for the relative merits of both and argues that the Mission combined them equally.[7] The 20,000 kilometres travelled from West to East Africa gave the Mission an extensive fieldwork study of numerous societies (across Senegal, French Sudan, the high Volta, Dahomey, Niger, Nigeria, Cameroon, Chad, Middle Congo, Oubangui-Chari and the Belgian Congo), while an intensive study was carried out in the places they stayed at, which gave them a more detailed specific knowledge about each of those instances. Even within the intensive method, Griaule incorporated an extensive observation through his insistence on the overall importance of teamwork, for which he argues emphatically in his essay. He makes the usefulness of teamwork clear in his example of observing an important public ceremony, where he argues that 'a single observer will be quickly overwhelmed ... It is often difficult for the same observer to put together the notes, to photograph, to film, to draw, and it is in any case impossible to be in the same instant in different places' (Griaule 1933: 8).[8] The advantage of a team, he says, is that it permits a *simultaneous* observation of the event by several observers with different tasks: 'If each of the members specialises in a determinant branch and if some between themselves assume several tasks, the team permits the simultaneous employment of procedures of investigation' (ibid.).

The implications for ethnographic observation were that, for instance, the study of funeral ceremonies of the Dogon should be observed simultaneously by several inquirers with tasks divided between them (for example, one to study the structure, functioning, graphic manifestations of the event, another the secret languages employed and a third to observe the music and choreography of the event). In terms of photography they had three cameras.[9] These could be used in different strategic positions from where the events could be effectively documented simultaneously. Such methods of course pre-date what is now a standard procedure in large- scale event television reporting or film work.

This multi-observation technique instigated by Griaule was part of his ambitious method to establish a cross-referenced data system intended to squeeze out any potential inaccuracies and mistakes in information, which threatened from all sides. It was a method that also had to be rapid – fast enough to *process* the observations. Hence, Griaule's solution is a division of work inside the specialist observer team: 'The quantity of results – one can add quality – that one can hope to attain is more than proportional to the number of workers' (1933: 9). The 'intrusion' of observers into the communities they were observing was not something that worried Griaule. Far from it, given that many of these peoples were already under a colonial administration, interfering in the culture was already an inevitable fact for him. His panoptic strategy was simply a necessary means to establish 'truth' from the many, rather than drawing on just one perhaps weak source. Thus for Griaule there was a kind of informational 'safety in numbers' that, together with the quite literal use of different points of view, was the necessary basis for factual and objective recording of the symbolic systems, rituals and objects of any cultural group studied. This was crucial, Griaule argues, because 'if all cultural activities are translated by their objects, it is theoretically possible to obtain knowledge of a society through what it creates and uses through a maximum of detail' (1933: 7). Here, Griaule subscribes to what his colleague Marcel Mauss (Jean Rouch's other teacher), called 'total social facts'. Loosely derived from Marx, this meant a conception of reality as 'a synthesis of many determinations' (Cousins 1989: 80). Griaule aimed to achieve this with a Fordist-type principle of the division into specialist labour across his team of workers. These methodological rules of Griaule's fieldwork underpin what appears in the *Minotaure* issue of the Dakar-Djibouti Mission.[10]

In *Minotaure*, different points of view within the various photographs are evident. Camera positions are varied, as is the subject matter, and framing and distance all differ. These are not 'scientific' photographs in the sense of having precise and fixed rules of composition (for example, a fixed subject-to-background distance regulated, a standard lighting and so forth), yet they do provide and yield 'information'. What we see in the photographs exceeds what is revealed by the written texts: the photographs show things beyond the written descriptions in what appears as a nascent *visual* ethnography.

Across the 88 pages of this smart, high-quality magazine, the reader was shown the objects, scenes and peoples, in short, the culture studied in its entirety. On the inside cover in *Minotaure* this ethnographic Mission represents the claim to a 'modern ethnography', where it is argued that it had never been so necessary to not separate science from art. The magazine purports to give the reader 'all the elements' to situate the published documents in their 'proper atmosphere' and to imagine their 'real roots'.

Yet if the spectator could imagine the 'proper atmosphere' through the photographs in *Minotaure* (and in the archives of the Mission), their meanings, in terms of social observation, are nevertheless anchored by the texts that Griaule and his team attach to them. Here the relations between images, their captions and accompanying essays became crucial in securing meanings. For example, the photographic image planted in the centre of the first page of Griaule's essay on method is accompanied by the caption: 'Jeune garçon Dogon habille des feuillage pour un rite saisoner' ('Young Dogon boy dressed in foliage for a seasonal ritual'), which serves to anchor the picture's meaning and place it as within a specific cultural framework – the words 'young boy', 'Dogon', 'dressed' and 'seasonal ritual' all have their own pre-existing connotations that provide vital knowledge for the viewer to locate the meaning of the picture. I may or may not understand the purpose of dressing up in what looks like a haystack, but the caption indicates that this is from another culture (Dogon) in which – I must presume – dressing like this is part of a normal 'ritual'. Griaule's caption (and Michel Leiris's, who edited the journal) is plainly aimed to be denotative speech, an 'object-language' avoiding myth.

Writing in 1931, the year the Dakar-Djibouti Mission started, Walter Benjamin took the ignorant photographer to court in his essay, 'A Short History of Photography': 'must we not also count as illiterate the photographer who cannot read their own pictures? Will not the caption become the most important component of the shot?' (1972: 25).

In this respect the captions and accompanying essays in *Minotaure* function to 'anchor' the photographs and keep the associative paths of the pictures strictly in the realm of ethnographic fact. Yet despite such texts around them anchoring their meaning by describing the scenes and objects depicted, many of the photographs in *Minotaure* have a signification that escapes us. While the viewer is given all the properties of a conventional photographic realism – a picture anchored by its caption – the scene pictured remains enigmatic. In a semiotic sense there is a struggle to attach a specific signified meaning, because the connotations are blocked due to my lack of cultural (Dogon) knowledge. In this photograph I can *see* a figure is dressed in foliage, I understand that, but any explanation about what this really means is not addressed. This might seem utterly basic. Yet this strange effect, of recognition without understanding, is amplified throughout the magazine. Where does this leave visual ethnography and its discourse?

What for Walter Benjamin was the crucial relation between picture and caption in photography becomes, in the cinema, the crucial relation between pictures in sequence and the soundtrack – through commentary. Marcel Griaule's strategy was to synchronise, as far as possible, the live sound recordings on phonographic cylinders to the visual film footage to play them together. Griaule's still photographs from the Mission were anchored with descriptive captions, as in the *Minotaure* magazine of 1933.

Writing much later in his essay, 'The Camera and Man', Rouch argues that in ethnographic films the relations between pictures and soundtrack have been subject to successive styles, which he describes variously as: 'colonial baroque', 'exotic adventurism' and the 'dryness of a scientific report' (1979: 59). Griaule's captioning of photographs on the Dakar-Djibouti Mission *aspires* to the 'dryness of a scientific report', no doubt as a positive defence against the other styles that preceded it. Rouch condemns the contemporary 'shameful distance of anthropologists not wanting to confess their passion for the people they study' and argues that commentaries should be *subjective*. For Rouch a soundtrack should not be 'objective' because 'instead of clarifying the pictures, the film commentary generally obscures and masks them until the words substitute themselves for the pictures' (1979: 58). Thus, in effect, the film becomes 'a lecture or demonstration with an animated visual background' (ibid.) Against this, Rouch argues the 'demonstration should have been made by the images themselves' (ibid.) and cites *Las Hurdes* (*Land Without Bread*, aka *Tierra sin pan*, 1933) by Luis Buñuel as a positive example. (Ironically this is the film Buñuel shot instead of going on the Dakar-Djibouti Mission, which Griaule had invited him to join.) Rouch argues that Buñuel's film was a good example of how images and sounds can be used together to create a 'cinematic life' (1979: 58). Cinema, he argued, should be as much a vivid experience of the adventures of those who are the subject of the film as that of the filmmaker. In that 'cinematic life' the verbal commentary should be there, Rouch argued, as a *counterpoint* to the visual images. Again, it is Walter Benjamin who reminds us of the conditions of this type of problem in his famous quote from Bertolt Brecht, again about photography:

For, says Brecht, the situation is 'complicated by the fact that less than at any time does a simple *reproduction of reality* tell us anything about reality. A photograph of the Krupp works or of the GEC yields almost nothing about these institutions. Reality proper has slipped into the functional. The reification of human relationships, the factory, let's say, no longer reveals these relationships. Therefore something has actually to be *constructed*, something *artificial*, something set up.' It is the achievement of the surrealists to have trained the pioneers of such construction. (1972: 24)[11]

In setting something up to achieve 'reality', Benjamin argues, we should turn our attention to the surrealists who were, in 1931, the pioneers of such a project.

The 'surrealist image', to which Benjamin alludes as something 'constructed', is a conflictual image, one that organises an image of the world that is, to use Benjamin's term, a 'profane illumination' (1992a: 228). Rather than re-presenting the world as in a conventional surface realism, Surrealism re-visions the world as one inhabited by images. This parallels Rouch's sense of a counter-point between images and sound and is in contrast to Griaule's image and textual *descriptive* realism, which is meant to increase verisimilitude and diminish the spectator's appetite for fantasy and imagination. Now it is possible to see why Griaule's 'scientific' approach to filming and photography, although providing a stable method for ethnography, fails to capture the imagination of either the surrealists or, later on, Jean Rouch.

Rouch's film work is different from the aims for ethnographic film laid out for it by Griaule. The subjective 'voice' of Rouch is in the camera positions, in the very production of the images and their inscription of the viewer within the events depicted, while the voice-over provides counterpoint 'captions' to those images – without reducing the images to illustrations of the commentary. This project is sympathetic to the fundamental aim of Surrealism, to bring psychical reality into play with material reality. The 'psychic automatism' of the surrealists (its founding definition in the *Manifesto*) invoked a state located between consciousness and sleep, a kind of daydream or pre-conscious consciousness in which sensibilities are open to material and psychical influences. Notwithstanding that this state might be the condition of the cinema or photography *per se*, Surrealism aspired to a modern experience of the world that, as it developed, increasingly recognised the problems and politics of this psychic automatist state as a means of recognising – and establishing – the realm of conflicts.

In this sense Rouch shared with the surrealists the value of an experience of images not burdened with the values of a worn-out realism. If visual images are closer to the structures of the unconscious, as Freud argued, both Surrealism and Rouch implicitly recognise this in their practices. To return to *Minotaure*, for example, it is a strange fact that the image of the young man dressed in foliage exceeds the descriptive rationality of the caption that surrounds it. Beyond the caption, any fixed meaning of the picture rampages a bit, there is no fixed signified. No specific *final* connotation can be placed upon it, despite the caption anchoring it. It is as though the supposed *pure difference* between a Western spectator looking at this photograph and what is depicted there always breaks down. While that is perhaps due to the returned gaze from within the picture, which creates a perpetual confrontation between looks, the spectator is left with the experience of a polysemic uncertainty so reminiscent of surrealist images.

As such, this structure opposes Griaule's theories and methods where images are pinned down by facts. We can reintroduce another figure here to this story of French ethnography and Surrealism: Michel Leiris. Thrown out of the surrealist movement by Breton in 1929, Leiris had affiliated himself with Bataille and the *Documents* journal before becoming the archival secretary on the Dakar-Djibouti Mission where he was responsible for writing up the history of the expedition. Leiris had also edited the Dakar-Djibouti Mission issue of *Minotaure*. A year after returning from the Mission he published his own diary written privately during the entire duration of the journey, which he called *L'Afrique fantôme*. In it, he problematised the observation methods of Griaule and produced his own more personal account of the voyage, displaying his sexual interests, private fantasies, resentments and even moments of boredom. This was a type of writing that Griaule certainly did not approve of and which made the two men fall out. No matter how problematic his approach, Leiris nevertheless brought this aberrant Surrealism to the ethnography.

Also in contrast to Griaule, the surrealists and Rouch both rejected any claim to objectivity, and in the context of ethnography it is interesting to see how Rouch argues for subjective involvement. It is different from Leiris's; Rouch recognises that there is no objective position and devises strategies to construct films as 'practical research' in a positive endorsement of understanding through images. Some of the differences in these techniques and attitudes may be due to the different historical moments in which these people operated. Griaule, Leiris and the surrealists worked in the politically turbulent French culture of the 1930s, a moment still enmeshed in colonialist political ambitions and a very different place to the post-World War Two context in which Rouch worked. By the end of the war, the European sense of self was dramatically changed, within and outside of itself, due to the onslaught of fascism and cultural, political and social devastation it wrought on everyone.

Where some have argued that when the impulse of European colonialism turns inwards (towards Europe), it is fascism that appears, we might say, in an opposing analogy, that when a European ethnographic impulse turns inwards, Surrealism is produced. Yet that would be to obscure the differences between Surrealism and ethnography. Ultimately, Griaule's ethnography aimed to familiarise 'us' with something unfamiliar: 'the other'. However, if Surrealism defamiliarised the world it is not in order to become – or know – someone else, but to have a better recognition of one's 'self' by incorporating its own others. It attacked familiarity with the other, but in order to render the familiar as other; the ethnography of Griaule attempted to render the other as familiar. It is perhaps the final testament to Jean Rouch's work that he opened another path, one that navigates between the two trajectories of French Surrealism and ethnography.

NOTES

1   Written in the year of Breton's death. Interview with M. Foucault by C. Bonnefoy, originally published in *Arts et loisirs*, 54, October 1966; reprinted in Michel Foucault (2000) 'A Swimmer Between Two Words', *Aesthetics: Essential Works of Foucault 1954–1984, Vol. 2*, ed. J. D. Faubion. London: Penguin, 172.

2   Rouch's family moved frequently, and by his eleventh year he was living in Casablanca, Morocco. After being sent back to Paris in 1930 he remained there until its occupation by Nazis in 1940. See Stoller 1992: 5.

3   See Clifford 1988: 117–51. For a sustained critique of Clifford's essay see Richardson 1993.

4   One suspects that Bataille and Breton were using the various issues of *Minotaure* to battle out their intellectual differences, though they both had to remember that neither of them owned it. See my previous discussion of this in Bate 2004: 235–7.

5   In Griaule's report on the Mission he says that Eric Lutten took the responsibility for filming, which was often simultaneous shooting from different directions by European and indigenous observer/operators. See Griaule 1932: 5.

6   The Mission had three cameras and one cine camera. One camera was a stereo 6 x 13cm camera, the second was a 9 x 12 camera and the third a Leica 35mm. According to the source cited, Jacques Mercier, much of the material has been lost. See Jamin 1996: 82, n.51.

7   We might note here that Griaule's formalised distinctions between *extensive* and *intensive* observation in ethnography were already operative as informal rules used by photographers outside of ethnography. (On Griaule's methods see also Paul Henley's contribution to this volume). The use of photography as documents for a social purpose also required such methods – a photographer like Lewis Hine, for example, who attempted to show the problems of child labour in the US at the beginning of the twentieth century, developed rules for systematically photographing and labelling the images. (Additionally, such categories might assist in distinguishing methods in contemporary documentary work: Martin Parr's tourist work is mostly extensive-based and Richard Billingham's family work, such as *Rays a Laugh*, uses an intensive method.)

8   My translation, as are all Griaule quotations .

9   The first production Leica was available in 1925.

10 Mary Douglas argues that the different interests expressed by English and French anthropologists in the opposing divinities of the Dogon cosmos (the English interest in Nommo, the French in Yourougon) is itself determined by, or reflects cultural factors to do with, the indigenous culture of the observers rather than anything external. Thus she demonstrates a further level at which the choice of phenomena to study is itself not 'objective'. See Douglas 1995.

11 Of course, five years later, Benjamin had grown pessimistic about the distraction with which the masses consumed images: 'The same public which responds in a progressive manner toward a grotesque film is bound to respond in a reactionary way to Surrealism' (1992b: 247).

REFERENCES

Bate, D. (2004) *Photography and Surrealism: Sexuality, Colonialism and Social Dissent*. London: I. B. Tauris.

Benjamin, W. (1972 [1931]) 'A Short History of Photography', trans. S. Mitchell, *Screen*, 13, 1, 5–26

_____ (1992a [1931]) 'Surrealism: The Last Snapshot of the European Intelligentsia', in *One Way Street and Other Writings*. London: Verso, 225–39.

_____ (1992b [1936]) 'The Work of Art in the Age of Mechanical Reproduction', trans. H. Zohn. *Illuminations*. London: Fontana, 219–253.

Billingham, R. (1996) *Rays a Laugh*. Zurich: Scalo.

Clifford, J. (1988) *The Predicament of Culture*. London: Harvard University Press.

Cousins, M. (1989) 'In the Midst of Psychoanalysis, Lévi-Strauss on Mauss', *New Formations*, 7, Spring, 77–87.

Douglas, M. (1995) 'Reflexions sur le Renard pâle et Deux Anthropologies: à propos du surréalisme et de l'anthropolgie français', in C. W. Thompson (ed.) *L'Autre et le sacré: Surréalisme, Cinéma, Ethnologie*. Paris: L'Harmattan, 199–218.

Foucault, M. (2000 [1966]) 'A Swimmer Between Two Words', in J. D. Faubion (ed.) *Aesthetics: Essential Works of Foucault 1954–1984, Vol. 2*. London: Penguin, 171–4.

Griaule, M. (1932) *General Report on Mission Dakar-Djibouti, 1931–1932*. Paris: Macon.

_____ (1933) 'Introduction Méthodologique', *Minotaure*, 2, 6–12.

Jamin, J. (1996) *Miroir d'Afrique*. Paris : Gallimard.

Leiris, M. (1981 [1931] *L'Afrique fantôme*. Paris: Gallimard.

Lewis, H. (1990) *Dada Turns Red: The Politics of Surrealism*. Edinburgh: Edinburgh University Press.

Richardson, M. (1993) 'An Encounter of Wise Men and Cyclops Women', *Critique of Anthropology*, 13, 1, 57–75.

Rouch, J. (1979) 'The Camera and Man', in M. Eaton (ed.) *The Films of Jean Rouch*. London: British Film Institute, 54–63.

Stoller, P. (1992) *The Cinematic Griot: The Ethnography of Jean Rouch*. London: University of Chicago Press.

From fieldwork in Bukina Faso, 1956

16 WAYS OF SEEING: DOCUMENTARY FILM AND THE SURREAL OF REALITY

Elizabeth Cowie

The Aristotelian categories are not indeed the only ones which exist in our minds, or have existed in the mind and have to be dealt with. We must, before all else, compile as large as possible a catalogue of categories; we must begin with all those which we can know that mankind has used. Then it will be seen that in the firmament of reason there have been, and there still are, many moons that are dead, or pale, or obscure. (Mauss 1979: 32)

For me, as an ethnographer and filmmaker, there is almost no boundary bet-ween documentary film and films of fiction. The cinema, the art of the double, is already the transition from the real world to the imaginary world, and ethnography, the science of the thought systems of others, is a perma-nent crossing point from one conceptual universe to another. (in Marshall & Adams 2003: 188)

Jean Rouch was both scientist and artist. He produced a body of work that has made an extremely important contribution to cinema as well as anthropology, yet which is both controversial and challenging as a result of the way in which he sought to dissolve the boundaries conventionally imposed on these domains. This has led to a certain compartmentalisation of his achievements into scien-tific ethnography, his films of visual record, his documentaries and his 'ethno-fiction' films. Rouch, however, saw his contribution in all of these activities as being informed by his early encounter with Surrealism whose profound effect influenced his subsequent scientific, intellectual and creative work. I will exam-ine here the legacy of this encounter and its influence on Rouch's work and ex-plore the relation between the documentary evidential and the realm of dreams, of imagination and of the irrational which are central to the surrealist impulse Rouch draws upon.

1.

Rouch recounts discovering in a library two issues of *Minotaure*, one about the Dakar-Djibouti Mission whose cover was a 'reproduction of a Dogon painting in red, black, and white'. The other one had a cover by Giorgio de Chirico and Rouch comments: 'I was very impressed by that. And I will remember all of my life the photography in that one issue – I think it was by Griaule – of the Dama masks dancing on the terrace. It was something very strange.' He continues: 'It was the same that was in the paintings of de Chirico, the same as you find in the first paintings of Salvador Dalí, in Max Ernst, in the collages. It was this way to "jump", to "imagine". And in the middle of that there was this strange ritual that nobody could understand' (in DeBouzek 1989: 303).

For André Breton, juxtaposition was a central concept in his Surrealist Manifesto of 1924 where he cites Pierre Reverdy's declaration:

> The image is a pure creation of the mind. It cannot be born from a comparison but from a juxtaposition of two more or less distant realities. The more the relationship between the two juxtaposed realities is distant and true, the stronger the image will be – the greater its emotional power and poetic reality. (Cited in Breton 1969: 20)[1]

This is not a juxtaposition brought together by the mind as a comparison – but a juxtaposition which imposes itself on the senses and brings about an imagining.[2] The juxtaposed realities must be encountered, and not invented, and the strength of the resulting image is not inherent in the 'found' realities, but in the subject who apprehends the juxtaposition. For surrealists the found object's re-contextualisation produces a tension, an impropriety and incongruence which disturbs rationality and prompts associations which may be unconscious as well as conscious. The 'found object' (*'objet insolite'*) is both a material entity encountered by chance and contingent on an arbitrary moment and context, and an image as it is grasped imaginatively by the conscious or unconscious mind.[3] Surrealism here is directly materialist and empirical in that reality is the scene of a physical encounter with objects, natural phenomena and human actions, through which imagining arises. Ethnography might be understood as the study of 'found cultures', and of the role of a culture's appropriation of 'found objects' in its philosophy, belief system and social practices. Function is deduced not from the qualities of the object but the qualities of its use, its deployment as 'found'. The ethnologist encounters the world he or she will observe as always unknown, as found – whether so-called 'pristine' or not – thus subject to a coming to understand through his or her 'imagining'. In this approach, documentation – as Marcel Griaule argued – is the first and foremost method and activity.[4] James Clifford has suggested that

> The surrealist moment in ethnography is that moment in which the possibility of comparison exists in unmediated tension with sheer incongruity. This moment is repeatedly produced and smoothed over in the process of ethnographic comprehension. But to see this activity in terms of collage is to hold the surrealist moment in view ... Collage brings to the work (here the ethnographic text) elements that continually proclaim their foreignness to the context of presentation. (1988: 146)

The incongruity of the found juxtapositions and their strangeness exists not in the objects or practices as such but in the context of their apprehension, both the context of the ethnographer's or spectator's cultural difference, and the context of a documentary re-presentation, which will always produce a new moment of juxtaposition and potential incongruity.

2.

Rouch sought to think outside of and in opposition to the division between material reality, rational empiricism and logical thought, and dreams and poetry as non-logical thought, as shown by the two stories that Rouch returned to in interviews and his writing. One concerned his professor of engineering, Albert Caquot, who formulated a new theory of resistance to stress in building materials through what Rouch calls 'poetry', that is, an imaginative understanding. For Rouch, then, thinking is an act of progressive imagining in relation to observed phenomena (the documentary, whether written or filmed) that is not simply and conventionally logical. It is a kind of thinking which is of the same order as poetry in making leaps of association (see Rouch 2003b: 112).

In a second story, Rouch recalls Griaule's observation regarding Dogon thought systems – which gives great importance in their mythology to the star Sirius and the two companion stars they ascribe to it – that what was remarkable was that Sirius does indeed have a companion star but it is not visible to the naked eye. Rouch reacted by declaring 'Well, then, they can't see it', for which he was called an ass by Griaule! What he understood by Griaule's retort was that he, Rouch, was reasoning within his own thought-system and not the Dogon, and Rouch goes on to explain: 'It's not renouncing our Cartesianism; it's considering the possibility that, besides our Cartesianism, besides our so-called scientific explanations, there are others. To ignore them means that we have an imperialist attitude.' Rouch speculates that: 'it was necessary for the Dogon observing

Sirius to introduce an element of disorder, a companion, which determines both the anomalies of the Sirius' trajectory and the anomalies of the [Dogon] creation myth' (2003b: 111–12). In holding together, juxtaposing, these two approaches to understanding a natural phenomenon, Rouch makes possible greater understanding of each (2003b: 113–14).

3.

In its critique of rationalism and its narratives of causality, Surrealism deployed the documentary evidential to produce unexpected connections which demand that we reassess our assumptions about the fact in its traditional, proper place, as a result of its new, improper, re-placing. Writing on Georges Bataille's contribution to the journal *Documents*, founded in 1929, Dominique Lecoq concludes that 'if logic masks the gaping inadequacies of the logos, Bataille, in impelling *Documents* to expose all the contradictions, chose both to uphold logic and to remove the mask' (in Brotchie 1995: 11). In Rouch's cinema, it is this double move that he, too, upholds.

Documents presented the new ethnography of Griaule and Michel Leiris emerging in France and, drawing on their work, the journal took examples from widely different cultures, and made connections appear where they were least expected. For co-founder Georges Bataille, in his contributions to the journal, the object was not art but evidence, not literature, but documents. It was a way of writing, Lecoq has suggested, that was capable of overturning the code of branches of knowledge without constituting in itself a closed, complete body of knowledge. Thus, he writes, Bataille 'called upon philosophy, ethnology, economics, psychoanalysis, not to borrow their results but to open up the notions they defined in new, illegitimate, unacceptable directions' (ibid.).[5] The object, and material reality, as referential and as the documentary evidential, are mobilised in ethnography, collage, art work or film, but as *re*-presented they are also displaced from their referential purposefulness. There is a change brought about by our imaginative understanding that Breton called a '*mutation de rôle*' (1972: 280). Evidence and the factual constitute the materiality of the documentary representation, therefore, not only as content but also as a form.

What arises is a 'seeing anew' in an estrangement through which the everyday and the taken for granted is re-presented. The documentary evidential is materially referential but, because brute reality is contingent and ephemeral, because it is something that just keeps happening, uncaused, it also exceeds the referential it invokes. While it engages us to make sense of and comprehend it as factual, the documentary evidential can also open us to the absence of meaning and the factual's appearance as uncaused.

The documentary film voices reality through organising its sights and sounds, but the space and time of the contingent reality recorded will nonetheless exceed the factual it is claimed to represent and, as a result, may engage us in an imaginative speculation as we become aware of what is not represented. This 'unrepresented' is what is off-frame, out of sight of the camera, and thus of the spectator, but which we can infer or speculate about, whether it is the rest of a landscape we are not shown, or the women workers whom we can see but never hear. It is an omission which we must evaluate: is it the result of chance or a deliberate act? Does it have aesthetic or political implications, or both? Representation, as Jacques Derrida has reminded us, both makes absent as it makes present, and it makes non-sense as it makes sense, or meaning, in representing. Documentary, like other forms of art, is concerned with the transformation of the ephemeral and the transitory into the significant through re-presentation and it, too, both anxiously commemorates as loss what is not preserved, recorded, remembered while disavowing it as significant, as necessary to its status as representing reality.

The unrepresented as the unacknowledged, unexplained and inexplicable in the contingent reality shown, negates the documentary feel of the images and sounds we see and hear, and as a result we may apprehend not merely the unrepresented but also the unrepresentable. Jacques Lacan has called this the 'real' in his tripartite scheme of the real, the imaginary and the symbolic (see Lacan 1977: 53) and which, while unrepresentable, nevertheless bears on us, palpable but unspeakable. Like the slips of the tongue or jokes that we make in our everyday lives, which Freud analysed as the 'return of the repressed' of the unconscious, the real can be felt in reality, encountered as the contingent, as the uncaused in reality that, while it may be named 'fate', nevertheless remains incomprehensible – that is, it is 'senseless' within our everyday common sense or rationality. The obviousness of reality, and of our look, which finds and possesses the world through our images in a logic of knowledge and understanding is put into question. For while forms of remembering may recollect 'cruel fate' into an orderliness of remembrance, however painful, it may also be re-encountered in the symptoms of trauma – that is, as the real which, while unrepresentable, is nevertheless made palpable by the way in which its absence, its non-representability, is signified.

4.

David Bate has argued that we must understand the surreal not as a type of image (or object) but a type of meaning or rather, of non-meaning, of a contradiction, ambiguity or veiling of meaning, enigmatic in fact (see Bate 2004: 23).[6] The surreal appears whenever we encounter the absence and thus failure of meaning which, much as nature abhors a vacuum, we seek to fill, yet for all the answers we may offer we cannot be certain which, or even if any, are true. The surrealist work – text, object or image – deploys reality to produce an encounter with that reality which is experienced as excessive and uncanny, disturbing our sense of what we expect the world to be like, appearing instead as unverisimilitudinous.

The surreal is experienced in our encounter with reality, or is that which we are brought to encounter through seeing again with the eyes of another – artist, photographer, cinematographer? This might be the 'found' as incongruities arising from natural but absurdist juxtapositions that jar and reverberate, challenging our expectations, which arise in Diane Arbus's work; or the visual traces of the unconscious, suggested in Brassai's *Rolled bus ticket* (1932), for example, as 'automatic image', documentary evidence of an unthinking action which betrays a psychological state to which the object bears no necessary or mimetic relation.[7]

In the documentary surreal we are grasped by the evidential as enigmatic signifier. Held by its unmeaning, we engage the traumatic, but spurred to make sense we embark on a process of translation through which we produce an account, an interpretation, which 'works'. Nowhere is this process made more necessary, and with more diverse interpretations, than in Luis Buñuel's film *Las Hurdes* (*Land Without Bread*, aka *Tierra sin pan*, 1933), which documents the circumstances of life – and death – of the communities in the Hurdes Altas region of Spain, notorious for the poverty of its land and people.[8] But the images alone could not show what Buñuel also observed, a 'land without bread, without songs', remaining obstinately enigmatic without the voice-over narration. For how else to convey how precious goats are, and how vulnerable they are to the dangers of the sheer mountain cliffs? Or that transporting the beehives to the mountains for the summer is a dangerous and risky journey for both the men and the animals carrying the bees? We see a harsh but awesomely beautiful landscape, yet we cannot see the physical and economic difficulties of scraping a living from this same landscape until it is intellectually rather than visually observed for us. The visible must be articulated as evidence.[9]

The work – and poverty – of *Las Hurdes* is narrated without, however, placing its story in a wider context through which we can understand causes: it is not explained as either natural and God-given, or the result of the peasants' ignorance, or solely due to the calumny of the exploiting classes of government and landowners. Failing to identify causes for the dire condition of the Hurdanos, the film's epistemological stance is scandalously neutral; it states just 'the facts' without making 'sense' of them, for example by resolving them into an account of the justice and injustice of the plight of the people, and thus the possible routes of action.[10] The life of the Hurdanos is 'made strange' by the film because, unexplained, it is inexplicable – how and why are these people without work, without land from which they can produce enough food to eat and without access to the medicines and education of modern society? The hardships the film relentlessly states are senseless and absurd in the perspective of modernism, that is, surreal.[11] In making apparent the non-sense of reality Buñuel challenges us to consider how we find meaning in the factual, that is, interpret it.

5.

The documentary evidential of cinema is firstly a space and a time, it is a *mise-en-scène* of action, reaction and of becoming. This is the ground of the present-tense of film that nevertheless includes its becoming past, as record. Film always shows both a 'now' and a 'then', so that the reality it re-presents – whether fictional story or documentary – is temporally inherently doubled. What is involved in documentary film surrealism is a 'found' *mise-en-scène* that brings into the same space what is not 'normally' adjacent, opening up associations and oppositions, inciting a certain horror, or pleasure, at the improprieties. Cinema as the art of the double and of dreaming enables a surrealism as well as a realism in its recording of reality. In Rouch's ethnographic films of record, as well as in his documentary fictions, a surrealism arises through the representing in his films rather than or as well as the represented; that is, through how we come to see, as well as what we see, as we apprehend the juxtaposing (collaging) and not only what is juxtaposed.

The found image or object is encountered in an experience which, whether brutal or beautiful, is equally captivating. Rouch has spoken of the importance for him of de Chirico's paintings, where the juxtapositions open the spectator to latent or potential meanings arising both in the cultural – and conventional – connotations of the depicted, and in the spectator's response to these *conjoined* connotations which thus spur further associations motivated by the spectator's emotional response. Describing de Chirico's lighthouse imagery, Rouch says 'this was an architecture of dream', through which the spectator will come to 'dream' herself, wakeful and as a kind of daydream. Rouch asserts: 'I've never considered craziness to be pathological, and I always considered it normal to dream. I've always been a very good dreamer; I've even written poems from my dreams' (in Taylor 2003: 132–3). For Breton, Surrealism was 'the resolution of these two states, dream and reality, which are seemingly so contradictory, into a kind of absolute reality, a *surreality*' (1969: 14). It was not only the external world that might provide 'found objects' but also manifestations of the mind's involuntary – unconscious – workings. Breton drew upon Freud's account of the unconscious and dreaming, as well as developing processes of 'automatic writing' as forms of 'controlled possession' through which to access the unconscious and that can be uncovered or revealed in reality. The dream, or image, can be read and analysed. It was Freud who gave voice and significance to the interpretation of dreams as access to knowledge about the unconscious, and who asserted the reality of fantasy and the imaginary in human psychology. Yet he was an ambivalent figure for Surrealism, for Freud also pathologised the unconscious and constituted psychoanalysis as a science and a hermeneutics.[12] Freud's project is deeply rationalist and, as Foucault has argued, in the West 'madness' as a category of human behaviour and psychology was constructed in opposition and as other to the rationality of sanity. Rouch himself has said of Freud: 'I saw that he was not a dreamer himself but was rather exploiting dreams – like Karl Marx' (in Taylor 2003: 132). Freud, however, in what he termed 'the navel of the dream', also asserted that there was a certain element in the dream which was uninterpretable, a non-sense (Freud 1961: 157). Here, as well as in his concept of disavowal, Freud affirms the way in which our relation to knowing, to the factual and the rational, is doubled and contradictory. Similarly Breton sees the contingent in the found object and image, which, as objective chance, is also ambiguous so that while it might be recorded and analysed, it retains a core of mystery or uncertainty. In his concept of the real Lacan drew on the insights of Surrealism (with which he was closely associated in the 1930s) while developing Freud's idea of an 'unplumbable' element in the unconscious.[13]

To Rouch, like Luis Buñuel, dreaming was a form of reality not only experienced in sleep in which one is other to oneself in a form of doubling: 'I brought dreams directly into my films, trying as hard as I could to avoid any analysis … The dream is just as real, maybe more so than reality. It's what I tried to do … jumping between the two' (Buñuel 1984: 92).[14]

6.

Rouch adopted the idea of a 'participatory camera' from Robert Flaherty, involving the people he filmed closely in the process itself, to produce, in Rouch's words, a 'ciné-dialogue', where there is no longer object and subject and 'knowledge is no longer a stolen secret' later to be consumed in another place, at another time, by another culture (2003: 185). This collaboration is also a work of transference and counter-transference in which filmmaker and participants variously may seek to provide what he or she understands – consciously or unconsciously – the other, the filmmaker, as wanting or desiring. Rouch commented that 'currently I am at the point of reflecting on my own role as a taker and giver of doubles, as an eater and shower of reflections … to clarify these roles in relation to the self of the ethnographer and ethnography itself' (2003: 184). Rouch is no longer an observer/camera but a participant who is in a form of trance, for 'the camera becomes a magic object that can unleash or accelerate the phenomena of possession' because it leads the filmmaker onto paths he would otherwise never dare to take, 'guiding him to something that we scarcely understand: cinematographic creativity' – in a form of automatism (ibid.). In filming *Les Tambours d'avant: Tourou et Bitti* (1971), Rouch suggests that the '*ciné-transe*' he experiences played the role of catalyst in bringing about the possession of the dancers.[15]

In his concept of the *ciné-transe* Rouch draws on the Songhay-Zarma theory of the person as split, 'founded on the notion of a "double" or *bia*, who represents shadow, reflection, and the soul, all at the same time', and which exists in a parallel world of doubles that is also the place of the imaginary (2003: 86, 183). This *bia* is tied to the body but may temporarily leave it during sleep, in dreaming, or when awake in a state of imagination or reflection; it also occurs in possession however, when the *bia* is replaced by the spirit or god, but is preserved in a protective fresh skin. The magician can voluntarily project his double who can then journey to the land of the doubles in order to guide or defend the community (though this is not without danger). The sorcerer, too, can project his double but here the purpose is for evil, to cause death by stealing the *bia* of victims. Rouch is possessed and thus separated from his *bia* in the *ciné-transe*, and also, like the sorcerer, is a hunter of doubles, while at the same time he is like the magician who directs his *bia*, and who returns the double – the filmed images – in a process which contributes to the community.[16] Both cinema, as a world of doubles, and Rouch's role as filmmaker/magician, were recognised by the Songhay-Zarma in their invitations to him to film their procession ceremonies, notably the *hauka*. For the camera is a magical other/double through which a world and an audience not present but imagined is addressed not only by Rouch but also by the participants. Cinema – documentary or fiction – is a production of a performing for others, a being seen and heard.

Rouch brings to his filmmaking his awareness of the concern of Surrealism with the split and multiple subjects, and retains a hesitation between rational and irrational explanation in his claims for the *ciné-transe*. Indeed, he emphasises that for the Songhay-Zarma the two worlds are so interpenetrated 'that it is almost impossible for the uninformed observer to distinguish the real from the imaginary in them. "I met Ali yesterday" can just as easily mean "I really met Ali yesterday" as "I dreamed about, I thought about, Ali yesterday". And when the observer gets used to this gymnastic, he disturbs the real as well as the imaginary' (2003: 96). Rouch's documentary fictions are therefore perhaps themselves special forms of *holey*, of 'play' and of possession in performing as one's double.

The reality given to the world of the imaginary is not delusion, but a certain kind of knowing or knowledge-relation which parallels Freud's notion of disavowal (see his essay 'Fetishism' from 1927), of knowing and not knowing, or of two knowledges each of which contradicts the other, which he saw as central to the splitting of the psyche.

7.

In *Les Maîtres fous* (1955) Rouch viscerally confronted audiences with the paradoxes of making sense of the reality we engage in as subjects and as spectators of his films. The film presents the juxtaposition of modernity – colonial British – and tradition in this *hauka* possession ritual of Songhay-Zarma migrants from French Niger in Accra, British Ghana. It is a documentary rather than simply a record, for it also presents the context of the migrants in Accra and their work, and introduces individuals who we will later see in the possession ritual, and the film then returns to this 'normality' at the end. Moreover, Rouch concludes the film with the claim that, in the mastering performed by *hauka* adepts, the participants have 'resolved, through violent crises, their adjustment to today's world' and thus he redeems the horrific scenes of the ritual. The possession rite is a weekly event, repeated just like their encounter with colonial modernity is repeated, and many of the spirits take the form of colonial figures – the Governor-General and so forth. The film aroused enormous criticism on its first viewing, and continues to powerfully divide viewers both regarding what we learn in the film and how we should understand the behaviour of the *hauka* adepts it shows us. The problem of interpretation makes palpable something of the real that the ritual itself also engages in relation to the process of possession. Tracing these problems of interpretation makes apparent the film's surrealism.

The ritual is undertaken within a carefully staged *mise-en-scène*, motivated by the forms taken by the spirits on entering their human 'horses'. A termite hill is painted to represent the Governor-General's palace, with a crude wooden likeness of him standing over the ceremony and patterned cloth representing the Union Jack flying overhead. There is also a cinema poster for three films, including *The Mark of Zorro*.[17] All these are kinds of 'found objects' whose redeployment produces a change of role, a '*mutation de rôle*'. Like all *holey* ceremonies it is highly theatrical and while this might appear burlesque to outsiders, its aim is neither parody nor critique. The ritual was interpreted by many – including the British authorities – as a parody of, and thus as also a resistance to, colonialism. However, while the *hauka* spirit world is peopled at least in part by colonial figures, this is not simply a self-conscious intention, since it is the spirit that chooses the adept (that is, the master) and not vice-versa. Moreover many of the spirits do not lend themselves to this interpretation, for example the truck driver and train engineer; here the *hauka* are possessed by the spirits connected to the new powers of technology. The eating of the dog, which breaks a taboo of the British colonial powers, enacts not mockery but an overcoming and absorption of that power, for the *hauka* show they are stronger. Previously it had been pig that was eaten, which is forbidden to Muslims like the *hauka* adepts. More importantly, as Rouch says in the film, these were 'powerful new gods who most certainly are not to be mocked'. The ritual's mimicry bears witness to the Songhay-Zarma encounter with the otherness of French and British colonialism, but also with Islam and North African and Arab culture. To read the ritual as motivated whether consciously or unconsciously by anti-colonialism is to offer a Western psychological explanation, as against the role claimed for it by the community itself. As Paul Henley shows, drawing on Rouch's ethnography, the *hauka* are one of six *holey* sects all of which associate spirits 'with alterity, exemplified by various ethnic Others with whom the Songhay have come into contact at certain moments in their history' (2006: 751).[18] The *holey* spirits are invoked to help protect or are consulted over problems for which their remedy is sought. Rouch's voice-over interpretation of the ritual can be related to its 'healing' role shown in the film in relation to the adept who confesses a transgression to the priest – that he has slept with his friend's girlfriend and subsequently has been impotent for two months – and is later possessed as 'Major Mugu'. As the film progresses and the ceremony finishes, the voice-over claims that he is cured and that his girlfriend is 'very happy' as a result. 'Possession, after all', as Rouch notes in commenting on Genet's *The Blacks*, 'was the original theatre, the idea of catharsis' (2003: 217).

What characterises the spirits is that they are otherworldly, and thus 'by very definition will behave in abnormal, outlandish ways' (Henley 2006: 755). The breaking of taboos marks the spirit as non-human, unrestrained by any rules. Henley suggests that the Songhay have looked to exotic Others to provide the models for the spirits because, 'in Lévi-Strauss's celebrated phrase with regard to Australian totems, these powerful Others are "good to think with", not about the nature of human beings, but about the nature of spirit beings' (2006: 752). Rouch asserts, 'there's an attitude of both mockery and respect in *Les Maîtres fous*; they're *playing* gods of strength' (in Marshall & Adams 2003: 189). As a result, Rouch suggests, the *hauka* were 'a fascinating model to follow' for young African students, as 'people who are afraid of nothing' (ibid.) just like the Europeans who do whatever they want, including breaking the taboos of others. Here he proposes what might be a self-conscious motive, yet the model can only be imitated through becoming possessed in a performance of unconsciousness.

What seems to be acknowledged through the *holey* sects is an otherness which enters the community but which it cannot direct or control, whether this is nature, incoming neighbours or Islam. The power of the other is signified in the deployment of its signs while it is also superseded by the superior power of the spirit, demonstrated by the inversion and transgression performed by the spirit through the *hauka* adept. The ritual presents an in-mixing of elements which remain distinct in a drama of their very juxtaposition, a conjoined image of embodied self and spirit, of power and weakness, where the abject and taboo are celebrated and valorised. The boundary of self and other is permeated as meaning and identity slips between, for the adept both is and is not the spirit, both partaking in the spirit's power and disowning it as much as he or she is disowned by it. Rouch comments: 'it was like Buñuel's attitude to the Church. You cannot feel sacrilegious if you do not respect your opponent. What the *hauka* did was very creative and implicitly revolutionary, just as the authorities feared' (2003: 218). It is a 'found' surrealism.

Henley uses the term 'thick inscription' to refer to film's capacity to show a detail and level of information that cannot easily be contained by explanatory voice-over, and is therefore especially appropriate in viewing *Les Maîtres fous*.[19] It should be added, however, that the 'meaning potential' arises not only from the complex and multiple reality recorded, but also in its juxtaposition across the film, and its impact upon audiences as shocking and impossible to assimilate within conventional (Western) understanding. As important as what we see is what we hear. The soundscape of the film includes much of the direct sound recorded, with the incantations of the *hauka* audible, as well as the single-stringed instrument used to call down the *hauka* spirits.[20] Rouch had sought to translate the speech but the glossolalaic mix of French and English made this impossible. DeBouzek describes how Rouch, having worked closely with one of the members of the cult on an interpretation of the events and recorded speech, 'decided to set his notes aside, doing the final voice-over without a written script. According to him, that first narration was part of his own "possession" by film, part of his personal ciné-trance' (1989: 308). Rouch's voice-over during the possession ritual both describes and explains, but he also re-enacts as he adopts the voices of the possessed dancers and the spirits that possess them; the pace and tone of his voice shifts, appearing perhaps to be as much possessed as the dancers themselves in this strange further doubling whereby the spirits, and the possessed, speak through Rouch as if he is also possessed. There is a marked contrast between his voice-over at these times, and where he is offering an explanatory description, at the beginning and end, and over the insert of shots of the British Governor, troops and the opening of the State Government.[21]

Rouch observed that 'every sort of force has attacked them [the *hauka*] and me for filming them – the colonialists who don't like the portrait, African revolutionaries who don't like the primitivism, anti-vivesectionists who don't like the sacrificial murder' (2003: 218). In the trance the adepts are indeed 'inhuman' for they are *hauka*, while nevertheless able to resume themselves as very much human, as Rouch shows in the film's closure. Is it not a Western gaze and its ideas of the world that can give rise to the fear Rouch claimed was experienced by the Senegalese director, Blaise Senghor? In Rouch's account, as he emerged from a public screening in Paris, Senghor felt that others in the audience looked at him with the thought: 'Here's another one who is going to eat a dog!' Such a gaze sees the possession ceremonies of the *hauka* as typical of all West African behaviour and it assumes a unified subjectivity to such 'dog-eaters', in contrast to the clearly doubled world of the *hauka* in which we are witnessing a theatre of performance that is unscripted or, rather, scripted by the *hauka* and not by the adepts. It is the spirit who eats the dog, not the man. The practice of possession and the philosophy of human and non-human it responds to undoes our sense-making of this film – we cannot produce a logic of cause and effect with reference to verifiable evidence. Prerana Reddy (2007) has argued that it is by exposing the constructedness of Western rationality that the *hauka* 'were making the most effective critique of all' but it is a critique 'found' by the 'Western' viewer – who might also be Nigerien and Muslim, not only white and Christian.

It is not the *hauka* adepts who are irrational, rather it is the spirits who are outside human sense, who are 'unreasonable'; that is, who act outside the decorum of what is proper, expected, human action. For what is held to be rational is more often a matter of verisimilitude, an action being either what we expect as likely, or being properly – with due propriety – motivated. The film juxtaposes two different orders of verisimilitude, two contexts of understanding in a collage that does not produce a mixing, that is not a dialectic that can be resolved into synthesis and that is not a dialogic encounter. The informed and anti-colonial Western viewer who can recognise that the ritual is a performance but where the performer is neither consciously acting the part, nor mad, but is acting on behalf of another, is nevertheless confronted by another non-sense which touches more closely the real. For who or what is this other directing the possessed?

Possession, like the automatic writing of the surrealists, as well as hypnosis and suggestion, opens the person to forces he or she is not self-consciously directing. In each case what we have is an observable phenomenon for which unverifiable explanations or understandings are offered. In Songhay-Zarma philosophy, the possession ceremony is a performance in reality by a possessing spirit who is not the double of the medium, but displaces this double in order to enter the medium's body and mind, who is therefore now other to herself. To the anthropologist, its benefit is a relation to the spirit whom the community can consult and receive advice from. For psychoanalysis, the possession is equally real – but as an effect of the processes of the unconscious, yet one in which a kernel of non-sense remains that Lacan calls the real.[22]

Rouch describes how disturbed he and the others involved in the filming were after recording the possession ceremony and that he said to Damouré Zika: 'We really made a bad film, it's very cruel.' They decided to go out the next day to see what the participants were doing and at Damouré's suggestion this became the epilogue, producing a closure for the filmmakers. Rouch also tells the story of his friend Tallou Mouzourane who was very shocked by what he had seen and declared that 'everything is fake. All this is fake', to which their driver answered that Tallou should be careful, or the *hauka* would take revenge. Two weeks later, Rouch claimed, Tallou was possessed (2003: 191). Not only is Rouch's own uncertainty as to the propriety of what he had seen and filmed shown here, but also the powerful impact of their experience of the ceremony. Rouch accepts the reality of the possession rites, and his own 'possession' during filming – and thus of a certain 'strangeness' of the self to itself – without resolving in this film, or in his later comments about it, what such possession implies for the person and for our notion of the person.[23] The interaction demonstrated by this film, and which is central to all Rouch's work, involves us as spectators in an encounter with the strangeness of ourselves and not only of the other. As in *Petit à petit* (1968–69) the surreal of reality is not only that of a non-Western culture for the European, but also of the Western culture for the non-European.

NOTES

1   Breton comments that, 'these words, however sibylline for the uninitiated, were extremely revealing, and I pondered them for a long time. But the image eluded me. Reverdy's aesthetic, a completely *a posteriori* aesthetic, led me to mistake the effects for the causes' (1969: 20).

2   Breton later argues: 'The principle of the association of ideas, such as we conceive of it, militates against it. Or else we would have to revert to an elliptical art, which Reverdy deplores as much as I. We are therefore obliged to admit that the two terms of the image are not deduced one from the other by the mind for the specific purpose of producing the spark, that they are the simultaneous products of the activity I call surrealist, reason's role being limited to taking note of, and appreciating, the luminous phenomenon' (1969: 37). For Breton Surrealism was, in its challenge to rationalism and traditional literature, a highly political project and this is an aspect in Rouch's work as well. Breton was, of course, a member of

the Communist Party between 1926 and 1933.

3   Such objects are not bizarre or strange until they strike us thus, that is, their bizarreness is a quality of perception in the viewer and not in the object itself. Hal Foster addresses this, and the fantasy as well as fetishism implicated in the formed and deformed surrealist image. See Foster 1995: 57–100.

4   That is, documentation using a wide variety of media, and which emerges from long-term fieldwork involving not only immersion in the culture but also 'initiation' through dialogue with informants'/'wise teachers'. See Stoller 1992: 19.

5   This is cited in *Encyclopaedia Acephalica*, a selection of works from both *Documents* and *Encyclopaedia Da Costa*, on which I have drawn for my summary here.

6   See more on the 'enigmatic signifier' in Laplanche 1999: 165.

7   For Rosalind Krauss, the surreal photographic object is a reality deformed and not simply found, since only in this way can the referentiality of the 'documentary' photograph be displaced (1981: 29). This view of course preserves the role of the artist-author. I am arguing, by contrast, that no visual record is simply referential – that is, its resemblance to reality may not affirm reality if the referent is unfamiliar, for here instead it risks appearing uncanny.

8   William Rothman points out that the film has traditionally been viewed as a 'social documentary', exposing society's problems, but is now more commonly viewed and taught as a 'mock documentary'. His account of the film makes clear its surrealist use of image and narration, but he sees the goal of its surrealism as being 'to reveal the truth, however it shocks us', whereas I am emphasising the failure of meaning, of any revelation of truth that thereby gives rise to our demand for it (1997: 37).

9   The film was shot silent. A soundtrack of voice-over commentary and music (Brahms) was only added by Buñuel in 1936, after the ban on the film was lifted and it was screened in France.

10 Buñuel described not just the tone of the voice-over but also the text itself as deliberately neutral (in Macdonald & Cousins 1996: 88). Rouch, who was strongly influenced by Buñuel's earlier films in collaboration with Salvador Dalí, spoke of *Las Hurdes* as an example of an ethnographic film 'where the commentary is in direct counterpoint to the images ... the violently subjective text brings the necessary oral cruelty to match the unbearably cruel visuals' (2003: 142). Rouch notes that Buñuel saw his film *Les Maitres fous*, saying that 'he was fascinated and afraid' (ibid.).

11 Thus, while many have seen this film as in sharp contrast to his earlier films made with Salvador Dalí, *Un chien andalou* (*An Andalusian Dog*, 1929) and *L'Âge d'or* (*Age of Gold*, 1930), Buñuel insists that in filming reality he was remaining within the spirit of Surrealism and says that although these first two films are 'imagina-

tive' and *Las Hurdes* is taken from reality, 'I feel it shares the same outlook' (in Macdonald & Cousins 1996: 88).

12 I have explored psychoanalysis, film and dreaming more extensively in 'The Cinematic Dream-work of Ingmar Bergman's *Wild Strawberries*' (see Cowie 2003).

13 In his book *Photography and Surrealism*, David Bate analyses with great insight the relation of Lacan's thinking to Surrealism and in particular to Breton's work. See in particular the chapter 'The Automatic Image' (2004: 54–87). Margaret Iverson argues that, moreover, Breton's 'found object' is the model for Lacan's notion of the *objet a*, that object by which the subject is enabled to separate from the real but which is thereby marked by the real at the same time as enabling desire (2004: 49).

14 Rouch comments of Buñuel, paraphrasing him, that 'his ability to cross the barrier between dream and reality is equally comparable: the sudden switch to the other side of the mirror. The dream is just as real, maybe more so, than reality. It's what I tried to do in *Moi, un noir* – or in *La pyramide humaine* – jumping between the two' (2003: 143).

15 See Michael Chanan's contribution in this volume.

16 The Songhay-Zarma, who are also Muslims, hold that this parallel world does not extend beyond death to the realm of the hereafter, managed by God.

17 Directed by Rouben Mamoulian, it is set around 1820, starring Tyrone Power as the son of a California nobleman returning from Spain to find his native land under a villainous dictatorship. The film might be read as itself anti-colonialist referring, as an American film, to not only Spanish but also to British colonial rule. The inclusion of the poster within the setting of the ritual thus references both doubling and transgression.

18 The essay is a valuable review of the ethnography of the *hauka* and the debate the film gave rise to.

19 Henley is here adapting Clifford Geertz's (1973) expression 'thick description'.

20 See also Michael Chanan's contribution in this volume.

21 The poetic nature of Rouch's voice-over arising from the rhythmic pace and repetitive structure that DeBouzek suggests is less apparent in the voice-over in English that Rouch recorded.

22 Jean-François Lyotard (1988) introduced the concept of the 'differend' to articulate the incommensurability of two views, two beliefs, that are held by opposed groups.

23 Rouch notes that in *hauka* possession adepts might be possessed by several spirits, but always the same ones and that 'it's a question of personal character, which suddenly decides what type of god will possess you' (2003: 190), implying that this is a matter of the psychology of the adept.

REFERENCES

Bate, D. (2004) *Photography and Surrealism: Sexuality, Colonialism and Social Dissent*. London: I. B. Tauris.

Breton, A. (1969 [1924]) 'Surrealist Manifesto', in *Manifestoes of Surrealism*, trans. R. Seaver and H. R. Lane. Ann Arbor: University of Michigan Press, 1–47.

____ (1969 [1936]) *Le surréalisme et la peinture*. Paris: Gallimard.

____ (1972 [1936]) *Surrealism and Painting*, trans. S. Watson Taylor. London: Macdonald.

Brotchie, A. (1995) 'Introduction', *Encyclopaedia Acephalica*. London: Atlas Press, 9–28.

Buñuel, L. (1984) *My Last Sigh*. New York: Vintage.

Clifford, J. (1988) *The Predicament of Culture*. Cambridge, MA: Harvard University Press.

Cowie, E. (2003) 'The Cinematic Dream-work of Ingmar Bergman's *Wild Strawberries*', in A. Sabbadini (ed.) *The Couch and the Silver Screen: Psychoanalytic Analytic Reflections on European Cinema*. London: Brenner-Routledge, 181–201.

DeBouzek, J. (1989) 'The "Ethnographic Surrealism" of Jean Rouch', *Visual Anthropology*, 2, 3/4, 301–15.

Foster, H. (1995) *Compulsive Beauty*. Cambridge, MA: MIT Press.

Foucault, M. (1984) *This is Not a Pipe*, trans. Richard Miller. Berkeley: University of California Press.

Freud, S. (1953 [1900]) *The Interpretation of Dreams. The Standard Edition of the Complete Works of Sigmund Freud*, vols 4 and 5. London: The Hogarth Press.

____(1961 [1927]) 'Fetishism', in *The Standard Edition of the Complete Works of Sigmund Freud*, vol. 21. London: The Hogarth Press, 152–9.

Geertz, C. (1973) *The Interpretation of Cultures: Selected Essays*. New York: Basic Books.

Henley, P. (2006) 'Spirit-possession, witchcraft and the absent presence of Islam: a re-appraisal of *Les Maîtres fous*', *Journal of the Royal Anthropological Society*, 12, 4, 731–61.

Iverson, M. (2004) 'Readymade, Found Object, Photograph', *Art Journal*, 63, 2, Summer, 44–57.

Krauss, R. (1981) 'The Photographic Conditions of Surrealism', *October*, 19, Winter, 3–34.

Lacan, J. (1977) *The Four Fundamental Concepts of Psycho-Analysis*. Harmondsworth: Penguin.

Laplanche, J. (1999) 'Interpretation between Determinism and Hermeneutics', in *Essays on Otherness*. London: Routledge, 138–65.

Lecoq, D. (1985) 'Documents, Acéphale, Critique: Bataille autour des revues', in Jan

Versteeg (ed.) *Georges Batailles, Actes du colloque d'Amsterdam*. Amsterdam: Rodopi, 117–30.

Lyotard, J.-F. (1988) *The Differend: Phrases in Dispute*. Minneapolis: University of Minnesota Press.

Macdonald, K. and M. Cousins (eds) (1996) *Imagining Reality*. London: Faber and Faber.

Marshall, J. and J. Adams (2003 [1977] 'The Politics of Visual Anthropology', in *Ciné-ethnography*, ed. and trans. S. Feld. Minneapolis: University of Minnesota Press, 188–209.

Mauss, M. (1979) 'Real and Practical Relations Between "Psychology and Sociology"', in M. Mauss (ed.) *Sociology and Psychology: Essays*, trans. B. Brewster. London: Routledge and Kegan Paul, 1–33.

Reddy. P. (2007) 'The Poesis of Mimesis in *Les Maîtres fous*: Looking Back at the Conspiratorial Ethnography of Jean Rouch', http://www.africanfilmny.org/network/news/TO1m2reddy (accessed 21 April 2007).

Rothman, W. (1997) *Documentary Classics*. Cambridge: Cambridge University Press.

Rouch, J. (2003a [1973] 'The Camera and Man', in *Ciné-ethnography*, ed. and trans. S. Feld. Minneapolis: University of Minnesota Press, 29–46.

_____ (2003b) [1978]) 'The Mad Fox and the Pale Master', in *Ciné-ethnography*, ed. and trans. S. Feld. Minneapolis: University of Minnesota Press, 102–26.

Stoller, P. (1992) *The Cinematic Griot: The Ethnography of Jean Rouch*. Chicago: University of Chicago Press.

Taylor, L. (2003 [1990]) 'A Life on the Edge of Film and Anthropology', in *Ciné-ethnography*, ed. and trans. S. Feld. Minneapolis: University of Minnesota Press, 129–46.

Still from the film *Cinémafia*, 1980

17 *CINÉMAFIA* – JEAN ROUCH WITH JORIS IVENS AND HENRI STORCK

Dirk Nijland

In 1980, Professor Adrian Gerbrands, an anthropologist and a filmmaker at the University of Leiden offered Jean Rouch an honorary doctorate in recognition of his contribution to visual anthropology as part of the 405th anniversary of the university. Jean Rouch refused, as he would not be seen in the traditional academic toga and, on a more serious note, he was very upset that Joris Ivens, the 'father' of Dutch documentary film, had been denied his Dutch citizenship for many years because of his left-wing politics and was never offered anything by a Dutch university in recognition of his work. Rouch wanted Ivens to receive the honour instead.

Rouch eventually did agree to receive the doctorate from Leiden University but asked that Ivens, Henri Storck, the 'father' of Belgian documentary film, and his old colleague Germaine Dieterlen attend the ceremony. He requested three rolls of film to make a record of Ivens and Storck as a way of honouring Ivens in Holland. One roll would be too little as the occasion may become rather emotional, as he explained.

Rouch used staff and ex-students from Leiden University to assist him with the production of *Cinémafia*. The film was edited by Rogier Busschots and Dirk Nijland (Professor Gerbrands' assistant) from Leiden.

Below is the dialogue of the film, wherein Rouch (behind the camera) is in conversation with Ivens and Storck. The filming took place in Katwijk, the Netherlands, on the North Sea shore where Ivens shot his only fiction film *The Breakers* in 1929.

Joris Ivens: Jean, this is nice, the lens and you...

Jean Rouch: Were you here in 1929?

JI: Yes, I filmed here *The Breakers* with Franken[1] and the actor and writer Jef Last.[2] The people from this village were going to church in their traditional Dutch costumes with those wide trousers. The women [in the village] were very beautiful with their golden decorations. Everybody came by [while Ivens was making the film], including John Ferno.[3] He was 15 years old at the time; this was one of his first film jobs. Other friends were also cooperating with me in making the film. Everyone was going into the church. But I never visited that church. I don't like churches.

JR: I don't like them either.

JI: But I understand that they are important for other people.

JR: And you, Henri? What were you doing at that time?

Henri Storck: I was filming in Ostende.

JR: Both of you filming by the seaside at the same time?

HS: Yes, I made a film about the sea and the dunes.

JR: What was the meaning of cinema for you both at that time? What was cinema? Was it play? Was it just a job? Passion, love?

JI: Once you start with it, it becomes everything, it is action, it represents life too. For me, it was also art. It was not a commercial proposition. I couldn't live off it. I earned money by working in my father's shop. I was selling cameras. Mostly photographic cameras. People didn't use film in those days.

HS: Yes, it was because his father was selling cameras, he wanted to play with them. He started very young, when he was nine.

JI: Yes, I made my first film when I was nine years old.

HS: For me, it was different. I came from a milieu of painters and writers. For me, the cinema was an art, the seventh art. A new form of art. It was the time of the avant-garde. People were very enthusiastic [about film]. I admired the way the painters in my hometown were painting the place. But a painting is static, and what seduced me in film was the movement and the possibility of bringing movement into images. One could not only represent the movement of the sea, the movement of the city and different sorts of actions, but also the camera. In my film [in Storck's film *Images D'Ostende*, 1929] the camera is often moving. I walk in the dunes and show them as a female body being caressed, or as waves frozen in their movement.

JR: What is the difference between your religious life and that of Joris's?

HS: He came from a typical Protestant, Calvinist environment.

JI: No, no I come from a Catholic family...

HS: From a Catholic family? Never mind. We never spoke about religion.

JR: Now you have the opportunity to do it! In front of the microphone and under the shadow of the church!

HS: You know, we just mentioned it to each other – Joris and I have known each other for nearly fifty years. We first met in November 1930.

JI: I will come again to Brussels to celebrate our first meeting there. Because we are here now for Jean, he must be invited too.

JR: What were your ideas about cinema in those days? What was the difference between the film made by Joris here and the film made by you, Henri, in Ostende?

HS: For me it was about painting. I wanted to make 'living' paintings. I wanted to express my impression of the sea, my love for the sea and its movement.

JR: And for you Joris, what was it about?

JI: With this film, *The Breakers*, I wanted to free myself from documentary. But after this film, I kept making documentaries.

JR: At that time, did you already use the word documentary?

JI: No, there were just films, as Henri already said. In the avant-garde you had film, architecture, painting, music etc. All that was part of one big movement – the avant-garde of the 1930s.

HS: Do not forget, it was the period of the Bauhaus and also of the French avant-garde with René Clair and the film of Fernand Leger...

JI: *Le ballet mécanique.*

HS: Joris and myself were very busy with Ciné-Clubs. In 1928 I founded a Ciné-Club in Ostende where the avant-garde films were shown, like *Un Chien andalou* by Buñuel. Joris started at the same time the Filmliga in Amsterdam...

JI: Not me alone, but with friends...

HS: Of course, together with friends. The Filmliga was a big Ciné-Club with its own screening room called 'De Uitkijk' ['The View'] – a space where you could see the outside world through the window of the screening room.

JR: And the man who was the co-director of the film you made here?

JI: Yes, that was [Mannus] Franken.

JR: What type of man was he?

JI: He was a great guy. He was a student in Delft and I was a student in Rotterdam. He made two very big outdoor theatre productions for his university's anniversary celebrations.

JR: Was his work influenced by Brecht?

JI: No, it was a more romantic and historical work. He actually started as the representative of the Filmliga in Paris. He lived mostly in Paris. There he made an excellent film: *Le Jardin du Luxembourg*. You must see that one.

HS: It is a wonderful film. Last year we saw it again. One of the most beautiful films about Paris.

JI: A must see for Parisians.

HI: Especially because the park of Luxembourg has not changed at all since. The film is timeless.

JI: Tell that to the Cinémathèque in Paris...

JR: When you made the film [*The Breakers*] here, was the monument already standing in the village?

JI: No. No.

JR: What is this monument for?

JI: For the murdered fishermen who were part of the resistance against the Nazis. The monument is of a woman with her child.

JR: Shall we walk towards the sea?

...

JI: I didn't start filming until the age of 28. I was a film technician, an engineer in photo-chemicals and an economist in the business of my father. It was only after the foundation of the Filmliga that I started making films. I saw films by [Walter] Ruttman and I thought: I too can make such films. I did know a lot about film technique so I started to use it.

JR: And in *Misére au Borinage*[4] [1933] did you both do the camerawork?

JI: Yes

HS: We used the Kinamo camera.[5]

JR: What was that?

HS: Yes, you should explain this. With that camera you made your first films: *Rain* etc...

JI: Yes, *Rain* and *The Bridge* [1928]. One used it hand-held. Like the Bell & Howell. Not on the shoulder, but you could hold it in front of your face. It did not have an electrical motor. You had to wind it every 7.5 metres. If you were very rich, you had two cameras. One person was winding the spring of the other camera and you did the camerawork.

HS: It was a 35mm camera.

JI: 16mm was not around yet. You are lucky Jean, you have 16mm, you have sound. You can express much more...

HS: We had 25-metre magazines. Less than a minute per magazine. You had to reload them often. We had nine, ten or more magazines with us at any one time. The film stock was excellent, from a German manufacturer.

JI: It was that famous Perutz film.

HS: The lenses were very high speed ones. I had a 1.8 lens. A fantastic lens.

JI: Those lenses didn't mount on the camera with bayonet fitting, but you had to screw them on very quickly. We always ran a contest with Johnny (Ferno) who could change the lenses the quickest.

JR: And who was the best?

JI: That varied. Johnny was very handy!

...

JI: This church [in the village on the seaside] was Catholic.

HS: And now it is Protestant.

JR: Joris, we are going into the sea...

HS: I lived till my 25th [year] near the seaside.

JI: I have a close relationship with the sea.

HS: I swore by the sea. I spoke to the sea and swore by the sea that I would film it.

JI: And did you say: Sea, I must tell now the truth?

HS: No. No.

JI: Did it understand you?

HS: I used to sleep in the dunes. I could think there in peace, meditating.

JI: Yes, and you can make love there too.

JR: And were you faithful to the sea?

HS: Yes.

JR: And you?

JI: Yes.

JR: Water, always water.

JI: In every film there is always water. Psychologists and psychiatrists love water.

JR: Water, water, water.

HS: And bridges, bridges.

JI: Water, fire, earth – those are important elements for the documentary maker. You can create a direct contact with the public as it always recognises the four elements. You must make that contact and try to show the public things they are not conscious of. Never let them 'fall asleep' with water and being lulled into familiarity.

JR: With me, it is also water.

HS: That is true.

JR: Even with the Dogon, between those steep rocks there are the water-spirits everywhere. Water is disorder and other crazy things.

JI: The sea is beautiful. But during [filming] *The Breakers*, we went mad when the sea was calm. We had to wait. Sometimes we had to wait for a week. There were very beautiful moments. I told Jean already how we filmed in the sea – underwater cameras didn't exist yet. We were using a bag of parchment with a piece of glass. Plastic didn't exist in those days either.

HS: No, it was rubber.

JI: Yes, a sort of rubber. You could see everything was very beautiful.

HS: Yes, you could see the waves.

JI: You could see also the beautiful light. Colour film didn't exist yet. I thought: I must have it in this way. I can enter the sea now in my underwear…

JR: And you, Henri, will you go into the sea?

HS: It is too cold.

JR: Otherwise, yes?

HS: Yes.

JR: You can change in those small huts over there…

JI: Oh, no, we must not exaggerate…

JR: Because to tell you the truth, it is my birthday today, the 31st of May.

HS: Yes, I know, it is your birthday.

JR: I am now 63. How old are you?

HS: 72.

JR: And you, Joris?

JI: 81. I congratulate you. You give me courage! Congratulations Jean.

JR: We will try something – I will change the viewfinder and we will try to embrace each other in front of the camera.

HS: This will not be on film?

JR: Why not?

HS: It will not be on film, but it will be on the sound.

JR: It will be on film, but it is not important. This will be 'Birthday on the Seafront', a nice series.

JI: For the next birthday we should go to Africa, because you are always filming there.

JR: No, in November first we should go to Henri's in Brussels. We will celebrate the fact that you two know each other for fifty years.

JI: And you will show us this film you are making now...

JR: If it does not come out, if we fail, we will film it once more. We can make mistakes, can't we?

JI: Yes, but it will be good.

JR: Where did you two first meet?

JI: In Brussels, where I saw Henri's first film, about Ostende.

JR: For the first time?

JI: Yes, [Jean] Vigo was there too.

HS: Yes, it was the 2nd Congress of the Independent Film.

JR: And Vigo was there too?

HS: Vigo, [Jean] Painlevé and Jean Lods.[6]

JI: There were filmmakers from all over the world. It was a very big event.

HS: Independent filmmakers...

JI: Independent and global...

JR: Boris Kauffman[7] was there too?

HS: Boris Kauffman, yes, I believe so. I don't remember. Yes, I believe so.

JI: [Hans] Richter too, wasn't he there?

HS: Yes, and others too.

JR: How did you see each other? Like friends?

JI: It was a Mafia because we knew each other very well. I mean, the international contacts were very good. It was like a 'complicity' – with Vertov, Pudovkin, Eisenstein, Ruttman, Grierson, Lods, Painlevé.

JR: And the old father Flaherty.

JI: He was our grandfather. He did not come often to Europe, but he knew how to make documentaries! He gave us the confidence that one could make also films without fiction which nevertheless touched the public. It was about 1925–26.

JR: The first film I saw was *Nanook of the North* [1922] with my father in Brest. I was seven years old then.

HS: [Seeing Flaherty's films] did determine one's life. I was so overwhelmed when I saw *Moana* in 1927. I was twenty years old. After that film I founded the Ciné-Club and started filming. I tell you a funny story: I was once with Rouquier[8] at a congress of German Ciné-Clubs in the Black Forest. Flaherty was there too...

JR: The wind is getting stronger. We'll continue Henri's story inside.

...

JR: Henri, what was the story the wind interrupted? The wind is our friend, but...

HS: After World War Two, in 1949, the German Ciné-Clubs organised a big seminar in the Black Forest. Chris Marker was there too and Bob Flaherty was there. That was great.

JR: How was he?

HS: Listen, when we begin about him ... blue eyes, twinkling eyes, always laughing and friendly. Open to everybody. He was always talking with young people, always being positive about their films, he was eager to see their films and to talk about them. He did good work. He encouraged you whilst others didn't do anything. George Rouquier was there too. He didn't speak English, but I felt he was very moved. At a certain moment he said, 'Can you translate something to Flaherty for me? I can't speak English. Can you say to him, that I saw *Moana* when I was twenty years old and that was the start of my film career?' The strange thing was that I too saw *Moana* when I was twenty years old and it made me decide to make films. So I did go to Flaherty and said to him, 'We both had the same experience and we want you to know that we were both twenty when we saw *Moana* which made us filmmakers.' He took both of us in one of his arms, pressed our bodies against his and said to us, 'My two boys.' He was like a father.

JR: And you, Joris, what could you tell us about him?

JI: He was a very generous man. He had white hair like me, but another style. He was typical Irish. He was also very strong. He taught me to drink Irish whiskey. He said, 'Joris, come with me to the explorers' club...'

JR: In London?

JI: No, in New York, where all those explorers came from the North Pole, the South Pole, or like you, from Africa ... But I said, 'I am not an explorer...' He said, and that was nice of Flaherty, 'No, no you are nevertheless working in the "social field", you are a kind of explorer too. I'll take you there with me to drink and meet the others.' So, I became a temporary member of this club. That was great. And that man ... sometimes one speaks about a man with a big heart – he had an enormous heart. He was hearty, cordial and generous, but he also knew his limits. When he could help young people, he did that. It was like Henri said. We talked a lot about our philosophical ideas. With Henri I didn't speak much about philosophy, but with Flaherty I spoke many times about it. I used to say to him, 'You are always looking at things somehow in the wrong way – all old things are good, and all the technical advances in the world make our lives more superficial and you are right in that.' But still, I said, 'When an Eskimo has put a lamp in his Igloo, that is surely a good thing!' 'Yes, that is okay', he said, 'but it depends who is installing those lamps – if a company is exploiting the people, it is not right, but when it is there really to help the Eskimo, it is fine.' That was the one time I got him a bit in a tight corner during our discussions. But later, when he had made the film *The Land* [1942], he said to me, 'Joris now I understand you better.' And I learned from him not to think in an orthodox way. He was always stimulating and encouraging me to continue filming. Political films sometimes do not succeed. This is the difficulty in my work – to try and unite political problems with art. Sometimes you succeed, sometimes you don't.

JR: So I am closing the circle. Thanks to Flaherty, I saw my first film ever. It was Frances Flaherty[9] who invited us to the Flaherty Seminar where I met Michel

Brault.[10] There I discovered the 'walking camera', which led to *Chronique d'un été* [1960]. That's how the circle is complete now.

JI: And it was *Nanook* which started it all.

HS: For me too.

JI: And I found my wife there, Marceline.[11]

JR: Love, the sea, birthdays, etc … I propose that we will do in November something like this in Brussels.

JI: We will try.

HS: Where there is a will…

JR: Of course.

JI: With one reservation, when I am filming in Florence, I can't come.

JR: We will try to get Luc de Heusch, to come too.[12]

JI: Everybody must come, Luc too.

HS: Luc will not be there. We must do it earlier, in September or October.

JR: We will try. We will try our best.

JI: It is very good. It is really good making a film with you!

HS: We must do it once more.

JI: Your camera [Rouch's] is a living, dancing camera, not only moving, but also living. It has become a person.

JR: Let's go to the sea…

Translated by Dirk Nijland and Joram ten Brink

Cinemafia 16mm, Colour, 33 min. (1980)
Crew 1
Camera: Jean Rouch
Sound: Robert Busschots
Crew 2
Camera: Rogier Busschots
Sound: Dirk Nijland
Editing: Rogier Busschots, Dirk Nijland
Mix: Han Panhuysen
Acknowledgements: Virginia Leirens, Willy Kessel, Jan de Vaal, Comité du Film Ethnographique, Paris, Musée du Cinéma, Bruxelles, Nederlands Filmmuseum, Amsterdam
Production: Department of Anthropology, Leiden, the Netherlands

NOTES

1   Mannus Franken (1899–1953), Dutch filmmaker, wrote and co-directed *The Breakers* and co-wrote *Rain* (1929) with Ivens. Franken and Ivens also collaborated on the film project *The Flying Dutchman* (an adaptation from a novel by Hendrik Marsman).
2   Jef Last (1898–1972), Dutch left-wing activist, writer and poet (wrote the original novel and acted in *The Breakers*).
3   John Ferno (Fernhout) (1913–87), Dutch filmmaker. Ivens' assistant cameraman and assistant editor on *The Breakers* and cameraman on *The Spanish Earth* (1937) and *The Four Hundred Millions* (1938).
4   A documentary film about the Belgian miners (Ivens and Storck, 1933).
5   A compact 35mm camera built from 1923 by ICA-AG which became in 1926 part of Zeiss Ikon-Ag in Dresden, Germany.
6   Jean Painlevé (1902–89), French filmmaker; Jean Lods (1903–74), French filmmaker.
7   Boris Kaufman (1887–1980), Russian/French cameraman (brother of Dziga Vertov).
8   George Rouquier (1909–89), French filmmaker and actor.
9   Frances Flaherty (1884–1972), wife of Robert Flaherty.
10 Michel Brault (1928–) Canadian cameraman, one of several cameramen on *Chronique d'un été*.
11 Marceline Loridan Ivens (1928–), French actress and filmmaker, took part in *Chronique d'un été*. Later became Ivens' wife.
12 Luc de Heusch (1927–), Belgian anthropologist, filmmaker and son-in-law of Henri Storck.

Tallou on camera and Mousa Amadou on sound, 1971

18 FROM 'CAMÉRA-STYLO' TO 'CAMÉRA-CRAYON' ET PUIS APRÈS...

Joram ten Brink

Few examples of writings on cinema have had as profound an influence on a generation of filmmakers as Alexandre Astruc's essay 'The Birth of the New Avant-Garde: La "Caméra-Stylo"' (1948). It is now considered a key moment in the development of French cinema in the past sixty years. The essay became a true manifesto ten years before the birth of the *nouvelle vague* itself. Its call for a change was prophetic. It became the agent provocateur of the *nouvelle vague* (see Gerstner 2003: 6). Although the essay's major impact on the world of fiction filmmaking is well documented, its impact on non-fiction film, seen primarily through the work of Jean Rouch and his *cinéma vérité*, has been given less attention. Rouch, partly through his affinity to Dziga Vertov's Kino-Eye, transformed 'Caméra-Stylo' (camera-pen) theory into a reality for the world of documentary filmmaking. Rouch himself talked often and at great length about Flaherty, Vertov and Vigo as his main inspirations. He rarely, and only then very briefly, mentions the 'prophet' Astruc.[1] Yet Astruc's 'Caméra-Stylo' had a much more significant impact on Rouch and through him on the world of non-fiction than he and others have acknowledged until now.

French cinema in the immediate post-war years was perceived as being in a state of stagnation. The disappointment was doubly felt when held in comparison to Italy where Neo-realism flourished bringing with it a sense of renewal and excitement that resonated strongly across Europe. As Louis Marcorelles, a key writer for *Cahiers du cinéma*, put it later: '[French cinema after the war] was missing the turning toward Neo-realism which it might have taken, it moved instead towards academicism and the great "machine constructions" of directors such as Clément and Clouzot' (1958: 192). The heavy reliance of post-war

French cinema on literature, its total dependence on professional scriptwriters and the lack of deep personal involvement by the filmmakers themselves in their work, established a beautiful and perfectly crafted world of studio-based cinema void of any human warmth or creative energy.[2] Gilles Deleuze attributes the stagnation in post-war French cinema to France's ambition to fully belong to the circle of victors after the war, seeking to restore pre-war French life and tenaciously holding on to the 'French Dream'; any renewal happened much later on in France, in comparison to Italy (see Deleuze 1986: 211).

Unlike mainstream fiction film, the documentary genre enjoyed a small renaissance during the immediate post-war years, with poetic documentaries and moving human stories, for example, in Georges Rouquier's *Farrebique* (1946), Jean Painlevé's films and Georges Franju's *Le Sang des bêtes* (*Blood of the Beasts*, 1949). *Farrebique* won the critics prize at Cannes in 1946. The film is a highly stylised documentary describing life in a small village in rural France, and tackles the problems of living in an isolated area and the pull of the big city. It tells the story of various members of the community (often using local dialect) and includes carefully constructed scenes during the four seasons of the year. *Farrebique* was shot like a fiction film with highly formal set ups, is very well-lit and accompanied by a symphonic soundtrack. Sections of the films are devoted to close-ups and fast-motion photography of flowers, trees and bees. Rouquier and other documentary filmmakers of that period were part of what Roy Armes (1985) refers to as the beautiful and perfectly crafted world of studio-based cinema, whilst their roots were in the small but active French pre-war avant-garde world (see also Goretta 1956/57: 156–8).

Astruc had written about the cinema since 1944, alongside his prolific writings on literature. He started making films himself (all fiction films) for cinema and television from 1952 onwards.[3] Many of his films were adaptations of literary works. Astruc's writings on cinema emerged in post-war France, as young French filmmakers and critics were gaining access to Hollywood films for the first time, after a long period of occupation. They set themselves in opposition to 'old Hollywood', as their views were irreconcilable with the Hollywood brand of cinema, yet they supported the new generation of Hollywood directors. They also objected to the old established home-grown cinema of the 1940s. Astruc's manifesto from 1948 was born from a recognition that cinema could be seen as an individual expression of artistic work in opposition to the tradition of Hollywood and the highly stylised home-grown French cinema. Eleven years later in 1959, Astruc defined the world of the artist as 'not the one that conditions him, but one which he needs in order to create and to transform perpetually into something that will obsess him even more than that by which he is obsessed. The obsession of the artist is artistic creation' (1985: 268).

In his manifesto Astruc coined the phrase 'Caméra-Stylo' to describe the directness with which the filmmaker should use the tools of the cinema to create a cinematic language in order to translate his or her ideas to the screen. In his pursuit of a new form for expression in cinema, he had already planted the idea of *mise-en-scène* as a way forward for French cinema (Astruc himself developed the concept later in his essay 'What is *mise-en-scène*?' in *Cahiers du cinéma*, first published in 1959). His desire for a new form in cinema can be seen from two points of view: a call for a new language to take cinema beyond the mere illustration or presentation of a dramatic scene, and a call for a new technological advancement towards smaller, more discrete tools of film production. The filmmaker is now, according to Astruc, in a position to look at the world in a different way and to be spontaneous with his 'writing'. He or she is able to react quickly to reality by 'jotting down notes' with a 'camera pen' (1968: 18). This, in Astruc's view, is similar to the novelist's mode of working with words to create literary work. The tyranny of heavy camera equipment and elaborate technical set-ups in film production were colourfully described by Jean Renoir in an interview with André Bazin as late as 1958 (in which Roberto Rossellini also took part):

> In cinema at present, the camera has become a sort of God. A camera is fixed on a tripod or a crane which is just like a heathen altar; about it are the high priests – the director, cameraman, assistants – who bring victims before the camera, like burnt offerings, and cast them into the flames. And the camera is there immobile ... and when it does move it follows patterns ordained by the high priests, not by the victims. (Bazin 1958/59: 26).[4]

The essence of the 'Caméra-Stylo', according to Astruc, would offer flexibility and a degree of subtlety to the filmmaker, unknown until now. He calls for a new type of filmmaking which emphasises above all the prominent role of the director as a creator of images. In 'Caméra-Stylo', images form the backbone of a film, escape the commercial industry requirements for entertainment, heavily influenced by literature, and the narrow definition of the avant-garde of the 1920s and 1930s as pure, poetic or surrealist cinema. In this, Astruc aims to broaden the term avant-garde to include films which use the 'Caméra-Stylo' (1968: 21–2). Astruc's use of the term 'avant-garde' gave post-war French filmmakers the confidence to leave behind 'cinema' – the only singular mode of expression – and develop other forms. Although the avant-garde did flourish in pre-war Europe it was always seen as a side show – an exploration of the moving image inside the art world. The fact that Astruc, a member of the mainstream film criticism fraternity of French film journals, made his call for this new language of cinema was even more significant.

Astruc does not mention non-fiction or documentary film in his manifesto for the future cinema of the 'Caméra-Stylo'. His world, as a writer and a film-maker, is the world of literature and film. His call for the new form of cinema is intended for his readers: post-war filmmakers and film critics who are all engaged in fiction filmmaking. In his essay he makes reference to the fiction films of the late 1930s onwards from Renoir, Welles and Bresson, which he claims were overlooked by contemporary film critics (1968: 17). One of the few times during that period in which Astruc referred to documentary film was in 1946, when he wrote of the 'renaissance' of Italian cinema with Rossellini's *Roma, citta aperta* (*Rome, Open City*, 1945) and discussing the up-and-coming screening of Rossellini's *Paisà* (1946) in Paris: 'The romantic documentary that has been developed in England as in France and America with the school of Cavalcanti seems to become the aesthetic of European cinema today – a formula full of possibilities' (1946: 5).

Astruc's writings and films had considerable influence on the *Cahiers du cinéma* critics and on the *nouvelle vague* group of filmmakers in general. Alongside Bazin, Astruc contributed articles to *L'Écran français* during and following the war years. When the Left took control of the magazine, Astruc followed Bazin, left the paper and joined the rival publication *Cahiers du cinéma*. Alan Williams describes Astruc's writings as a critic and, in particular, in the 'Caméra-Stylo' essay, as the 'glue' that enabled the dramatic change in French cinema for years to come (1992: 306). In an interview in 1962 in the pages of *Cahiers du cinéma* Jean-Luc Godard defined the critics within the *nouvelle vague* as allied with 'uncle' Astruc (1986: 60) – one of the direct consequences of Astruc's 1948 essay was Truffaut's 1953 manifesto 'A Certain Tendency of the French Cinema'. In it Truffaut continues with Astruc's attack on the established role of the script-writer and the prominence of literature in French cinema: he speaks harshly of the scriptwriters of the established order wishing only for some pictures to illustrate their (literary) stories (1976: 233). In his manifesto he echoes Astruc's idea of the importance of the personal voice of the filmmaker in expressing a strong worldview, and in 1957 Astruc's essay was cited as having had a major influence on the *nouvelle vague* in Pierre Kast and Jacques Rivette's conclusion in 'Six characters in search of auteurs' (Bazin *et al.* 1985). They argued that film-making had dramatically changed and was now going to be produced 'by hand', comparing this to the process of writing a novel. Thus, the distinction between scriptwriter and director became blurred, leading to the birth of 'auteur cinema'. The same article made clear that Astruc's manifesto from 1948 was as influential on contemporary French filmmaking as were his films from the early 1950s, which paved the way for younger directors to make more personal works and tackle contemporary issues concerning young people's ambitions. Rouch clearly followed this throughout his work in the 1950s and 1960s in his African ethno-fiction films and, more crucially, in his Parisian work – *Chronique d'un été* (1960), *La Punition* (1962) and *Gare du Nord* (1966). Pierre Kast and Jacques Rivette also remarked, referring especially to Astruc's films, that as a result of the birth of the new cinema the technical quality of filmmaking had become questionable (see Bazin *et al.* 1985). It is similar to the criticism often levelled at Rouch's work in Africa in the 1950s, or in *Chronique d'un été* as a very innovative, if somewhat technically flawed work.[5]

Bazin further developed Astruc's 'Caméra-Stylo' idea in the early 1950s, declaring that: 'the filmmaker is no longer the competitor of the painter and the playwright, he is, at last, the equal of the novelist' (1971a: 40). One of the few early mentions of the 'Caméra-Stylo' in the context of documentary film can be found in Bazin's essay on the film *La Course de taureaux* (*The Bullfight*, 1951), which was screened with a commentary written by the surrealist and ethnographer Michel Leiris. The film was made by Pierre Braunberger, who later became an influential producer in France (producing among other films Rouch's *La Pyramide humaine* and *Petit à petit* (1968–69)). Bazin's article looks at the extraordinary experience of watching the film and the representation of death in cinema. He defines the work as an example of what he also sees in Braunberger's other documentary film, *Paris 1900* (directed together with Nicole Védrès in 1948) – a development of the techniques of the 'Caméra-Stylo' in the editing process, similar to the new Hollywood cinema of Welles or Italian Neo-realism (2003: 28). Another rare use of the 'Caméra-Stylo' term in the context of the documentary genre was apparently from Alain Resnais. His lost film, *Ouvert pour cause d'inventaire* (1946) is often referred to as his first. Mostly a non-narrative, semi-surrealist work, it is a documentary on the city of Paris. Later on, Resnais himself described it as 'a sort of diary; later that sort of thing was called "Caméra-Stylo"'. Angès Varda, who saw the film, commented that 'it was a succession of pure sensations which never really reach the state of consciousness' (in Gianvito 1999/2000: 41).[6]

Documentary film in France in the 1950s developed a more poetic, personal style through, among others, Chris Marker, Alain Resnais and Roberto Rossellini. Following the 'Caméra-Stylo' assertion that cinema is a tool of subjective expression, personal documentaries produced by an artist became the 'new' documentaries. Marker's and Resnais' early films were shot as silent documentaries and were given 'literary' commentaries created during the editing stage. *Letter from Siberia* (1957) by Marker came to the attention of Bazin in 1958 as a type of film that had not been seen before in France: 'How can one present *Letter from Siberia*? At first one must do this in a negative way, by noting that it resembles nothing which has hitherto been made in the way of documentary ("topic-based") films' (1983: 179). Although superficially the film looks like another travel report from the USSR, Bazin claims that this is a wrong description of the film and suggests his own definition: '*Letter from Siberia* is an essay in the form of a cinematographic report on Siberian reality past and present ... An essay at once historical and political, even though written by a poet' (1983: 180). Bazin continues his argument by recognising that the filmmaker's presence in the film defines its form. Rossellini's documentary film project made in India in 1959 – the first large-scale 16mm film documentary series produced for European television – was another personal commentary-led work.[7] Through his commentaries, which accompanied the transmission of the series on French and Italian television, Rossellini delivers his perspective on travelling and on India, looking at everyday life rather than the 'mysteries' of the country, its religion and temples. According to Fereydoun Hoveyda, who travelled to India with the director, Rossellini was inspired by Vertov and planned to follow *Paisà* with his Indian documentary project (see Hoveyda 1998). Hoveyda describes Rossellini and his cameraman hiding in street corners, behind buildings and on balconies to record their extensive documentary images of daily life in India.

Yet a real radical change in documentary film in France arrived with Rouch's *cinéma vérité* and his creation of a new language of documentary cinema assisted by important technological innovations. Rouch, with *cinéma vérité*, and in particular in *Chronique d'un été*, uses the camera in true 'Caméra-Stylo' fashion – taking the writing principle further into an active creation of the world in front of the camera with the camera as his writing tool. No more hiding in street corners in Siberia or India to record daily life, no more literary texts or personal commentaries on the soundtrack. Rouch asks Marceline Loridan to walk through Les Halles and improvise her story in front of the camera. The camera provokes, changes and interferes with reality to produce the truth of the cinema – the real 'Caméra-Stylo' film, using a hand-held camera-pen in the possession of the artist. Deleuze describes the changing role of the camera with the *nouvelle vague* and uses Rouch's work in documentary film as an example:

> The fixity of the camera does not represent the only alternative to movement. Even when it is mobile, the camera is no longer content sometimes to follow the characters as merely the object, but in every case it subordinates description of a space to the function of thought ... Hitchcock's premonition will come true: a camera-consciousness, which would no longer be defined by the movements it is able to follow or make but, by the mental connections it is able to enter into. And it becomes questioning, responding, objecting, provoking ... in accordance with the functions of thought in a *cinéma vérité*, which as Rouch says, means, rather, the truth of cinema. (1989: 22)

Thus the artist becomes the creator and producer of truth, because 'truth is not to be achieved, formed or reproduced; it has to be created' (1989: 146). Incidentally, Deleuze also remarks that the Rouchian 'truth of cinema' enables Rouch to move easily into the worlds of dreams and possession, and he quotes Jean André Fieschi: 'What Rouch films, and he is the first to do so, is no longer behaviour or dreams, or subjective discourses, but the indiscernible mixture which links one to the other' (in Deleuze 1989: 302). Deleuze also identifies the years after World War Two as the beginning of a new era in cinema. Although he arrives at a different set of conclusions about what is new, he shares with Astruc the notion that the 'old' or 'classical' cinema has become inadequate (1989: xi). According to Deleuze, a new set of film characters emerge from the ashes of the war: they are 'seers' and not mere 'actors' (ibid.). In one sense, *Chronique d'un été* is the ultimate film of 'seeing', of witnessing Europe in the immediate post-war landscape. 'Are you happy?' is the central question of the film.

Rouch's use of synchronised sound in combination with a lightweight hand-held camera, starting with *Chronique d'un été*, further enhanced the sense of the 'Caméra-Stylo'. Gone are the days when the image only determined the length of the shot, which in the past, no doubt, gave rise to a very innovative development of the documentary form. The synchronised sound created open-ended shots, longer takes and injected a sense of adventure and uncertainty into filmmaking.[8] Sync sound offered the filmmaker complete control over the process of making or 'writing' films for the first time. The new experience of sound also enhanced the sheer pleasure in using a camera and a microphone as a direct means of expression, the experience of employing the 'Caméra-Stylo'.

Chronique d'un été is the ultimate 'Caméra-Stylo' film, where its themes, technological innovations and the new language of the documentary film all converge. Rouch, after completing the work, describes his camera and tape recorder as his tools: 'as indispensable as a note pad and pencil' (2003a: 267). He declares that writing about cinema has become a very difficult thing for him. He believes that film 'is such a personal thing ... that the only implicit techniques are the very techniques of cinematography: sight and sound recording, editing the images and recordings' (2003a: 266). By constantly referring to itself and reflecting on its construction, the film is Rouch's most reflexive work and this reflexivity is a direct consequence of the 'Caméra-Stylo'. In *Chronique d'un été*, Rouch investigates throughout the notion of using the building blocks of cinematic language – image, sound and editing – to its fullness. Rouch and Morin, directly to the camera, and implicitly in most of the film's scenes, constantly question their method, the film's themes and their own roles in the production. Their 'self', either visible or obscured, is often a reference point, and inseparable from the 'text' of the film. The directors stand in the centre of an often eclectic and fragmentary work. Astruc's call for 'writing' films as they occur to the writer or the filmmaker has been fulfilled with *Chronique d'un été*.

The image-writing essence of the 'Caméra-Stylo' was preceded as a cinematic tool by Rouch's other main inspiration, Dziga Vertov. Vertov described himself as 'a film writer. A cinépoet. I do not write on paper, but on film' (in Geduld 1967: 97). In 1929, introducing the term 'Kino-Eye' Vertov wrote: 'Kino-Eye is the documentary cinematic decoding of both the visible world and that which is invisible to the naked eye' (in Michelson 1984: 87). In his writings about his film *The Man With the Movie Camera*, Vertov describes in detail his effort to establish the Kino-Eye as an experiment in the creation of an autonomous genre, separate from fiction, theatre, literature and documentary techniques which all existed prior to his work (in Michelson 1984: 82–91). In *Chronique d'un été*, Rouch also develops further Vertov's work on board the Lenin train and later on board the Red Star steamer. Vertov's filmmaking techniques progressed from straightforward Kino-Eye productions to much more complex operations. Instead of sending rushes to be edited in Moscow, Vertov saw the value in setting up editing rooms on board the train and steamer in order to create feedback sessions with the workers and farmers who were the subjects of the films.[9] Rouch showed the rushes of *Chronique d'un été* to its participants and went one step further than Vertov by incorporating these feedback scenes in the film itself.[10]

Chronique d'un été of course also mirrors Vertov's production of the film *Entuziazm* (*Enthhusiasm*, 1930), in which Vertov worked closely with a team of technicians to create the first mobile sound recording device.[11] Rouch's continuous drive to try to perfect the notion of writing with the camera and his work on the development of the lightweight sync-sound camera for *Chronique d'un été* in 1960 is well documented.[12]

Rouch, in his seminal essay 'The Camera and Man' from 1973, talks in detail about the technical developments in the years after World War Two. The development of the 16mm camera and, from 1951, the development of smaller sound recorders created a new breed of ethnographers who became at once director, cameraman, sound recorder and editor. Rouch describes that he realised only later that a new cinematic language had been invented. He quotes himself writing in *Positif* in 1955: 'The spectator can suddenly understand an unknown language without the gimmick of subtitles, moments where he can participate in strange ceremonies' (2003b: 35). With the development of the lightweight camera Vertov's Kino-Eye became a 'walking eye' or, in Rouch's term, a 'living camera' (2003b: 38). In this the film is able to penetrate reality in a physical sense rather than standing as an observer from the sideline. For Rouch, the resulting 'walking cinema' is the synthesis of Vertov's Kino-Eye and Flaherty's participating camera (2003b: 39). Rouch continues to describe it in terms of embarking on the shoot without prior knowledge, moving constantly in and out and around the scene – thus, one can argue, the writing quality of Astruc is being fully achieved. Rouch also mentions the over-indulgence of the new audio-visual world. His response is Astrucian, but again he only discusses Vertov's Kino-Eye when he describes the old 'pen hands' transformed into the contemporary 'ciné-eye' (2003b: 43). The cameraman, Nestor Almendros, who shot in 1964, on 16mm, most of the short films that made up *Paris vu par...* (except Rouch's contribution), describes his experience working with the new lightweight portable 16mm camera as an 'interesting experiment' in which the technical results left much to be desired. He observes that Rouch was the only one among the group of six *nouvelle vague* directors involved in the production of *Paris vu par...* who really understood and exploited the new possibilities of the camera in combination with direct sound. Rouch fully used the new tool by filming only two uncut shots, following the actors from interior to exterior locations (Almendros 1985: 51–3).

Astruc also predicted in his 'Caméra-Stylo' essay the radical change that 16mm would provoke. Films would no longer be projected as big 'events' in cinema. The portable projector and the television set would make the experience of watching films far more intimate, and closer to daily experience (1968: 19). It would not be possible to speak about cinema, but only a multitude of cinemas (ibid.).[14] The portable projector became an important new element in the creation of Rouch's new world of ethnographic film.

Many of Rouch's films echo the call by Astruc to extend the definition of the avant-garde to include the new form of 'Caméra-Stylo'. Astruc sees that the contemporary viewer of films is 'in danger of getting blunted by those everyday films which, year in and year out, show their tired and conventional faces to the world' (1968: 17). Astruc calls to stop 'going on for ever ploughing in the same fields of realism and social fantasy which has been bequeathed to it by the popular novel' (1968: 18). Rouch, with his first-hand experience of Surrealism in 1930s Paris, talks repeatedly about the need to incorporate the world of dreams as part of the reality portrayed in his films. He attributes many of his ideas to Buñuel's cinematic treatment of dream (2003: 143). In this, Rouch shares Astruc's sentiment expressed in his call to move to 'Caméra-Stylo' cinema, partly based on the avant-garde.

Astruc's most dramatic impact on the world of the *nouvelle vague* generation of fiction filmmakers after the publication of the 'Caméra-Stylo' article, was most likely his call for the scriptwriter to direct his own scripts and for the traditional role of a scriptwriter to be abolished (1968: 22). Rouch's own fiction work, starting as early as the 1950s, with the ethno-fiction films in Africa, and with most of his fiction work in France, followed this advice to its extreme. Not only was the division between scriptwriter and director eradicated, but a traditional fiction film script itself was never written. Rouch's work with his actors in Africa can be described as a pure form of Astrucian 'Caméra-Stylo', where actions were 'written' directly on camera by Rouch and his acting team (but nevertheless improvised and discussed at length in advance).

The remarkable change in French documentary films since Rouquier's *Farrebique* which came as a direct result of Rouch's 'Caméra-Stylo', is clearly manifested in two works produced immediately after *Chronique d'un été* by Mario Ruspoli: *Les Inconnus de la terre* (1961) and *Regard sur la folie* (1962). Both were shot by Michel Brault. Ruspoli acknowledges *Chronique d'un été* as the main influence on the production of his two films. Using Brault's 'marvellous flying and strolling [camera] technique' and Rouch's sound assistant Roger Morlilère's 'tactfully recorded soundtrack' enabled him to work for long periods of time among his subjects and avoid 'altering the behaviour of those we were filming' (1963: 157). In a striking similarity to *Farrebique*, Ruspoli's film, *Les Inconnus de la terre*, tells the story of an isolated rural community in the French countryside. But in sharp contrast to *Farrebique*, *Les Inconnus de la terre* uses available light and employs the hand-held camera technique, and many of the villagers talk directly to camera and refer continuously to the presence of the filmmaker. In *Regard sur la folie* the filmmaker reflects on his working with his subjects by showing the viewer the camera and the Nagra and by inserting long heart-searching question-and-answer sessions in roundtable discussions, 'in the style' of *Chronique d'un été*. The film ends with the cameraman turning his lens towards the viewer, reaffirming his role in 'writing the film'.

In 1963 Rouch predicted that the power of the camera as a writing tool would be so great as to replace any other form of anthropological record making – that is, writing books. In fifty years time, he claimed, there would be no more anthropological books, only anthropological films (see Shivas & Cameron 1963: 23). In his 1973 essay, 'The Camera and Man', Rouch's conclusion pointed to the future of the video system, in which portable picture and sound recording are merged into one and coupled with a playback facility, which would also fulfil the feedback component of the new cinematic language (2003b: 46). In 1978 Rouch spoke of developing his style by combining Flaherty's participatory camera and Vertov's Kino-Eye (see Yakir 1978: 7). He spoke enthusiastically of the new Super 8 format and video with single sound system as the next step for filmmaking: 'One will have no need for a crew and will create a face to face cinema' (ibid.). The filmmaker is not himself anymore, he has a camera and a microphone – a mechanical eye and electronic ear. The filmmaker arrives at a state of ciné-trance, creating a new truth, a new *cinéma vérité*, which is no longer entrenched in reality. It is the truth of the cinema. The new Super 8 and video also make it possible, according to Rouch, to make extremely cheap films

– Astruc's 'Caméra-Stylo' will become a 'Camera-Crayon' – the camera pencil that can be put in everybody's hand (Yakir 1978: 10), or as he puts it elsewhere: 'the democratic, cheap, Bic ballpoint will replace the expensive Parker fountain pen' (in Bellour & Frydland 1963: 153). Rouch's vision for the future at that time is very clear: 'Maybe in some years there will be truly a one-man system. A film-maker will be able to work in the field by himself over a long period of time. With a small two-track Nagra, a microphone on the camera ... and an earphone to monitor sound as he is filming ... [the future will bring] the new race of film-makers' (in Anon. 1978: 78).

Yet Rouch himself never made the transition to video. His eagerness ex-pressed above to push the 'Caméra-Stylo' to its ultimate frontiers never mate-rialised. He expressed on numerous occasions, from the early 1980s onwards, his strong reservations about the quality of the video recordings and screenings, and resisted for many years video projections at the Musée de l'Homme. He be-came increasingly isolated due to his attitude to video, especially among visual anthropologists and the new generation of his students.

In an interview with Enrico Fulchignoni published in 1981, one of the most comprehensive and revealing interviews ever given by Rouch, he expressed for the first time his dissatisfaction with the new technological inventions: 'Despite all the advances, the dream of new cinema had not been achieved. We should go somewhere else, we should slip on the winged shoes of Arthur Rimbaud and go off somewhere else ... and in spite of Kudelski, Coutant, Brault, Beauviala or Leacock ... we are still constrained to something terrible, formal, for example, we make films that have a set framing' (in Fulchignoni 2003: 148).

As early as 1948 Bazin pointed out very clearly the inherent contradiction in the drive to make the camera more real through the addition of sound and colour (1971b: 26–7). He accepted that in the future, enjoying ever-improving technical innovations, cinema will return purely to reality. Yet he also saw the pitfalls in the new world dominated by the camera: 'actually, the art of cinema lives off this contradiction. It gets the most out of the potential for abstraction and symbolism provided by the present limits of the screen, but this utilisation of the residue of conventions abandoned by technique can work either to the advantage or to the detriment of realism' (Bazin 1971b: 27). All of this points to Rouch, in 1981, echoing his nervousness about realism and cinema's aesthetic as Bazin had done in 1948, the year of Astruc's 'Caméra-Stylo' manifesto.

NOTES

1   In a text accompanying the script of *La Pyramide humaine* (1959), Rouch (1960)

refs to Astruc in a very interesting way: 'It's not for nothing that our friend Astruc invented the "caméra-stylo", without ever using it' (1960: 27). Furthermore, Rouch mentions Astruc only briefly in an interview with Raymond Bellour and Maurice Frydland (1963); in an interview with Dan Yakir (1978); and in his own work, 'The cinema of the future?' (2003a: 269).

2   See Armes 1985: 127–45 for a detailed account of the immediate post-war years.

3   Full details in Astruc 1992.

4   Interview in *France Observateur*, translated in *Sight and Sound*. Renoir also adds in this interview, ten years after Astruc's essay, his belief in the benefit of what he calls 'going back to the roots of cinema', abandoning its technical over-layers and giving the filmmaker the simple tools of film production to work with: 'Like in the early days of cinema, cinema will reclaim its role as an art form' (1958/59: 26). Renoir describes during the interview the new method he would like to use: he wishes he could work like a documentary newsreel cameraman who follows the actions rather than having the actors follow the camera operator's instructions.

5   See Hoveyda 1986: 254. Rouch himself often expressed his disdain of 'la belle image' ('the pretty picture'): see DiIorio 2005: 122.

6   The story of the lost Resnais film is told in Gianvito 1999/2000: 40–1.

7   *J'ai fait un beau voyage* (*I Had a Fine Trip*), 1959, ten episodes, ORTF France.

8   See Joris Ivens' strong reservations about the use of sync sound, following his first viewing of *Chronique d'un été*, retold in the interview with Marceline Loridan Ivens in this volume.

9   This process was extensively used in his film *Shestaya chast mira* (*The Sixth Part of the World*, 1926).

10 A moving account of the making of *Chronique d'un été* is given by Rouch in 1979: 'When Edgar Morin and myself decided to make the film, a new experience in *cinéma vérité*, our sole intention was an homage to Dziga Vertov. We did not realise, however, that we were meddling with a cinema whose smouldering ashes were waiting to reignite in our hands. And the friendship and wisdom of George Sadoul was absolutely invaluable in helping us separate the damp fuses from the real Molotov cocktails' (in Anon. 1979: 29).

11 See Fischer 1977: 25–34 for a detailed account of the film's process of production.

12 See Winston 1996: 82–3 for a detailed account of Rouch's close co-operation with André Coutant in Paris over the design and modification of the new lightweight 16mm camera, and his experimental use of new Nagra equipment for sync-sound shooting.

REFERENCES

Almendros, N. (1985) *A Man with a Camera*. London: Faber and Faber.

Anon. (1978) 'Interview with Jean Rouch', Educational Broadcasting International, 11, 2, 76–8.

____ (1979) 'Interview with Jean Rouch', *Framework*, 5, 11, 26–30.

Armes, R. (1985) *French Cinema*. London: Secker and Warburg.

Astruc, A. (1946) 'Renaissance du cinéma Italie – *Rome, ville ouverte*', *Combat*, 16 November.

____ (1968 [1948]) 'The Birth of the New Avant-Garde: La Caméra-Stylo', in P. Graham (ed.) *The New Wave*. London: Secker and Warburg, 17–23.

____ (1985 [1959]) 'What is *mise-en-scène?*', in J. Hillier (ed.) *Cahiers du cinéma, Vol. 1*. London: Routledge, 248–59.

____ (1992) *Du stylo à la caméra*. Montreal: l'Archipel.

Bazin, A. (1958/59) 'Interview with Jean Renoir', *Sight and Sound*, 28, 1, 26–30.

____ (1971a) *What is Cinema?, Vol. 1*. Berkeley: University of California Press.

____ (1971b) *What is Cinema?, Vol. 2*. Berkeley: University of California Press.

____ (1983) *Le Cinéma français de la libération à la nouvelle vague (1945–1958)*. Paris: Éditions de L'Étoile.

____ (2003 [1958]) 'Death Every Afternoon', in I. Margulies (ed.) *Rites of Realism*. Durham: Duke University Press, 27–31.

Bazin, A., J. Doniol-Valcroze, P. Kast, R. Leenhardt, J. Rivette and E. Rohmer (1985 [1957]) 'Six characters in search of auteurs', in J. Hillier (ed.) *Cahiers du cinéma, Vol. 1*. London: Routledge, 31–47.

Bellour, R. and M. Frydland (1963) 'Aux sources du *cinéma vérité* avec Jean Rouch', *Cinema*, 63, 72, January, 151–3.

Deleuze, G. (1986) *Cinema 1: The Movement-Image*. London: Athalone.

____ (1989) *Cinema 2: The Time-Image*. London: Athalone.

DiIorio, S. (2005) 'Notes on Jean Rouch and French Cinema', *American Anthropologist*, 107, 1, 120–2.

Eaton, M. (1979) (ed.) *Anthropology-Reality-Cinema*. London: BFI.

Fischer, L. (1977) '*Enthusiasm*, from Kino-Eye to Radio Eye', *Film Quarterly*, 31, 2, 24–34.

Fulchignoni, E. (2003 [1981]) 'Jean Rouch with Enrico Fulchignoni: Ciné-ethnography', in J. Rouch, *Ciné-ethnography*. Minneapolis: University of Minnesota Press, 147–87.

Geduld, H. (ed.) (1967) *Film Makers on Film Making*. Bloomington: Indiana University Press.

Gerstner, D. A. (2003) 'The Practice of Authorship', in D. A. Gerstner and J. Staiger (eds) *Authorship and Film*. New York: Routledge, 3–26.

Gianvito, J. (1999/2000) 'Remembrance of Films Lost', *Film Quarterly*, 53, 2, Winter, 40–1.

Godard, J.-L. (1986) interview with, in J. Hillier (ed.) *Cahiers du cinéma, Vol. 2*. London: Routledge, 59–67.

Goretta, C. (1956–57) 'Aspects of French Documentary', *Sight and Sound*, 26, 3, 156–8.

Hoveyda, F. (1986) 'Cinéma Vérité, or Fantastic Realism', in J. Hillier (ed.) *Cahiers du cinéma, Vol. 2*. London: Routledge, 236–48.

____(1998) *A Tribute to Cinémathèque française*. On-line. Available at: http://hoveyda.org/india.html (accessed 21 October 2006).

Marcorelles, L. (1958) 'French Cinema, the Old and the New', *Sight and Sound*, 27, 4, 190–5.

Margulies, I. (ed.) (2003) *Rites of Realism*. Durham: Duke University Press.

Michelson, A. (1984) *Kino-eye*. London: Pluto Press.

Nichols, B. (ed.) (1976) *Movies and Methods*. Berkeley: University of California Press.

(1958–59) 'Interview', *Sight and Sound*, 28, 1, 26–30.

Rouch, J. (1955) 'A propos des films ethnographiques', *Positif*, 14/15, 143–6.

____ (1960) '*La Pyramide Humaine*: Scenario', *Cahiers du cinéma*, 112, 15–27.

____ (2003a [1960]) 'The Cinema of the Future', in *Ciné-ethnography*, ed. and trans. S. Feld. Minneapolis: University of Minnesota Press, 266–73.

____ (2003b [1973]), 'The Camera and Man', in *Ciné-ethnography*, ed. and trans. S. Feld. Minneapolis: University of Minnesota Press, 29–46.

Ruspoli, M. (1963) 'The lightweight synchronised cinematographic unit', *Arab Cinema and Culture*, ed. E. Fulchignoni. Beirut: The Arab Film and Television Centre, 2, 121–73.

Shivas, M and I. Cameron (1963) 'Interview with Jean Rouch', *Movie*, 8, 23, 17–28.

Truffaut, F. (1976 [1953]) 'A Certain Tendency of the French Cinema', in B. Nichols (ed.) *Movies and Methods*. Berkeley: University of California Press, 224–37.

Williams, A. (1992) *History of French Filmmaking*. Cambridge, MA: Harvard University Press.

Winston, B. (1996) *Technologies of Seeing: Photography, Cinematography and Television*. London: British Film Institute.

Yakir, D. (1978) 'Ciné-transe: The Vision of Jean Rouch', *Film Quarterly*, 31, 3, 2–11.

Damouré Zika, Ghana, 1954

19 INVENTING THE INTERVIEW: THE INTERROGATORY POETICS OF JEAN ROUCH

Michael Uwemedimo

On 7 September 1944, *Libération* devoted over a quarter of its front page to carrying the results of '*le "Gallup" français*' that interrogated and interpreted the nation's attitude towards the Liberation and offered its readers 'the exclusive results obtained from the first survey that the French Institute of Public Opinion [IFOP] have carried out since September 1939'. From the end of the war through to the 1960s, opinion polling, surveying and various species of sociological study were to become an ever more visible aspect of France's post-war reconstruction and process of modernisation.

What I want to do here is to situate Jean Rouch's experiments with the interview form, and, more broadly, what could be termed his interrogatory poetics, in this context. I want to sketch out the ways in which his 'interrogatory scenes' are moments of a new cinema's shared concern with surveying, polling and interviewing, and the ways in which these concerns are symptomatic of a national culture anxiously questioning the meanings and nature of modernisation, decolonisation and, ultimately, 'Frenchness'.

When, in the closing months of 1957, *L'Express*, announced the arrival of the *nouvelle vague*', its coming, as with the Liberation, was discerned, defined and marked by a wave of opinion polls and *études psycho-sociales* that signalled both a crisis and a celebration of national identity.[1] In partnership with IFOP, who also carried out a number of 'depth interviews', the journal tried to reach some eight million young people across the nation with its questionnaire. The 3 October 1957 edition carried 'une grand enquête nationale' across a full centre spread; the results were run almost weekly in the months that followed. Its enquiries ranged from questions of health and employment to those around culture and politics.

The *nouvelle vague*, then, in its first incarnation as a generational phenomenon, was launched on a wave of popular social scientific and journalistic experimentation whose central methodological instruments and rhetorical forms were the questionnaire and the survey interview.

The interview also played an important role in the *Nouvelle Vague*'s next incarnation as a specifically cinematic phenomenon. Two of the *Nouvelle Vague*'s inaugural works feature interview scenes – François Truffaut's *Les Quatre cents coups* (*The 400 Blows*, 1959) and Jean-Luc Godard's *À bout de souffle* (*Breathless*, 1960) In *Les Quatre cents coups* Antoine (played by Jean-Pierre Léaud), in a striking and sustained direct address, answers the off-screen questions of a psychologist (whom we never see). In *À bout de souffle*, one of the *Nouvelle Vague*'s model *auteurs*, Jean-Pierre Melville, in a cameo as the author Parvulesco, holds forth at Orly airport in a scene that stages the celebrity interview as farce.

If each film signals the presence of the interview in the new cinema, then each also points to the implication of the interview in key areas of contemporary culture: Truffaut's to the rise of the interview in the human sciences; Godard's to the significance of the interview to the new press and media (and the celebrity culture that was critical to its economy). Furthermore, when one considers the importance of the interview to *Cahiers du cinéma*'s *politique des auteurs*, and the role of that policy in opening a critical space for the *Nouvelle Vague*, the irony of Godard's parodic treatment of the 'interview-with-the-great-author' suggests a way in which the innovations and tendencies of the new film press were very much a moment in the broader developments in the post-war media. Indeed, the *Nouvelle Vague* issue of *L'Express* carried an interview with Jean Renoir in its '*Paris en parle*' feature section.[2] But the 'feature-length' director's interview was one of the conspicuous achievements of *Cahiers* criticism and by 1962 the journal had published 59 interviews with 45 directors. The interview, then, was significant to the new cinema as both content and context.

In an avowedly experimental mode, the survey interview is central to the films of that period on the cusp of art, anthropology, sociology, research and essay, by directors such as Rouch, Godard and Chris Marker. Three of these directors' films illustrate the ways that the interview and the survey more broadly were both the *vehicle* and the *object* of critique in this cinema: *Chronique d'un été* (1960), *Le Joli mai* (1963) and *Masculin/Féminin* (1966) (Godard has called these films a 'Paris trilogy').[3]

Even when interview scenes are not directly featured in this 'Paris trilogy' (as they often are), the impulse to survey frequently seizes the camera – as crowds of commuters and lines of traffic traverse the frame, the camera itself seems to conduct a series of street surveys, to offer a random, but somehow representative, sample of the Paris streets. Not just the image, but the language of these films is inflected by the terminology and forms of the statistical survey and survey interview – 'statistical lyricism' (a tendency to quasi-scientific, quasi-surreal enumeration) and an insistently *interrogative rhythm* marks their voice-overs and dialogues. The list in Chris Marker's *Le Joli mai*, enumerating everything from annual sunlight hours to litres of wine drunk, from number of births to kilowatts of electricity consumed, is a sublime parody of this 'statistical lyricism' and a number of contemporary critics commented on the interview-like exchanges of *Masculin/Féminin*.[4]

From the outset, the work of Rouch, Godard and Marker was involved in, and attempted to critique, that moment when the interview in France was a discursive practice at the conjunction of social science, market research, political polling and popular culture. Combining journalistic opportunism, scientific pretension and political purpose – the enthusiastic surveying of *L'Express* typifies this moment.

Of these three directors, it was Rouch, as a professional ethnographer whose initial investigations had been guided by the topics of ethnographic questionnaires provided by his mentors, Marcel Griaule and Germaine Dieterlen, who was working most directly with, and against, the procedures and implications of regimes of directed questioning.[5] Of Rouch's films, the densest with experimental 'questioning scenes' is undoubtedly the one he made with Edgar Morin, in Paris, in 1960: *Chronique d'un été*. The extended project involves the interview throughout – not just the film which stands at its centre, but promotion, public debate, post-production research and a publication whose preface included a long excerpt from an interview Rouch and Morin gave to *France Observateur*, and whose epilogue is a post-production questionnaire of the film's participants (see Rouch 2003: 274).[6] This project lends itself well to a consideration of the manifold implications of the interview in Rouch's practice, and of that practice's relation to a culture in which the interview was ever more pervasive.

Indeed, it is significant that the first person to be interviewed in this film was herself a professional interviewer. Marceline Loridan explains that she did 'psychosociological surveys for an applied social psychology firm'. She goes on to detail, 'I do interviews, analyse the interviews and eventually write up summaries of them' (in Rouch 2003: 276). That this interview serves to frame the entire film is both a declaration, and a performance, of the project's reflexivity. Not only does the film open with professional questioners asking questions about asking questions, but the interviewee is also a professional questioner. As in the subsequent films of the 'trilogy', here the interview is both a medium and a focus of critique.

Loridan's itinerant interviewing was made possible by newly portable tape recorders; the roving interrogations of the film she features in were made possible by the synching of such recorders to lightweight and responsive 16mm cameras. These new technologies took the interviewer into the streets. But, more than anything else, it was the new media of television (as well as the more established medium of radio) that brought the interviewer into the home. So did the telephone. Every week, the opinion poll department of RTF (French Radio and Television) would call thousands of viewers to survey their viewing habits (perhaps interrupting their evening's enjoyment of an interview with some pop star or politician). Graduates in social psychology and marketing, as Jérôme Bourdon notes, 'were head-hunted by Jean Oulif in 1964' (1991: 187). Oulif, who started off as a radio news journalist, was in charge of the opinion polls department at French radio and television from 1950–72 (see Méadel 1991: 174). Bourdon goes on to note that

> Jean Oulif, anxious to modernise his department, pleaded for the creation of posts for his social psychologists … He reminded his superiors that this practice was now recognised and laid down, not only in France, but in other countries, and gave examples of social psychologists working in businesses, carrying out 'motivational research'. (Bourdon 1991: 187)

Thus, the institutionalisation of audience research in the organs of the post-war media was part of a busy exchange between academic social science, commercial and market research and rapidly expanding spheres of communication and political modernisation. As the opinion survey and interview became an ever more popular feature of the output of post-war media, various interview scenarios were staged with increasing regularity both behind-the-scenes and as a scene.

As opinion polling established itself in key institutions, the interview scene gained a particular profile in contemporary French life. The interview was suddenly everywhere – in the newspapers, on television, in the clinic, the courtroom, the police station, the laboratory.[7] The professionalisation and increasing publicity surrounding the interviewer and pollster during this period gave rise to both widespread *fascination* and *suspicion*. Both these attitudes are evidenced in the early scenes of *Chronique d'un été*, where two young women take to the Paris streets with microphone in hand to quiz a curious and cagey public. The street interviews in these scenes repeat again and again the seventh question of the famous *L'Express* questionnaire: 'Are you happy?' The parallels between these two projects are suggestive. Certainly, what both film and journal illustrate is that the new press and the new cinema, each self-consciously experimental, had grasped the interview scene not only as a novel journalistic or sociological technique, but also as a novel form of *representation*. The interview scene (and survey culture more broadly) generated new rhetorical, graphic and narrative forms to which the experiments of filmmakers such as Rouch were responding, and to which they contributed.

Such survey specialists as those Oulif recruited could be found conducting interviews in the most unlikely places, so that interviews were performed by experts not only in the psychiatric clinic, police station, television studio and employment office, but on suburban street corners, at supermarket checkouts, at the factory gates, in prison.[8] The interviewer became a recognisable 'type', featured not only on the glossy sheets of the new press and in the films of a new cinema, but between the covers of 'serious' literature also. Both the main characters of Georges Perec's book, *Les Choses* (*Things: A Story of the Sixties*, 1965), are market researchers. The other main character is *L'Express*, the magazine itself. Of the two human protagonists, Perec writes:

> Their work, which was not exactly a trade nor quite a profession, consisted of interviewing people by various different techniques, on a range of subjects … Motivation research had emerged in France several years earlier … New [research] agencies were springing up by the month, out of nothing, or almost … Instant surveys, called mini tests, earned a hundred francs each … they spent a few months handing out survey questionnaires, [then] set off … with their tape-recorders under their arms [they were introduced] to the techniques of the open interview and the closed interview … they learned how to make other people do the talking and to weigh their own words carefully; they learned how to unearth from people's muddled hesitations, perplexed silences and shy hints the lines that needed pursuing. (1965: 27–30)

Just as Jerôme and Sylvie set off in Perec's novel, Rouch and Morin send Marceline and Nadine off with tape recorders over their shoulders into the streets of Paris. The scene from *Chronique d'un été*, in which a mechanic and his wife are being interviewed on issues of tax and vacations, could very well be edited into the scene from Marker's *Le Joli mai* in which the director quizzes a tailor about similar topics (including the question of happiness). That these two scenes could be cut together without too great a sense of disjunction attests to the fact that by the beginning of the 1960s certain interview *topics* had become commonplace (and by 'topic', I mean both subject and site): the street interview, the round table, the talking head, the question of happiness, standards of living, work and leisure, national character, sexual practice – all of which feature in *Chronique d'un été* – were common scenes on the televisual terrain.

Yet there was still an air of novelty, and indeed, as I will come to later, *foreignness*, to the interview. While Rouch and Morin, through directly calling the interview into question, and Marker, through the deployment of an ironic register, introduce a critical reflexivity, there is as much celebration as critique in their relationship with the interview; there is a palpable excitement about the novel possibilities the interview presents. Certainly, one of the reasons why Marceline and Nadine are sent out to ask Parisians if they are happy is because they can – there is an evident excitement here, about new technological possibilities, an excitement about reflecting back to itself the live mood of the streets, the capital and the nation – this excitement, and indeed, this reflexivity, is shared with journals such as *L'Express*.

Nevertheless, a certain anxiety clearly attends this enthusiastic impulse to survey – it is evident in the nervousness and tension of Rouch and Morin's initial questions and in their final ruminations, as they pace the corridors of the Musée de l'Homme at the end of the film. Some of these anxieties are voiced by Jerôme in Perec's novel, and echoed again in the final film of the 'Paris trilogy' – Godard's *Masculin/Féminin*. The central character of this film, Paul (again played by Léaud), has drifted like Jerôme into market research. Over shots of Paris streets crowded with shoppers, Paul provides the following voice-over:

> From January to March I continue asking questions of the French on behalf of the IFOP. Why are vacuum cleaners selling badly? Do you like cheese in tubes? How much do you read? What is your cadre? Poetry, does that interest you? And winter sports? What do you think of short skirts? When you see an accident, what do you do? If your fiancée dropped you for a negro, would it make any difference to you? (Godard 1969: 172)

There is a surreal poetry to the list of questions that Paul reels off. It calls to mind the random responses to *Chronique d'un été*'s first enquiry about happiness, which range from the trivial to the pathetic. Indeed, both *Masculin/Féminin*'s interrogatory enumerations and *Chronique d'un été*'s roll of responses are in many ways reminiscent of the surrealist researches.

Michel Leiris, author of *L'Afrique fantôme* (1934), should be mentioned in this connection, for one can trace in his work genealogical links between the aesthetic and methodology of the surrealist researches and those of Rouch (see Thompson 1995). The surrealist researches involved questionnaires and group interviews, and were published in the pages of journals such as *Document*, *Minotaure* and *La Révolution surréaliste*.[9] These investigative ventures simultaneously appropriate and parody the protocols, prestige and ambitions of the scientific survey.

Leiris was a member of the 1930–31 Dakar to Djibouti expedition sponsored by the Musée de l'Homme, and headed by Rouch's mentor Marcel Griaule. Leiris, like Rouch, was moved by the impulse to disrupt the rigid systems of anthropological taxonomy, the determination to call into question the discursive instruments of ethnographic enquiry, the desire to initiate a conference and exchange between documentary and fiction, and a critical concern about the colonial implications of the discipline. Rouch is very much of Leiris's line.

It is precisely a methodology of surrealist ethnography that informs the research agenda behind the street interviews in Rouch's film, *Petit à petit* (1968–69). The impulses and aims that I have noted that Rouch and Leiris share are all evidenced in a scene in the film of brilliantly absurd 'reverse anthropological' fieldwork. Outside the Musée de l'Homme, on the windswept plaza of the Trocadero, Damouré Zika (who has travelled from Niger to research skyscraper construction) accosts passers-by and, in the name of a 'sociological survey', insists on inspecting their teeth with a ballpoint pen, measuring their craniums with callipers while interviewing them and occasionally muttering generalisations about how fat and ugly the French are.

All the familiar ethnographic topics and methodological imperatives of 'scientific' interview technique are immediately identifiable in Rouch's anthropological parody. It was against these rigidly prescribed topics, and in an attempt to explore different rhythms of interrogatory exchange, that social scientists such as Rouch (who was deliberately working against the rigid questionnaire mould of the Gottingem School of Visual Anthropology) and Morin experiment with the poetics of the interview.[10] Rouch's search for a looser, more *responsive* interrogatory form, is one aspect of a series of explorations of which his unplanned camerawork is another.

This desire for responsiveness, for an increasingly *dialogical* interview form, and the influence of a surrealist poetics, can be discerned in the following comment by Morin (made in 1967 in a report on a survey in a French village):

> The interview, regarded as a drudgery by sociologists and market researchers, was for us one of the essential means of communication. The 'dives' with tape recorder as oxygen tank and microphone as harpoon led us to the secret dimension of lives that seemed two-dimensional at first sight. (Morin 1971: 258)

Against that two-dimensionality, Rouch deploys the methodological imagination of the surrealist survey. At one point in the series of *Petit à petit*'s reverse anthropological encounters, Damouré measures the breasts and hips of a young Parisian student. The uncomfortable prurience of the exchange not only calls into question the erotic ethics of the ethnographic encounter, but also gestures to the wave of 'sensational sex surveys' that were becoming ever more popular in contemporary France. The sociologically-inflected title of Godard's *Masculin/Féminin* also signals the way in which moments of the new film culture simultaneously appropriated and parodied the scientific and sensationalist impulses of the new survey culture – the title is a clear allusion to the rash of popular 'sociological' and 'psychosocial' studies into sexual mores and behaviour. Consider, for example, the 1961 survey in which the central figures of *L'Express* were all involved, *Patterns of Sex and Love: A Study of the French Woman and Her Morals*. Here is an extract from the book's back cover:

> Some years ago Dr Alfred C. Kinsey published his now famous report on the morals and sexual behaviour of the American woman next door ... Now, from the country of Brigitte Bardot, comes a study that is no less surprising. Its findings have brought facts to light that startle even Frenchmen. Based on in-depth interviews it provides a valuable contribution to our knowledge of the patterns created by the sex drive in the human female. (FIOP 1964)

The book is subtitled: 'A study by the French Institute of Public Opinion, with comments by Michel Audiard, Marcel Aymé, Françoise Giroud, Félicien Marceau, Jacques Robert, France Roche and Christiane Rochefort'. With the single exception of Marceau, all of the commentators are, or were at some stage, journalists; and with the exception only of Aymé, and Marceau again, all had written film scripts. The conjunction here of a new magazine culture, a new cinema and the survey is clear.

The interview scene brought into focus certain anxieties about sexuality and national identity. In a scene in *Chronique d'un été* the conversation is directed from the 'problem' of interracial love rather than sex, to the Algerian war and a pervasive concern about the 'state of the nation'. It is an emblematic scene, which is replayed in a number of Rouch's films – the conversation on the boat in *Petit à petit* has much the same format, and deals with much the same concerns: sex, race and national identity.

But it was not just that the interview brought these preoccupations into focus, it was also itself the focus of such preoccupations. So, looking again at *The French Woman and Her Morals*, it is notable that the study deliberately associates itself with, while differentiating itself from, the Kinsey reports, involved as it is in an attempt to define and discern a national character:

> Most of us are familiar with the studies published in the United States by Dr Alfred C. Kinsey and a team of interviewers from Indiana University ...

The study you are about to read is different in nature: leaving physiological matters aside, it deals only with the psychological and social elements of the problem of the French woman and love. (FIOP 1964: 11)

The French woman was not American – this is the claim the survey purports to demonstrate. It is the same claim made by Parvulesco in the interview featured in *À bout de souffle* – when asked by a young female reporter, 'Do French and American women differ in their attitudes?', Parvulesco replies, 'French women are totally unlike Americans. The American woman dominates the man. The French woman doesn't dominate him yet.'

The interview in France, at crucial stages of its cultural adoption and institutionalisation – particularly during the third-quarter of the nineteenth century and again after World War Two – has been bound up with arguments about Frenchness and foreignness. Since its inception the interview, as a popular journalistic form, had been perceived as an American invention and institution. In *The Power of News* Michael Schudson observes:

French writer Paschal Grousset [in 1884] compared the French press unfavourably to the British, noting that it had borrowed too freely 'that spirit of inquiry and "espionage"' from the Americans. 'The mania for interviewing, which is so rampant in America, and which has a tendency to acclimatise itself here, will never take root in England.' (1995: 76)

Certain quarters of interview culture in France consciously distanced themselves from 'quantitative' and 'behavioural' approaches, perceived as American in character, and favoured the 'open' interview, which, they held, suited a uniquely French sensibility. As Oulif has commented:

Certain opinion polls with a strictly commercial aim, carried out in the USA in particular, and based solely on the immediate reactions of the television viewers ... are unpleasantly reminiscent of the physiological experiments practised on dogs in laboratories; the dogs' opinion is not asked for, but its reactions are observed. Our opinion polls appeal to the discernment and taste of the French. (In Méadel 1991: 161)

Rouch and Morin, too, favoured 'deep' and 'open' interviews. The staging of such dialogues profoundly shapes the *mise-en-scène* of the film they made together. Indeed, when one mentions Rouch and the interview in the same breath, one immediately thinks of *Chronique d'un été* – the images and dialogue of that film seem somehow emblematic and representative, and radiate out across his oeuvre. However, and this is perhaps a little surprising, when one then turns to reviewing that oeuvre, one does not find as much as one might expect of what is immediately identifiable as interview form. The interview in various manifestations in fact features more in the films of Godard and Marker. *Chronique d'un été* seems to have been the focal point of Rouch's experiments with the interview and at least the most *visible* focus of his methodological use of the interview.

At first glance, it appears that the further Rouch's films move from the 'centre', the less interrogatory discourse they contain. Of course, *Chronique d'un été* itself is a focus on the colonial centre, an *anthropology of the centre*: an attempt to investigate the 'Parisian tribe'. And in the modern metropolis that Rouch's camera interrogates, subjects are quizzed and challenged, provoked in quite extraordinary, and sometimes disturbing, ways. Yet it is a point of note that while Rouch often spoke of 'the catalytic camera' participating in, and precipitating, performances of various kinds, it rarely acts as an incitement to speech when it is far beyond the metropolitan circle.

In Paris, Rouch arrogates to himself the authority to question, and to call into question the answers he elicits. Indeed, he (half-)jokingly alludes to the good cop/bad cop routine in the opening scene of *Chronique d'un été*. His interrogatory position here is one of sceptical sympathy – conspiratorial, yet critical.

Such a critical pitch is absent from the films that deal with traditional aspects of various West African cultures – while these films are full of responsive curiosity and fascination, their purpose seems to have been not so much to *question* as to *record*, even if as a participant rather than as a detached observer with pretensions to objectivity. In those rural areas of West Africa, the camera does not so much incite speech as participate in other, typically non-verbal and ritualistic types of performance.

Some commentators have found this problematic, and in an interview with Dan Georgas, Udayan Gupta and Judy Janda, Rouch is challenged on this issue (interviews, significantly, are where we get much of Rouch's own reflections on his practice): 'It struck us that your film about France emphasises how the European thinks, while your films on Africa emphasise how the African behaves' (in Rouch 2003: 214). The implicit charge is clear: for Rouch, the Parisian subject, the metropolitan subject, is a complex and *responsible* subject, one that can be challenged to critically reflect on an interiority, one whose prejudices can be called into question; simply, a subject able to answer a question. Whereas, *over there*, it is not speech that counts, but behaviour.

Now this is telling criticism, though rather imprecise. For it is by no means true that there is no African voice in Rouch's films. As Rouch remarks with regard to a particular film, 'Omuarou approved the change of the title from *Tre-ichville* to *Moi, un noir [1958]*. It was the first time that a *noir* was speaking on film – and he was speaking about his own life, or rather about images of his own life' (Rouch 2003: 140). *Jaguar* (1967) is a film of Africans speaking as, and to some extent, for, themselves. *La Pyramide humaine* (1959) voices the encounter between Africans and Europeans. Indeed, the more strictly ethnographic films contain much speech also, albeit more often than not of a ritualised form.

And so when Georgas, Gupta and Janda go on to ask Rouch, 'aren't Africans as articulate as Europeans? Isn't there a modern African society as creative as the group that called itself Socialism or Babarism?', the answer of his films, clearly, is 'yes' (in Rouch 2003: 214). It is not that an African voice, or a black tongue, has been excluded. Indeed, in his film of the 'centre', *Chronique d'un été*, some of the voices are African, and while perhaps not central they are by no means margina-lised. What one finds, however, moving out from *Chronique d'un été* and Paris, is that the further one travels from a fraught and uncertain process of moderni-sation, the less subjects are questioned and the more they are captured. So, in *La Pyramide humaine, Jaguar* and *Moi, un noir*, in films where there is a city, and a dialogue between modernity and tradition, there is an interrogatory poet-ics. However, as the production sites move further from a metropolitan centre and certainly as they encounter the Bandigara Cliffs (a geographical feature that seemed to shelter the Dogon from outside influence and to offer the anthropolo-gist the kind of tightly defined cultural formation that the discipline is perhaps predicated on), questions – at least questions posed on and by the camera – are much less frequent.

The interview, then, for Rouch seems to be a methodological instrument and rhetorical form bound up with an interrogation of modernity – at least this is so for the *filmed* interview. For, in fact, it is not the case that Rouch does not interview members of rural African societies. In his *written* anthropology there are indeed interview transcriptions. Focusing on the role of the interview in Rouch's work encourages one to consider relationships between these aspects of his practice that tend to be dealt with discretely – his film work, on the one hand, and his written ethnography on the other.

As Rouch remarks in the preface to his major thesis on Songhay religion and magic, it was 'the very useful questionnaire [sent by Griaule] which guided my first investigations' (1989: 13).[11] His attitude towards these pre-formulated questionnaires was ambivalent: they served him as tenplate and means of en-gagement. Of such a questionnaire provided to him by Germaine Dieterlen, he remarks:

She sent me a model questionnaire on the cult of the water spirits. I will al-ways remember one of the questions: 'Do the victims of the water spirits have their nostrils and their navel cut?' Without believing it at all, I asked Kalia

[Zika's grandmother], who, to my great surprise said, 'Of course! But if you already know such things, why bother me with all these simple questions?' (2003: 107)

The question contained the answer and the interview served as an initiation. Though, even in this example, it seems that Rouch is echoing the sense of the questionnaire's excess that his respondent voices. And so he seems to have regarded such questionnaire-based interviews as a sign of profanity rather than initiation. One senses a certain impatience, from both Rouch, the interviewer and his respondents:

> I will never forget certain remarks of the wise Damouré Zika exasperated with the implacable mechanics of questionnaires: 'Eh ansara! This is wasted time: you want to dismantle men and devils like a broken truck, but afterwards you won't know how to put it back together again, and it'll be you who's bust.' (1989: 319)

Nevertheless, one finds responses to interview questions (and references to the interviews themselves) worked into the text itself. One also finds interview transcriptions in their entirety as supplementary texts (these interviews seem to have been led for the most part by Damouré Zika).[12] So the interview is in evidence, even if it is regarded with a degree of impatience, frustration even.

Indeed, we would be surprised not to find interviews in these texts. The interview is one of the three primary methods of social research that, according to Justin Stagl, all others can be reduced to: direct observation; interviewing those that have directly observed; and inference from phenomena (2004: 3). It is clear that in his films with traditional African cultures, Rouch privileges the first of these research methods because the object of his enquiries are to a large extent observable – that is to say, ritual practices, performances and procedures. Whereas, in the centre he privileges the second because it seems that his object is not publicly visible: subjective experience (in the Cartesian tradition, directly observed by the subject), which a certain kind of interrogatory discourse promises to reveal. The register of his interviews with the Dogon, then, were *informational*, whereas in the metropolis they tend to be *confessional*.

In both registers, the interview for Rouch is a richly productive form that serves as a *technique* (of direction, or of generating dialogue, for instance), as a *structural principal* (inflecting not only the rhythm of dialogue but the pattern of the *mise-en-scène*) and as a *scene*. Common to Rouch's approaches to the interview in different contexts, and informing all aspects of his interrogatory poetics, is this imperative: 'Try to ask good questions, the answers to which will open up new questions ... human beings [are] the strangest beings in the world, and we can only ask questions' (2003: 143, 146).

NOTES

1 'La Nouvelle Vague' was the banner under which L'Express ran its survey and through which it branded itself as the organ of this wave. The survey questions were first published on 3 October 1957, and the results published weekly between 10 October and 14 November. Concluding commentary and the IFOP analysis were published in the 5 and 12 December issues; the following issue ran a critical analysis of the survey by Henri Lefebvre and a response to its questions by Françoise Sagan.

2 L'Express, 3 October, 1957, 24–5.

3 Godard makes this claim in an advertising pamphlet for Masculin/Féminin titled, 'Godard's Chronicle of a Winter'. It is reproduced in translation in the English-language version of the screenplay (Godard 1969: 222).

4 For instance, Pauline Kael's review in The New Republic not only notes that the film's rhythm is marked by an interrogatory to and fro, but that employing interrogation as dramatic method 'was prefigured by the psychiatric interview in Truffaut's The 400 Blows ... the celebrity interview in Breathless, and cinéma vérité movies by Jean Rouch and Chris Marker' (1969: 286).

5 Rouch remarks in the preface to his thesis, '[Griaul] had sent me a very useful questionnaire which guided my first investigations' (1989: 11 [my translation]). Elsewhere, Rouch notes, 'as well as encouraging me to continue enquiries into these things, [Dieterlen] sent me a model questionnaire on the cult of water spirits. I will always remember one of these questions' (2003: 107).

6 'The Point of View of the "Characters"' was originally published as 'Le point de vue des "Personnages"' (Rouch & Morin 1962).

7 The popular, the administrative and the disciplinary – the voice of the people, the word of power and the sentence of the law – were each articulated and implicated by the interview.

8 It is worth mentioning that the main character in Truffaut's, Une belle fille comme moi (A Gorgeous Bird Like Me, 1972) is a sociologist with a tape recorder, and that an extended interview articulates the narrative thread, as he pursues his erotically-charged interrogations of criminal women.

9 See, for instance, the questionnaire-based project that was published in two issues of La Révolution surréaliste: 'Enquête. Le suicide est-il une solution?', La Révolution surréaliste 1 (1924), 2; and 'Enquête. Le suicide est-il une solution?', La Révolution surréaliste 2 (1925), 12–13.

10 Professor Christopher Thompson brought Rouch's resistance to the 'Gottingem methodology' to my attention in one of several discussions we had as I was preparing this chapter. He also pointed out many interesting connections between Rouch's interrogative poetics and that of the surrealist researches.

11 My translation.

12 See, for instance, 'La Mythe de Dongo Raconté par Dawda Sorko – film et commentaries: Jean Rouch; enquête: Damouré Zika', in Rouch 1997: 251.

REFERENCES

Bourdon, J. (1991) 'The Growth of Opinion Polls in French Television, 1958–74', in B. Rigby and N. Hewitt (eds) *France and the Mass Media*. London: Macmillian, 177–94.

Godard, J.-L. (1969) *Masculin/Feminin: A Film by Jean-Luc Godard*, ed. and trans. P. Billard. New York: Grove Press.

FIOP (1964 [1960]) *Patterns of Sex and Love: A Study of the French Woman and Her Morals: A study by the French Institute of Public Opinion, with comments by Michel Audiard, Marcel Aymé, Françoise Giroud, Félicien Marceau, Jacques Robert, France Roche and Christiane Rochefort*, trans. Lowell Bair. New York: Panther.

Kael, P. (1969 [1966]) 'The *New Republic* Review', in *Masculin/Feminine: A Film by Jean-Luc Godard*, ed. and trans. P. Billard. New York: Grove Press, 208–88.

Méadel, C. (1991) 'The Arrival of Opinion Polls in French Radio and Television, 1958–74', in B. Rigby and N. Hewitt (eds) *France and the Mass Media*. London: Macmillian, 147–76.

Morin, E. (1971 [1967]) 'The Multidimensional Method', in *Plodémet: Report from a French Village*, trans A. M. Sheridan-Smith. London: Allen Lane, 254–63.

Perec, G. (1965) *Les Choses*. Paris: Julliard Collection 10/18.

Rouch, J. (1989) *La Religion et La Magie Songhay*. Bruxelles: Editions de L'Université de Bruxelles.

_____ (1997) *Les Hommes et Les Dieux du Fleuve: Essai Ethnographique sur les Populations Songhay du Moyen Niger 1941–1983*. Paris: Editions Artcom.

_____ (2003 [1978]) 'The Mad Fox and the Pale Master', in *Ciné-ethnography*, ed. and trans. S. Feld. Minneapolis: University of Minnesota Press, 102–26.

Rouch, J. and E. Morin (1962) 'Le point de vue des "Personnages"', *Domaine Cinéma 1*. Paris: Interspectacles, 154–66.

Schudson, M. (1995) 'Question Authority: The History of the News Interview, 1870–1930', in M. Schudson *The Power of News*. Cambridge, MA: Harvard University Press, 72–93.

Stagl, J. (2004) *A History of Curiosity: The Theory of Travel 1150–1800*. London:

Routledge.

Thompson, C. W. (1995) *L'Autre et le sacré: surréalisme, cinéma, ethnologie.* Paris: L'Harmattan.

From fieldwork in Niamey, Niger, 1961

20 DISBELIEVING DOCUMENTARY: ROUCH VIEWED THROUGH THE BINOCULARS OF MARKER AND RUIZ

Ian Christie

If Robert Flaherty gave birth to the myth of 'innocent' documentary, both in subject and method, then Jean Rouch may count as the first great doubter – questioning whether what is filmed can ever be true; whether merely showing is enough; and what happens to 'reality' when we start to make, or watch, a film. The importance of Rouch to questioning documentary as a form is underlined by considering the views of two other sceptics, Chris Marker and Raul Ruiz, both of whom have at times been involved in the same business of what the critic Jean-André Fieschi has called 'repudiation' (1979: 72).

I should point out that the Rouch under discussion here is not quite the same as the real Jean Rouch, who sadly died in an accident in 2004.[1] My 'Rouch' is more like the structure or position named after the real Rouch, in the way that Peter Wollen (1972) put it in his clarification of the 'auteur' concept. Why raise this old theory issue? Because discussion of documentary is still often conducted as if there was an organised debate between different philosophical positions, such as those of Flaherty, Vertov, Grierson and Rouch. In reality, of course, the positions were more fluid and pragmatic, and often much less considered than they may appear to later scholars. Rouch himself came to believe in later life that invoking Dziga Vertov in relation to the project of *cinéma vérité* in *Chronique d'un été* (1960) was probably a mistake, since it bred endless confusion and controversy (1971: 13). Vertov had named his pioneering newsreel *Kino Pravda* after the Bolshevik newspaper *Pravda* ('Truth') in the early 1920s, and Vertov's example was invoked, through the slogan *cinéma vérité*, when filmmakers in France and elsewhere started to use lightweight equipment to film unobtrusively in the early

1960s. Yet this invocation was more as homage than any deliberate attempt at emulation; for neither Rouch nor Vertov would have wanted to claim that their films offered 'the truth' in any absolute sense, although both believed in film's capacity to evoke or elicit truthfulness. And just as considering Vertov's actual practice, alongside his stream of polemical writings, throughout the 1920s yields important insights into the changing focus of his work, so too the 'real' Rouch raises illuminating and awkward issues which complicate any purely theoretical view of his position.[2]

Rouch, however, began not as a filmmaker but as an anthropologist, making the kind of records that anthropological fieldwork has used since Alfred Haddon's pioneering expedition to study the Australian Aborigines of Torres Strait in 1898 (see Long & Loughren 1993: 33). And for much of his career, he held posts within international anthropology and at the Musée de l'Homme in Paris, even though some of his films were supported by commercial producers and seen at non-specialist festivals from as early as 1955 (see Eaton 1979: 4–5). This might lead us to consider the historic relationship between anthropology and cinema which makes Rouch's transgressions more than merely idiosyncratic. Rachel Moore has explored the strong correlation between the early theorisation of film and an interest in the primitive or the magical in her book *Savage Theory: Cinema as Modern Magic*. Moore starts from the well-established debt that modernist artists owed to the primitive 'as a source of affects that modernity itself lacked' (2000: 14), and the coincidence between the rise of Modernism and the appearance of the founding works of social anthropology. Thus, for instance, in the years between Picasso's *Les Demoiselles d'Avignon* (1907) and Stravinsky's *The Rite of Spring* (1912), there appeared such key texts as J. G. Frazer's *Totemism and Exogamy* and Lucien Lévy-Bruhl's *How Natives Think* (*Les fonctions mentales dans les sociétés inférieures*), both in 1910, and Franz Boas's *The Mind of Primitive Man* in 1911. By the 1980s, this correlation had become a familiar field of study; and Moore cites influential essays by James Clifford (1981) and Hal Foster (1985) which explore the ambiguities of 'the primitive' in art and anthropology.

The next stage in Moore's argument is to note the high incidence of references to the 'primitive' in early theorisations of cinema, from Vachel Lindsay's *The Art of Moving Pictures* (1916), in which he compares movies to 'stone-age picture writing' and to Egyptian hieroglyphics, to Béla Balázs's view that the mass appeal of cinema was due to 'its clumsy primitiveness' and that, being linked to primitive gesture language, it offered access to 'non-rational emotion' (Moore 2000: 50). Moore also argues that two other key early theorists, Jean Epstein and Walter Benjamin, while stressing the mechanical nature of cinema, also both drew attention to its uncanny 'doubling' of the real world. Following our tendency to read this psychoanalytically, in terms of Benjamin's 'optical unconscious', there is, she suggests, a consistent conflation which makes the archaic 'both primal and primitive' (2000: 21), as indeed it was for Freud when he developed the concept of the unconscious from primitive animistic beliefs.[3] We might also recall Benjamin's earlier essay 'On Language as such and the Languages of Man', dating from 1916; and Epstein's 1923 declaration: 'The cinema is polytheistic and theogonic. Those lives it creates ... are like the life in charms and amulets, the ominous tabooed objects of certain primitive religions' (1981: 23). For Epstein, the cinema is 'an eye independent of the eye' – a modern, yet magical form of mediation, as it was also for Benjamin, who, while sharing much of Vertov's disapproval of capitalism's appropriation of cinema, could also appreciate how the camera 'makes strange' its habitual subjects: the film stars (1973: 233).

Many other examples could be given from the writings of the pioneer theorists of cinema: from Sergei Eisenstein's attempts to trace the sources of representation and narrative in 'primitive' practices, informed by his extensive knowledge of anthropology and by his encounter with Mexico; Siegfried Kracauer's 'redemption of physical reality' as the central thrust of cinema's claim to artistic status; and André Bazin's conception of film as fulfilling a 'guiding myth [of] recreating the world in its own image ... unburdened by the interpretation of the artist'.[4] The point, then, is clear enough: much of the theorisation of cinema that is still influential rests upon some kind of equation between film and the 'primitive'. And this belief has helped to maintain the 'naturalistic fallacy' of documentary: a deep-seated belief that it is, or can be, a form of direct access to reality – subject to the mechanism of cinema; yet also, magically, *un*mediated. This equation was undoubtedly reinforced by the canonic position accorded to Robert Flaherty, as the 'founder' of the documentary tradition with his *Nanook of the North* (1921). Even if Flaherty was no ethnographer, but an explorer turned expeditionary filmmaker, the example of his career helped to buttress a belief in exotic documentary as – however contrived and compromised – none the less embodying the authenticity of first-hand contact with the primitive. Bazin spoke of 'witness' and 'authenticity' in reflecting on the superiority of even imperfect films of exploration to their studio-made counterparts; and the residual value of films brought back from distant lands is no doubt their evidential value – faults that bear witness to authenticity, in Bazin's terms (1967b: 162).

Rouch might have remained within either the ethnographic or the expeditionary tradition. But with *Les Maîtres* (1955) and *Moi, un noir* (1958), he moved to a distinctively critical position which would ensure that he could no longer be comfortably placed in either of these genres, and would also remain at a tangent to conventional fiction cinema. Both of these films, shot in Africa, start from the premise that the 'primitive' can only be understood in dialectical relationship with the 'civilised'. In the former, members of the *hauka* cult of Niger are shown in relation to the colonial regime that drives them to seek escape in bizarre ritual, in a kind of parody of the rituals of colonialism. In *Moi, un noir*, the first of Rouch's films to be shown as a theatrical feature, dockers in Abidjan are shown to have developed a kind of protective or compensatory urban subjectivity through imagining themselves as Hollywood stars.

Rouch, then, can be seen as embodying the passage from the ethnographic 'primitive', located in distant, exotic places, back to the spectators of the first world, reminding them that Africans inhabit a world that they have helped shape, and which in many ways they both share, at least through the overarching culture of cinema. As Epstein wrote in 1926: 'the young black who used to kneel in worship before the headlights on explorers' cars is now driving a taxi in Paris and New York. We had best not lag behind him' (Epstein 1981: 21). Having shown that Africans were in many ways as sophisticated about film as first-worlders in *Moi, un noir*, Rouch was invited by the sociologist Edgar Morin to 'make a film about white people'. The result was *Chronique d'un été*, made in France in 1960, using a technique not of passive observation, but of provocation. With the microphone as its tool, and the camera often tactfully hidden, it challenges a cross-section of the natives of Paris to reveal themselves: first in a series of street encounters, then in more intensive solo and group interviews.

To some extent, *Chronique d'un été* may have been eclipsed by the subsequent widespread use of its basic strategies, especially in television documentary. Yet what remains striking and distinctively Rouchian is the filmmakers' willingness to reflect on their own practice *within* the film; and the use of different strategies to yield self-revelation, including the now-famous 'interior monologue' delivered while walking through Les Halles by Marceline Loridan, a survivor of the concentration camps who would later become Joris Ivens' partner and collaborator. Historically and ideologically, it marks a point in the evolution of documentary at which techniques formerly used to interpret the 'exotic' are returned to their point of origin; but even more importantly, the fact that the film is seen *in progress*, reflecting its impact on the lives of those being portrayed, calls into question the very idea of a stable subject or situation *to be shown*. Going beyond the simple idea of the non-professional or 'real person' within a film, *Chronique d'un été* proposes that filming can never be neutral, but unavoidably creates a dynamic of representation and self-presentation. This has sometimes led to the conclusion that Rouch is, in effect, making fiction, since he is using many of the strategies of fictional narrative and the audience is responding similarly to the interpersonal drama of these characters. But this is surely simplistic. *Chronique d'un été*, no less than *Moi, un noir*, remains rooted in an ethnographic perspective on society; but its work as a film is to deconstruct the practice of documentary, while rejecting the consolations of fiction. We are left with a film that obstinately reveals its shifting conditions of production and leaves us with more questions than answers.

And of course Rouch was not alone in raising such questions in the early 1960s, especially in a France that was awaking bloodily and divisively from its imperial dream.[5] Chris Marker's progress from his early diary and essay films towards feature-length, and increasingly fictionalised, works offers a striking parallel with Rouch.[6] Indeed Marker's *Le Joli mai* was avowedly a response to *Chronique d'un été* – taking the temperature of France at a crucial moment in the process of decolonisation, in mid-1962, after the Algerian war formally ended, and using the same Coutant-Mathot 16mm camera with synchronous recording, which Marker would call the 'living camera' (see Sadoul 1979: 296). Most of Marker's films would continue to be cast in the genre of insider-reporting from exotic locations, ranging from Siberia and China to Israel and Cuba, and following somewhat in the French literary tradition of the journal, taking inspiration from those of Stendhal and Gide, with elements of the social criticism of Montesquieu's *Les Lettres persanes*.[7] But in the late 1970s and 1980s, he would return to the long form of *Le Joli mai* in the reflective chronicles of *Le Fond de l'air est rouge* (*The Base of the Air is Red*, 1977) and *Sans soleil* (1982).

While the former consists of an enquiry into the progress of revolutionary movements and socialism in the decade between 1967 and 1977, it is in *Sans soleil* that Marker created his definitive disavowal of documentary. The film's protagonist is a global traveller who takes trips to the far corners of the world, filming marginalised Koreans in Japan and pauperised inhabitants of Guinea-Bissau, and visiting the locations of Hitchcock's *Vertigo* (1958) in San Francisco. He is, of course, Marker himself – the actual creator of the images we see – although we never see him, and he is addressed only as 'you' by the film's female narrator, as if in a romantic fiction. Here the literary tradition of the traveller reaches its climax, with a visit to the arch-romantic site of Iceland; yet the film also contains an elaborate unpicking of the presumptions of documentary, with asides on the ethics of subjects looking back at the camera ('those who wait and have nothing' in the Cape Verde islands) and a deliberate invocation of the 'resurrectionist' myth of cinema in the *Vertigo* sequence. Marker's 'disbelief' in naturalistic documentary lies in his simultaneous acknowledgement of his own presence, which marks every episode of this film, with erasure of his own visibility outside of his filmmaking.[8] Latterly, he has become, in effect, a modern 'techno-shaman', offering his globalised sensibility as a grid through which we can make sense of the overload of images and sounds that reach us through other channels.[9]

Marker's method of creating a fictional persona who is active in the pursuit of remembering (which is not just the opposite of forgetting) and memorialising, notably in his films about the Soviet filmmaker Alexander Medvedkin, might seem to place him at the opposite pole to Rouch's outward-looking inquiries.[10] Certainly it would be difficult to imagine Marker wishing to show his material to those he has filmed, and to take account of their responses, as Rouch insisted the ethnologist-filmmaker must do (see Eaton 1979: 58).[11] Ultimately his omnivorous curiosity, wide experience and insider knowledge seems turned inward, serving the sensibility which is organising it like a latter-day Symbolist hero: Axel or des Esseintes. But what he shares with Rouch is the problematisation of any film's point of view and a rejection of the transparency or self-sufficiency of the image to 'explain itself'.

Another perspective on Rouch is provided by the Chilean filmmaker Raul Ruiz, who has lived in France since 1974. Ruiz was originally a director of neo-realist drama and what were sometimes obliquely 'militant' films under the Popular Unity regime of Salvador Allende.[12] Arriving in France as a political exile, he became a prolific documentarist for French television in the late 1970s, maintaining an 'outsider' stance, partly by inclination and partly in accordance with the terms of his refugee status in France. One film from this period, *Great Events and Ordinary People* (*De grands événements et de gens ordinaires*, 1979) embodies much of Ruiz's scepticism towards the documentary tradition. In what began as a commission from the Institut national de l'audiovisuel to make a 'personal' film about local elections, seen from an outsider's point of view, Ruiz moves at accelerating speed through the conventional strategies of the television documentary, interviewing a cross-section of local people on the street and in their homes. But the film soon admits that this reveals little about the electoral process; and instead its subject becomes the form of documentary itself, with a series of sequences built around 360-degree pans, which also make ironic reference to the culture of cinema in France (one of these circular tours takes place in the editorial office of *Cahiers du cinéma*, hinting at the insularity of French cinema discourse).

In its final sections, Ruiz's film addresses the relationship between documentary and society in terms of power. A Canadian filmmaker explains how difficult he has found it to gain access to French politicians and intellectuals, who resist the collusion with the media found in other societies – and the power wielded by the filmmaker in Third World societies. Documentary, Ruiz reflects through his unseen narrator, is in fact a colonial form, founded on the ability of the colonising world to impose its vision on dependent peoples and lands. Although documentary may try to move with the times, it rarely exposes its own terms of reference: its failures as well as its lucky accidents. Elsewhere, in his *Poetics of Cinema*, Ruiz has argued against the 'conflict-centred' model of cinema, with its belief in narrative efficiency, proposing instead a 'shamanistic' approach, influenced by the aesthetics of the Baroque and of Surrealism (1995: 73). The roots of this radical relativism arguably lie in Rouch's original disavowal of naturalistic documentary. Identifying himself as a filmmaker from the Third World, Ruiz enters into a triangular dialogue with Rouch and Marker, in which the very concept of documentary can no longer be used unproblematically, any more than it can be opposed to fiction.

Both Marker and Ruiz have thoroughly confounded the documentary/fiction distinction, producing works that establish their own specific terms of reference. Ruiz describes this as making 'poetic objects', with rules 'that are unique to each film and must be rediscovered by every viewer' (1995: 77). Although much of Rouch's filmography appears to consist of films 'about' specifiable subjects, closer examination will usually show that each is unique in its premise, anticipating the approach advocated by Ruiz. After *Chronique d'un été*, Rouch's career would zig-zag between the first and third worlds, taking him back to Africa for many more films that would continue to explore the power dynamics of colonial, and increasingly post-colonial, societies, while also giving him opportunities to develop the practice of a 'shared anthropology' in films made in France.[13] Late in his career, and no doubt frustrated by the continuing problem of finding forms that would allow his films to circulate outside specialist circles, he undertook an ambitious attempt to explore the roots of ritual in *Dionysos*, co-written with the Martinique-born filmmaker Euzhan Palcy. Spun out of a slight fable about an American professor who has come to Paris to research a thesis on Dionysos, and in effect becomes a modern Dionysos, as the film tries to explore the presence of the primitive, or primeval, in contemporary society. Cast adrift from documentary as a basis, the carnivalistic form is sometimes embarrassing (in the way that Ruiz's baroque inventions can also be) and may count as an honourable failure within Rouch's oeuvre. Yet it is also a true *apologia pro sua vita*, and ends with a touching dialogue in which, true to form, Rouch interrogates or reveals himself. Asked by 'Dionysos' what he is doing, he replies, while filming, that he is 'continuing to look for the imaginary between space and the seasons'.[14] A far cry indeed from 'mere' documentary; but a good manifesto for the utopian ideal of film.

NOTES

1 An early version of this chapter was given as a paper at a conference on Rouch, at the Institute of Contemporary Arts in London, in June 2000, at which the filmmaker was present, along with other leading pioneers of 'direct cinema' and *cinéma vérité*, including Albert Maysles and Richard Leacock. This made distin-

guishing positions from people a more urgent priority than it might otherwise have been; but the point remains valid.

2   The large Vertov retrospective at the 2004 Giornate del Cinema Muto in Sacile made it possible to understand Vertov's progression from early actualities to increasingly elaborate structures in the late 1920s.

3   See also Sigmund Freud, 'The Uncanny', 1985: 365.

4   On the evolution of Eisenstein's aesthetics, see, for instance Christie & Taylor 1993. Kraucauer's aesthetic is most fully expressed in Kraucauer 1960. Bazin's underpinning of his aesthetic appears in 'The Myth of Total Cinema', 1967b: 21.

5   In 1954, France withdrew from Indochina after eight years of escalating war with Ho Chi Minh's liberation movement; and in the same year Algerian nationalists launched a guerrilla campaign that would continue until 1962, when Algeria gained independence.

6   Four years younger than Rouch, Marker started making films in the early 1950s, and the first of his 'foreign reports', *Dimanche à Pekin*, in 1955.

7   *Les Lettres persanes* (1721) purports to be a collection of letters by Persians visiting Europe in the 1710s and commenting on the institutions and customs they find – a veiled form of social criticism practised by Montesquieu.

8   Marker has rigorously censored the appearance of any portraits of himself and maintained close control over the circulation of his films.

9   He has also moved 'beyond' cinema in gallery installation works and in the CD-ROM *Immemory*. For discussion of this, see Tode 2005.

10 Marker followed his first portrait of Medvedkin, *Le Train en marche* (*The Train Rolls On*, 1971), with an extended account of Medvedkin's – and by extension the Soviet system's – life in *Le Tombeau d'Alexandre* (*The Last Bolshevik*, 1992).

11 This practice is continued by some other observational filmmakers, notably Michael Grigsby.

12 For an account of Ruiz's work in Chile, see the interview by Malcolm Coad and Ian Christie (1979).

13 Rouch originally used this phrase and 'anthropological dialogue' in an article in *Le Monde* on 16 June 1971.

14 Dialogue quoted from a text by Daniel Boitier, 'Et toi, Jean, qu'est-ce que tu fais?', http://www.jean-rouch.de/texte.html (accessed 14 November 2006).

REFERENCES

Balázs, B. (1952) *Theory of the Film*. London: Dennis Dobson.
Bazin, A. (1967a [1953]) 'Cinema and Exploration' in *What is Cinema?*, ed. and trans. H. Gray. Berkeley: University of California Press, 17–22.

_____ (1967b [1946]) 'The Myth of Total Cinema' in. *What is Cinema?*, ed. and trans. H. Gray. Berkeley: University of California Press, 154–63.

Benjamin, W. (1973) 'The Work of Art in the Age of Mechanical Reproduction', in *Illuminations*, trans. H. Zohn. London: Fontana, 211–44.

Bullock, M. and W. Jennings (eds) (1999a [1912]) *Walter Benjamin: Selected Writings*. Harvard, MA: Belknap/Harvard University Press.

_____ (1999b [1912]) 'On Language as such and the Languages of Man', in *Walter Benjamin: Selected Writings*. Harvard, MA: Belknap/Harvard University Press, 62–74.

Christie, I. and R. Taylor (eds) (1993) *Eisenstein Rediscovered*. London: Routledge.

Clifford, J. (1981) 'On Ethnographic Surrealism', *Comparative Studies in Society and History*, 23, 4, 539–64.

Coad, M. and I. Christie (1979) 'Between Institutions', *Afterimage*, 10, 103–14.

Eaton, M. (ed.) (1979) 'Chronicle', in *Anthropology-Reality-Cinema: The Films of Jean Rouch*. London: British Film Institute, 1–6.

Epstein, J. (1981) 'On Certain Characteristics of *Photogénie* (1923–1924)', trans. Tom Milne, *Afterimage*, 10, 20–3.

Fieschi, J.-A. (1979) 'Slippages of Fiction', in M. Eaton (ed.) *Anthropology-Reality-Cinema: The Films of Jean Rouch*. London: British Film Institute, 67–77.

Foster, H. (1985) 'The "Primitive" Unconscious of Modern Art', *October*, 34, 45–70.

Freud, S. (1985 [1919]) 'The Uncanny', *Pelican Freud Library* 14, Harmondsworth: Penguin, 339–76.

Kraucauer, S. (1960) *Theory of Film: The Redemption of Physical Reality*. Oxford: Oxford University Press.

Long, C. and P. Loughren (1993) 'Australia's First Films: Facts and Fables, Part Six: Surprising Survivals from Colonial Queensland', *Cinema Papers*, 96, 32–6.

Moore, R. (2000) *Savage Theory: Cinema as Modern Magic*. Durham: Duke University Press.

Rouch, J. (1971) 'Cinq regards sur Vertov', in G. Sadoul *Dziga Vertov*. Paris: Editions Champ Libre, 11–14.

_____ (1979 [1973]) 'The Camera and Man [extract]', in M. Eaton (ed.) *Anthropology-Reality-Cinema: The Films of Jean Rouch*. London: British Film Institute, 54–63.

Ruiz, R. (1995) *Poetics of Cinema*, vol. 1, trans. B. Holmes. Paris: Editions Dis Voir.

Sadoul, G. (1979 [1963]) 'Un miroir qui réflechit', *Chroniques du cinema français*, Paris: Union générale d'éditions/Collection 10, 18, 296–302.

Tode, T. (2005) 'Film – That was Last Century! Chris Marker's CD-ROM *Immemory*', *Film Studies*, 6, 81–6.

Wollen, P. (1972) *Signs and Meaning in the Cinema*. London: Secker and Warburg.

From fieldwork in Niger, 1946–47

21 ADVENTURES ON THE ROAD: SOME REFLECTIONS ON ROUCH AND HIS ITALIAN CONTEMPORARIES

Anna Grimshaw

Although Rouch's influence on developments in European cinema has often been noted, his work is conventionally bracketed off as part of the tradition of ethnographic film. The African context of his practice has served to place the work in a specialised category which engages a very particular – and limited – audience. As a result, anthropologists and film critics have not spent much time exchanging ideas about the scope and significance of Rouch's cinema. On the one hand, this has created a rather uncritical celebration of Rouch among ethnographic filmmakers, who have tended to overlook problems of race, gender and power in favour of an easy acceptance of his claims to have subverted conventional anthropological hierarchies. On the other, his relegation to a footnote by many commentators on European cinema has pre-empted proper consideration of his place within a broad landscape of filmmakers, one that includes not just the French *nouvelle vague* but figures like Rossellini, De Sica, Antonioni or Fellini.

A quick glance at some of Rouch's most notable films, *Les Maîtres fous* (1955), *Jaguar* (1967), *Moi, un noir* (1958), *La Pyramide humaine* (1959) and *Chronique d'un été* (1960), made between 1954 and 1960, reveals a significant coincidence of dates. Of course, these were years in which many classic films of European cinema were released – Fellini's *La Strada* (1954) and *Le Notti di Cabiria* (*Nights of Cabiria*, 1957), Resnais' *Hiroshima, mon amour* (1959), Antonioni's *L'Avventura* (1960) and, of course, Truffaut's *Les Quatre cents coups* (*The 400 Blows*, 1959)and Godard's *À bout de souffle* (*Breathless*, 1960). This overlap in dates surely suggests the possibility of an interesting conversation across areas of disciplinary specialisation.

I want to suggest some of the ground on which anthropologists and film critics might begin to productively engage. I propose a juxtaposition of Rouch with his European counterparts as a way of bringing into new focus certain key concerns of post-war cinema. Despite their different geographical and cultural location, Rouch's films raise questions about subjectivity and society that resonate strongly with issues explored by figures such as Rossellini, De Sica, Fellini or Godard. The African site of Rouchian cinema, however, reconfigures these questions in a number of interesting ways. Looking more carefully at what is shared and what is different in the work of Rouch and his Italian or French counterparts enables us to begin to construct a more expansive history of post-war cinema, one in which the conventional relationship between the centre (Europe) and periphery (Africa) is rendered unstable. At the same time, placing Rouch alongside Fellini or Godard serves to enrich anthropological understandings of his particular innovations as a filmmaker. No longer an isolated, self-invented figure whose work exists in a kind of vacuum, we can begin to situate his practice beyond the narrow confines of ethnographic cinema.

My own approach to Rouch has been profoundly shaped by the writings of the West Indian historian, C. L. R. James. Drawing on classics such as *The Black Jacobins* (1938), *American Civilization* (1950) and a number of other essays, I have sought to work with Jamesian ideas as a way of exploring the complex interplay between historical location, substantive focus and aesthetic experimentation in the cinema of Jean Rouch. In bringing these two figures together, I am prompted by a significant overlap in their work. For the conditions in which Rouch forged his particular identity as a filmmaker were central to James's thinking and writing during the 1950s and 1960s. At this time James was preoccupied with independence movements in Africa and the Caribbean. He was especially interested in the relationship between democracy and creativity, believing that new aesthetic forms emerged at certain moments in history, when existing conceptions of social and political life were being challenged by movements of popular resistance. He was unusually sensitive to the role of artists and writers in these moments of transition, while remaining mindful of the easy danger of falling into a kind of crude reductionism. Moreover, James perhaps more than anyone else was quick to point out that developments in areas that might be considered to be 'peripheral' or 'marginal' were often in advance of the 'centre' and served to challenge it (see in particular, along with those works noted above, *Nkrumah and the Ghana Revolution* (1977)).

Although there is much to explore in terms of Rouch's relationship to the *nouvelle vague*, it is the relationship with Italian filmmakers – especially De Sica and Fellini – that I find especially intriguing in developing a more expansive conversation about Rouchian cinema. Not least Rouch's playful, somewhat theatrical, personality seems to have much more in common with De Sica and Fellini than with his French equivalents. But beyond this there are a number of points of similarity – and difference – that I believe are worthy of further exploration. These relate to notions of subjectivity, the city and the notion of the journey as a structuring principle of cinematic narrative. I will briefly consider Rouch's films of the late 1950s in the context of the work of De Sica and Fellini – suggesting that we consider *Les Maîtres fous*, *Jaguar* and *Moi, un noir* as part of a shared landscape that includes *Ladri di biciclette* (*Bicycle Thieves*, 1948) *Umberto D* (1952), *La Strada* and *Nights of Cabiria*. The point of departure for my discussion is Rouch's film, *Jaguar* and Fellini's *La Strada*. I have long been intrigued by the overlaps between these two works – the close proximity of dates, the use of picaresque narrative and the shared interest in the lives of people moving around the edges of mainstream society.

Rouch's *Jaguar*

The cluster of films that Rouch made between the mid-1950s and early 1960s have always seemed to me to constitute the creative core of his work. Here Rouch established the major preoccupations of his cinema (cities, people on the move, migrant subjectivities) and forged an innovative film practice that profoundly unsettled the conventional categories of documentary and fiction, reality and the imagination, Europe and Africa.

Jaguar is critical to the group of films inaugurated by Rouch's controversial *Les Maîtres fous*. If much less problematic than *Les Maîtres fous* – indeed almost irresistible in its energy and playful good humour – *Jaguar* shares with the earlier film a concern with the lives of migrants as they move, geographically and psychologically, across the rural and urban landscape of West Africa. Like *Moi, un noir*, made in the same period, *Jaguar* is much celebrated as an example of a hybrid form, 'ethno-fiction'. All of these films demonstrate the potential of Rouch's camera to serve as an active agent in the expansion of subjectivity. *Jaguar* follows Damouré Zika, Lam Ibrahima Dia and Tallou Mouzzourane as they set forth from the countryside for the great adventure of African cities. Travelling through strange places, encountering strange people, telling tall tales, the three friends eventually reach the Gold Coast where they establish a small market stall, 'petit à petit'. Here they fully realise themselves as actors in the theatre of the city. But Rouch does not leave his subjects here. Returning to their villages, the filmmaker likens Damouré, Lam and Tallou to the heroes of history, men transformed by experiences afar and whose adventures accord them special status in the eyes of those left behind in their village. Rouch continues his story of these characters in a later film, *Petit à petit* (1969–69). This time his subjects travel to Paris, undergoing a whole series of humorous encounters with girls, sports cars, skyscrapers and other symbols of modernity. I confess that I have always found the sequel much less convincing than *Jaguar* – more contrived and forced than the open, engaging spirit of the earlier work. Following James, I attribute the contrast between *Jaguar* and *Petit à petit* to the changed historical conditions of the films' making – a point I return to below.

Adventures on the Road

Fellini's film, *La Strada*, tells the story of the relationship between a brutish circus performer, Zampanò, and Gelsomina, the young woman he purchases from her mother at the beginning of the film, and who travels with him along the road, enduring his humiliations and neglect until he cruelly abandons her as she sleeps. Critical in their journey, their restless movement from one place to another is the spiritual awakening of Gelsomina. Her experiences serve to clarify the innocence and purity of her own being. Her encounter with the Fool is an important turning point. The Fool's violent death at the hands of Zampanò is followed by Gelsomina's abandonment on the wayside. Continuing alone, Zampanò learns of her death many years later. In the closing scene of the film, Fellini suggests the possibility of Zampanò's redemption as he weeps for his loss.

La Strada was the first film in what Peter Bondanella calls Fellini's 'trilogy on spiritual poverty' (1991: 30). The other two films, *Il Bidone* (*The Swindle*) and *The Nights of Cabiria* followed in 1955 and 1957 respectively. Critics were sharply divided in their responses to these films. Fellini was widely attacked by those on the Left who accused him of abandoning the political commitment of Neo-realism in favour of fantasy and mysticism. Other commentators, most notably André Bazin, recognised *La Strada* as an example of a 'neo-realism of the person', acknowledging the films' fundamental continuity with, if important extension of, established concerns in Italian cinema (in Bondanella 1978: 57).

Placing *La Strada* and *Jaguar* alongside one another throws into relief a number of questions about contemporary society that Fellini and Rouch share. Given the cultural locations of their work, however, each filmmaker articulates a profoundly different understanding of the world in which they live. At one level the two films are remarkably similar – both document a journey, a voyage of discovery that leads to a metaphysical truth. The characters in *La Strada* and *Jaguar* encounter obstacles and challenges; and, as a result of their adventures on the road, they undergo a transformation, emerging at the end of the film with a profoundly different understanding of their own subjectivity. But if Fellini's moments of redemption are pre-eminently individual, Rouch's moments of redemption are always social, found within the context of cinema itself.

Fellini's film came only a few years after works like De Sica's *Bicycle Thieves* and *Umberto D.* Already these two pieces expressed a very different conception of the post-war world than was to be found in films like Rossellini's 'war trilogy'. As Millicent Marcus explains it, the sense of heroism, optimism and collective endeavour that animated films like *Roma, città aperta* (*Rome, Open City*, 1945) or *Paisà* (1946) had dissipated, and was replaced by what she calls the 'banality' of existence (1986: 55). Antonioni famously articulated the changing agenda of filmmakers at this time:

> The Neo-realism of the post-war period, when reality itself was so searing and immediate, attracted attention to the relationship existing between the character and surrounding reality. It was precisely this relationship which was important and which created an appropriate cinema. Now, however, when for better or worse reality has been normalised once again, it seems to me more interesting to examine what remains in the characters from their past experiences. (Quoted in Bondanella 1991: 108)

Fellini shared with Antonioni a desire to explore subjectivity as a more subtle and complex phenomenon than had been possible within classical neo-realist cinema, with its location of characters in concrete social and economic circumstances. In *La Strada*, Fellini sets his characters free – of both history and society. Gelsomina, Zampanò and the Fool move through different spaces and different encounters on a journey that is neither linear nor progressive. The episodic movement of the narrative symbolises the allegorical nature of the tale. The journey is a spiritual quest that involves moments of insight rather than any cumulative development of understanding.

La Strada was made in the context of post-war consolidation. No longer active participants in the collective effort of remaking society, Italian filmmakers were now located differently, increasingly positioned as detached observers of a world that set individual and society against one another. Filmmakers believed themselves to be faced with a choice. For Fellini, it seemed impossible to imagine a full and creative exploration of subjectivity that also took society or history into account. The subjective life of his characters can only unfold outside time and space. In *La Strada*, he abandons the city and conventional narrative – 'the plot' – to construct instead a picaresque story assembled from episodes and individual moments. As Bazin observed, events 'befall' Fellini's characters rather than 'happen' to them. Bazin goes on to suggest that Gelsomina's transformation is built upon what he calls 'vertical' gravity rather than 'horizontal' causation.

By this he draws attention to the fact that subjectivity is no longer shaped by context but emerges in response to misfortunes and events outside the subject's control (1972: 84).

In turning his back on the world, however, Fellini precludes the possibility of development in his cinema – there is only *repetition* (represented by Zampanò) and *transformation* (represented by Gelsomina). There are 'breakthroughs', flashes of insight that remain quintessentially personal. What we discover is that the detachment of subjective experience from society and history, understood by the filmmaker as a liberation – existentially and aesthetically – for himself and his characters becomes ultimately a check on the possibilities of subjective expansion itself.

By contrast, Rouch's cinema of the 1950s appears much more fluid and inventive. Specifically, it was not bound by the same dualities or oppositions between subjectivity and society that came to divide Italian cinema. *Jaguar* was made in the midst of colonial independence. We may recognise that this was a classic Jamesian moment in which all established categories were giving way, a moment in which the relationships between Europe and Africa, cinema and life, political upheaval and artistic expression were posed anew. But positioned 'off-centre', in Africa, rather than in Europe, located in a period of chaos not one of consolidation, Rouch's cinema offers a different interpretation of questions that animated – and divided – the Italian filmmakers. We can see that in *Jaguar*, as well as in *Les Maîtres fous* and *Moi, un noir*, Rouch's subjects are profoundly aware of themselves as agents in history and society. At the same time, however – and this is important – their subjectivity is neither defined nor confined by time and space. In place of the opposition between city and countryside, history and the imagination, society and the soul that Fellini builds at the heart of *La Strada*, *Jaguar* reveals the effortless movement of Damouré, Lam and Tallou across these categories.

Rouch's filmmaking practice was forged in conditions not unlike those existing in Europe after 1945, when directors like Rossellini celebrated the collective solidarity of people rebuilding society from the ruins of fascism and war. Rouch's subjects are engaged, too, in the struggle to create new forms out of the collapse of the old, but his conception of people in the world is quite different from that expressed in *Rome, Open City*, *Bicycle Thieves* or *La Strada*. For example, Rouch shared the same fascination with urban space that marked the work of some his Italian counterparts – that is, he conceived of the city not as a backdrop to human action but as a significant expression of it. If, however, the Italian directors increasingly depicted the city as a vast, disorienting and impersonal place which isolated and rendered powerless its inhabitants, Rouch saw it differently. For him, these very qualities of the city (its surreality) were integral to its power as a space for the invention and reinvention of the self. Unlike the father and son of De Sica's *Bicycle Thieves* or the old man in *Umberto D*, Rouch's African migrants flourish in the city. They are not tiny figures dwarfed by a large, anonymous world. People like Damouré or Lam or Tallou are pre-eminently *players*, and luck is always on their side. What Rouch shared with Fellini (and Antonioni) was a commitment to exploring subjectivity, conceptualised as a complex interior space that stretched far beyond its social manifestation to encompass the imagination, fantasy and the unconscious. But his vision did not involve a retreat into a sort of redemptive cinema (Fellini) nor into a world of subjective isolation and despair (Antonioni).

To conclude, my approach to understanding the work of Jean Rouch has its origins in the tradition of ethnographic film. I have found that anthropologists are rather uncritical in their celebration of Rouchian cinema, overlooking its unusual historical location and insulating their discussion of it from broader debates about post-war cinema. By suggesting we work with Jamesian ideas as a way of exploring how cinematic practices are embedded in certain historical moments, I am anxious not to be understood to be advocating a closing down of possibilities. Indeed quite the reverse. One of C. L. R. James's greatest strengths was that he never lost sight of the complex interplay between social context and individual personality. I would be the first to admit that any attempt to pin Rouch down, so to speak, immediately runs into the problem of the fugitive nature of the subject. Like the characters of his films he was pre-eminently a 'player', constantly in movement, at once elusive and deeply subversive of conventional understandings. Like all good footnotes, he continually threatens to unravel the text.[1] In proposing that we remove Rouch from his marginal place in the narratives of cinematic history, I do not intend to check his disruptive potential – rather I want to release it.

NOTE

1 Not least, Rouch's work raises the possibility that the origins of the *nouvelle vague* lie in Africa, not Europe.

REFERENCES

Bazin, A. (1972) *What is Cinema? Vol. 2*. Berkeley and Los Angeles: University of California Press.

_____ (1978 [1955] 'La Strada' in Bondanella, P. (ed.) (1978) *Federico Fellini: Essays in Criticism*. New York: Oxford University Press, 55–84.

____ (1991) *Italian Cinema from Neorealism to the Present.* New York: Continuum.

James, C. L. R. (1977) *Nkrumah and the Ghana Revolution.* London: Allison and Busby.

____ (1980 [1938]) *The Black Jacobins.* London: Allison and Busby.

____ (1994 [1950]) *American Civilization.* Oxford: Blackwell.

Marcus, M. (1986) *Italian Film in the Light of Neorealism.* Princeton: Princeton University Press.

On set, *Petit à petit*, 1968–69

22 THE CONFIDENCE ISSUE: ROUCH AND KIAROSTAMI

Charles Warren

If one starts, it is hard to stop thinking about Jean Rouch's *La Pyramide humaine* (1959) and Abbas Kiarostami's *Nema-ye Nazdik* (*Close-Up*, 1990) as two films that press the question of what we are seeing in a film. In Rouch's film we are introduced to some black and white teenagers in Abidjan, Ivory Coast, and told that they have agreed to improvise and act out a story of interracial friendship and romance, in the process expressing racial views they may or may not hold. Near the end of the film Rouch tells us that the young people have made discoveries about themselves, that fiction has become reality. What have we in fact seen? In *Close-Up* we meet a Tehran confidence man interested in film. He may not set out to be a confidence man, but he leads a bourgeois family down the garden path, encouraging them to think he is the famous film director Mohsen Makhmalbaf and that they will be involved in a film production. *Close-Up* offers to show us a mix of documentation of real events as they happen, and honest re-enactments. Like *La Pyramide humaine*, or Rouch and Morin's *Chronique d'un été* (1960), *Close-Up* makes strong suggestions that the making of the film before us has shaped the lives of the people we see on film. Again, what are we in fact seeing, and in what direction does it go?

La Pyramide humaine and *Close-Up* are unusual films. They push to the fore and make unavoidable, questions about what it is we are seeing. Rouch tells us in voice-over that the students, the actors we see, are doing a certain thing and that they end up changed people. And *Close-Up* does not present itself simply as a window on reality. The film's scenes come in different styles – re-enactments, interviews, the following of ongoing events, a courtroom scene that, inexplicably, looks like video or a different kind of film stock than the rest. The opening re-enactment, of a taxi ride through Tehran, is not made clear as being a re-enactment until well after we have viewed the scene. The film is possessed of a restlessness and self-consciousness that carry over to the viewer; it would keep us conscious, asking what it is that we are seeing.

Close-Up and *La Pyramide humaine* are unusual in being so forthrightly provocative about, we might say, their state of being. Yet they raise questions for all of film – fiction and non-fiction. Are they an odd pair to take on such a role? One can suggest not, with an invocation of Jean-Luc Godard. In 1965 Godard named *La Pyramide humaine* the second-best French film since the Liberation, placing it just after Max Ophuls's *Le Plaisir* (1952) and just ahead of Cocteau's *Le Testament d'Orphée* (*The Testament of Orpheus*, 1960), Renoir's *Le Testament du Docteur Cordelier* (*Experiment in Evil*, 1959) and Bresson's *Pickpocket* (1959) (much mixing of documentation and fantasy in this list) (see Godard 1986: 210). The films of Jean Rouch – especially the sequence *Moi, un noir* (1958), *La Pyramide humaine* (1959), *Chronique d'un été* (1960) and *Jaguar* (1967) – kin to but different from Italian Neo-realism, doing something more daring, more conscious – had a powerful effect forming and confirming the French *nouvelle vague*.[1] Recently the eternally productive Godard, of films and of ideas, has said that cinema begins with Griffith and ends with Kiarostami.[2] To look at cinema through the lens of Godard is not the only way to look, but it is a revelatory way. Godard and the French *nouvelle vague* proceeded with an awareness of all of film and an impulse to think about film: their films think about film. Their work is a centre of consciousness, where everything exists in a present. We can go to these filmmakers and critics to learn about film, to open ourselves to it. T. S. Eliot proposed that Baudelaire and subsequent French poetry led us into John Donne and the English seventeenth century, and of course into the future, all the books existing in one time, or out of time, as it were under the eye of God.[3] This may be a proposition outrageous to historians, but Eliot's point, and his effect, is to open us to poetry. History cannot show us all that is going on in a poem, a book or a film. *La Pyramide humaine* opens the door to film consciousness – to *one* consciousness, I would say again – this film whose title is that of the fairy tale-like, heated, delirious Paul Éluard prose poem that is read on-screen and seems to make everything happen in the film. And for a certain film consciousness Kiarostami is the end of cinema. What can this mean except that he makes an impression to be reckoned with, like Griffith, as Godard would have it, inventing cinema day by day on the set of *The Birth of a Nation* (1915) (1986: 117)? Kiarostami, paradoxically, seems uninterested in the history of cinema, and just proceeds from his experience making advertisements and instructional films, his love of children and his deep involvement with classic and modern Persian poetry.[4] As the situation keeps hinting, the matter of these films and their implications is a matter of poetry, poetry in the Heideggerian sense of a radically new, in each instance, unstoppable, uncontainable creative force. Eliot felt compelled to call poetry 'a superior amusement' (1950a: 8). One thinks of Ingmar Bergman's remark about Stravinsky, that he was always urging 'restraint' because he knew he had a volcano inside (1988: 35).

La Pyramide humaine and *Close-Up* are documentaries, and they have something important to suggest about fiction, specifically film fiction. With documentary there is always the confidence issue. One cannot decisively know that the images are what they purport to be, that what the film says, is true. Even with the single image as certifiable as one likes regarding content, there come into play the human factors of deciding what to film and where to place the camera, and deciding where the shot will begin and end and the placing of the shot into a context of other shots, making a fabric. The truth cannot but come as a creative act; and perhaps truth here is an impossible vanishing point.

It may be that our best approach to documentary is one that can find some footing in philosophy's response to the broad problem of scepticism, scepticism as to whether the world exists as it appears – I may be only dreaming it – and scepticism as to whether others exist and are like me. There is no proof. We cannot know the world and others in a way that would satisfy a sceptic. But we can examine the means by which we do live in the world and with others. We can dig for answers that we know but mostly repress or overlook, in the numbness of everyday living or in the face of relentless questioning. Inspired by Wittgenstein's *Philosophical Investigations* (1953) and J. L. Austin's study 'Other Minds' (1979), Stanley Cavell has developed the concept of acknowledgement as opposed to knowing. There is no simple formula for this. Cavell takes many hundreds of pages in *The Claim of Reason* (1979a) to say what acknowledgement is, to point us towards it, examining philosophers' arguments, producing examples from life, invoking myths, dramas, poetry. Our great resource is the ordinary – not something we all know perfectly well, but a deep trove the door to which we tend to keep shut.[5] Over the past half century what is called ordinary language philosophy has evolved as a procedure for insisting on what we are able to say, and do realise, against metaphysical claims, as Wittgenstein called them, that would limit us or hold us to a logical standard, all this enterprise amounting to a simplification and distortion of life. As literature and the arts, film among them, have become subject more and more to restrictive conceptions and sceptical questioning, some lately – Martha Nussbaum a well-known name among them – have wanted to place their work, and encourage more work, under the rubric of ordinary language criticism (1995). One could say this is really a revival, calling attention to new philosophical underpinnings, of a practice of criticism long since established and always carried on, though for some time now feeling the forces of repression. The repressed, if it matters, does not go away. It comes back.

With a film making claims to truth, the issue of giving confidence is inextricably tied up with evaluation – not the testing of a film's claims with hope of reaching a decisive outcome, but the making of a judgement that we ought to have faith. Making such a judgement is a matter of a total impression, involving thinking and more than thinking, all of which begins early in the experience of watching a film, and never ends – we go on and on and never make up our minds finally. This is good enough and more than good enough. This is how we live, or how we might live, as Wittgenstein, Austin and Cavell would have it. If we look at works of art – films – as we look at the world itself and at others, giving scrupulous attention to the experience at hand and drawing on a broader experience, indeed on all our experience, then we must be prepared to admit that any case may be different from all others, that the case at hand may demand a reconstitution of any sense of rules we may have for making evaluation. We live by drawing comparisons. But the world, the work, the film, comes in a creative guise, ever new. Critical engagement needs to be creative, improvisatory, for all the cultivation of faculties that goes behind it. Wittgenstein's *Philosophical Investigations* paints a complex, almost novelistic, picture of how we live and think and make formulations. There is about the book a strong sense of realism and sanity, as well as a terrifying openness to the winds of madness. Wittgenstein works to find bearings in life, and for many readers projects a delicate sense of rules. Yet to read through the *Philosophical Investigations* is to be struck at the seemingly infinite possibilities, the creative possibilities, of ordinary language, of the speech, the life we in a sense already have. And the *Philosophical Investigations*, this hard-won account of our life, written in intense fragments with energies leaping out from the gaps between, is itself a creative work. It is peculiar, – to some unreadable – even a utopian work, seeking freedom, like the work of the surrealists and Jean Rouch. Indeed, it is like the work of all film, if we see the medium itself as essentially surreal, at once engaged and displaced, in the spirit of the *nouvelle vague*.

In *La Pyramide humaine* Rouch is perhaps the confidence man, seducing the students (are they students?) to participate in his film, giving them who knows what guidance, telling the viewer directly what is pretended here and what becomes real and will stick. In *Close-Up* Kiarostami presents a version of Rouch, in the confidence man Sabzian, who seems at least provisionally to let himself believe he is a filmmaker, as he leads a family to believe they are getting involved in a film. Also, Kiarostami presents a version of Rouch in himself, Kiarostami, whom we see and hear around the margins of the film, coordinating things, like Rouch in *Chronique d'un été*, *La Pyramide humaine* and other films. Sabzian entreats Kiarostami, when they meet in the jail, 'make a film about my sufferings', which is what Kiarostami does, as well as making a film about the middle-class family who want to be in a film. Sabzian's film in a sense gets made – it is *Close-Up* – just as the family's film gets made. But *Close-Up* is also a film about the interest in cinema and what this can do to people (as Kiarostami justifies it in the film to the judge of whom he asks permission to shoot a trial). The same can be said about the making of Rouch's peculiar film of his young friends who want to go through with the making of it at his suggestion. Kiarostami as director finds an alter-ego in Sabzian and thereby acknowledges a certain madness and extra-legality in himself. That one must lose one's mind to a degree to find one's way is a lesson Rouch knew well, as did Wittgenstein.

La Pyramide humaine gives no particular reason to distrust Rouch, though a sceptic could never be sure about it all. I would suggest that Rouch's words in voice-over and his conversations with the students stay in the mind in something of a suspended, provisional, uncertain state, while the rest of the film goes on to do its work more directly, as in the episodes with the students alone, which form an alternating pattern of rather claustrophobic scenes of discussion of race relations or romantic complications, and then explosive physical activity, outdoors and on the move. (*Close-Up* also follows a pattern of confinement breaking out into the open – film seems to confront reality and then to change it.) The plan for *La Pyramide humaine* and even the comment on its outcome are a means of setting up the episodes, and perhaps no more than that; Eliot said of poetry that the meaning is like the meat the burglar throws to the housedog, to satisfy and divert one habit of mind so that the poem can do its real work (1961: 151). In *La Pyramide humaine* we see young people in groups and pairs talking heatedly, perhaps sincerely, but with an overly verbal quality. Then, repeatedly, we see actions spun out in the various settings of Abidjan, as if words and thoughts need the test of physicality: guitar playing, soccer, long walks, dancing at night, a bike ride, the exploration of a beached ship. People apparently fall in love and get jealous and upset. The very point of the film seems to be to get us to ask whether what we are seeing can be just pretending, whether this acting does not become a reality of sorts, though it may not be the reality we have fixed ideas about – neither a lie nor the old understood reality, but something of a third reality, a film reality that must be reckoned indeed a reality. Here it is. People do undergo metamorphosis, which is easy to see in the young, who are so full of hope – we remember at the beginning the students, black and white, introduce themselves in class, most giving an anticipated profession: sociologist, musicologist, philosophy professor, pharmacist, entomologist (making one think of Buñuel). Film always amounts to a displacement, a transfiguration, of the world. Those on film undergo metamorphosis inevitably. *La Pyramide humaine* provokes a certain uncertain change in its subjects, and perhaps reflects, documents, change such as it is always occurring. Film cannot be disentangled from life. What we live is film.

The historical sense might say, what we live now is film. But Godard suggests film is a realisation of impulses always there in the arts and in life (throughout his criticism of the 1950s, Godard relates film to Diderot and other eighteenth-century moralists). Cavell says that film – a world that is there and not there – was born in a crisis of scepticism, as was the thinking of Wittgenstein.[6] It is not that life now is new, but that the regard of life asks to be reformed, given a new form.

La Pyramide humaine suggests of all film taking the world as it is – documentary film if you like – that it is a co-operation between the world and film, that the world never simply *is*, but comes to us in metamorphosis, that the metamorphosis of film is reality. This is not to say that a film may not seem fake, and be fake. The world is creative, and film's creation of the world, or creative registering of the world, is what the world asks. This seems somehow signalled by the student's voice-over a third of the way through *La Pyramide humaine*, saying that everything – the access of feeling and change – began with the classroom reading of the Éluard text, 'when poetry entered our hearts like a marvellous poison'.

Poetry had already entered the picture, of course, at the moment Rouch said, 'let us make a film'. Soon thereafter the students introduce themselves, and the film makes its first break to the outdoors, viewing Nadine and Alain in a travelling shot as they ride on a motorbike, with Nadine's voice-over talking of *vacances* (holidays) and the possibilities they bring, anticipating the later part of *Chronique d'un été*. The *vacances* are film, adventure, poetry. The shot of the motorbike ride says eroticism, which is at the crux of life, change, creation, poetry. Editing Nadine's voice-over onto the image is poetry. So is the ensuing flow of scenes: the first interactions, two guitar players, their music carrying over onto a soccer game, additional voice-overs as the students make their lives. The film, with its decided gestures, asks: is this poetry not the way to get to life in its truth? If the students are to be what they are, must they not become caught up in a poetic act?

La Pyramide humaine's ultimate signal that poetry, film poetry, is the true direction for life, comes with the crashing sea around the beached ship at the end. A protracted discussion of the romantic match-ups and then of race and African politics breaks out to the magical scene of a film projection, with Rouch's voice-over saying that the students view footage of their story so far and decide to 'go all the way' with the experiment, putting it 'to the test of tragedy', meaning the enacted death of Alain in the sea after his dive from the beached ship. Tragedy is not cruel obliteration, but a transforming trauma or death, like that of Oedipus or Agamemnon, or the *actus tragicus* of the crucifixion of Christ. Tragedy is ritual, a way of moving life forward, indeed of living, as in the many rituals filmed –

and in part provoked – by Rouch over the years among the Songhay and Dogon, or among Europeans in *Chronique d'un été* with their own *vacances*. Alain in *La Pyramide humaine* presumably does not die – we see him resurrected, walking on the street at the end – unless this is a trick of editing, giving footage taken before an actual death. But Alain does go into the sea, in this act or performance that, Rouch says, means so much to everybody, taking things all the way, 'freeing those who believe too much in their roles'; making it possible to move on, free from the constrained roles of life before the experiment of the film, and free from the film itself. And the sea is the emblem of film, of film poetry, as the sea and water more generally have been on so many occasions – *Bronenosets Potyomkin* (*Battleship Potemkin*, 1925), *A Day in the Country* (1936), *Man of Aran* (1934) and in Tarkovsky's work – where water's reflecting surface and its broader transformative imagination play a major part in provoking us to keep watching the film. Rouch's filming of the sea, and the rhythm of his editing of these images – pure documentary if you like – is the most arresting thing about *La Pyramide humaine*, and sends one back through the film to think it out.

In the jail in *Close-Up* Sabzian says to Kiarostami: 'What I did looks like fraud.' And to Kiarostami's question 'what is it really?', Sabzian's only reply is, 'I'm interested in cinema.' Cinema, documentary or whatever it is, if scrutinised may look like fraud. But perhaps there is a good fraud, and a good credulity, a necessary way of life, of acting and communicating and understanding. We are in the realm of Herman Melville's novel *The Confidence Man* (1857), which suggests that over-confidence is less dangerous than no confidence, which is not to endorse confidence *tout court*. *Close-Up* changes people's lives. It seems even to affect the conciliatory judge in court and the humiliated family in their decision to forgive Sabzian – all seem to do what Kiarostami wants, what the film wants. This film, like *La Pyramide humaine*, sparks change, allows change, documents change as something more than the film could invent – the desire on the part of life to approximate film, to become film, and such a desire to be able to be realised.

In *La Pyramide humaine* people offer to enact a fiction. In *Close-Up* people interested in fiction find themselves caught up in a peculiar film of unclear provenance, not what they expected (or did Sabzian expect it?). What these films say about fiction is that it is a possibility. Some fiction films one wants to call fake. But valid fictions are experiments, a test against reality, showing that an imaginative idea can come about as, in Wittgenstein's formulation, a form of life. We see people say the words and do the acts, we see objects, we see a world, on the plane of a third reality, as it were, not a lie and not the reality we had supposed as such, without thinking. Film is thinking. What in film could be more thoroughly created than the work of Mizoguchi? Yet *Saikaku ichidai onna* (*The*

Life of Oharu, 1952) comes down to the nub of the loving but unobtrusive camera following Kinuyo Tanaka's uncanny pained, slow, dignified way of walking in that first scene among the ageing prostitutes in a suburban wasteland – a seventeenth-century one that we know is also the post-Hiroshima wasteland. And at the centre of *Le Plaisir* is a document of movement, as Danielle Darrieux's prostitute – young but feeling the weight of flesh – sidles and backs easily but restlessly about the farmhouse room she is given for the night. How can Darrieux be a poor provincial prostitute? This film, which ends contemplating the sea as does *La Pyramide humaine*, is in its big central story largely about Darrieux's playing of a role, and by making an issue of this opens possibilities in our view of the role and of the 'real' woman Darrieux. *Le Plaisir*, with much location shooting, is hardly more a fiction than those other films Godard named, of Rouch, Cocteau, Renoir and Bresson.

The great English literary critic F. R. Leavis proposed, to the disgruntlement of some historians, that every valid work of literature speaks to the question 'what for?' – that is to say, what is life for? ('we get, not what we are likely to call an "answer", but the communication of a felt significance' (1969: 46)). We might say that every valid film, fiction, documentary, is a provocation. What are we seeing? Where does it go? Where are we as we witness – perhaps at once within ourselves and displaced from ourselves? Where might we go?

NOTES

1   See Godard 1986: item 53, 'Jean Rouch Wins the Delluc Prize', 104; item 68, *Moi, un noir*, 129; item 72, 'Africa Speaks of the End and the Means', 131–4; and item 93, 'Interview with Jean-Luc Godard' (1962), 180, 194.

2   This statement was bandied about a good deal at the time *Ta'm e guilass* (*Taste of Cherry*, 1997) won the Palme d'Or at Cannes. Kiarostami acknowledges the statement and comments on it in an interview, saying Godard made it after seeing *Zendegi va digar hich* (*Life and Nothing More…*, 1991) in the early 1990s (The *Guardian* Interviews at the National Film Theatre, Abbas Kiarostami: 28 April 2005, http://film.guardian.co.uk/interview/interviewpages/0,,1476326,00.html (accessed 17 November 2006)). The statement appears on the front cover of Alberto Elena, *The Cinema of Abbas Kiarostami*, 2005. Thanks to Daniel Morgan and Tom Gunning for help in tracing this Godardian remark.

3   Eliot 1950b. See also 'Tradition and the Individual Talent' in Eliot 1950a.

4   Hamid Dabashi (2001) gives a good account of Kiarostami's involvement in poetry. Laura Mulvey (2006) makes an interesting connection of Kiarostami to Rossellini and to Italian Neo-realism more broadly.

5　See especially chapter 13, 'Between Acknowledgement and Avoidance', 327–496.

6　Cavell begins this line of thought in *The World Viewed: Reflections on the Ontology of Film* (1979b).

REFERENCES

Andrew, G. (2005) 'Guardian/NFT Interview with Abbas Kiarostami', *Guardian* Unlimited On-line, 28 April. On-line. Available at: http://film.guardian.co.uk/interview/interviewpages/0,,1476326,00.html (accessed 7 October 2006).

Austin, J. L. (1979) 'Other Minds', in J. O. Urmson and G. J. Warnock (eds) *Philosophical Papers*, third edition. Oxford: Oxford University Press, 76–116.

Bergman, I. (1988) *The Magic Lantern*, trans. J. Tate. New York: Viking Penguin.

Cavell, S. (1979a) *The Claim of Reason: Wittgenstein, Scepticism, Morality, and Tragedy*. Oxford: Oxford University Press.

____ (1979b) *The World Viewed: Reflections on the Ontology of Film*. Cambridge, MA: Harvard University Press.

Dabashi, H. (2001) 'The Making of an Iranian Filmmaker: Abbas Kiarostami', *Close-Up: Iranian Cinema, Past, Present and Future*. London: Verso, 33–75.

Elena, A. (2005) *The Cinema of Abbas Kiarostami*, trans. B. Coombes. London: SAQI.

Eliot, T. S. (1950a [1919]) 'Tradition and the Individual Talent', in *Selected Essays*. New York: Harcourt, Brace & World, 3–11.

____ 1950b [1920]) 'The Metaphysical Poets', in *The Sacred Wood*. London: Methuen, 241–50.

____ (1961) *The Use of Poetry and the Use of Criticism*. London: Faber and Faber.

Godard, J.-L. (1986) *Godard on Godard: Critical Writings by Jean-Luc Godard*, ed. and trans. T. Milne. New York: De Capo Press.

Leavis, F. R. (1969) *Anna Karenina and Other Essays*. New York: Simon and Schuster.

Mulvey, L. (2006) 'Abbas Kiarostami: Cinema of Uncertainty, Cinema of Delay', in *Death 24 x a Second: Stillness and the Moving Image*. London: Reaktion, 123–43.

Nussbaum, M. (1995) 'The Window: Knowledge of Other Minds in Virginia Woolf's *To the Lighthouse*', *New Literary History*, 26, 4, 731–53.

Willemen, P. (ed.) (1978) 'Interview with Max Ophuls' in *Ophuls*, trans. J. Batchelor. London: British Film Institute.

Wittgenstein, L. (1953) *Philosophical Investigations*, trans. G. E. M. Anscombe. New York: Macmillian.

Still from *Chronique d'un été*, 1960

23 ROUCH'S 'SECOND LEGACY': *CHRONIQUE D'UN ÉTÉ* AS REALITY TV'S TOTEMIC ANCESTOR

Brian Winston

Without prejudice as to whether or not *Chronique d'un été* (1960) is, in autuerist terms, more the work of Edgar Morin than of Jean Rouch, there is no question that the latter's on-screen presence, albeit far more shadowy than Morin's, is at times crucial. When the young men gather at the table, not for the first time in the 'commensality' phase (as Morin was to call it) of the shoot, it is Rouch who pushes Morin to encourage them into a discussion of the Algerian War, a topic which they had so far assiduously avoided discussing (see Morin 1985: 7, 11; Feld & Ewing 1985: 56). When, at another table, Marceline Loridan reveals her distaste at dancing with a black man during *Le Quartorze Juillet* (1953) it is Rouch who quickly intervenes in the conversation to ask Landry, the Ivorean who, for the film, is an explorer from Africa investigating 'the strange tribe that lives in Paris', if he has ever noticed the number tattooed on Marceline's arm (in Morin 1985: 13). The seeming inconsequential query is not, of course, to change the subject, but to reveal that the racist Marceline has herself been the victim of extreme racism, a Jewish casualty of the Nazis who deported her as a child to a concentration camp during World War Two (as the tattoo indicates).

Such overt on-camera manipulations of the conversation in the direction he felt the film needed to go was entirely within Rouch's expanded notion of legitimate documentary intervention, since his purpose was to make manifest the *mentalités* of his subjects for the camera. This interventionism, it can be argued, is one of the two formal outcomes of *Chronique d'un été*'s rich, albeit largely unacknowledged, legacy for the Anglophone documentary. It stands behind the interventionism of much of what we today call 'reality TV'. The other better-known formal outcome, of course, is the idea of filming the filmmakers à la Vertov.

Is this distinction between two legacies a distinction worth making?

The first legacy

I am not seeking to contradict the fact that in the protean oeuvre of Rouch's work *Chronique d'un été* is not as central as his reception in the Anglophone world has made it. Be that as it may, the fact is that for most of us, *Chronique d'un été* has been, more or less, the Rouch oeuvre in its entirety; and it is pretty meaningless to question the impact of the man (at least on the mainstream of Anglophone documentary production over the last half century) in terms that stray much beyond *Chronique d'un été*.

The distinction between documentaries where a filmmaker is seen on-camera, which can be designated *cinéma vérité*, and its contemporary alternative, the observational ('fly-on-the-wall') 'direct cinema', was to be more often than not blurred over the next half century. Nevertheless, at the outset in the early 1960s, the desire to observe in as unobtrusive a way as possible, which animated direct cinema practitioners, significantly marked them apart from a minority group of filmmakers who, in the name of *cinéma vérité*, put themselves (and thereby the filmmaking process) in the frame. (The *locus classicus* of the former is *Primary* (also made in 1960) and of the later *Chronique d'un été*.)

However, there was, and is, an Anglo-Saxon misunderstanding of the distinction. This initially arose from the confusion of terms between *cinéma vérité* and direct cinema (*cinéma direct*) which attributed the central idea of the latter (even as it reduced that idea to a mere matter of long sync takes in available light), to the former. (In the Anglophone documentary tradition, the hand-held long take with available sound and light style becomes, of course, far more the legacy of *Primary* – of Drew/Leacock/Pennebaker – than of Rouch.) More significant than these linguistic misappropriations was the fact that *cinéma vérité* in mainstream Anglophone television usage was anyway itself bastardised. Direct cinema shooting ratios were well beyond the norms of television production except for the chosen few – Roger Graef in the UK, Frederick Wiseman in the US, for example. The rest had to make do with a mixed style which used limited long takes and still deployed interviews, commentary, added music, 'B' rolls and all the rest of the Griersonian tool-box. In the UK this was termed 'vérité', in effect distinct from both *cinéma vérité* and direct cinema (see Winston 1995: 210–18).

In received professional opinion at the time, 45 years ago, all Rouch was seen to be adding to this direct cinema/*vérité* 'fly-on-the-wall' approach was merely to put himself in the frame. And what was the point of that? This was very much a step too far for mainstream North American and UK television – then more or less the only game in town. This was after all the era when British crews were given to demanding: 'Do you want this shot properly or in "wobblyscope"? Do you want to be able see this or is shooting it in the dark alright? Mumbles OK or shall I mike people properly?' and so on. Filming oneself as a guarantee of truthfulness was a bridge too far.

Of course, such reflexivity anyway strikes the Anglo-Saxons as a bit arch, a bit cerebral, a bit – dare we say – Continental? After all, Grierson and company had had no time for Vertov and his games thirty years before, regarding *Man with a Movie Camera* (*Chelovek s kino-apparatom*, 1929), for example, as a *reductio ad absurdam* – 'too clever by half', Grierson had suggested at the time (1981: 141); 'We didn't take it seriously, quite frankly', Paul Rotha recalled half a century later (quoted in Marris 1982: 7). While *Cahiers du cinéma* greeted *Chronique d'un été* with references to Heisenberg's uncertainty principal, Richard Leacock, a one-time camera-assistant to Flaherty and a physicist by education as he never tired of saying, was muttering about it being nothing but a recording instrument (say a seismograph) – which he did to such good effect that Godard for one thought Leacock's camera lacked 'intelligence' – an extremely unfair judgement, but one brought upon Leacock by himself (see Goldmann 1979: 66; Godard 1963/64: 140; Blue 1965: 16).

It is no wonder then that Rouch's life-long project problematising the nature of reality and its representations was absorbed by the Anglo-Saxon mainstream, in so far as it is absorbed at all, in a pretty simple-minded way: take as a random example of this, Michael Moore's presence in *Roger and Me* (1989). The film starts with the Moore home movies of Michael as a young child as he explains in voice-over that he is the scion of a family of General Motors assembly-line workers who grew up in Flint, the decline of which is the film's subject. There is, though, no sense that Rouch's broader attack on the implicit fraudulence of the unproblematised documentary image is in play here. Moore, an old-time agitprop journalist, is merely writing himself in, in time-honoured fashion, to es-tablish his proletarian *bona fides*. Although such authoring has been part of An-glophone television documentary's approach to the real from the establishment of current affairs as a genre in the mid-1950s, it is curious that it so often takes this Mooresque tone – a somewhat self-consciously knowing comic stance. It does so most notably in the films of Nick Broomfield (who as a graduate of the National Film School in Britain in the 1970s was certainly aware of Rouch and the implications of his approach in a way that Moore, as the director of *Roger and Me* making his first film with no such background, probably was not). Both their on-screen presences, despite Broomfield's handsome British upper-class foppishness being at odds with Moore's blue-collar American boorishness, function in more or less the same ironic/comic mode.

Broomfield is, arguably, the master of the Anglo-Saxon transformation of Rouch's strategy in *Chronique d'un été* – to use the image of the filmmaker as a totem of the problematised image – into the documentarist as a species of comic Holy Fool. After the austerities of his engaged early work (from *Juvenile Liaison* (1975) to, say, *Soldier Girls* (1980) Broomfield developed an on-camera persona of charming ineptitude. In *Tracking Down Maggie* (1994), for example, he appears to be unable to obtain an interview with Mrs Thatcher even though she is in the middle of her by-then usual post-prime-ministerial round of publicity activities. The Anglo-Saxons have in effect created a self-fulfilling prophecy around the first of *Chronique d'un été*'s legacies. Having understood reflexivity in terms of the crude presence of the filmmaker on screen, they could then easily demonstrate (at least to their own satisfaction) that this presence within the frame was, as they had always suggested, no guarantee of truthfulness at all. It was no guarantee of anything. In fact, Broomfield's on-screen persona in this phase of his work is pretty much an act – as was revealed by the climactic moment from *Kurt and Courtney* (1997), when he coolly seizes the microphone at a huge banquet of *le tout Hollywood* to harangue Courtney Love, the star guest. Broomfield's voice-over explains the hysterical wavering of the camera by saying his operator was terrified. Broomfield (here far more James Bond than Hugh Grant) was, despite the previous accumulation of bumbling images we have of him, clearly not remotely phased. What we have got from those Anglo-Saxons who followed Rouch onto the screen – Moore, Broomfield, Ross McElwee and untold television journalists and presenters of long-form series – is nothing less than a species of, if not lying, then certainly somewhat unreliable narrator.[1]

A second legacy?

For the past 45 years, the filmmaker in the frame has been the most overt legacy of *Chronique d'un été* but since the rise of reality television there is another aspect of Rouch's filmmaking strategies which demands consideration from the Anglo-Saxons. It is not that we see Rouch on screen; it is that we see him on screen overtly intervening to direct the conversation – to 'direct' action both as a participant in it and, of course, as the film's director. Rouch can be seen to be 'constructing' the film in ways above and beyond the Anglo-Saxon norms of documentary 'construction'; but as Morin said, 'The great merit of Jean Rouch is that he has defined a new type of filmmaker, the "filmmaker diver" who "plunges" into real-life situations.' Rouch's first legacy is, thus, his presence on the screen; his second, which logically does not depend on seeing him in the frame at all, is his willingness to push his subjects into places they would not otherwise occupy in the name of understanding their inner selves better. The first is concerned with the filmmaker, the second with the filmmaker's subjects.

The Anglo-Saxon interventionist norm was, prior to direct cinema, a matter of reconstruction which had no such Rouchian ambitions. It was deployed simply to capture what the camera had missed. At the outset, the basis of reconstruction for both Flaherty, and subsequently Grierson, was that these missed events reconstructed for the camera had been as far as possible authenticated by prior witness – not necessarily by the filmmaker but by somebody, somewhere. In the case of *Nanook of the North* (1922), it is the memories of 'Nanook' (played by Allakarialuk) concerning his father's generation and their life – igloo building, harpoon hunting and the rest – which provides this 'witness'. This is without prejudice to the reality of the Griersonians' obedience to such a 'rule' of prior witness along these lines. In fact, they were to play increasingly fast and loose with it until the coming of the Canadian National Film Board, Drew, Leacock and Pennebaker in the late 1950s and early 1960s rendered the whole strategy illegitimate by demanding nothing be reconstructed for the camera – ever. What had been missed remained so in direct cinema.

Central here is the fact that prior witnessed reconstructions are scarcely the same as Rouchian interventions designed to provoke responses illuminating the *mentalités* of a film's subjects. The interventionism of Rouch, whether conducted on or off camera, could not (and does not) need the legitimacy of prior witness. As with the journalistic interview, the results on the screen (or the page) would not exist but for the intervention of the filmmaker (or the journalist). The press interview, developed as a technique by American reporters from the 1830s on, had still not quite been absorbed into everyday journalistic practice by the second half of the nineteenth century. There were persistent misgivings as to its validity. As late as 1884, in the London evening daily, the *Pall Mall Gazette*, the editor W. T. Stead wrote that 'one of the superstitions of the English press … is that interviewing is a monstrous departure from the dignity and propriety of journalism' (in Silvester 1993: 7). The direct cinema practitioners eighty years later felt exactly the same and eschewed interviews in their documentaries because they too felt them to be improper. That the interviewers, Rouch and Morin, were on the screen in *Chronique d'un été* was not for them a guarantee of truth but yet further cause for concern. But the real worry was the picture presented by the film of 'the strange tribe that lived in Paris'. At a critical meeting in Lyon in 1960 to discuss the then new revolutionary lightweight 16mm sync-sound equipment, Leacock pronounced *Chronique d'un été* as being beyond pointless 'since the only thing that's happening to them [the film's subjects] is the fact they are being filmed' (in Shivas 1963: 18). For a filmmaker whose guiding principle was to let the event be more important than the filming, how could he be impressed by such an effort? What was the point of a series of events which had no existence outside the film they were part of, if that film was to be considered a documentary.

The arrival of the breathtakingly misnamed 'reality television' brings this somewhat obscure argument centre-stage. The initial (and in many quarters sustained) professional reaction to this television programming development was to dismiss it as illegitimate, undignified and improper. It is seen as a prime site of what Jon Dovey has memorably termed 'a freakshow', a contemporary continuation of the long tradition of 'trash TV' (see Dovey 2000). (*Candid Camera*, after all, was on US television by August 1948.)[2] But beyond a distaste of populism and a more visceral dislike of the inherent voyeurism and exploitation of most of reality television's output, finding a theoretical justification for denting such programming's documentary status has proved more difficult. It can be argued that a central reason for this is, exactly, this second legacy of Rouch's.

Does this definitional problem matter?

It does, because as with all theoretical issues around the documentary, the ideological power of any claim on the real, made by documentary or broadcast news, is of considerable consequence to the political economy of the media's systems of representation. Without a claim on reality, the evidentiary truth of any image is denied. If new genres or sub-genres of programming raise serious questions as to the nature of the 'evidence' the image provides (as arguably reality television shows do), in turn such questioning undercuts (or runs the risk of undercutting) the evidentiary *bona fides* of news and documentary – 'evidentiary television', as these might be called. This is, of course, not necessarily a bad thing since it is not entirely irrational to ask whether or not any 'truth' is (or can be) actually on offer even in the most sober documentary and news productions. Critics of the established order might therefore be pleased with programming that in the long term possibly subverts the ideological force of mainstream 'evidentiary television'. Be that as it may, there can be no question that the possible impact of reality television on the mind of the audience attuned to watching 'evidentiary television' is a matter of some importance.

Reality television primarily puts 'real' people, that is non-professional actors, in unscripted situations created by the producers. The current vogue for such programming is normally traced to the long Writer's Guild strike in the US in 1988, which forced the networks to move formats such as *America's Most Wanted* (1988–) and *Rescue 911* (1989–96) to prime-time. These programmes use footage of disasters and arrests amongst others (often amateur or surveillance) as well as reconstructions and studio presentations. They are distant from the observational norms of documentary although they do contain elements of actuality. Reality game shows (or 'gamedocs') too (apparently) use the actuality of surveillance to focus on 'a series of "real-life" exchanges between a group of carefully selected individuals gathered together in a highly contrived, made-for-TV environment and required to respond to a number of challenges dreamt up by members of the production team' (Kilborn 2003: 58–9). Soon reality television was being used to describe not just these programming forms but 'make-over programmes, talent contests, docusoaps, dating shows, court programmes, tabloid news magazine shows, and reality-based sitcoms' (Murray 2004: 1900). The development of these programmes has been considered as a positive: 'For its supporters, reality TV may be championed as the vanguard heralding a new, more democratic era of TV within a multi-channel environment' (Biressi & Nunn 2005: 2).

Among its most fervent champions are, of course, those who produce the programmes. Their totemic ancestor, Allen Funt, *Candid Camera*'s 'host', explained his intentions in 1985 in *Psychology Today* as wanting 'to go beyond what people merely said, to record what they did – their gestures, facial expressions, confusions and delights' (in Loomis 2004: 443). Funt's tendentiousness in this is, of course, to ignore (as do those who today echo such arguments) that his basic purpose was to cause embarrassment, distress even. It must be noted, however, that his intention was never to illuminate the inner person, as was Rouch's. The filmmakers' actions are the same – establishing the situation and then guiding it for the camera – but the intentions are opposing ones: to cause embarrassment versus illuminating the human condition.

It could be, though, that intention is beside the point. Rouch's second legacy might be in play despite the difference of intention because however different the objectives of the producers, the outcome might still be similar. For Jon Dovey, who does not share elitist disdain for reality television in any form, even the least documentary-like of reality television programming – a reality television 'game' show such as *Big Brother* (2000–) – has the capacity to illuminate life as much as does Rouch, or for that matter any other 'sober' (as Bill Nichols would call them) documentarist:

When *Big Brother* in the United States gets tangled up in debates and arguments about race, it's reflecting something significant about America. When the Portuguese *Big Brother* sparks a national debate about domestic violence after an incident on the show, we are seeing a culture in the process of modernisation coming to terms with contemporary European culture ... Although the reality TV game show does not set out to do public service work, far from it, it nevertheless can be seen to reflect and produce debates that raise questions about the way we live now, in terms of identity, relationships, genders and ethics. (2004b: 246)

If an astute critic can make a plausible cause for the social worth of reality television games, then reality television series devoted to observing events, in the approved dominant fly-on-the-wall documentary manner, can also easily be seen in the same way.

Take *Wife Swap*

This exercise, presented as a series of *vérité* documentaries, involves episodes in which two families swap mothers for two weeks – as mums, of course, not as conjugal partners. Only the title is swinging, otherwise its 'no sex please we're British'. The attractions for the audience would appear to be the *jouissance* of voyeurism; the frisson arising from the clash, comedy, friction – and potential trauma – of different sorts of lifestyles being artificially brought together. It is produced by Stephen Lambert who used to make respectable fly-on-the-wall BBC television series about such things as the Foreign Office and he edited the BBC's prestigious documentary slot *Modern Times* (1995–2001), a strand of traditional social documentaries. Now he has moved into the more lucrative world of reality television and stands ready to defend this (to my mind) unedifying, asinine exercise in exploitative and potentially psychologically damaging spectacle:

> Certainly we wanted people who were going to contrast strongly with each other but we try to be as neutral as possible when we film it … Many TV reviewers launched vicious attacks on the people in the show, and we did not do that. So it was very hypocritical of them. (In Thorpe 2003: 14)

'We try to be as neutral as possible.' Well, having cast, for example, a racist woman who has a bit of a thing about miscegenation to live for two weeks with a spliff-smoking black man, of course you can afford to be 'neutral'. Surely otherwise you would be over-egging the pudding somewhat? And of course, having exposed these people to hatred, ridicule and contempt, the hatred, ridicule and contempt they then attract is nothing to do with you. That will be the fault of hypocritical newspaper hacks and the 5.7 million who tuned in to see the fun and games. Responses, outcomes – none of these are apparently much the responsibility of Stephen Lambert, no longer a television producer, now more an 'engineer of souls' (as they used to call Stalin) – or a 'filmmaker diver' (albeit unseen) as Morin called Rouch.

It is not far-fetched to claim that Lambert, however unknowingly, is a recipient of Rouch's second legacy. The programmes cannot be dismissed as documentaries even though, in my view, they are ethically outrageous and disgustingly exploitative. Nevertheless, they could still illuminate *mentalités* – that is, exhibiting precisely the quality we admire in Rouch's documentaries. This is exactly as Dovey sees it: for him *Wife Swap*

> brings up questions about who does what kind of domestic work, how work outside the home is gendered, how this new status of women in the work force effects parenting and attitudes to parenting ... These fundamental questions of life politics around who does what work, emotional, domestic and paid, are exactly the issues thrown up by the analysis of reflexive modernity made by sociologists like Anthony Giddens. (2004b: 246)

This show and other programmes in the same mould have been designated by Lambert as 'manipulated' or 'constructed' documentary (in Thorpe 2003: 14). Lambert's concept of a new 'manipulated' or 'constructed' documentary is breathtakingly ahistorical. He seems to have a charmingly naïve belief in the direct cinema rhetoric of the 1960s that pure observational filming really does have the capacity to produce unmanipulated and unconstructed films. This was (and remains) impossible of performance – a difficulty ignored then, and, as Lambert and many others demonstrate, continues to be ignored today. Mindless observational filming is not documentary, it is surveillance. The very point of documentary, what makes it different from other forms of non-fiction filming, is exactly that it is manipulated and constructed – that it is, as Grierson's 1933 definition has it, 'the creative treatment of actuality' (in Paget 1998: 117). But Grierson would not acknowledge that what Lambert is doing in *Wife Swap* – what might be called 'the creative treatment of created situations' – had to do with documentary at all.

The danger to the Griersonian documentary tradition (and the news as well) is not that such a high degree of manipulation undercuts the pretensions of evidentiary television. It is that reality television does so essentially by exploiting the same techniques of observational realism as documentary uses. On the screen they look identical. Therefore, reality television, where every frame arises from fundamental producer manipulations however observational it appears, calls into question thereby the authenticity of every frame of (supposedly un-manipulated) evidentiary television. Lambert's concept of 'manipulated' or 'constructed' documentaries, however ill-articulated, involves *cinéma vérité* levels of producer interference. That, after the initial set-up, these arrangements are veiled, as it were, by the usual observational direct cinema style – or in the bastardised *vérité* television equivalent of that – is not the point. As with the newspaper interview, the events in *Wife Swap* are certainly witnessed – that is what Lambert means by the filming being 'neutral', observational – but they would never have occurred had Lambert and his team not dreamt up the initial situation. So Lambert's strategies, and the strategies of much reality television in this documentary mode, overlap with Rouch's procedures. In the same way, the events in *Chronique d'un été* are witnessed but would never have occurred had the filmmakers not set them up.

Reality television's use of 'ordinary' people also matters on the moral front and here again *Chronique d'un été's* second legacy is in play. Engineering souls is an ethically dangerous business and it is not hard to envisage that the ship of reality television could be disastrously holed at any time on a legal iceberg. Legal opinion about these programmes is quite clear: 'There will always be the risk of harm' (Matheson & Calow 2003: 6). Positive outcomes arising from appearances on reality shows have been noted – the decorator faking it as an artist deciding afterwards to become one, and the like – but just as common is the parade of the sobbing and the distraught – a commonplace of reality television – not all of whom are 'C-list' celebrities putting on a style (see Freeman 2002: 8). Some participants have successfully sued for misrepresentation (see Hill & Ahmed 2003: 19). One *Wife Swap* subject was moved to begin (but not pursue) divorce proceedings when she returned to her authoritarian spouse (see Nosowicz 2003: 21). (On the other hand, another in the US was reported as mending her selfish ways (see Orr 2004: 13).) In the United States, there have been actions for harassment and for injury (see Usborne 2003: 11), despite the fact that the injured party willingly collaborated in the stunt, and it is an old principle of common law that one cannot actually ever agree to one's own injury.

There have been even more serious outcomes. Sinisa Savija threw himself under a train four weeks after being expelled from the Swedish version of *Survivor* (see Addley 2002: 2). In the States, Najai Trupin shot himself three weeks before *Contender*, the series in which he had agreed to participate, began transmitting. 'Nothing changes', said producer Mark Burnett. 'I'm not even going to make any edits because it's real' (in Timms 2005: 19). It is hard not to think that being the defendant in a manslaughter trial would do wonders for Mr Burnett's moral education, but the legal chain of causality in that situation, as in all others thus far, has been too stretched. However, it would be foolhardy to anticipate that this will remain the case forever.

Although many of these moral problems arise in programming at the 'games' end of the reality television continuum rather than from 'constructed' documentaries, nevertheless Morin and Rouch did themselves court disapprobation because of their interventions in the lives of the subjects of *Chronique d'un été*.

Morin's on-camera treatment of the obviously emotionally fragile Marylou was seen as an invasion of privacy by others involved in the film. Hostile comments along these lines were included in the famous penultimate sequence where the subjects gather in the cinema of the Musée de l'Homme to watch a cut of the film (see Feld & Ewing 1985: 69). Morin and Rouch also included in the finished film the story of how Angélo, the Renault worker, was threatened by his bosses because the crew had followed him to work (Feld & Ewing 1985: 61). The film, however, does not document that he was actually sacked, nor does it show their further interventions, finding him another job at a film studio only to have him lose it because of his unionising activities (see Morin 1985: 21; Yakir 1978: 9).

The evidentiary versus the simulated

The attempts to clear the theoretical undergrowth post-reality television have been partial but the most persuasive suggestion (to be found in the work of Jon Dovey) had been to move reality television away from evidentiary claims about pre-existing independent realities towards a new position where such programmes are considered a species of simulation. For Dovey, simulation is not necessarily mimetic but does involve 'representing what is unobservable' (2005: 240). He draws on the work done on the computer modelling of social phenomenon for his picture of what simulation might mean in the context of reality television. Dovey quotes Nigel Gilbert's explanation of the validity of the use of simulation in sociology:

> We wish to acquire knowledge about a target entity T. But T is not easy to study directly. So we proceed indirectly. Instead of T we study another entity M, the 'model', which is sufficiently similar to T that we are confident that some of what we learn about M will also be true of T... Computer simulation is an appropriate methodology whenever a social phenomenon is not directly accessible either because it no longer exists ... or because its structure, i.e. its behaviour, are so complex that the observer cannot directly attain a clear picture of what is going on. (Gilbert & Conte 1995: 4, 2)

By analogy, then, the reality television shows, wherever they are placed on a continuum from observational documentary (*Wife Swap*) to species of game show (*Big Brother*), are essentially ways in which the 'target entity T' (human behaviour) is modelled as 'M'; and what we learn from M applies to T. This is why the shows, which cannot be justified as legitimate in terms of traditional evidentiary television have been so popular – 'water-cooler TV': they model truths about our *mentalités*.

Rouch and Morin in *Chronique d'un été* were similarly concerned with simulation using men and women who, in Rouch's initial voice-over 'gave a period of their lives over to a new experience of *cinéma vérité*'. Morin described the film as 'research', an 'experiment' (1985: 4). Dovey hereby provides a context into which their effort can also be placed. Although, as he points out, there are considerable differences between *Big Brother* and *Chronique d'un été* (as to their distinct modes of production and exhibition, tone and ambition and so on) nevertheless they do share the fundamental assumption that the production can itself provoke and create the action, as well as a certain fascination with questions of identity and experience within the realm of the banal and the everyday (2005: 243). In the same way, *Wife Swap* too mimics *Chronique d'un été* in the willingness of the producers to conduct social 'research' and 'experimentation'. In some sense, then, it is not too extreme to claim a relationship, a consanguinity between *Big Brother* and *Wife Swap* (and therefore the rest of reality television) and the second legacy of *Chronique d'un été*; for *Chronique d'un été* is the template for provoking action and then observing the consequences. If such interventionist proceedings threaten evidentiary television (and they do) then so does *Chronique d'un été*. Yet for this to be a true threat we would have to demonstrate that the audience could not tell the difference between watching evidentiary programming or simulation, that is a screen displaying, say, a particularly iconic image of *The Sims*. It would require that the audience had no inkling of the underlying difference between the evidentiary and the simulated – rather, as we know, a minority have difficulty distinguishing fact from fiction and seem to believe, for example, in the independent reality of soap opera characters.

Although there is no evidence in audience research that viewers are sophisticated enough to embrace the concept of simulation as a ground of difference between evidentiary and reality television, there is research showing that they do understand gradations in the representation of the factual. Annette Hill's latest findings, for example, reveal that audiences have an active view of what she terms 'categorisation', seeing 'a fact/fiction' continuum:

At the far end of the fact/fiction continuum are more traditional types of factual programming such as news and current affairs [which I would call the 'evidentiary'], whilst at the other end of the scale are new reality programmes such as *Big Brother* or *Joe Millionaire* [2003]. A myriad of other types of factual programming, from popular documentary to hidden camera formats, are somewhere in the middle of the fact/fiction continuum … Audiences watch popular factual programming with a critical eye, judging the degree of factuality in each reality format based on their experience of other types of factual programming as a whole. (2005: 173)

Hill's interviews reveal that her informants are more than capable of interrogating what they see, understanding the producer's role in creating the image as well as evaluating the honesty of a subject's 'performance'. However, the possibility of confusion between the evidentiary and simulated is not laid to rest. Her informants do not appear to be sophisticated enough to fully absorb Dovey's distinction and so his attempt to distance reality television from documentary, while theoretically engaging, is unlikely to address the main issue: definitional confusions do matter and the audience, as far as we can tell, is confused.

The irony is that – however unconvincingly – initially *Chronique d'un été* never presented itself as documentary. As Morin wrote in the film's official synopsis: 'This film is research … It is not a fictional film. This research concerns real life. This is not a documentary film. This research does not aim to describe; it is an experiment lived by its authors and actors' (1985: 4).

It 'does not aim to describe'; that is to say, it is not evidence of a pre-existing independent reality. It is a document of an experience – the experience of being filmed. The initial French response to *Chronique d'un été*, in contrast to Leacock's disdain at the essential pointlessness of such an exercise, was to immediately see the richness of the intellectual framework of the 'research' the filmmakers had undertaken. The original *Cahiers du cinéma* review of *Chronique d'un été* cited not simulation and games theory but the older principles of experimental physics to explain what Morin and Rouch were about: 'They are honest enough to enter the arena … They set before us all the conditions of the experiment' (Fereydoun 1979: 249).

Perhaps here is the elusive clue to the difference that makes a difference between *Chronique d'un été* and reality television after all – that Rouch and Morin were 'honest enough to enter the arena'. It is not then a matter of the second legacy, which Rouch shares with reality television, but the first, which he does not share. It is the on-screen presence of Rouch, 'the filmmaker diver', that justifies and legitimates this level of intervention but allows the result still to remain within the realm of documentary – a document of an experience whose validity we can judge because it exposes the processes of its creation. Conversely, it is exactly the on-screen absence, the 'transparency' of *Big Brother* and Stephen Lambert and the rest, which de-legitimates their efforts as documentary. Rouch's presence within the frame in *Chronique d'un été* might be shadowy, but it is crucial.

In fact, there is no second legacy in play without the first also being deployed if the result is to be considered legitimate as documentary.

NOTES

1   However, it must be said that in his more recent work (such as *Biggie & Tupac* (2001) or *Aileen: The Life and Death of a Serial Killer* (2003)), Broomfield has emerged once again as a far more serious and trustworthy figure.
2   Following a radio precedent, *Candid Microphone* (1951–52).

REFERENCES

Addley, E. (2002) 'Sinisa's Story', *Guardian* G2, 26 July, 2–3.

Biressi, A. and H. Nunn (2005) *Reality TV: Realism and Revelation*. London: Wallflower Press.

Blue, J. (1965) 'One Man's Truth: An Interview with Richard Leacock', *Film Comment*, 2, 3, Spring, 15–23.

Dovey, J. (2000) *Freakshow*. London: Pluto Press.

_____ (2004a) 'From Verite to Simulation', paper given at 'Building Bridges: The Cinema of Jean Rouch', conference, Institut français, London, 8–10 October 2004.

_____ (2004b) 'It's Only a Game Show: *Big Brother* and the Theatre of Spontaniety', in E. Mathijs and J. Jones (eds) *Big Brother International*. London: Wallflower Press, 232–49.

Feld, S. and A. Ewing (1985) '*Chronicle of a Summer*' [Transcript], *Studies in Visual Anthropology*, 11, 1, Winter.

Fereydoun, H. (1979 [1963]) 'Cinéma-vérité ou réalism fantastique', trans. J. Hillier, *Cahiers du cinéma*, 125, November.

Freeman, H. (2002) 'My Brush with Fame', *Guardian* G2, 26 September, 8–9.

Gilbert, N. and R. Conte (eds) (1995) *Artificial Societies: The Computer Simulations of Social Life*. London: University College London Press.

Gilbert, N. and J. Doran (eds.) (1994) *Simulating Societies: The Computer Simulation of Social Phenomena*. London: University College London Press.

Godard, J.-L. (1963/64) 'Richard Leacock', trans. P. Graham, *Cahiers du cinéma*, 150–1, December/January, 139–40.

Goldmann, L. (1979) 'Cinema and Sociology: Thoughts on *Chronique d'un été*', in M. Eaton (ed.) *Anthropology–Reality–Cinema*. London: British Film Institute, 64–6.

Grierson, J. (1981) *Grierson on the Movies*, ed. F. Hardy. London: Faber.

Hill, A. (2005) *Reality TV: Audiences and Popular Factual Television*. London: Routledge.

Hill, A. and K. Ahmed (2003) 'TV, Public School and Ryan's Fall', *Observer*, 11 May, 19.

Hillier, J. (1986) *Cahiers du cinéma in Translation II*. London: British Film Institute.

Kilborn, R. (2003) *Staging the Real: Factual TV Programming in the Age of Big Brother*. Manchester: Manchester University Press.

Loomis, A. (2004) 'Candid Camera', in Horace Newcomb (ed.) *Encyclopedia of Television: Vol. 1*. New York: Fitzroy Dearborn, 443–4.

Marris, P. (ed.) (1982) 'Preface', in *Paul Rotha*. London: British Film Institute, 3–4.

Matheson, C. and D. Calow (2003) 'I'm a Liability, Get Me Out of Here', *Observer Business*, 1 July.

Morin, E. (1985) 'Chronicle of a Film', trans. S. Feld and A. Ewing, *Studies in Visual Anthropology*, 11, 1, Winter.

Murray, S. (2004) 'Reality TV (US)', in H. Newcomb (ed.) *Encyclopedia of Television: Vol. 3*. New York: Fitzroy Dearborn, 1900–02.

Nosowicz, D. (2003) 'Programme Note', *Observer TV*, 28 January, 21.

Orr, D. (2004) 'Redemption through Reality TV? It can be done', *Independent*, 27 November, 13.

Paget, D. (1998) *No Other Way to Tell It: Dramadoc/Docudrama on Television*. Manchester: Manchester University Press.

Shivas, M. (1963) 'Interviews: Richard Leacock', *Movie*, 8, April, 21–3.

Silvester, C. (ed.) (1993) *The Penguin Book of Interviews*. Harmondsworth: Penguin.

Timms, D. (2005) 'US Reality TV Contestant Kills Himself', *Guardian*, 16 February, 19.

Thorpe, V. (2003) '*Wife Swap* Director Raps Hypocrisy of TV Critics', *Observer*, 26 January, 14.

Usborne, D. (2003) 'Reality Check for TV Producers as Humiliated Contestants Sue', *Independent*, 8 January, 11.

Winston, B. (1995) *Claiming the Real: The Documentary Film Revisited*. London: British Film Institute.

Yakir, D. (1978) 'Ciné-transe: The Vision of Jean Rouch', *Film Quarterly*, 31, 3, Spring, 2–11.

INDEX